WHAT HEALTH EXPERTS ARE SAYING

"In *Never, Ever, Ever Give Up—Health Is on the Way,* visionary Rod Burreson takes us on a journey into healthcare as it will be practiced in the 21st century. His keen insight into the physical, nutritional and mental aspects of life offer a roadmap to health that everyone will find informative and uplifting. This book is a must read for doctors and patients who wish to experience a vibrant and healthy way of living."

—Paul Nash, D.C., N.D., CCN

"Rod Burreson has created an extremely practical, informative road map for anyone interested in improving his or her health. The information contained in this guidebook should be helpful to relatively healthy people who wish to achieve optimal health as well as sick people with minor or even major ailments. It can be used as a reference book for healthcare practitioners who wish to incorporate nutrition, nutritional supplements, exercise and lifestyle approaches to healthcare into their practices."

—Michael B. Schachter, M.D., CNS

"After reading *Never, Ever, Ever, Give Up* from cover to cover, I found it to be one of the most exhaustive treatises ever written on the subject of diet and nutrition and their relationship to health and disease. This book should be must reading for all doctors, and no home should be without a copy."

—Angelo P. John, Director
A. P. John Institute for Cancer Research

"We can heal ourselves regardless of what we have been programmed to think. Nontoxic, noninvasive and inexpensive therapies are a reality . . . This information has been kept from the majority of the population for too long. Eventually the truth finds a way to surface!"

—Valerie Sheppard, President
The Sheppard Foundation

NEVER, EVER, EVER GIVE UP—HEALTH IS ON THE WAY

NEVER, EVER, EVER GIVE UP— HEALTH IS ON THE WAY

—

Rod Burreson
with Paul Ward, PED

NORGE PUBLICATIONS

The following publisher has generously given permission to use extended quotations from copyrighted works. From "The Rise and Fall of the Killer Drug Rezulin" by David Willman. Copyright 2000, *Los Angeles Times*. Reprinted with permission.

Norge Publications
16841 Armstrong Avenue, Irvine, California 92606
(949) 476-8675/F: (949) 476-8682

Individual Sales. This book is available through most bookstores or can be ordered directly from the Publisher at the address above.

Quantity Sales. Special discounts are available on quantity purchases by corporations, associations, and others. For details, contact the "Special Sales Department" at the address above.

Printed in the United States of America

Cataloging-in-Publication Data
Burreson, Rod, 1933-
  Never, ever, ever give up—health is on the way / Rod
Burreson with Paul Ward.—1st ed.
  p. cm.
  Includes index.
  LCCN: 2001135842
  ISBN: 0-9714507-1-4
  1. Nutrition—Popular works. 2. Health—Popular
works. 3. Dietetics—Popular works. I. Ward, Paul,
  PED. II. Title.
RA784.B87 2002   613.2
               QB101-201182

Cover Photograph: Greg Porter, Porter Creative Group
Cover Design: Emily Brand and Sherli Babakani, Kani Designs
Editorial Services: PeopleSpeak

This book is dedicated to the thousands of people who faithfully listen to my daily health and nutrition radio show and to the wonderful people who have attended my annual seminars. It is your support that has made this book a reality.

This book is also dedicated to the memory of my son, Rex, who was such a great people person and whose untimely death caused me to redirect my life to the path I travel today. It has been more than ten years since his tragic accident, and every time I think of him, it brings tears to my eyes and a smile to my face. Rex epitomized my love and concern for all the young people of this great country.

CONTENTS

Foreword

It is my pleasure to write this foreword to *Never, Ever, Ever Give Up—Health Is on the Way* by Rod Burreson, whom I have known for many years. Rod's passion has been to find a fountain of youth, and he has been responsible for developing a successful anti-aging company, Roex, Inc. Rod has tremendous energy and is persistent in his untiring efforts to help others in their quest for health as well. He has developed nutraceutical products to improve health for most of the systems in our body: brain, mind, heart, lungs, gastrointestinal system, liver, urological and reproductive system.

As a neurologist (professor of neurology at the USC School of Medicine), I am deeply involved in the use of conventional medicine to treat disease. However, I appreciate the role of complementary/alternative medicine in health promotion and disease prevention. I am also trained in Ayurveda and yoga and have been involved in various clinical and academic organizations, including the National Center for Complementary and Alternative Medicine (a division of the National Institutes of Health). I appreciate how Rod brings to this book the best concepts in mind-body, nutrition, and other aspects of alternative health for prevention of disease and development of a healthy life.

American medicine is undergoing major changes with regard to issues of cost, access, and quality of care. Along with this transformation in U.S. healthcare, the public, payers, and providers are trying to find safer and less-expensive alternatives that complement conventional medicine.

This book discusses the importance of all aspects of health, including the physical, mental, and spiritual conditions that need to be considered. This patient-centered approach promotes healing of the whole patient. Complementary/alternative healthcare in such a system involves the utilization of a broad range of healthcare modalities that include modern medical techniques complemented by nutraceuticals, herbs, yoga, meditation, relaxation, biofeedback, acupuncture, and Ayurveda. The use of herbs dates back to early forms of medicine, and many herbs have now been scientifically proven to be effective in treating a variety of conditions. They are used in much the same fashion as pharmaceuticals; in fact, about 25 percent of our modern-day pharmaceuticals are derived from plants.

In spite of the advances in modern allopathic medicine, there are a number of areas where it has failed to gain control in a consistent manner: chronic disorders of stress, headaches, and pain. Patients who are overweight or have AIDS, cancer, arthritis, cardiovascular disorders, memory disorders, and various addictions continue to suffer greatly. In addition, the high cost, and often negative side effects, of common forms of conventional treatment have led us to search for less-expensive and safer alternatives. Many forms of complementary therapies that serve as effective and low-cost preventive treatments are likely to become more accepted in the future.

The growing need for health promotion and disease prevention has provided added impetus to the complementary healthcare movement. Public awareness and acceptance of unconventional therapies is widespread, according to a scientific report by David Eisenberg, M.D., published in 1993 in the *New England Journal of Medicine*. Also, certain aspects of complementary medicine are gaining acceptance in leading academic health science centers, such as Harvard Medical School, Stanford University, USC, UCLA, New York University, Columbia's College of Physicians and Surgeons, the University of Florida, and the University of California in Irvine, to name a few.

The geriatric population is increasing worldwide, but the number is growing at a faster pace in Western developed countries, including the United States. The exact biological basis of aging has been elusive throughout the history of civilization. Many have tried to find the fountain of youth. A great deal of work has been done to understand the basic mechanism and to retard the aging process in modern Western medicine. In spite of the progress made, there is a lot more to learn in both the basic and applied aspects of aging.

By the year 2030, the number of individuals 65 and over will reach 70 million in the United States (about 20 percent of the total population). Those who are 85 years and older will be the fastest growing segment of the population. This dramatic increase has various ramifications, particularly from a healthcare perspective.

Various factors that are responsible for delaying and easing aging include proper nutrition, exercise, genetics, and active social and psychological involvement with life. Proper handling of some of these factors could lead to better solutions for optimal health and longevity. This means that full aging is an art, as well as a science. Successful management of the aging process begins in early childhood and proceeds through the various stages of life.

Human life is associated with miracles that take one from conception to birth, then to sexual maturation and throughout adulthood, with continual healing and cell renewal. *Never, Ever, Ever Give Up* reminds us of our important role to encourage and support the body rather than hamper its natural abilities. This book is an excellent motivator and tells us if we set our mind on wellness, we will achieve it.

Never, Ever, Ever Give Up can help individuals who are interested in maintaining their health and retarding the aging process.

The book contains a great deal of important information that is factual and scientifically based. Rod has a simple, common-sense approach that we all can learn from and be inspired by.

Health is something we should not take for granted. It is something we all need to work at and strive for. This book not only tells a human story but is a book that can be used as a valuable reference and resource guide for years to come. Rod deserves special congratulations for a job well done!

SHRI K. MISHRA, M.D., M.S. (Administrative Medicine)
Professor of Neurology and Coordinator Integrative Medicine
USC School of Medicine, Los Angeles, California

Acknowledgments

Every time I sat down to write this book over the last year, I considered how fortunate I was to have so many intelligent, honest people provide me with their points of view and assessment of the content and presentation. The title, *Never, Ever, Ever Give Up*, came about because of my attitude in life and the fact that one of my most constructive critics, Julie Lynch, was so emphatic about getting the right name on the cover. I want to thank her for her unwavering critical review, writing knowledge, and guidance. Sharon Goldinger, the editor, provided me with such timely professional guidance and critical evaluation that I often reflect what might have been had we not had her input. Dr. Paul Ward, whose knowledge and contribution have been invaluable to the content, has helped make this book a one-of-a-kind masterpiece. Many other people have been involved in one or more aspects that make this book a great work, and I thank all of them for their review, evaluation, and input.

Finally, I want to thank Chris Bolduc and Emily Brand for the many hours they spent designing the cover, reviewing the content, and coordinating the different people involved with the production of this project. I am sure that Chris will be a very happy person to see this project completed. Little does he know, but his work has just started, for now we must get it out to the people, and that is an even bigger project.

NEVER, EVER, EVER GIVE UP— HEALTH IS ON THE WAY

Introduction

Never, Ever, Ever Give Up is built upon the concept that the decisions you made yesterday dictate how you look and feel today. The decisions you make today will dictate how you look, feel, and live tomorrow.

Look at where you are today and the decisions you made to get here. Now picture what you would like to look like tomorrow and consider the decisions you need to make today to get there. This book is like a road map or guide to living, survival, and rehabilitation. Of course, the end result should be to slow down the aging process and to be viable and healthy the rest of your life. I want to help you get on the right road to health so that you can enjoy life to its fullest.

I have counseled many, many people on health and nutrition. I have done several thousand radio shows on the subject (e.g., *Roex Health Update*) and have listened to the stories that callers tell about the problems that they face, the decisions that they consider making, and, of course, the courage they must muster to change their lives. This has given me a vivid view of where the general population is in regard to health today and how much help is needed.

I want to pass on the information I have worked so hard to learn. I also want to help you understand yourself a little better and help you understand that nobody is perfect, certainly not me.

Think about what you really want out of this world. What are you willing to do to achieve these goals? And, finally, what are you willing to give back to the world?

This book can help you see the "big picture" and is a great guide to help you meet your goals. This book is not overly sophisticated, and the data is presented in reasonably simple terms.

Never, Ever, Ever Give Up might be considered a reference book for people who are really serious about extending and renewing their lives. The data in the book is factual and well substantiated. However, this book is not intended to be a "know-it-all" book—I am far away from knowing it all, but what I know *works!*

Many books discuss health and nutrition, the mind and the body. They tell you all about vitamins, minerals, herbs, psychotherapy, hypnosis, and so on. Most of them speak to you from a theoretical point of view, not a practical one. Instead, I want to describe how all of these factors work in the body, how you can work with them, and *why* you need to work with them if you're going to survive the terrible onslaught of chemicals, drugs, toxins, and other substances that influence your health. As you progress through the book, I believe you will get a clear picture of how I see health and life, as well as some of the mistakes that I have made and what I've learned to get this far in life.

I am 69 years old and in pretty good health. I work hard at it, but I don't work hard enough. I work continuously at it, but I don't work consistently enough. I'm always striving to do better, and you should do the same. Since we are not perfect, we should all strive to do better.

Goal setting is a good way to accomplish this. However, if you set goals that are too high, you will seldom reach those goals. If you set realistic goals, then those goals can, and in most cases will, be accomplished. Each time you reach a goal, set another, higher goal—not too high, but high enough so you have to stretch some to get there. Realize that you need to constantly readjust your goals and your road map to attain them. As you do this, you will see results that bring courage, desire, and enthusiasm to continue.

Rehabilitation is emphasized throughout the book, and because I've had to go through rehabilitation so many times, I feel like I am somewhat of an authority on the subject. Rehabilitation is tough, it takes courage, it takes a great deal of time and effort, and it takes perseverance. Most of all, you can never, ever, ever, give up. Consequently, you will find this book very helpful as a guide to reinstating your body and reaching your goals.

Throughout this book you will see how fortunate I feel to know what I know and how aware I am of how much I don't know. The more I learn, the more I know I don't know. Actually, the less you know, the more you don't know you don't know.

It's a real disappointment when you listen to some people speak and it becomes obvious that they don't know they don't know. Yet they are passing on false information to many other people. Dozens, thousands, or millions of people may be functioning on false information because the people they rely on for guidance don't know they don't know.

Even intelligent people make stupid comments once in a while. This includes doctors, lawyers, you, me, and everybody else. Nobody is perfect, but if you go through life with some influence over other people, you bear a certain amount of responsibility to make sure that the information you are passing on is correct. As a consequence, I have done a lot of research: I've read hundreds of newsletters and books and counseled with doctors, biochemists, pharmacologists, scientists, and many other learned people to find out the correct answers to my questions and those that people ask me.

Sadly, a lot of people giving advice to others would rather not say, "I don't know." Instead, they'll give you false information or couch their response in innuendoes to confuse you and belittle you in order to alter your opinion. I am sure you have heard a doctor scoff at a question that you asked or a comment that you made.

You will not find intentionally false information or arrogant attitudes in this book. First of all, if we don't know, we won't comment on it. Second of all, many areas require further study and research before we can address the issues with confidence. Until we get that confidence, we are just not going to address those issues or we will tell you what we do know, even though it may be of limited value in the overall picture.

Never, Ever, Ever Give Up is a guide for you, the reader, on how to approach life with confidence, knowing that a great deal of research from many different sources and years of practical experience have gone into the preparation of this book.

The Bible, by the way, is also an incredible source of wisdom, knowledge, and encouragement. You will see several favorite scriptures of mine and my co-author's throughout the book. The Bible has answers to all of life's questions, and it can be helpful no matter what your personal beliefs are. The Bible is, after all, the best-selling book of all time.

A cheerful look brings joy to the heart,
and good news gives health to the bones.
—PROV. 15:30

A very important part of this book is the mind-body connection. The Bible tells us to be joyous in all things—not some things but all things. We can learn something from even the worst experience we have gone through, or we can take that experience and help others because of what we have gone through. A negative attitude is not good for anyone! Our attitude, how we think, is so powerful that we can actually change things with the mind both in the body and in the environment.

Your mind plays a very important role in this drama called living. I want you to visualize how you want to change things with your mind and with your body. I want you to recognize the importance of exercise, the air you breathe, sleep, nutrition, water, the love and affection that you need from your family and friends, and, most of all, your relationship with the Almighty. All of these are needed for a strong body and mind and a successful cruise through life. Many areas in this book will help you realize the picture of health that you envision.

Remember, *whatever the mind can conceive and believe, it can achieve*. If you can believe and visualize that you are going to be healthy, you will get healthy. Your mind is so powerful! Your mind can actually release chemicals into your body that are so powerful they can reinstate your health more effectively than anything else in the world today. In combination with the mind, proper supplementation that addresses structure and function in the body can help you reach your goal a lot faster. Consequently, when your mind and the supplements work together in your body, you really have what it takes to get there. You have an anti-aging powerhouse working in concert toward one ultimate goal—your health!

We all need help in this world, whether we like to admit it or not, and I have had some great help with this book from Dr. Paul Ward. His contribution, knowledge, and push have made this book possible. He is my very learned partner, whose help and assistance and wealth of information and understanding give you some content not previously presented by any writer. We have worked together to bring to you what we consider a masterpiece. I do hope you will feel the same as you finish this book and incorporate some of its wisdom and knowledge into your life. I just want all of you to know how much I appreciate my colleague's efforts and input.

I've had some really bad experiences in my life, most of which were my fault, and I've had some wonderful experiences in my life. All of these experiences have brought me to where I am today. As you read this book, you will, hopefully, begin to see that the place you are in today is the result of the decisions you made yesterday.

God has played a substantial role in my life, my survival, and my destiny. If you don't believe in God, you may be able to see him through my eyes. I thank God every day for his strength, protection, and guidance. He has given me so much, and I am truly grateful. I wish to acknowledge him in all that I do, and I hope that you will, too.

This book will give you a road map to what you can and should do if you want the 21st century to be a wonderful, rewarding, and healthy experience. Starting today, develop a plan to maintain or regain your mental and/or physical health. While it is very difficult to be all-inclusive in a single book like this, I'll try my best to tie everything together. So sit back, get comfortable, and continue reading to see how we can work together so that you can reach your goals and objectives of tomorrow. *Note: This book mentions various brand-name products available from Roex, Inc. For more information about these products, please see the appendix near the end of the book.*

PART 1

A Road Map to Health

God's greatest creation, the human body, is designed with an amazing innate ability to heal itself. It, however, cannot perform this miraculous achievement without our support.

The body must be balanced to be healthy. Numerous self-help books have been written on achieving balance in life. Our very existence depends upon millions of electrochemical processes that balance the physiological processes that take place in the body every day.

ARE WE KILLING OURSELVES?

The natural human life span is believed to be at least 120 years, yet most of us die prematurely at age 73 for men and at age 77 for women. Why? If we do not provide the body with what it needs to function properly, we cannot adequately fight off illness and disease. We become vulnerable to recurrent or degenerative conditions or those concentrated in specific organs, such as the lungs, heart, or reproductive system. Eventually, cancer, AIDS, or some other opportunistic degenerative disease takes over.

Good health should not be thought of as the absence of disease. We should avoid this negative disease-oriented thinking and concentrate on what we must do to remain healthy. Health results from supplying what is essential to the body on a daily basis, while disease results from living without what the body needs. We are responsible for our own health and should take control of it. When we are in control of our health, disease cannot take over. Remember my motto, *"If it is to be, it's up to me."*

WHO IS IN CHARGE OF OUR HEALTH?

Each individual is in charge of his or her own health. Our health is supported by new, creative developments in the healthcare industry; however, we are currently feeling the effects of our poor decisions in the management of new technology over the past five decades.

Your present state (mental and physical) of health is closely associated with the decisions you made yesterday. The decisions you make today will greatly influence your state of health tomorrow.

LET US WORK WITH THE BODY

The natural approach to health and healing is consistent with the body, working with it rather than against it. This was the philosophy of many traditional remedies that have now been lost or replaced.

However, not all so-called natural remedies are the answer to every ailment. Numerous companies make inappropriate, unsubstantiated claims for their products just to increase sales. We need to be able to sort through the mass of information and misinformation to make educated decisions for ourselves.

Realize that there are no miracle cures. Supplements can only support the body and its innate ability to heal itself.

The natural approach maintains that the constant effort of the body's life force is always in the direction of self-cleansing, self-repairing, and positive health. The philosophy maintains that even acute disease is a manifestation of the body's efforts in the direction of self-cure. Disease, or downgraded health, may be eliminated only by removing the real cause from the system and by raising the body's general vitality so that its natural and inherent ability to sustain health is allowed to dominate. In short, this means taking control of your immune system and balancing all body functions. To do this, you very likely will need to detoxify the liver, kidneys, and colon.

The natural philosophy maintains that chronic diseases are frequently the result of the body's inability to cleanse or heal itself. It is unable to get back into balance because of certain deficiencies or toxic overload or because it is otherwise suppressed. Thanks to the research stimulated by Dr. Linus Pauling and other nutrition forefathers, we now realize the astounding health-protective, immune-stimulating factors of vitamin C and other substances found in nature. In a sense, we are moving back to basics. The best medicine may have been under our noses the entire time. Natural medicine is the least expensive—and most compatible—that can gently lead our body back to homeostasis, or balance.

More research is needed on an endless array of natural compounds to determine their potential benefit to our health, but such research is expensive. While pharmaceutical companies fund a large number of health-related research studies, they are not so interested in funding research for natural products that cannot be patented—no matter how effective they are, no matter that they are without side effects, no matter that they are what God created for us to use.

. . . and the leaves of the tree were for the healing of the nations.

—REV. 22:2

An allopathic physician is a doctor who treats disease and injury with active treatments, such as medicine or surgery. The treatment is meant to have the opposite effect from that caused by the disease or injury. Allopathic medicine is largely symptom and drug related. It has no component of disease prevention or support of the body's natural response to fight illness. It has no component of nutrition. In spite of the huge amount of scientific evidence supporting proper nutrition, most doctors today have had little more than a few classroom hours of basic dietetics.

Good nutrition plays a large role in the naturopathic approach to health. Good nutrition is essential for normal organ development and functioning, reproduction, growth, optimal energy and efficiency, resistance to infection and disease, and the ability to repair bodily damage or injury.

Our responsibility is to feed ourselves properly. We cannot expect to maintain optimal functioning as living human machines if we feed ourselves junk—calories devoid of crucial nutrients. As a nation of convenience, we have grown accustomed to what is fast and easy. Frozen, prepackaged, boxed, quick-cooking, and fast foods have replaced what once took our grandmothers all day to prepare. These fast foods lack vital nutrients, fiber, and enzymes, which we need for optimal health and immunity.

In the next several chapters, the significance of a good diet, exercise, the mind-body connection, and rehabilitation and their impact on good health are reviewed in more detail. My exercise program shows you the road to improvement in all the basic physical fitness attributes while improving functional flexibility. Over time, exercise will dramatically reduce your body fat, especially when combined with sensible eating. You will also accrue the mental benefits that go with a commitment to regular physical activity.

You will learn how to think about your body, how to program your mind for success and the future, and how to rehabilitate yourself physically. The decisions you made yesterday are now manifested in how you look and feel today. The decisions you make today will dictate how you look, feel, and live tomorrow.

My people are destroyed for the lack of knowledge.
—Hos. 4:6

—1

My Story

It was a beautiful, sunny afternoon in late June 1974. The sun was hot and I was doing one of the things I enjoy most—riding my motorcycle, hill climbing. I had just ridden up a steep hill, and as I reached the top, I shut down the throttle and stopped. I stood on my right leg as I looked back over my left shoulder and down the hill to see where the rest of my group was. All of a sudden, my right knee buckled, and over backwards I went with the motorcycle down the hill. When I finally came to a stop, the bike landed just beside me, hitting me in the chest and left shoulder as it came to rest.

As I lay there in the sweat, the dust, and the heat, thinking, "What happened?" I realized I had just broken my right knee for the fourth time. Within minutes, my knee was so big from fluid and swelling that it almost felt like it would burst. Of course, I had tight jeans on, adding to the discomfort.

The feelings and experience you go through right after you break a bone, sprain an ankle, or have an accident are overwhelming. The break of a bone causes a rush of fluid to that location as the body attempts to protect itself. You can easily go into shock. Nothing feels right. As you realize what has happened to you, the pain increases.

The others in my group got me and my bike back to the truck, the city, and my home. The following day, I headed for my doctor's office. After one look, Dr. Mullolly shook his head and said, "Rock, you did it again."

The x-ray explained what had happened. A ligament (which is like a strap) runs along the outside of the knee and connects to the bone. The connection near my joint broke, causing my knee to buckle. As a result, the cartilage in my knee was crushed as well. The doctor said, "Rock, we've got to go to surgery." So to surgery we went.

Following surgery, I spent eight weeks in a cast that extended the full length of my leg. Once Dr. Mullolly took the cast off, he said, "You know, we need to talk. Your knee joint is in such terrible shape, you really need a knee replacement. I want you to go home and consider this because without it, you're not going to be able to walk off a curb or go up and down stairs and you're going to have to wear a brace for the rest of your life. It's just not a viable way to live as a young man." With that thought in my mind, I left his office on crutches. My right leg muscles had atrophied badly. For support, my knee was wrapped tightly with Ace bandages. Immediately after Mullolly removed my cast, I started my rehabilitation program at my gym at home. I quickly found out how weak my leg was and how loose the joint was as I tried to work with my leg. It was scary. I couldn't do anything.

I started thinking about what causes a bone to deteriorate like that. What causes bone reabsorption? Right then, I decided to go to the University of California at Los Angeles (UCLA) Medical Center Library and start learning about bones. From there, I began an enormous search to understand how, if it's even possible, to rebuild bone, muscle, and joints.

What I learned was amazing. I learned about the osteoblast process, where your body pushes minerals into the bone structure, and the osteoclast process, where your body pulls minerals out of the bone structure. It made sense to me to begin replenishing the mineral supply in my body. It seemed obvious that I was deficient in minerals or wasn't absorbing them properly.

I knew the manager at Lindbergh Nutrition Center, a very popular health food store in Woodland Hills, California. Talking to her about the issue, we decided that I should start taking bone meal supplements. We searched for the best bone meal in the world and found out that New Zealand was probably the best place to get it. I got my first large batch of bone meal tablets and started taking 20–30 tablets a day for about a year and a half.

In just six months, I was walking without a brace. My knee was feeling a lot stronger, and I was working out regularly. By December 1975, within a year and a half of my surgery, I was back in karate classes.

I had been taking nutritional supplements for years and thought at the time that I was fairly knowledgeable. I didn't realize then how much I didn't know. After learning about bone reabsorption and how to reinstate the skeletal structure, I was on a new road. From that time on, I was intently learning about nutrition. With my new understanding of bone structure, I realized that certain nutritional deficiencies (specifically, vitamins A and D) were the reason I had broken so many bones in my life.

I don't believe many people have broken more bones than I have, except Evel Knievel and a few other unfortunates. I've broken most of my ribs on both sides, my floating rib on my left side, several bones in my left foot, my right knee (four times), my shoulder, my toes, several fingers and bones in both hands, and I have had multiple fractures in my face. It is amazing how resilient the body is, even in the worst circumstance.

The first time I broke my right knee was in 1954 when I was a member of the Navy's touring wrestling team in Alameda, California. I had just gotten an appointment to the Olympics in Greco-Roman wrestling in the 191-pound weight class. In this type of wrestling, no holds below the waist are allowed. Competitors have to be very strong in the arms, upper body, and legs, which I was. I wrestled an exhibition match at Berkeley Auditorium in Berkeley, California, the day before I was supposed to leave for the Olympic tryouts in Panama. At that exhibition, I had my opponent up in a fireman's carry and my left foot slipped off the mat. As my left foot slipped, I dropped my opponent on my right leg. My right leg broke at the knee just like a wishbone. What a mess! The ambulance took me to Berkeley Hospital, but the staff found out I was in the military, so they wouldn't treat me.

Treatment was delayed until I was transferred a few days later to Oak Knoll Naval Hospital. There, in the orthopedic ward, my knee had swollen to twice its normal size and the pressure was almost unbearable. The doctor came in and said, "I want you to sign this form because we're gonna tap your knee to relieve the pressure, then we'll do surgery." This was 1954—doctors knew very little about knees back then. I was skeptical and said that I wanted to think about it for a while. The doctor got very upset with me and said, "Fine, I'll be back tomorrow morning."

Later that day I talked with other patients in the orthopedic ward, who were returning from the Korean War. I mentioned what the doctor had told me, and one of the patients said, "Man, that guy's a butcher." He pointed out a man who'd had his ankle worked on by this doctor. He could no longer raise and lower his foot. It hung down so he had to wear a brace just to keep from breaking his ankle. I saw that and said, "That's it. I am not having surgery."

The doctor came into the ward the next morning with the forms. I told him, "I'm not signing them. I'm not having this surgery until I know just how bad off I am."

He retorted, "Well, when the pain gets bad enough, you'll sign them," and walked away. Now keep in mind that the pain was so bad that I couldn't touch my knee. A fly once landed on my knee and it felt like I had been hit by an ax. This went on for several days, and each morning the doctor would come in and say, "You had enough yet?"

Each time, I replied, "Nope, I'm not signing." A young nurse, a first lieutenant, on the night shift felt so sorry for me that she came in one night and tapped my knee to relieve the pressure. It was like taking a huge load off my knee. The relief was incredible.

The next morning when the doctor saw that someone had tapped my knee, he was enraged. He wanted to know who was responsible. He never did find out who did it, as nobody in the ward would tell him. Looking back, I thank God that I didn't allow that doctor to cut on me.

I spent several more weeks in the hospital until the swelling went down and I could actually walk around. It turned out I had cracked the bone and had "maximum internal derangement" of my right knee. The doctor, still angry, said, "I'm going to fix you, Burreson." He had me transferred through the commander at my base in Alameda to Midway Island. I couldn't imagine anyone being that vindictive. It took a few weeks to get all the paperwork together to get me transferred. But it turned out to be a blessing. By that time, my rehabilitation was going very well. My knee was getting stronger as I was in the gym daily. This was my first major rehabilitation program, and I learned a lot from a young therapist who helped me.

After the Midway Island transfer, I was put in charge of the electrical shop in the Air Rescue hanger. I had been assigned to the Sea and Air Rescue Group based on one of the smallest islands in the South Pacific. I quickly got to know the people on the island: the parachute riggers, the machinists, everyone. With their help we designed a knee brace—one of the first that had metal on both sides. It laced up and was hinged for free leg movement. Because of the way we designed it (through much trial and error), I was able to function normally, despite all of the internal derangement that had taken place in my knee, and I started rebuilding my leg muscles with weights through leg extensions and squats for the first time. During my 14 months on Midway Island, I built up the strength in my knee, my legs, and my whole body tremendously. I worked out almost every day and developed a lot of power.

When I got out of the Navy in 1955, I enrolled at the University of Minnesota. I tried out for the wrestling team and did very well, but my knee would swell up badly as it could not withstand the pressure. I knew there was something wrong, but didn't know what, and I wasn't about to have surgery to find out. I never did get on the University of Minnesota wrestling team, much to my chagrin, but I graduated in 1960.

Through the years, I have had many injuries, breaks, and sprains. I became interested in nutrition because I instinctively knew that it was the right direction to go for rehabilitation and support.

I knew about the significance of nutrition even before I broke my knee. When I first went into the Navy, in July 1951, I went to boot camp in San Diego. We wore only whites, which were made of cotton. I was transferred from San Diego to Florida and still wore only whites as it was warm there all year long. When I graduated from aviation electricians school in Jacksonville, the Navy transferred me to Alameda Naval Air Station in Northern California. There, for the first time, I had to wear dress blues. The first time I put them on, within a couple of hours I broke out in a red rash. It itched so bad that I could hardly stand it. When I went to the sick bay, the staff did not know what caused the rash so they referred me to Oak Knoll Naval Hospital.

The staff at Oak Knoll discovered that I had a vitamin A and D deficiency. They put me on A and D supplements for about three months. During this time they tried to get me a medical discharge, which I did not want. I probably feared I would end up back in the little town in Minnesota that I grew up in. They said that if I couldn't wear dress blues, I obviously couldn't be in the Navy. I tried all sorts of "remedies"—I even took apple cider vinegar baths for weeks. After several months, when the fat-soluble vitamins were re-established in my body, I was able to wear the dress blues—and able to stay in the Navy. I suspect that the problem was a sensitivity to the dye used.

My first period of rehabilitation was actually back when I was only four years old. I was with my father, a bricklayer, who was building a basement for a house in Minnesota. I was standing at ground level and he was 10 feet down on the concrete floor of the basement. All of a sudden, the ground under me gave way and I went headfirst into the basement, hitting the left side of my head. My dad rushed me to the doctor. This was 1937, so most doctors didn't have x-ray machines. I had a concussion and was sent home.

After a few weeks, however, my left eye began to cross and I eventually lost the forward vision in that eye. Apparently, I had damaged the optic nerve or some part of the sight mechanism from the eye to the brain. Over the next nine years, during the summer months I wore an eye patch over my good (right) eye to see if I could re-establish the left eye's link with the brain. Throughout my grade- and high-school years, I had two nicknames: "Rocky" and "One Eye." "Rocky" came from my beating up all the kids who teased me for walking around with a patch over my eye. (You know where "One Eye" came from.)

In the summer of 1946, at age 13, I had eye surgery at the New Ulm Minnesota Hospital by Dr. Fritche. He was convinced he could restore the sight in my left eye. After the surgery, I was blindfolded (both eyes) for four months. When the bandages were removed, the room was dark and then the light was gradually increased. I'll never forget the disappointment on my father's face when, after surgery and four months of literally being blind, the end result was, it didn't work.

I was glad it was all over and I could go back to school and sports. From then on, however, I was very sensitive to the things that people said. I could hear little inflections in the way they spoke, which gave me much more insight into individuals than most people could imagine or understand.

When I got married in 1957, I was attending the University of Minnesota on the GI Bill. My wife and I worked hard to pay for my education. I worked 40 hours or more per week—nights on the freight docks loading and unloading trucks so we could make ends meet. I also carried a full load of university credits. Following my graduation, we moved to California. We eventually bought a house and had our first child, a girl we named "Shelli."

I was 31 years old at that time. A doctor in Van Nuys (Dr. Kratz) was very optimistic that surgery on my eye would have a good chance of realigning my eye and maybe even restoring my forward vision. When I got home from the hospital, I had both eyes covered, again. My wife went to the grocery store and left me to tend to our nine-month-old daughter. It was a beautiful, warm summer day and I was sitting in the shade under the patio cover next to the pool in our backyard.

Shelli was just starting to walk pretty well. All of a sudden, I heard a big splash and I knew she had fallen into the pool. I jumped in where I heard the noise. A voice inside my head told me, "Pull off those bandages so you can see her." I ripped them off. The bright sun blinded me so I could hardly see, but I caught a slight glimpse of her. Once I had her safely in my arms, the rest was easy and we got out of the pool. By then, my eyes were burning from the bright sun and pool water. When my wife got home, we returned to the hospital. That surgery was also unsuccessful; however, over time my sight has improved in my left eye. My peripheral vision is perfect, but I still have 20/200 vision in the left eye, which is legally blind.

In 1965, life was good. I was making money, we had three children, and I was working out regularly and in good shape. I had just bought a beach house, or actually a "tear-down" on the beach.

One Sunday afternoon in early summer of that year, my brother, Dennis, and I were loading his motorcycle onto the front of his truck. We were in front of the garage and I was on the street side. We were just setting the motorcycle into the hangers on the front bumper when Dennis yelled, "Rock, look out!" I turned and saw an out-of-control car coming at me. Fortunately, it first hit the truck's fender before it hit me. I flew up in the air and landed on my back in the middle of the street. There I lay, in shock. The car came to rest about 100 feet past the truck. A young sailor got out of the car. He lost control of his bowels and bladder when he saw what he'd done. I lay in the street until the ambulance arrived and took me to St. Joseph's Hospital in Oxnard.

The doctors x-rayed me from head to toe. By that time, the entire lower part of my body was black-and-blue. My brother and his family and my wife and family were all there when the doctor said, "I can't believe it, but Mr. Burreson does not have a single broken bone. However, he has ruptured and bruised so many blood vessels that he cannot move his legs for a couple of weeks."

I had just started my own business and had purchased a real estate project with every cent I had. There was no way I was going to lie around and wait to go broke. So three days later, as difficult as it was, on crutches, I went back to work.

I had been working hard on my legs and had them in great shape before this accident. By the time I could resume working out, my right knee was giving me terrible problems again with stiffness, swelling, and pain. I went to see Dr. Mullolly in Van Nuys for the first time. He x-rayed my right knee and asked, "What in the world have you been through with that knee?" He tapped the fluid and said, "Rodney, that knee is in very bad shape. You must be very careful with it from now on. No more weightlifting with your legs."

Of course, that advice went in one ear and out the other. I had injured or broken that knee before, and I felt I knew what it took to rehabilitate it again. For several years, my knee got progressively better. I worked hard again on my legs. I always wore a large knee brace when I worked out because the right joint was weak and loose, but I still worked out.

In 1973 my whole world started to fall apart. By 1974 I wasn't working out much and I had just gone bankrupt in a large real estate venture. I was drinking too much, worrying too much, and literally destroying myself. From 1974 to 1992, I was very mixed up. I had trouble making money. My personal life and my business life were both not going well, and it was all my own fault.

You must learn how to think before you can learn how to live.
　　　　　　　—ERNEST HOLMES, *The Science of Mind*

My thinking was all wrong. In May 1988, I was in Los Angeles and I had just sold a real estate property that I was a partner in for a sizable profit. After we finished the contract, my partners and I had drinks together. I must have had 10 beers or more. Then at one o'clock in the morning, I was dumb enough to think, after that many beers, that I could drive from Los Angeles to Palm Springs.

I was driving down the Pasadena Freeway approaching an interchange when I fell asleep and went head-on into a big concrete abutment at about 70 miles per hour.

When I woke up, I was in Huntington Memorial Hospital in Pasadena, California. My face was so swollen you wouldn't have recognized me. My right knee was twice its normal size. My right shinbone had a large dent in it. My right shoulder was about two inches lower than my left with the right clavicle hanging on by a thread and swollen like a golf ball. My back was out. I really couldn't move and could barely breathe or talk. There I lay, trying to remember what had happened. Not long after I awoke, the doctor came in and said, "I want you to sign this form so we can x-ray you and check you out." I signed it. But it turned out that the doctor really had me sign a California Highway Patrol form giving my consent to take a test for blood alcohol content. My results showed a high alcohol content—over .10 percent.

The staff x-rayed my shoulder, my knee, my shinbone, and my back but not my face. They said, "I can't believe you haven't broken a bone." They didn't realize I had broken my face in many places. The doctor admonished me, "You don't need medical attention, you need Alcoholics Anonymous," and he kicked me out of the hospital that morning in the condition I was in.

I called my son, Rex, who was living in Palm Springs, to come pick me up. He had to literally carry me into the wheelchair and from the wheelchair into the truck to get me home. I was really hurting and should never have been released from the hospital. In fact, I later sued the hospital and that doctor. The lawyers got most of the money, but the hospital relented and agreed I shouldn't have been released.

Ten days later, my face was still hurting and swollen and I couldn't eat. The maxilla (upper jawbone) on my left side was hanging down about a quarter of an inch, so I couldn't chew or even close my mouth all the way. So, back into the hospital I went.

I underwent major surgery to push my face back in line. The doctors wired my mouth together to try to pull the maxilla back in alignment. It was quite a horror to wake up and find I couldn't open my mouth. I couldn't eat and could hardly breathe. I almost panicked. After eight weeks, the wires were removed from my teeth and my jaw, but the maxilla still didn't fit together properly (as we had discovered the problem very late). I still couldn't get my teeth together.

The solution offered me was to cut my jawbone to alter it. Of course, I didn't allow that. I spent the next two years going to the dentist, who cut and filed my teeth until my bite fit together better. Today I have lots of crowns and my teeth don't quite fit together properly, but going to the dentist was far better than having my jawbone cut.

After getting the wires off my jaw, I decided to go back to work on my body. I went to the gym and was so weak, I couldn't move the 45-pound bar off the rack without having it slam onto my chest. It took me another year to get my body in shape again. All that time, I was going to the dentist three or four times a week.

The period from 1988 to 1993 was especially tough. I was working on a large, difficult real estate project while also working hard to get myself back in shape mentally and physically. My son, Rex, was my partner in the project and was also a real estate broker. On a Sunday evening, July 1, 1990, I received a call from my brother informing me that my son's airplane had crashed in Lake Havasu, Arizona, and he and his two friends were killed. Rex was twenty-six years old. My brother's son, Derek, was there and saw the whole thing. Imagine the devastation and the depression that I felt. The terrible feeling of being lost hit me. After the funeral, I spent the next two years drinking beer and crying. My son and I had been extremely close. I felt very cheated and lonely.

Then one day I decided, "Rock, you've got to shape up. You've just got to get yourself together. You must let go." In 1992 I started working for my brother in insurance, while I figured out what I was going to do and how I was going to do it.

Early in 1993, on a business trip to Denver, I met a doctor named Tom. He told me about a product from France, a powerful antioxidant called "grape seed extract" or proanthocyanidin,[1] that had so many wonderful effects on people's health in Europe. Our conversation excited me so much that I ended up calling France to learn more about the extract. Tom had given me the names of some doctors and biochemists to contact who were doing research on the extract. I ordered some and then started taking it. I began to see amazing results. I then gave it to several friends with various health problems, and even I couldn't believe the incredible results at first. They kept asking me for more because they knew it was helping them. I decided the product was so good that I had to get it out to the American public, and that was the beginning of Roex, Inc., and PC-95.

The company started with me selling the product (I called it "PC-95" for 95 percent pure proanthocyanidin) from the trunk of my car. I won't tell you all the problems I went through at the beginning, but I will tell you it is definitely because of God that I am here. Today the company has developed into one of the most unique, aggressive, and viable nutrition companies in the country.

One reason we have done so well and are so successful is because the products really work. I won't sell a product I don't believe in—and I can't believe in a product that doesn't work.

The second reason for our success is a man named Fred, who came to me from out of nowhere. Fred called me one day in early 1995 and explained that he used to be a runner, but he had developed a sore heel and had to quit running and even walking. He had been to several doctors and was very discouraged by their advice and poor results and the fact that he was constantly getting worse. He had done everything including receiving cortisone injections and taking prednisone, but nothing helped. He said he had been referred to me by a friend who advised him that maybe I could help.

I suspected his problem was due to inflammation of the nerve in his heel, but I am no doctor. I told him that if I were him, I would certainly try PC-95 because of its powerful anti-inflammatory properties. He came to my little office in Irvine, California, and bought two bottles of PC-95 and left. I suggested he take at least 10 tablets per day—the therapeutic dose in Europe. About two weeks later, Fred called me again and said, "I can hardly believe it, but my heel is getting better and I need some more product," so I sent it to him.

About a month later, Fred called again and said he was doing his daily walk again and was very pleased! He then told me that he worked for KIEV radio and said, "Rod, you must get on the radio and tell people about PC-95." The first few weeks I did a show once a week for 15 minutes. After each show I would race back to the office to see if there were any phone calls—we got lots of calls. Then I began doing a half-hour show once a week, then three times a week, and finally I was doing several shows every day on different stations. Now I am on the radio across the United States.

Back on July 1, 1994, exactly four years to the day after my son, Rex, was killed, my younger sister, Marilyn, at age 58, had a major stroke and was hospitalized. After the stroke she was in terrible shape. She had difficulty speaking, the right side of her face was sagging, and she couldn't really use her right hand.

The doctors had determined that her right carotid artery was over 90 percent blocked. In September of that year, Marilyn had carotid artery surgery. When she came home from the hospital, my brother and I were there. Of course, I wanted her to start taking PC-95 immediately. The doctors sent her home on Coumadin (a blood thinner) and an aspirin a day and said that they had done all they could do for her. The rest was up to time—maybe she would get better and maybe not.

That was all the fuel I needed to get her started on PC-95. I had to argue with her husband as he strongly felt that if the doctors didn't prescribe it, she shouldn't take it. We almost got into a fist-fight over this issue. Finally, he relented and Marilyn started taking four tablets a day of PC-95. I wanted her to take much more, but that was as far as they would agree to go. Soon she noticed a little improvement and then agreed to take six tablets per day.

On December 17, 1994, she phoned me from her home in Minneapolis, Minnesota. She was crying but very excited. She said, "Rock, listen to me. I can now say the words I want to say, and I looked in the mirror and my face is no longer sagging. And besides that, I can now use my right hand. I don't have full use of my fingers, but at least I can sign a check." Then she said, "I am so excited. I am going back to work."

That day was one of the happiest days of my life and hers, too. I then knew that all the research that I had read and all the stories I had heard about people benefiting from proanthocyanidin (PC-95) would change my life forever. I made a total commitment that day to introduce the world to the benefits of PC-95, and I asked God for help. I knew that with his strength, protection, and guidance I could go forward. Roex would bring the highest quality products available from around the world, like PC-95, to the public for their great good. I thank God because today, we are well on our way.

It has been difficult to educate people on the importance of PC-95. I strongly feel that everyone should be taking PC-95 every day. It is so beneficial to the cardiovascular system and our health in general. It is 50 times more effective as an antioxidant than vitamin E. I hope someday soon, the news media will realize how important antioxidants and proanthocyanidins are to our health and that they will help us educate the public. When that happens, think of all the people who have had strokes or heart attacks or have diabetes, eye problems, cancer, and so many other health problems who will benefit from taking PC-95. Our job has just begun, but our destination is obvious—to educate everyone on the importance of taking antioxidants, vitamins, minerals, essential fatty acids, and PC-95!

—2

The Mind-Body Connection

The Missing Link to Health, Wealth, and Happiness

As a man's understanding of the mind increases and his capacity to utilize the subtle laws of nature grows, he will gradually be set free.
—ERNEST HOLMES, *The Science of Mind*

The mind-body connection is proving to be the most important misunderstood relationship within our society. In America and most other countries of the world, we know more about space and its complexities than we know about the human mind. The human mind is the least understood, the least researched, the most feared, and yet the most important connection to the evolution of life and health.

The medical community and the pharmaceutical companies, until recently, have prevented the general public from learning much about the correlation of the mind to the health of the body. We must understand how the mind works in order to free ourselves from the bondage of illness and disease and overall human suffering.

25

THE BRAIN

Most people believe the mind resides in the brain and they are one and the same. This is not true. To help you understand, let's take a look at the brain.

The brain is about 3–3.5 pounds. It contains trillions of brain cells (neurons), which communicate by means of neurotransmitters. These cells control everything from our breathing and heartbeat to all other autonomic (involuntary) activities and also our senses (hearing, vision, smell, etc.), speech, memory, imagination, communication, and overall health.

The brain is often described as consisting of a left hemisphere and right hemisphere. The left hemisphere is considered the logical, analytical, and rational side of the brain, which controls speech, reasoning, and so on. The left hemisphere mode then is the sequential mode, the objective mode, the verbal mode, and yet it can process only between six or seven simultaneous inputs. When we learn a profession, becoming an engineer, architect, physician, lawyer, or scientist, it is the left side of the brain that is primarily involved. This is also where the conscious mind resides.

The right side of the brain, or the right hemisphere, is considered the subjective side, the intuitive side, the nonrational and involuntary side. It involves imagination, spatial relationships, deductive reasoning, and memory. It is capable of processing and combining about two million simultaneous inputs of information. This is also where the subconscious mind resides. We see things in this mode through the imaginary side of the brain, the subjective side (i.e., through the right hemisphere). Artists, musicians, and poets have occupations that require more integration between the left and right sides of the brain than many of the more functional professions, such as lawyers, accountants, and scientists.

THE MIND

The *mind* is the *thinker*.

The *brain* or the soul is the *executor* of the thought.

The *body* is the *manifestation* of the thought.

To examine the mind and how the mind uses the brain to carry out its thinking, we must examine the following components:

- *Conscious mind:* This is the objective mind.

- *Unconscious mind:* This is the subjective mind, including memory storage and what is called "the mental law."

These two distinct parts of the mind are responsible for your makeup as an individual—your individuality and how you perform as that unique individual. These two sides of the mind are basically divided into intuition and emotions on the right side and thinking and intellect on the left side.

- *Critical faculty (the conscience):* This is the screening factor that controls the passage of information from your conscious mind to your subconscious mind. It helps you decide what is right or wrong—for you.

In my study of hypnotherapy, I learned people will not do something under hypnosis (like remove their clothing in a room

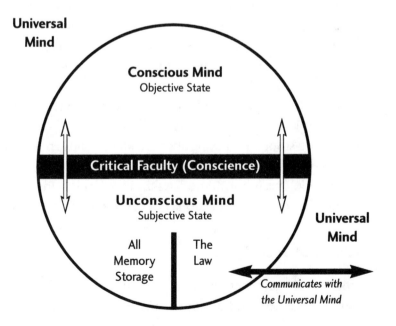

full of people) that they would not do consciously. This is because the critical faculty will not allow it.

- *Universal mind (the collective unconscious):* This is made up of all the individual minds of all time, much like the ocean is made up of billions of drops of water.
- *Mental law:* This is our connection with the universal mind. This law includes physical laws of nature (such as gravity), which we have no control over, as well as the mental law of our creator.

The illustration above will help you understand the way I see the conscious and the unconscious mind and their relationship to each other. While this picture fairly represents the mind, you should now correlate the conscious mind with the left hemisphere of the brain, the unconscious mind with the right hemisphere, and the critical faculty with your conscience.

The Unconscious Mind (Subconscious)

Have you ever had a feeling when meeting somebody new that you really like that person? This can work the other way, too—you know there's something about the person you just don't like, and later you find out that you were right to trust the "feeling" you had. That is your unconscious mind, the intuitive side of your mind, connecting with you.

Have you ever tried to think of a name or an answer to a question that you know, but you just can't think of it? And then later, after you have stopped thinking about it, all of a sudden it comes to you. It comes to you through the unconscious mind from your memory bank. This is one of the ways the mind works. Incredibly, the mental law dictates our actions directly and indirectly.

The Power of Thoughts

Do not allow negativity to be a part of your thinking. It can lead to many imbalances and disappointments in your world. *If you think you can, you will, and if you think you can't, you won't.* Either way, you are right.

By thinking, we can bring into reality whatever we desire. *Whatever the mind can conceive and believe, it can achieve.* If you think about this statement, you will come to realize its power. An individual, through conscious thought, can bring into his or her life whatever he or she believes. Your thoughts manifest through the condition of your body, your health, your family, your relationships, your happiness, and your world. Your unconscious mind can be your best friend or your worst enemy, depending on your thoughts. The unconscious mind executes your thoughts according to this strict mental law. Your individuality is what makes you different from every other person and is based on how you use this mental law, i.e., the way you think.

Be Very Careful What You Think

For this reason, I am telling you; whatever you ask for in prayer, believe that it is granted to you, and it will be yours.
—MARK 11:24

The following is an example of how your thoughts can work against you. We often hold certain individuals (such as medical doctors) in a position of prestige. Because of this respect, we may give very little thought to questioning their decisions and statements, thus allowing them to easily pass through the critical faculty.

For discussion purposes, let's say you have cancer and have been undergoing alternative therapy and are beginning to feel much better. You go to see your doctor, who, however, has no respect for this therapy and says, "Why spend your money? It will do you no good. You have terminal cancer and the best thing you can do is go home and get your affairs in order."

Because of your prestigious view of the doctor, you assume he is right and you give up. Sure enough, you soon die. But you died because your conscious mind accepted his statement as fact, and your subconscious mind carried out the will—the thought—of your conscious mind. We must all be on guard as to what we think about and what we accept to be true. The reason is this: The thoughts from your conscious mind are executed by your servant, the unconscious mind, according to a strict mental law.

This mental law works for all people the same way. When you understand how the mind works, you can draw into your life what you think. Consequently, to learn how to think is to learn how to live. If we understand the mind, we can learn how to live by using the mind.

Life reveals itself to each person as we understand this mental law, and the evolution of human consciousness (awareness) brings with it endless powers and possibilities. We must utilize the mind more effectively in our daily lives and strive to reach an understanding of the mind-body connection.

Your life is much like a ship at sea. A ship without a rudder can spin around aimlessly, getting nowhere; but when you use a rudder, you can steer the ship and aim for your destination. The unconscious mind is like a rudder and works to steer your thoughts from your conscious mind. Your unconscious mind executes your thoughts. Your body and your life, as they presently exist, are manifestations of your past thoughts. Anything the mind thinks, it can "unthink" or change. If, therefore, by the law of cause and effect, we have produced unpleasant conditions in our lives, we should be able by this same law to produce an entirely different effect. Consequently, as we bring thoughts into our subconscious mind we initiate this universal law, which must and will respond as long as we believe, and the thoughts are manifested in and through our bodies and our lives.

GOAL SETTING

Setting and reaching a goal is a good example of the use of this mental law. Here is how it works: Select a goal and write it down. Outline the steps you need to take to reach your goal. Think about your plan and modify these steps until you're certain your goal will be obtained. During this period, your conscious mind is giving instructions to your subconscious mind, directing it to put all its powers in motion to reach this goal. From here on, the mental law is at work, moving you unconsciously toward this goal. When it is reached, you must immediately set another goal. Your unconscious mind is your servant and wants to serve. Should you not set another goal, the unconscious mind has no task at hand. Many people make this mistake. With no goal to pursue, your subconscious mind is free to do what it wants, including going back to old bad habits. Your best friend can become your worst enemy.

> *As a man thinketh, so is he.*
> —ERNEST HOLMES, *The Science of Mind*

The power of suggestion is very strong. Positive affirmations can be very helpful as well. When you say something out loud and repeat it, it makes that thought concrete. You start to believe it, and then you begin to take action accordingly. If you do this, it is much more likely to happen.

The Bible tells us that *faith without works is worthless*. If you believe something, you also have to follow through with the appropriate action. For example, if you truly believe that you are going to be a golf pro, you had better get out on the golf course and spend time swinging those clubs. Nothing worthwhile comes without hard work—but you also have to believe!

IT'S ALL IN YOUR HEAD

In psychosomatic illness, the mind influences the body to create or exacerbate illness. More importantly, the mind can also influence the body to heal itself. Most of the time, we do not even realize that this is going on as it is on a cellular level and not easy to visualize or feel.

Deepak Chopra has written extensively about connecting the mind, body, and spirit. He makes several interesting points. In his book *Ageless Body, Timeless Mind,* Chopra writes:

Unfortunately, our culture has made the mistake of deciding that the human body is a machine, an inert lump of matter that works without any intelligence of its own. This misconception led to a second mistake—that most spiritual people must be those who renounce the body, deny its passions or at the very least attempt to control its desires.

This kind of prejudice against the body runs contrary to the way that Nature fashioned us. Nature balanced mind, body and spirit as co-creators of our personal reality. You cannot do a single thing, from falling in love to uttering a prayer to metabolizing a molecule of sucrose, without affecting everything you are. The body is a platform that allows any experience or energy to see the light of day. It is a 3D projection of billions of separate processes going on at any moment including a process as profound as coming to know the reality of God.[2]

STRESS AND YOUR HEALTH

The field of medicine is just beginning to use the mind-body connection for healing. Psychosomatic medicine is the study and the recognition of how the mind influences the body and health. Psychoneuroimmunology is the scientific field that investigates linkages between the brain, behavior, and the immune system and the implications of these linkages for physical health and disease.

The central nervous system and the immune system, communicating through the neuroendocrine system (which produces various hormones), are closely involved in an individual's adaptation to the environment. Recent evidence suggests that stress (either natural or produced in a laboratory) can alter the human immune system. Measurable immune system parameters can be influenced by strategies involving self-regulation, including relaxation and imagery techniques, biofeedback, humor, and hypnosis and conditioning. Many studies report significant immune parameter changes as a result of these various strategies. Knowledge of the mind's effect on the body is rapidly expanding and may be important for achieving improved immune system functioning and health.

A woman with breast cancer, which had metastasized, was under the care of her regular physician, but her treatment was having no beneficial effect on her condition. She stopped the treatment and started seeing a physician experienced in psychosomatic medicine, who began working with her mind with positive affirmations and other therapy. In six months, her cancer was completely gone. This was confirmed by her previous physician, who also told her that the cancer would return. She believed him and soon it did. She returned to the other physician, who again helped her to eliminate the cancer in 12 months. These types of examples are abundant, but they usually are not recorded in the scientific literature. Most physicians are highly skeptical of such events and often claim that there was some misdiagnosis.

Chronic stress increases our vulnerability to infectious disease. The role of stress in the course of other conditions, such as inflammatory bowel disease, remains unclear. Because there are large individual differences in people's psychological response to stress, it is important to consider the role of mental and physical responses to stress. Depression has been associated with the immune system, and a person's attitude, perceived control, view of self, and view of the future have been associated with immune parameters and health in some studies.

USE THE MIND TO OVERCOME PAIN

Many people are able to use the mind to overcome pain. Your mind can be the best painkiller there is! When individuals experiencing severe pain are given a placebo with the explanation that it is a painkiller, 30 percent will experience the same pain relief as if a real painkiller had been administered. The placebo effect is powerful, indeed.

The same placebo pills can be used to stop excessive gastric secretions in an ulcer patient, to lower blood pressure, or to fight cancer. All the side effects of chemotherapy, including nausea and hair loss, can also be induced by giving cancer patients sugar pills while assuring them that they are receiving a powerful anticancer drug. There also have been incidences where injections of sterile saline have led to remissions of advanced malignancy because the patients believed. Research indicates that the pills or injections themselves may be meaningless; the power is in what the patient believes.

The placebo effect is about healing. The human healing process can be substantially influenced in actual medical practice by appropriate kinds of caring, communication, and patient empowerment.

We all need to be in control of our thoughts. Use your mind to bring health, wealth, and happiness! Remember, if it is to be, it is up to me!

Nutritional Supplementation Today

The Real Story

Scientific evidence is overwhelmingly in support of nutritional supplementation. Research has shown that vitamins and minerals, often in doses higher than those recommended by the daily value (DV, formerly recommended daily allowance, or RDA), may protect against a wide range of health problems, including cataracts, heart disease, stroke, diabetes, cancer, birth defects, and even aging.

It is estimated that almost three out of every four Americans (over 70 percent) regularly take vitamin and mineral supplements. This demonstrates the clear opinion of the public that they are indeed an important part of a healthy lifestyle. Unfortunately, too many vitamin peddlers have swamped the marketplace, making outlandish advertising and labeling claims and pushing questionable-quality pills simply to make a fast buck at the expense of your health.

As a result, most health seekers are confused and overwhelmed by too many choices. They need to fight back. They need to know what they are spending their hard-earned dollars on and that what they are taking is actually doing them some good.

Many people are taking supplements by the fistful, but they're not getting well. There may be a number of reasons for this. Few people today really understand what they are taking and why. We all have a responsibility to our bodies to know what we are putting in them.

The major issues the consumer needs to be aware of when selecting nutritional supplements are

- Quality control
- Raw materials
- Delivery system
- Advertising claims
- Dosage

QUALITY CONTROL

The quality of the raw materials used in making supplements is of the utmost importance. Most studies are designed to obtain the best possible results, so they usually use raw materials of the highest quality possible. If a product contains substandard material, the results are not likely to be the same as those seen in scientific studies using superior materials.

This is especially true for herbs. Standardized herbal extracts have a much higher concentration of the active ingredient compared to an herbal supplement that contains the whole plant ground up. Therefore, the standardized extract is likely to be more potent in its pharmacological effect.

This issue of quality control is a common problem. Consumers may get frustrated with the product they are using, thinking that it doesn't work, and may even come to the conclusion that all nutritional supplements are a waste of money. This is very unfortunate as it may be that what they need to do is switch to a more reputable company that uses high-quality ingredients in its products.

We can all learn from the experience that Bill from Boston had in dealing with his rheumatoid arthritis. Bill suffered from pain and discomfort for years. For the last four years he had been using many popular supplements to aid his degenerative condition: MSM (methylsulfonylmethane—dietary sulfur), chondroitin and glucosamine (sulfates), and flaxseed oil. He said his condition had improved somewhat, but he still struggled. He agreed to try PC-95 (proanthocyanidin from a leading supplier of premium-quality botanicals), vitamin C powder (pharmaceutical grade), and MSM powder (the patented material from Dr. Stanley Jacob, the world's top researcher in this field), all supplied by Roex. After about three weeks he called me and said, "Rod, my pain is gone, it's just gone."

This clearly demonstrates how important it is to use superior-quality materials. If the supplements you are using are not helping you, switch to a brand that contains superior-quality materials and see for yourself the difference it can make.

RAW MATERIALS

The form of raw materials selected can have a direct effect on the quality and effectiveness of a supplement. For example, the majority of calcium supplements sold today are composed of calcium carbonate, which is chalk. This is the cheapest form of calcium. It is also hard to digest and poorly absorbed, especially for older individuals, because it must first bind with hydrochloric acid before it can be utilized by the body.

A double-blind, placebo-controlled, randomized trial demonstrated the effect of calcium carbonate and calcium citrate on bone loss in healthy postmenopausal women. Half of the women had a low dietary calcium intake (below 400 milligrams [mg] per day), and the other half had a moderate intake (400 to 650 mg per day). The women received either a placebo, 500 mg calcium carbonate, or 500 mg calcium citrate malate per day for two years.[3]

In women who had undergone menopause five or fewer years earlier, bone loss from the spine was rapid and was not affected by supplementation with calcium carbonate. In the postmenopausal women (six years or more) and those who were given the placebo, bone loss was less rapid in the group with the higher dietary calcium intake. In those with the lower calcium intake, calcium citrate malate prevented bone loss during the two years of the study; its effect was significantly different from that of the placebo.

Healthy older postmenopausal women with a daily calcium intake of less than 400 mg can significantly reduce bone loss by increasing their calcium intake to 800 mg per day. At the dose tested, supplementation with calcium citrate malate was more effective than supplementation with calcium carbonate. From the research that I have read, a person could benefit by taking several different forms of absorbable calcium plus other minerals in proper balance, using 1,200 mg of total calcium for even greater benefit.

Some forms of calcium, such as calcium citrate and hydroxyapatite, are far more usable by the body and more effective than other forms of calcium, such as calcium carbonate or oyster shell calcium. When you hear statements like "Calcium is good for your bones" or "MSM is good for your joints," you need to find out what type of calcium or what source of MSM.

I am appalled by the many health resources that continually recommend the use of calcium carbonate over other, more bioavailable forms. Yes, calcium carbonate has the highest amount of elemental calcium and is comparatively inexpensive, but you must ask yourself why you are taking calcium in the first place. If it is doing little good, aren't you really doing your own body a disservice?

Another concern with other sources of calcium such as bone meal or seashells is high lead content. These inexpensive sources of calcium may contain appreciable levels of lead. Long-term exposure to lead may cause kidney damage, high blood pressure, or birth defects.

DELIVERY SYSTEM

Many people want to know, "Which are better, tablets or capsules?" The answer is, it depends upon the product. Some formulas and raw materials provide better delivery and assimilation in tablets, while others are more effective in capsules. This is a very important question because an improper delivery system can interfere with the assimilation and effectiveness of the product, as well as your ability to tolerate the formula or product. Both tablets and capsules can be good when properly manufactured. Which ones should be used depends on the raw material.

Some products can serve multiple purposes when presented by different delivery systems, such as digestive enzymes, probiotics (beneficial bacteria), and colostrum (a natural immune modulator). For example, you can open up colostrum capsules and pour the contents directly into your mouth and around your teeth and gums. (This is one of the best products I know of for gum disease.) Don't swallow it right away, but let it sit there and mix with your saliva. Some of it will be absorbed through the thin mucosal membranes of the mouth. Also, digestion starts in the mouth, so chewing digestive enzymes can greatly enhance digestion and assimilation of the foods we eat.

ADVERTISING CLAIMS

The sad truth is that some companies will say anything to get you to buy their products. If a company cannot support their product claims with scientific documentation and a product sounds too good to be true, then it probably is. Today, with Internet access to medical libraries, medical journals, and other respectable data banks, there is absolutely no excuse for companies making false claims, but they often do.

It is our responsibility to educate ourselves and search out what supplements can be beneficial for our own specific health concerns. This information is readily available in books such as this one and many others, the Internet, and other places. Look for scientific documentation supporting claims made for supplements and the benefits they provide. Don't take everything you hear and read at face value.

DOSAGE

Proper dosage is also a very important consideration in regard to obtaining optimal benefits from nutritional supplements. Many people will not take a high enough dose in order for a supplement to be effective. And in other cases, individuals will go overboard with the dangerous attitude that "more is better." This may create toxic side effects or waste money, as more does not mean better.

If you want a supplement to have a therapeutic effect, you may need to research what the proper therapeutic dose is. This may vary with your age or body weight. Sometimes you will need to take a higher dose for the first few days or weeks to reach a saturation point and then reduce to a "maintenance" dose.

Many people become discouraged, thinking that their supplements are not working, but in fact, they are not using them correctly. They may not be taking an adequate amount of a supplement or may be improperly combining it with another supplement. For example, mineral supplements should not be taken at the same time as a fiber supplement. It is also important to find out which supplements work best on an empty stomach and which should be taken with food. (See part 3 regarding specific health problems.)

MY DAILY NUTRITION PROGRAM

People continually ask me, "Why do you take so many different vitamins every day?" I tell them, "We are what we assimilate!" In other words, we may take into our bodies many different food groups, but how much nutrition is in them and how well do we absorb (assimilate) those nutrients? As we age, our ability to assimilate the nutrients in food diminishes. Medications can also hinder assimilation, as do various health problems, including diabetes, arthritis, and alcoholism. The poor quality of the foods we get today from most sources is also a major problem. These factors combined can create a need for a significant number of vitamins, minerals, and antioxidants just to protect ourselves and support the many structures and functions of the body.

A healthy body is a guest-chamber for the soul;
a sick body is a prison.
—FRANCIS BACON

The primary reason most people get limited results from nutritional supplements is they take inadequate amounts to actually address deficiencies. The second reason is the quality of the supplements.

The third reason is most bizarre. Studies tell us that nearly 75 percent of the people taking nutritional supplements take a multivitamin. Think about this and ask yourself if you honestly believe that you can get all of your daily nutritional requirements from one little tablet. If you believe that marketing scam, you deserve what you get—nothing! Give the money that you spend on such items to your church or favorite charity; it will do you more good.

Unfortunately, another issue heavily influences many people about nutrition—*scare tactics*. Many false and misleading statements are made that scare and confuse people. For example, several studies performed under questionable circumstances now have people worried that they may be getting *too much* vitamin C.

This is the kind of nonsense that drug companies and the media are foisting on you. Dr. Linus Pauling, perhaps the foremost authority on vitamin C, ingested approximately 20 grams of vitamin C daily for 30 years or more with very strong scientific evidence to support his program. Many other very learned doctors and scientists have also proved how effective vitamin C is in the body in large quantities both for antioxidant protection and liver functioning, as well as collagen manufacture. It disgusts me to read misleading news releases (specifically, the one issued by Dr. James Dwyer from the University of Southern California) about how vitamin C enlarges or increases the walls of the arteries without telling the whole story. It absolutely increases these and other cell walls. But that is good, not bad. Cell wall deterioration is one of the primary complications of diabetes, cardiovascular disease, and many other health problems, but for some reason, the researchers don't tell you that.

A growing body of research supports massive doses of intravenous vitamin C in cancer therapy, yet the media and orthodox oncologists ignore it. Why? Maybe it works too well and it is terribly inexpensive. Researchers around the world are now studying vitamin C, olive leaf extract, grape seed extract, and other antioxidants and seeing amazing results, yet we get little if any news of their benefits to humanity.

Can the medical and pharmaceutical industries be that scared about the public getting so healthy that it would affect their profits? We know how the government has tried to regulate and control the sale of amino acids and other harmless natural substances. In fact, nutrition companies are not allowed to recite most health benefits on their labels or in their marketing literature. This is not right, but the situation is improving.

An abundance of new research on vitamins, minerals, and antioxidants demonstrates their wonderful benefits. (I am dedicated to bringing you the latest research from around the world that can have a profound effect on your health and your life through my daily radio show, *Roex Health Update*, that can be heard in major cities throughout the country.)

Happiness is more a state of health than of wealth.
                                             —FRANK TYGER

If you fall into the "drugs and surgery" trap, you may suffer the consequences. In fact, you may die about the same time you run out of money and/or benefits. It is not that drugs and surgery have no importance; they can be very important and even lifesaving. In my opinion, however, drugs and surgery should be a *last resort*, not the first, and they should not be used for the general health and maintenance of the human body. The proper approach to good health involves nutritional supplementation on a daily basis and bringing the body back into balance.

For all who read this book with skepticism: I am 68 years old as of this writing. I take no medications. I have addressed many personal health problems simply with nutrition and exercise. I thank God every day that I am alive for the great learning experience I have gone through in my life.

Most of you would shudder to think of having to go through all the health- and injury-related issues and rehabilitations that I have. Yet without having gone through them, I wouldn't be here today with this knowledge to share with you.

Keep in mind that what I do for myself may not be exactly right for you, but through 30 years of study, trial and error, the program outlined below has certainly done wonders for me. You can easily adjust your individual program according to your personal needs.

My Daily Program

As you read through and study my nutrition program, please refer to part 2 of this book for explanations of the different supplements mentioned below.

1. First thing in the morning (every morning with rare exception):
   - PC-95 (6 tablets or more)
   - Oleuropein (4 tablets or more)
   - Distilled water (8 oz or more)

   This provides me with the antioxidant protection for the day and helps stimulate the elimination system.

   Children can benefit from taking one PC-95 daily. To be healthy, children need antioxidants as much as adults.

   Note: In my opinion, PC-95 is the single most important nutrient to put in your body every single day of your life with the exception of pure water. If you can afford only one supplement, it should be PC-95.

2. Thirty minutes later:
   - Ester-C® (vitamin C) (4–6 tablets)
   - MSM (4 tablets or 1 teaspoon of powdered MSM in water)
   - CitriGenics I (3 tablets)
   - Immortale (2 tablets)
   - Colon Essentials (2–3 capsules)

   This is excellent for abundant energy—whether it's for exercise, work, shopping, or family activities. Within

30 minutes I start my exercise program. As I begin, my energy level starts to rise and stays high all through my workout and into the next several hours.

3. Exercise:

I try to work out for 45–60 minutes at least four times per week. I would like to do it daily, but my schedule is just too demanding. Be careful not to overdo it. When you are tired, you become more vulnerable to colds and flu.

4. Power Drink (my breakfast):

I pour 6 oz or more of apple juice (you can substitute any juice you prefer) and an equal amount of distilled water into a blender. Then I add the following:

- 2 scoops whey protein
- 1 raw egg (I have been eating a raw egg almost daily for 30 years.)
- 1 scoop (approximately 4,000 mg) glutamine powder
- 1 tablespoon psyllium husk powder or ½ cup ground flaxseeds for extra fiber
- 1 banana or any other fruit
- 2 tablespoons natural cultured yogurt
- 1 rounded teaspoon MSM powder

Next, I blend and drink. It's great!

I also take the following supplements with my drink:
- B complex (1 tablet)
- Calcium/mineral formula (6 tablets)
- Colostrum (4 capsules)
- Immortale for Men (2 tablets)
- Livalon (2 capsules)
- Vitamin A/D (1 capsule)
- EFAs (essential fatty acids) (5 capsules)
- Advanced Men's Formula (2 tablets). This prostate support formula, I believe, is one of the best in the world. I strongly encourage its use for every man over the age of 35 (and maybe younger).

5. Midmorning:
   - Colon Essentials (3 capsules)
   - Colostrum (4 capsules)
   - Ester-C® (4 tablets)

6. Lunch:

   For lunch I usually have an apple and some raw trail mix—that is, unless I have a luncheon appointment.
   - B-complex (1 tablet)
   - Immortale for Men (2 tablets)
   - Colostrum (3 capsules)
   - Advanced Men's Formula (2 tablets)
   - Digestive Balance Chewable Enzymes (3 before lunch and 3 after lunch). *People must learn the importance of adding enzymes to their diets.* Our foods are enzyme deficient, so we rapidly deplete our enzyme reservoirs. That leads to so many problems, including a significant portion of the 500,000 estimated gall-bladder removals annually in the United States.

7. Midafternoon:
   - Oleuropein (2 tablets)
   - Ester-C® (2 tablets)
   - Colostrum (4 capsules)
   - MSM (1 teaspoon) in distilled water
   - Vitamin C powder (1 teaspoon with the MSM)

8. Dinner:

   I usually eat a medium to large salad containing lots of raw vegetables: onions, peppers, avocados, tomatoes, lettuce, and whatever else I can put into it. It's great, healthy, easy on the body, and nonfattening. I prefer a homemade dressing consisting of olive oil, flaxseed oil, apple cider vinegar, fresh lemon juice, garlic, and black and cayenne pepper.

9. After dinner:
   - Digestive Balance Chewable Enzymes (3)
   - WOW (2 or more capsules)

- Hurricane (2 capsules)
- Advanced Men's Formula (2 tablets)
- CitriGenics II (5 tablets)
- Immortale for Men (2 tablets).
- Livalon (2 capsules). I think every adult in America could benefit from Livalon, the great liver detoxifier.

10. Bedtime:

- Melatonin. I like to cycle it by taking 1 tablet one night, 2 tablets on the second night, 3 tablets on the third night, and then I don't take any for a couple of nights.
- Calcium/mineral formula (4–6 tablets)
- Colostrum (4 capsules)
- Advanced Men's Formula (2 tablets)
- Immortale for Men (2 tablets)

11. All day:

I try to drink at least eight 8 oz glasses of distilled water daily. When you drink distilled water, it is a good idea to ingest about ¼ teaspoon of iodized sea salt daily or eat an apple with a little iodized salt (table salt). The salt will help hold the water longer in the cells. Note: If you have high blood pressure or do not drink distilled water, you should not take extra salt in your diet.

If you need more fiber and you are not allergic to shell-fish, you can take more CitriGenics II on an empty stomach during the day. It helps the body manage cholesterol—it helps raise the HDL (high-density lipoprotein, also called "good cholesterol") level, lower the LDL (low-density lipoprotein, or "bad cholesterol") level, and normalize total cholesterol.

I recommend that before starting this or any other nutrition program, you start a journal and write down anything and everything that bothers you—aches and pains, eye problems, circulation problems, diabetes, or allergies. Note any medications you take and their doses. Write down how often you are taking any type of pain reducers or other medications.

After 30 days on the program, open up the journal and see what has changed or fallen off the list. Make your notations and then close the journal. Stay on the program for another 60 days and return to the journal. When you review your journal entries from the beginning, you will hardly believe how your health has changed and improved!

Please note: This is *my* nutrition program. I do not recommend that you follow my program; it is merely a guide to help you understand my view of the importance of taking these products and what they are doing for me. If you take medications of any kind, be aware these supplements are potent products and they may cause medications to work more effectively in some cases. If you observe any side effects while taking these products, please check the side effects and contraindications of your medications. Your goal is to be medication free, but it takes time for the products to bring you back into balance. Please *do not stop* any medications without the advice of your doctor.

—4

Caveat Emptor

The Drugging of America

We live in a drug-oriented society, and drugs—both legal and illegal—are widely available and accessible. In fact, our entire external environment is filled with drugs, or unphysiological substances, that pervade our entire beings, and in many cases, we do not even realize it or recognize them!

In our culture, there are three categories of drugs:

1. Medically prescribed drugs and antibiotics, usually used for a condition, ailment, illness, or disease.

2. Recreational drugs. Examples of these drugs are alcohol, heroin, cocaine, "poppers" (amyl nitrate), marijuana, LSD, and numerous others, including nicotine, caffeine, and sugar.

3. Toxic chemicals, not usually considered drugs. These are chemical pollutants, contaminants, pesticides, additives, colorings, dyes, herbicides, fungicides, insecticides, organic phosphates, PCBs (polychlorinated biphenyls), heavy toxic metals, and the like. In fact, we are exposed to approximately 80,000 chemicals daily that are really toxic substances. They lead to much suffering, deterioration, degeneration, and premature death.

An abundance of these drugs and chemicals exists in our air, water, soil, and food supply. We eat them, drink them, and breathe them all the time. Add to this recreational and prescription drugs (including antibiotics, hormone replacement therapy, etc.) and we are placing quite a large burden upon the liver and body.

It is often easy to develop physical, physiological, as well as psychological dependency upon these chemicals, and we then become "addicted." If one suddenly stops consuming one of these drugs, uncomfortable withdrawal symptoms are usually experienced by the person. A craving and search for a "fix" occurs. Once it's procured, the symptoms of withdrawal dissipate—temporarily, that is. As the level of the addictive substance drops too low, withdrawal symptoms return and the search for a "fix" begins once again. On and on it goes. Coffee (caffeine) is a good example.

The food, chemical, and pharmaceutical industries have combined their advertising skills to woo Americans to purchase and frequently consume their products on an ongoing basis. They earn big money by keeping the unknowing and unsuspecting public addicted and drugged. We have all heard or seen the advertising statement "Ask your doctor if this drug is right for you."

Americans must recognize that there is a way to reverse this process. It requires changes in lifestyle: a diet composed of natural and organically grown foods, the appropriate nutritional supplements in optimal doses, pure water, detoxification, and cleansing of the entire body and brain. Anaerobic and aerobic exercise, creative work, genuine friends and friendships, and a meaningful relationship with love, respect, and admiration are also very beneficial.

Because of toxic external environments and toxic internal environments, millions of Americans develop allergies—hidden, unsuspected, compulsive allergic addictions and irritations. So we crave the same foods, drinks, and chemicals on a regular basis or lack the ability to consume many good foods. The various involved industries (food, milk, dairy, meat, chemical, and pharmaceutical) each take advantage of us and advertise their wares, reaping tremendous financial profits at the expense of our life, health, well-being, and pocketbooks. By keeping us drugged, toxic, and malnourished, these industries perpetuate our constant addictions. Is there a connection between cancer and all of these drugs and toxins? I certainly think so.

A NATION OF ADDICTS

If we pay attention to advertising on television and radio and in newspapers and magazines, we find out that there are drugs to give you energy, drugs to calm you down, drugs to perk you up, drugs to lift your depression and relieve your anxiety and tension, drugs to relax you, drugs to eliminate your headache, drugs to lessen and remove your pains, and drugs to treat your arthritis, cancer, diabetes, heart disease, premenstrual syndrome (PMS), and menopause. There are antibiotics to treat your infections, drugs to thin your blood, drugs to stimulate or suppress your immune system, and drugs to overcome the side effects of the other drugs you are taking into your body.

You must protect yourself and your family from exposure to and consumption of drugs that are so widely available, accessible, and prevalent in our society today. Are you seeking ways to cut down or eliminate medically prescribed pharmaceutical drugs and find safe, natural, alternative substances? Are you aware that you have "hidden" addictions to caffeine, tobacco, alcohol, sugar, and other harmful substances, as well as allergies to common foods?

You are no doubt aware that addictions are widespread and encompass a wide variety of harmful substances. You have no doubt heard, read, or seen that the conventional approaches to problems, diseases, and allergies in the medical community are drugs, surgery, and radiation. Does this make any sense to you?

Alcohol rehabilitation centers use counseling and unknowingly substitute five common substances for alcohol. They are widely available at AA (Alcoholics Anonymous) meetings: caffeine, sugar, doughnuts, sodas, and cigarettes. Nutritional supplements and hypnotherapy would be very beneficial here yet are not allowed.

In the medical and mental health fields, people who display incorrect or inappropriate symptoms, unusual behaviors, and abnormal thought patterns all need drugs, according to the pharmaceutical industry. (See chapter 5 on ADD/ADHD.)

The *Physicians' Desk Reference* (PDR) is a 3,000-page listing of the names and descriptions of all the drugs commonly prescribed by physicians around the United States. The PDR also lists harmful side effects and contraindications of each drug and the name and address of the manufacturer. When you read the side effects of these drugs it becomes very apparent that many times the side effects are worse than the problem you are trying to solve. Also, almost all drugs are toxic to the liver.

Most adults in Westernized countries are addicted to a variety of drugs, both legal and illegal: caffeine, tobacco, sugar, salt, sodas, alcohol, and other "legal" drugs. Each is widely available and easily accessible. And each has deleterious side effects. So buyer beware.

Finally, there is a group of individuals who have survived life the longest—elderly senior citizens. A staggering number of U.S. seniors are prescribed and use multiple medications each day. Most frequently, and sadly, the last drug prescribed was needed to lesson the side effects of the previously prescribed drug, and so on.

All of these drugs merely suppress symptoms, and few, with rare exceptions, deal with eliminating the underlying cause or causes of the difficulty. The great majority of seniors have multiple conditions; hence, they take several medications to cover their various conditions rather than address the underlying imbalance or deficiency.

Kill the Pain

People don't like pain. Right or wrong, the prevailing philosophy seems to be "If it hurts, numb it." Pain is a signal from the body that something is wrong. Painkillers (drugs) do what they say— they stop the pain. They don't make the problem go away, they just help you deal with it. Unfortunately, in order to accomplish such a task, they numb much more than the pain. They numb our minds, reflexes, motor skills, and the ability to function optimally mentally or physically. Painkillers are also highly addictive.

Think about how many people you know who are using such drugs. Four of the top 10 selling pharmaceutical drugs are pain-killers: codeine, Tylenol-3® (with codeine), Darvocet® (propoxy-phene), and prescription strengths of ibuprofen (Motrin®) and naproxen (Naprosyn®). Others include morphine, Percocet®, Per-codan®, Vicodin®, Demerol®, and Darvon®.

Anyone who has experienced arthritic pain knows how won-derful it is to find relief, even though temporary, from aspirin, ibuprofen, or some other NSAID (nonsteroidal anti-inflamma-tory drug). After a while, however, the pain returns, and your first inclination is to take another dose of the NSAID. As long as this is only occasional, it would seem no more dangerous than taking an aspirin for an occasional headache. The problem arises when the need for painkillers is frequent and perhaps growing, as in a chronic disease such as arthritis. Every year, about 3,000 Americans die from the side effects of substantial doses of aspirin and other NSAIDs. Another 41,000 people wind up in the hospital as well.

For short-term use, NSAIDs serve a very useful purpose. But for long-term use at high doses, as in osteoarthritis, they can be very dangerous. Problems they can cause include

- Kidney damage
- Liver damage
- Hypertension
- Gastrointestinal damage
- Asthmatic attacks
- Ringing in the ears

Another painkiller, acetaminophen (Tylenol®) is not actually an NSAID. It has its own problems, however. For example, you should never consume alcohol when you are taking aceta-minophen because of the very toxic effect on the liver.

Why Are We Drugging Our Children?

One of the most commonly prescribed drugs for our children today is Ritalin. Over four million children are currently using this or a similar drug. Ritalin is a psychostimulant often prescribed for children with ADD (attention deficit disorder) or hyperactivity. It can also be called "speed," although in children who are hyperactive, it has a calming effect and increases attention span. Side effects include irritability, nausea, appetite suppression, weight loss, and insomnia or other sleep disturbances. About 10 percent of those who take Ritalin complain of headaches, and about 9 percent develop tics and dyskinesia (impairment of voluntary movement).[4] The next chapter includes more on this disorder.

America Is Addicted to Sugar

Sugar is much like a drug in that it has addictive properties and adverse side effects. Sugar is not a whole natural food. It is refined, fragmented, denatured, and completely stripped of all nutrition present in its original form. Sugar cane and sugar beets, the primary sources for sugar, are natural and contain minerals, vitamins, trace elements, enzymes, fatty acids, and amino acids. The final result of the refining process is a pure crystallized form of sucrose, a white, "pharmaceutically pure" chemical.

Sugar is *absolutely worthless* to our essential dietary needs. Eating sugar actually creates a loss of essential nutrients required to metabolize it in the body, such as B vitamins and chromium. Interestingly, in the processing of raw sugar cane and sugar beets, over 90 percent of the naturally occurring chromium is lost. Chromium is required for insulin to bring glucose into the cells to be used as fuel. Without chromium, we can't burn these calories, so instead they are converted to fat and stored.

In addition to causing weight problems, sugar is a major contributing factor in the growth of many degenerative conditions, such as diabetes, heart disease, tooth decay, periodontal disease, and osteoporosis. Sugar consumption has also been associated with hyperactivity in children and with criminal behavior.

Overreliance on Drugs

We have been programmed by the pharmaceutical industry to believe that we need drugs to maintain our health. Drugs are not the answer for optimal health, immunity, and long lives. In fact, they often create more problems than they help. Drugs may give us quick relief—a bandage to cover up what we do not want to deal with. Pain is a symptom that something is wrong, that our immune system is unable to "keep up." Instead of looking at our diets and lifestyles and listening to our bodies, we turn to

- Painkillers to numb the pain instead of fix what is causing the pain.
- Antihistamines and nasal sprays to mask the symptoms of colds, allergies, and sinusitis.
- Antibiotics, especially for children who need to develop an immune system on their own, to ward off infections or to clear up acne.
- Alcohol, tranquilizers, or Valium to relieve stress and help us sleep.
- Antacids to dull an overworked digestive system due to over-consumption. Use of antacids diminishes our ability to break down our food, leads to "acid rebound," and has other side effects that can lead to stomach ulcers and even cancer.
- Crash diets or diet pills to help us lose weight.
- Caffeine and sweets to give us quick energy.

Refined concentrated sugar is rapidly absorbed into the bloodstream and quickly raises the sugar in the blood to a dangerously high level. At this point, one will feel an abundance of energy. The pancreas practically goes into shock. It is forced to compensate by producing and releasing high amounts of insulin, a hormone that allows the sugar to enter the cells so it can be burned.

The excess insulin not only rapidly brings the sugar level down, it lowers it far below normal. The term associated with this is "hypoglycemia" (or low blood sugar).

Something to Think About

In 1900, sugar consumption was less than 10 pounds per person per year. Now it is 150 pounds.

In 1900, the United States was rated first in health of 100 countries. Today it is 37th (in spite of the fact that we spend more per person on healthcare than any other country in the world).

Many adults have poor insulin function. Normal amounts of insulin are produced, but because of the high-sugar diet, this hormone is present more often than not. The cells eventually become less sensitive to the continual presence of insulin. This is analogous to the situation where the first few times the fire alarm goes off, we jump in response to it, but if it keeps ringing, we eventually ignore it.

Sugar accounts for approximately 24 percent of our total caloric intake. On average, Americans consume over 30 teaspoons of sugar per day. Some people are very careful and consume hardly any at all, so that means others are taking in more than the average.

We all know that candy, desserts, and sweets contain sugar, but do you realize how much? Sugar can be found in many places we would not even dream of looking: salt, peanut butter, bread, fruit juices, instant oatmeal, meat products, canned vegetables, mayonnaise, toothpaste, baby food, and more. If you think that you are avoiding sugar, take a look at how much is hiding in these popular foods:

Estimated teaspoons of sugar per serving:

Cola beverage (12 oz)	10
Hard candy (4 oz)	20
Apple pie (1 slice)	12
Sherbet (½ cup)	9
Flavored yogurt (8 oz)	7
Ice cream (4 oz)	5

Orange marmalade (1 tbsp)	5
Canned corn (5 oz)	3
General Mills Honey Nut Cheerios (⅔ cup)	2.5
Kellogg's Fruitful or Raisin Bran (⅔ cup)	2.25
General Mills Raisin Nut Bran (⅔ cup)	2
Ketchup (1 tbsp)	1

Percentage of refined white table sugar by weight:

Kellogg's Sugar Smacks	61
Nondairy creamer	60
Kellogg's Apple Jacks	55
Post Cocoa Pebbles	54
General Mills Lucky Charms	50
Milk chocolate candy	50
Salad dressings	up to 30

Note: Many manufactures try to "hide" sugar by giving it other names—corn syrup, corn syrup solids, maple syrup, molasses, cane syrup, fructose, dextrose, maltose, lactose, and so on.

Antibiotics

Antibiotics are still over prescribed, although it is well known that the indiscriminate use of antibiotics for every real or imagined illness leads to the development of resistance in the invading organisms. We are already having difficulty treating penicillin-resistant strains of gonorrhea. The penicillin-resistant disease first emerged in the Philippines, where even the most potent antibiotics are sold without a prescription and where prostitutes regularly take penicillin as a prophylaxis against venereal disease.

Antibiotics may be needed in certain situations, but they disrupt the natural homeostatic balance of necessary bacteria throughout the entire body. Antibiotics not only eliminate "disease-causing" bacteria, they also kill healthy bacteria that are needed by the body. When the use of antibiotics is absolutely necessary, probiotics should always be used as a follow-up to promote the replenishment of healthy bacteria in the digestive tract. (This is discussed in part 2.) One of the best probiotic formulas is Colon Essentials from Roex, which has three very powerful bacteria that benefit the colon and helps reinstate homeostasis in the body.

Sleeping Pills

Barbiturates and other hypnotics (sleep inducers) have a high risk of abuse. Many, many people either cannot fall asleep without sleeping pills or think they can't. While effective, these drugs reduce necessary REM (rapid eye movement) sleep, which is the type of sleep when we dream and when the mind and body repair themselves.

We need good quality sleep nightly for the body to recover from all the stress we put it through during the day. The immune system functions best when we are asleep, for example, which is why when we get sick, it is best if we just go to bed and let the body recover. However, if the sleep you get is not natural—that is, drug induced—the quality of your sleep will suffer and so will you.

Mark Hughes of Herbalife died recently because he had a sleep disorder and his physician prescribed antidepressant medication that became toxic when taken with alcohol. Why do so many people turn to dangerous drugs when many safe alternatives are available? Melatonin, a natural hormone, and other natural sleep aids without side effects are discussed in part 3.

Drugs control peoples' behavior, mind, perception, thinking, and learning abilities to the serious detriment of their health and well-being, yet the drugging of Americans continues at an unprecedented pace.

For a frightening story about the dangers of this situation, turn to "The Rise and Fall of the Killer Drug Rezulin" in appendix B. The story is taken from an article published in the *Los Angeles Times* on June 4, 2000.

—5

Attention Deficit Disorder/ Hyperactivity Disorder

The American Epidemic

One example of the drugging of America involves our children. Approximately four to six million school-age children and millions of adults display the many signs and symptoms of attention deficit disorder/hyperactivity disorder (ADD/ADHD), which is reaching epidemic proportions. Children who display inattentive, noncompliant, or hyperactive behaviors do not necessarily have a disease or disorder in the orthodox sense; instead, they may be experiencing abnormal brain chemistry due to a number of possible factors.

ADD/ADHD is defined as age-inappropriate impulsiveness, lack of concentration, and sometimes excessive physical activity. ADD/ADHD has been associated with learning difficulties and lack of social skills. Obviously, what constitutes "normal" in these areas covers a wide spectrum, and thus it is unclear which children suffer true ADD/ADHD and which children are just more rambunctious or rebellious than others. No objective criteria exist to accurately confirm the presence of ADD/ADHD.

Once ADD/ADHD was medically defined, pharmaceutical companies raced for an answer in the form of a drug. Unfortunately, the most successful treatment thus far has been central nervous system stimulants, such as Ritalin (methylphenidate). While these drugs appear to be effective for psychological, educational, and social disorders, many professionals feel they offer only a temporary solution since these drugs do not permanently change behavior patterns.

Worse, Ritalin can cause side effects. It is an amphetamine (speed) related to cocaine. While these drugs are stimulants in normal individuals, they often have a calming effect in those with ADD/ADHD. According to the *Physicians' Desk Reference*, Ritalin can cause a number of harmful symptoms, including

- Nervousness
- Insomnia
- Tachycardia (racing heart)
- Loss of appetite
- Memory impairment
- Headaches
- Stunted growth
- Zombie-like, robotic behavior
- Increased risk of cancer
- Depression

With continued use, the drug can even lead to psychotic episodes, dependency, and perhaps addiction. As tolerance increases, drug doses also may need to be increased, and stopping treatment suddenly can cause serious side effects.

Ritalin is a controlled substance. Besides cocaine, other drugs in this class (schedule II) include methamphetamines and methadone, all of which are categorized for their high abuse potential and severe side effects.

Dr. Mary Ann Block reported in *Energy Times* magazine that recently a teenage boy who had been taking Ritalin for 10 years died of a heart attack. The medical examiner attributed the death to Ritalin. Physicians responded by saying Ritalin could not have caused the heart damage. Because Ritalin has been used for so many years it must be safe, they claimed.

According to the National Institutes of Health (NIH), studies with Ritalin were conducted for only a short period, up to three months, before its approval. At that time, many believed that the affected children would outgrow the disorder, but we now know that this is not the case, and many individuals have been taking the drug for 15 years or longer.

Ritalin produces pharmacological effects similar to those produced by cocaine. Cocaine and Ritalin go to the same receptor sites in the brain and have the same effect on the heart as well. If any young person using cocaine daily for 10 years had a heart attack, there would be no question that the heart attack was caused by cocaine use.

FRIGHTENING NEWS

When Ritalin was given to cocaine users, they couldn't distinguish the Ritalin high from a cocaine high! In addition, one study out of Berkeley found that Ritalin users were three times more likely to develop a taste for cocaine.[5]

Despite this readily available information, America increased its administration of the drug 200–300 percent from 1991 to 1995. Another source stated that from 1990 to 2000, prescriptions for Ritalin increased by 600 percent.[6]

What is also very alarming is the increase in the prescription of Ritalin, as well as Prozac and clonidine—adult antidepressants— to children as young as two to four years old! The safety of these drugs has never been tested on such young children. Two-, three-, and four-year-olds are *supposed* to be hyperactive! The fault should not be focused only on the physician—consider the kind of parents who would drug their two-year-old because the toddler is active and prone to get into trouble.

It also should be noted that only here in the United States are Ritalin and these other drugs given to "hyperactive" children to such a great extent. Prescription sales for Ritalin in the United States are five times higher than in all other countries combined. In most countries, if a child is bored in school, he or she is likely

Ritalin Fraud?

On May 1, 2000, the firm of Waters & Kraus, LLP, filed a class-action lawsuit in Texas entitled Civil Action No. B-00-082, *Hernandez, Plaintiff, Individually and on Behalf of all Others Similarly Situated v. Ciba Geigy Corporation, U.S.A, Novartis Pharmaceuticals Corporation, Children and Adults with Attention-Deficit/Hyperactivity Disorder (CHADD), and the American Psychiatric Association.* The suit states allegations based on fraud and conspiracy. It highlights the four-year period from 1991 to 1994 in which CHADD allegedly received $748,000 in donations and contributions from Ciba/Novartis while actively increasing the sales and supply of Ritalin (methylphenidate) in the United States. For more information, visit www.ritalinfraud.com.

to be challenged with a more difficult assignment. Children who are labeled with ADD/ADHD are not lacking in intelligence; in fact, they often have higher IQs than their peers.

Recently, the Food and Drug Administration (FDA) allowed the use of Concerta, a new drug for children with ADD/ADHD. The drugging effect of each dose of Concerta lasts for 12 hours. Other harmful and toxic drugs prescribed to treat ADD/ADHD include Adderall, Catapres, Paxil, Zoloft, and Prozac. Each of these has numerous side effects and contraindications. None of these drugs address the underlying root cause of the problem, and the number of children classified with ADD/ADHD is growing at an alarming rate. Why don't doctors and the FDA look at sugar consumption? I think that is where we should start.

WHY NOT DEAL WITH THE CAUSE OF THE PROBLEM?

Instead of treating symptoms with drugs, it makes much more sense to examine the core problem and then build a solution based on the cause of the problem. While most sources maintain that the cause of ADD/ADHD is still largely unknown, a number of progressive researchers have narrowed down the possibilities to several key factors. Top suspects include

- Nutritional deficiencies
- Neurochemical imbalances
- Food allergies
- Hypoglycemia

Other related factors include poor eating habits, synthetic food additives and preservatives, and environmental toxins. Based on these findings, ADD/ADHD should be addressed by providing affected children with adequate nutritional support, while also monitoring their diet and environment.

Keep in mind that during a child's early years, the delicate nervous and endocrine systems are still in the developmental stages. Researchers have found that in children with ADD/ADHD, these systems may not be developing correctly due to specific nutritional deficiencies. The most commonly implicated deficiencies include essential fatty acids (EFAs), phospholipids, antioxidants, and vitamins and minerals—all of which are essential for healthy brain, nerve, and endocrine function.

Essential Fatty Acids

A deficiency of several EFAs has been observed in some children with ADD/ADHD compared with unaffected children. The EFA docosahexaenoic acid (DHA), a polyunsaturated omega-3 fatty acid commonly found in fish and flaxseed, is perhaps the most important nutrient needed by children suffering from ADD/ADHD.

DHA is concentrated in the brain, where it is critical for the healthy transmission of nerve impulses and cell membrane functionality. DHA is provided in breast milk but was not included in infant formulas until only the last few years. Without it, optimal development of the brain (and also the eyes) cannot occur.

Researchers at Purdue University compared boys with ADD/ADHD to boys who were considered normal and found that the ADD/ADHD boys had significantly lower serum and red blood cell levels of DHA than the normal boys. Several studies have shown that DHA supplementation has a positive effect on the symptoms of ADD/ADHD and related disorders.[7]

Abnormal Conversion of EFAs Suspected

Several researchers have hypothesized that some children with ADD/ADHD have altered fatty acid metabolism.

The Hyperactive Children's Support Group in England has found a connection between ADD/ADHD and EFA deficiency. The group's researchers suspect that hyperactive children might have a problem with an important pathway in the body that converts EFAs to prostaglandins—hormone-like substances that control all bodily functions at the cellular level. Their research demonstrated that many children cannot metabolize nor absorb EFAs normally. The EFA requirements of these children are thus higher than normal. An EFA deficiency results in some serious symptoms, many of which look like those of ADD/ADHD. Other common symptoms are eczema, asthma, and allergies.

The following points suggest the involvement of EFAs in ADD/ADHD–like behavior:

- Hyperactive male children outnumber females by three to one. They required two to three times more EFAs than females to prevent signs of EFA deficiency. Males may have more difficulty converting EFAs to prostaglandins.
- About two-thirds of children with EFA deficiencies have abnormal thirst.
- Asthma and eczema and other skin problems are more common in hyperactive children due to the defective formation of prostaglandins.
- Many children with ADD/ADHD are zinc deficient. Zinc is required for the conversion of EFAs to prostaglandins.

• Wheat and milk can adversely affect some children. These foods can block the conversion of EFAs.

Fatty acids must be converted in order to be used. Diet plays a key role in the process because it takes adequate zinc, vitamins C and E, niacin, and vitamin B_6 to convert omega-6 fatty acids to omega-3 fatty acids. Other factors that can interfere with this important conversion process are chronic illness, stress, and the consumption of large quantities of saturated fats and hydrogenated oils, which contain trans-fatty acids and drugs.

Phospholipids

Phosphatidylserine (PS), a natural phospholipid found in the brain (and foods such as lecithin and eggs), is another important nutritional compound for children with ADD/ADHD. It plays an important role in several metabolic and pharmacologic functions, and studies have documented its positive effects on the brain neurotransmitters (such as acetylcholine, serotonin, norepinephrine, and dopamine) that are intimately linked to behavior. This may be one explanation why PS supplementation can help improve behavior, cognitive function, concentration, attention, and memory.

B Vitamins

B vitamins, particularly vitamin B_6, have also been used for children with ADD/ADHD. Low levels of B_6 have been detected in some ADD/ADHD patients. A study of six children with low vitamin B_6 levels found that B_6 and Ritalin were both effective at reducing symptoms; of course, only the vitamin B_6 corrected the vitamin deficiency.[8]

One double-blind, crossover study found vitamin B_6 to actually be more effective than Ritalin in calming a group of hyperactive children.[9]

Certain B vitamin deficiencies are directly associated with reduced mental performance. These vitamins are essential for the proper development of the nervous system, metabolism, and psychiatric health. Vitamin B_6, B_{12}, and folic acid deficiencies are specifically implicated in behavioral problems, as well as in depression and personality disorders.

Vitamin B_6 is essential for optimal brain function, in part because it acts as an important coenzyme for the synthesis of the brain neurotransmitters GABA (gamma-amino butyric acid), dopamine, and serotonin. Researchers in Spain observed that vitamin B_6 and folic acid supplementation clinically improved both behavior and school performance in students exhibiting problems in these areas.[10]

With vitamin B_{12} deficiencies, neurologic and psychiatric disturbances are often present, along with symptoms of depression and dementia. This was observed by scientists at Baylor University Medical Center, who noted that patients with low levels of vitamin B_{12} and folic acid had diminished neurotransmitter function, which ultimately contributed to neurologic and psychiatric conditions.[11]

Minerals

Other research shows that certain mineral deficiencies can contribute to ADD/ADHD, and other abnormal behaviors. The results of a Canadian study, for example, showed that adolescents with behavior problems often had marked iron deficiencies.

Some children with ADD/ADHD have lowered levels of magnesium. In a preliminary but controlled trial, 50 ADD/ADHD children with low magnesium levels (as determined by red blood cell, hair, and serum levels of magnesium) were given 200 mg of magnesium per day for six months. Compared with 25 other magnesium-deficient ADD/ADHD children, those given magnesium supplementation showed a significant decrease in hyperactive behavior.[12]

About 80 percent of American children are believed to have magnesium deficiencies, so this is not likely to be the entire solution to the problem.

What are the symptoms of a magnesium deficiency in children?

- Excessive fidgeting
- Restlessness
- Anxiety
- Psychomotor instability
- Learning difficulties in the presence of a normal IQ
- Low calcium assimilation

Foods high in magnesium include fresh green vegetables, raw wheat germ, soybeans, whole grains, seafood, figs, and almonds. How often are significant amounts of these foods included in a child's diet?

Zinc deficiencies are also common among individuals with ADD/ADHD. Zinc is important for conversion of EFAs to prostaglandin hormones, which help the brain deal with cortisol, often referred to as the "stress hormone."

In addition to magnesium and zinc, other common mineral deficiencies seen in ADD/ADHD patients are iron, copper, and calcium.

Mineral deficiencies, in conjunction with chronic exposure to heavy metals, can also lead to mineral imbalances that affect neurological function. If the body lacks the minerals that it requires, it may accept and store dangerous metals such as lead, mercury, and aluminum instead.

Sugar

Some parents believe that sugar and refined carbohydrate foods may exacerbate ADD/ADHD. One study found that avoiding sugar reduced aggressiveness and restlessness in hyperactive children. Girls who restrict sugar intake have been reported to improve more than boys who do the same. Glucose tolerance tests on several hundred hyperactive children found that the majority exhibited abnormalities in glucose metabolism. These imbalances often develop into hypoglycemia, which provokes the release of adrenaline and other hormones that can trigger hyperactive behavior.[13]

Research has firmly established that several nutrients and herbs can help promote favorable sugar metabolism. For example, the trace mineral chromium, which plays a key role in balancing blood sugar, can help the body to regulate insulin. Olive leaf extract also improves blood sugar imbalances. In fact, European studies show it can help normalize blood sugar by optimizing serum insulin levels.

Antioxidants

Antioxidants that cross the blood-brain barrier (such as PC-95 and lipoic acid) can also help ADD/ADHD.

The following was reported by Dr. Steven W. Heimann in the *Journal of the American Academy of Child & Adolescent Psychiatry* (April 1999):

> J.M. was 10 years old when care was transferred from a colleague, who maintained the patient on dextro-amphetamine (a stimulant) for ADD/ADHD. Significant developmental delays in early childhood prompted an evaluation at a well-respected autism center, whose doctors did not support the presence of a pervasive developmental disorder but rather ADD/ADHD. The patient had difficulties with hyperactivity, impulsivity, and inattention. Poor social skills led to frequent physical altercations at school.
>
> Stimulants provided only a slight improvement in ADD/ADHD target symptoms. Without notifying the treating psychiatrist, J.M.'s parents began to give him proanthocyanidins in addition to his prescribed dextroamphetamine. The parents noted significant improvement in target symptoms during the manufacturer-mandated algorithm-defined two-week titration phase.

The parents reluctantly agreed to give J.M. a trial period off of proanthocyanidins for four weeks to compare the effects of the stimulant plus proanthocyanidins to the stimulant alone. Within two weeks of withholding the proanthocyanidins, the patient became significantly more hyperactive and impulsive, marked by numerous demerits in school. He was also involved in several physical altercations, which previously had abated with proanthocyanidins. J.M.'s regimen of proanthocyanidins was reinstated, and again he demonstrated significant improvement in ADD/ ADHD target symptoms within three weeks.

Antioxidants that cross the blood-brain barrier are known to benefit the central nervous system and conditions such as Parkinson's disease. It is certainly possible that similar oxidative damage to receptor sites, autoreceptors, neurotransmitters, or second-messenger systems contribute to the neurobiochemical basis of ADD/ADHD. Therefore, the use of antioxidants such as PC-95 could have a role in the treatment of ADD/ADHD. Well-controlled studies are needed, but hundreds of scientific and anecdotal reports can be found claiming the benefits seen in individuals with ADD/ADHD.

In his book, *The Antioxidant Miracle*, Dr. Lester Packer writes:

When experiments in my laboratory first revealed that proanthocyanidins had a modulating effect on nitric oxide [a free radical], I hypothesized that it could be a potential treatment for attention deficit and hyperactivity disorder (ADD/ADHD), a condition that is characterized by the inability to concentrate, impulsivity and hyperactivity. No one knows the cause of ADD/ADHD, but at least one major study showed that people with ADD/ ADHD have less blood flow directed to the part of the brain that helps to organize behavior. Since nitric oxide is instrumental in circulation, it seemed probable that an imbalance of nitric oxide could be at the root of this common problem.

Clinical studies also show that lipoic acid can help normalize blood sugar levels by increasing cellular uptake through the burning of glucose. These two supplements can be used individually or together in children with behavior problems.

Food Allergens

Food sensitivities also play a role in behavioral disorders; therefore, affected children should be tested for the most common food allergies. The top five include milk, wheat, corn, chocolate, and citrus. Parents should also prevent their children from consuming any foods with preservatives, additives, and colors.

The number of studies linking ADD/ADHD and poor diets is mounting. In one study, 59 of 78 children (75.6 percent) referred for "hyperactive behavior" improved on an open trial of an elimination diet. Nineteen of them were studied in a placebo-controlled, double-blind challenge protocol.[14] In a study published in *The Annals of Allergy*, the benefits of eliminating reactive foods and artificial colors in children with ADHD were reported. The report concluded, "Dietary factors may play a significant role in the etiology of the majority of children with ADHD."[15] In a review of studies at California State University, implementation of "nutrient dense diets" in 813 state facilities "resulted in significantly improved conduct, intelligence, and/or academic performance."[16]

Lifestyle Changes

Smoking during pregnancy appears to increase the risk of giving birth to a child who develops ADD/ADHD. Also, a newborn or developing child should not be exposed to secondhand smoke.

Exposure to lead and other heavy metals has been linked to ADD.

Breast-feeding is highly recommended for all newborns to ensure optimal brain development. Having mothers supplement their diets with essential fatty acids before pregnancy and throughout breast-feeding is also helpful.

—6

Sex
A Giant Three-Letter Word

Sex is the most talked about and thought about three-letter word in our vocabulary outside of the word *you*. We see and hear more about sex today than anytime in history. There are many reasons for this popularity, but three of the most significant reasons are given below.

First and foremost, we are constantly being bombarded by electronic and print media about sex. Sex sells! It gets people's attention, and advertising executives and those concerned about ratings know this. Second, because of its intrigue, young people today are very interested in experimenting with sex. The third point is the most worrisome. Sex education in our schools may be creating more problems than it is solving by not encouraging morality, which should be taught side by side with the subject. The result of all of this is a rise in sexually communicable diseases, which causes great concern to all the people in multiple relationships as well as the Centers for Disease Control (CDC).

Why are so many people interested in improving their sex lives? Why are there so many commercials on television (and everywhere else, too) for products to boost sexual performance?

SEX PROBLEMS

One of the reasons so many people have sex problems today is the sad state of health in this country: poor circulation, hormone imbalances (particularly, low testosterone levels), prostate problems, side effects of medications, nutritional deficiencies, and other stumbling blocks such as weight problems, depression, impotence, and frigidity. Unfortunately, our lifestyle, stress, diet, and relationships influence our sexual life, performance, and enjoyment. In addition, the mind can either be our best friend or our worst enemy in a sexual relationship, and this aspect is often overlooked.

With the geometric rise in diabetes, kidney disease, chronic alcoholism, multiple sclerosis, atherosclerosis, chronic fatigue, and vascular disease, it is no wonder there is such a problem with sex. Between 35 and 50 percent of all men with diabetes experience impotence to some degree, and one in four men over the age of 50 are impotent to some degree. Many of these men have turned to the medication Viagra. It apparently works quite well but can cause a sudden, substantial drop in systolic and diastolic blood pressure, which can lead to dangerous conditions or even death. (Note: If this situation were to happen with a nutritional supplement [and I doubt it would], I'm certain government authorities would have it taken off the market immediately.)

Many medications can cause sex problems. Antihypertensives (high blood pressure medications) greatly inhibit libido. These include Aldomet, Aldoril, Apresoline, Capoten, Catapres, Corgard, Inderidem, Lopressor, Lozol, and Minipress, just to name a few. Diuretics also can cause loss of sex drive, and these include Aldactazide, Aldactone, and Maxzide. Antidepressants such as Triavil (also known as amitriptyline) and Navane, also list impotence as an associated side effect. Obviously, the generics, if available, of these drugs have the same effect.

INFERTILITY

Infertility is generally defined as an inability to conceive after six months to one year of trying. An estimated 20 percent of couples have trouble conceiving. While it appears that falling sperm counts may be part of the problem, rising maternal age is certainly a factor, and as women are having babies later in life, the risk of infertility rises.

Treating infertility has become a huge medical industry during the past few decades, with doctors doing everything from prescribing fertility drugs to arranging for test-tube babies (in vitro fertilization). These well-publicized procedures can cost up to $10,000 apiece or more, and it may take several years for some women to see results, if at all.

Scientific studies have linked infertility with deterioration in sperm quality (sperm count and morphology). The decline of sperm quality in industrialized nations is a controversial issue; however, a Swedish infertility study tested the morphology and total count of sperm in like populations of men in 1956, 1966, 1976, and 1986. A significant reduction was observed in both parameters.[17] A similar study compared 185 consecutive spermiograms from men of infertile couples in 1980–1981 to age-matched controls of a group tested in 1960–1961. The study found that both sperm volume and count sharply decreased. Further analysis suggested larger decreases for men living in urban versus rural environments.[18] The results are not shocking when you consider the increased exposure to toxins in industrialized nations. Those faced with infertility issues may have success by incorporating nutritional supplementation. Results from many studies including those at the University of Iowa, the University of Wisconsin, and the University of Grenoble, Tronche, suggest that nutritionally deficient diets contribute to low sperm count.[19] (Note: Ingredients found in Immortale have been shown to support sperm production and increased feelings of well-being.)

In addition, researchers investigating the cause of the decline in sperm counts have reported some alarming findings. Evidence suggests that pesticides and other pollutants are estrogenic, meaning that they have chemical effects that mimic those of the female sex hormone. Exposing the male of a species to enough estrogenic chemicals for an extended period produces a feminization effect, including a lower sperm count. A growing number of scientists are calling for controls on all of these estrogen-like chemicals, but so far nothing is really being done about them.

Here's some of the evidence that feminization is, in fact, taking place: In Lake Opopka, Florida, a big spill of an estrogenic pesticide occurred in 1988. Subsequently, male alligators developed abnormally short penises, reproductive impairment, and female-like hormone levels. In the lower Columbia River in the Northwest, juvenile male otters have testicles that are only one-seventh of the normal weight. They, too, show evidence of exposure to estrogenic chemicals. Florida panthers were exposed to the estrogenic pesticide DDT for years, and they ate other animals that were also exposed. Panther fatty tissue was found to have high levels of DDE, a DDT breakdown product. The panthers also have an unusually high incidence of abnormal sperm, low sperm counts, undescended testicles, and thyroid dysfunction.

The use of such chemicals is a strong reason why it is so important to drink distilled water and to eat organically grown, nongenetically modified foods. This is also why it is so important to maintain a healthy liver. Supplements that can help support the liver and rid the body of harmful chemical compounds include Livalon (milk thistle extract) and PC-95 (proanthocyanidin).

REJUVENATING HERBS AND NUTRIENTS FOR A GREAT SEX LIFE

No magic aphrodisiacs exist that work for everyone, but some great formulas and tonics can rekindle the spark in your sex life. They can help accomplish the following:

1. Increase the blood flow to the genital organs to prolong or enhance arousal. (This is the strategy of Viagra.)
2. Balance hormone levels and increase the amount of testosterone in the blood to promote desire in both men and women.

3. Improve the nerve endings and nerve conduction in parts of the brain that control pleasure, making touch more enjoyable and heightening sensation.

For Men

This section describes some specific herbs, extracts, vitamins, and minerals that can benefit the body for enhanced physical, mental, and sexual performance.

Puncture Vine Leaf and Fruit (Tribulus terrestris) This plant is native to eastern Europe. Clinical research has shown that *Tribulus* generates a tonic effect on sexual organs and hormones, assisting the body in healthy sperm production, promoting an increase in sexual drive, and maintaining healthy testosterone levels. This is due to the nutritional support that *Tribulus* provides to the body's production of hormones. The extract of the plant is recognized as a diuretic and aphrodisiac. It has anti-oxidant and hypolipidemic (lower blood lipids) activities. *Tribulus terrestris* extract has also been effectively used for nonspecific impotence and aging for men in both Europe and Asia. All the pharmacological properties of *Tribulus terrestris* are clinically proven.

A much desired additional benefit is its ability to enhance lean muscle mass development in both men and women. The last significant benefit *Tribulus terrestris* can have is its very powerful and favorable influence on the entire urinary tract for both men and women. You will find it in both Immortale for Men and Immortale for Women.

Wild Green Oats (Avena sativa) Oats make horses frisky and have long been considered to be a male sexual energizer, hence the phrase "sowing his wild oats." In folk medicine and among current herbalists, green oats are used to treat nervous exhaustion, insomnia, and "weakness of the nerves." Wild oats contain alkaloids that are believed to account for oats' relaxing action. The more you use this herb as part of an enhancement formula, the more effective it can become.

Korean (Panax) Ginseng Panax ginseng has been revered in Asia for centuries as a male potency and longevity tonic. It stimulates sexual function in both males and females. Studies confirm that the long-term administration of Korean ginseng enhances erectile capacity and sexual performance. Researchers state that the effects of saponin, extracted from ginseng, on the smooth muscle of erectile tissues suggest a possible breakthrough in the treatment of erectile dysfunction, bringing hope to many sufferers. An Italian study of 66 adult males recently showed that ginseng may enhance levels of sex hormones, such as testosterone, and sperm volume and motility.[20]

Korean ginseng works by affecting the nervous system, cholesterol and lipid metabolism, and endocrine activity. Ginseng has a tonic effect on the entire body, helping the body to adapt. This herb increases analytical and overall mental performance while diminishing fatigue. Ginseng has been called the "king of all tonics" because it has been shown to help the body strengthen normal functioning and to assist in overcoming the effects of stress and fatigue, promoting health and vitality. Among the significant components of ginseng are the phytochemical triterpenoid saponins (chemicals with medicinal properties), known as ginsenosides. Many researchers believe these phytochemicals may be helpful in assisting the body to normalize hormone balance.

Muira Puama (Prychopetalum olacoides) This herb is native to the Brazilian Amazon. Indigenous tribes of Brazil use this plant internally as a tea for treating sexual debility and impotency, neuromuscular problems, rheumatism, grippe, cardiac asthenia (weakness), and gastrointestinal asthenia and to prevent baldness. It is also used externally in baths and massages for treating paralysis and beriberi.

In a French study, Muira Puama was given to 262 men with a lack of sexual desire and inability to attain or maintain an erection. Within two weeks, with a daily intake of this herb, 62 percent of the men claimed marked improvement in these areas. In other studies, 66 percent (62 out of 94) of the participants reported an increase in the frequency of sexual intercourse. One Brazilian study claimed effectiveness in over 70 percent of the people studied.[21]

Proanthocyanidins (PC-95) Proanthocyanidins are known to enhance circulation throughout the body. PC-95 is a great complement to any formula or program for enhancing blood flow. This herbal extract performs best when taken by itself or with one or two other antioxidants, such as olive leaf extract and vitamin C.

Ginkgo (Ginkgo biloba) This herb has a high flavonoid (antioxidant compound with medicinal properties) content. Many scientific studies on ginkgo involve its flavonoid action on the vascular system. This effect can be found throughout the body, especially in the brain, making ginkgo the most famous herb for improving brain function. It has been shown to be very useful for stimulating blood supply in impotent men, improving the duration and quality of erections. At low doses it can improve both mental behavior and sexual function in elderly patients who originally showed problems with alertness.

Ginger (Zingiber officinale) According to reports of research with animals in Saudi Arabia, ginger significantly increased sperm count and motility. There are no known studies on humans, but ginger is so safe and tasty that it definitely is worth trying. Ginger does have some mild antioxidant properties, which can only help.

Horny Goat Weed (Epimedium spp.) This plant is used in Chinese medicine to enhance male sexual function and performance and to correct reproductive disorders. It is being prescribed for impotence, infertility, premature ejaculation, low sperm count, and reduced sex drive and is used to nourish the male sexual area. *Epimedium* has been studied extensively and has been demonstrated to increase the levels of corticosterone, cortisol, and testosterone. These studies have concluded that its androgen-like effects stimulate sexual activity, increase sperm production, and heighten sexual desire.

Sarsaparilla Root (Smilax reglli) This is a plant containing saponins, which may aid in hormone balancing. It has been used for centuries in North and South America as a male sexual enhancer. Athletes find sarsaparilla can benefit performance and increase testosterone levels.

Yohimbe (Coryanthe johimbe) Yohimbe is a tree that grows in West Africa. The bark has been used for centuries (or longer) to make a tea to amplify male virility and sexual prowess.

The active component, yohimbine, has been used for over a century in the treatment of erectile dysfunction. Yohimbine is approved by the FDA for treatment of male impotence, whether due to vascular problems, diabetes, or psychogenic causes.

Systematic studies have shown that it has a remarkable positive effect on sexual performance. Yohimbine (though not the whole herb) has been the subject of at least two dozen scientific studies, most of which have confirmed its ability to increase blood flow to the penis and cause erectile stimulation. The few controlled, randomized human studies conducted have consistently shown the advantage of yohimbine (compared to a placebo) as a sexual stimulant for impotent and healthy males.

Yohimbine stimulates the central nervous system, increases resting heart rate, and slightly raises body temperature. It dilates small arteries in the skin and increases blood flow to peripheral parts of the body. In men, the surge of arterial blood to the penis is accompanied by slight compression of veins there, thus preventing blood from flowing out of the organ.

Yohimbe may cause side effects similar to those of other stimulants, including anxiety, restlessness, jitters, dizziness, headache, and insomnia. Higher doses may lead to more serious symptoms, such as rapid heartbeat and a dramatic rise in blood pressure. Those who should not use yohimbe include children, pregnant women, and the elderly; people with psychiatric conditions; anyone with a history of problems related to the heart, liver, or kidneys; and persons who have gastric or duodenal ulcers.

Yohimbine is present in significant quantities in almost all over-the-counter herbal yohimbe products. While most of the testing on yohimbe has been done on men, it seems it may hold promise for women as well. (I do not use it because it may cause inflammation of the genitals in men.)

Damiana (Turnera aphrodisiaca) Damiana contains a volatile oil that is known to stimulate the genitourinary tract—the basis of the claim for its aphrodisiac properties. It also may provide a sex-hormone balancing effect. Damiana may be a very good component of any formula for sexual enhancement for both men and women.

Maca This is a radish-like tuber that grows in the mountains of Peru, where it is used in traditional Andean culture for male impotence, especially for increasing sexual desire or as an aphrodisiac. The active ingredients consist of glucosinolates, sterols, and saponins. These sterols are precursors to hormones, especially sex hormones—the ones we want to awaken for healthy passion. It has also been effective for menstrual and menopausal symptoms in women. Other traditional uses include increasing energy, stamina and endurance in athletes, promoting mental clarity and improving chronic fatigue syndrome. (I have personally tried this herb and found that *Tribulus terrestris* is much more effective.)

L-arginine This amino acid plays a number of important roles in the body, including stimulating the pituitary gland and thymus. The resulting glandular secretions may affect sperm formation, muscle building, and immune function. Arginine may also promote heart health by helping to improve blood cholesterol profiles, relieve heart-related chest pains (angina), and control blood pressure.

Arginine has also been shown to act as a body stimulant for the production of nitric oxide. A gas molecule, nitric oxide has a number of potential effects on body cells, including relaxing arteries and small blood vessels. This can benefit sexual response by maintaining blood flow to the penis or clitoris, for example. Although researchers are still exploring its actions, there is some indication that nitric oxide may also function as a sex-enhancing neurotransmitter.

Numerous studies over the past decade have explored the role of nitric oxide in sexual response. Nitric oxide has been shown to increase erections in primates, dogs, cats, rats, rabbits, and other animals. Animal studies have also determined that long-term oral administration of arginine has potentially beneficial effects on erectile response. As one study concluded, "These data support the possible use of dietary supplements for treatment of erectile dysfunction."[22] A few animal studies have also shown beneficial effects for both nitric oxide and arginine on female sexual response.

A more limited number of studies have looked directly at the effects of arginine on human sexual response. For example, a small 1994 study in which men took 2.8 grams of arginine every day for two weeks showed a significant improvement in erectile function.[23] The clinical efficacy and acceptance of L-arginine HCl was tested in 40 infertile men. All of these men had a normal number of spermatozoa but a decreased motility; this decreased motility was not due to infection or to immunological disorders. The treatment consisted of 80 milliliters of 10 percent L-arginine HCl administered daily for six months. L-arginine HCl showed to be able to improve the motility of spermatozoa without any side effects.[24]

Most recently, a study published in 1999 followed for six weeks 50 men with erectile dysfunction. Among those who took a high (5-gram) daily dose of arginine, 31 percent reported significant (subjective) improvements in sexual function, compared to only 12 percent of those taking a placebo.[25]

Foods high in arginine include sunflower seeds (one of the richest dietary sources), as well as other nuts and seeds, such as peanuts, sesame seeds, soybeans, almonds, and Brazil nuts.

Niacin This vitamin is well known for increasing circulation, evidenced by the tingling feeling one gets on the skin after taking it. Increasing blood circulation can help deliver to the sexual organs the nutrients needed to perform better. Several studies have shown that niacin can help in sexual function for both males and females.

Zinc This mineral is required for normal testosterone and sperm production. It has been hypothesized that high levels of impotence in American males may be due to chronic zinc deficiency. This may explain why in ages past, oysters, which are loaded with zinc, were thought to be an aphrodisiac.

Good sources of zinc include spinach, papaya, collards, brussels sprouts, cucumbers, string beans, endive, cowpeas, prunes and asparagus.

Vitamin C For treatment of male infertility caused by sperm abnormalities or clumping, vitamin C supplementation has been shown to be as effective as several fertility-enhancing drugs.

Vitamin B$_6$ People who advocate micronutrient supplementation often recommend vitamin B$_6$ for infertility. The best sources of this nutrient include cauliflower, watercress, spinach, garden cress, bananas, okra, onions, broccoli, squash, kale, kohlrabi, Brussels sprouts, peas, and radishes.

Choline Scientists at the University of North Carolina School of Medicine in Chapel Hill have found that in male rats, a deficiency of dietary choline, one of the B vitamins, is associated with infertility.

Lecithin is an excellent choline source. Herbal sources of choline include fenugreek leaves, shepherd's purse, ginseng, horehound, cowpeas, English peas, mung beans, and lentils.

Note: Men also need to address prostate health. See the segment on prostate health in part 3 for more understanding of the importance of maintaining this gland and supporting its function.

For Women

Most of the substances described for men also apply to women, and vice versa, with a few exceptions. Both men and women should look for enhancement formulas that include many of these ingredients. For women, the following products may be helpful and beneficial:

Dong Quai (Angelica sinensis) This herb is classified as having a tonic action for both men and women but especially women (mostly seen in its ability to tone the blood). This is the most commonly used herb in Asia to regulate menstrual function and to tone the female organs. Dong quai has been shown to both contract and relax uterine muscles and is also used to increase sexual activity in females. It has the reputation for keeping the female system *female*.

Damiana (Turnera aphrodisiaca) Damiana contains a volatile oil that is known to stimulate the genitourinary tract—the basis of the claim for its aphrodisiac properties. Damiana provides a hormone balancing effect.

Other constituents of damiana include arbutin, a known antimicrobial agent for the urinary tract; thymol, useful against fungus, intestinal worms, and parasites; copaene and cadinene, which are useful for lung inflammation; and sitosterol and gonzalitosin, which have mild antitumor effects. In summary, this is one incredible herb that needs to be a part of any formula for body function, sexual enhancement, and overall health protection.

Kava (Piper methysticum) Kava comes from the Polynesian islands, where it is reputed to be very useful in helping women relax for increased sexual pleasure. Kava is excellent for treating stress and tenseness in the body so one can be more receptive to his or her partner. This herb also has a relaxing function on the entire pelvic area. It is being employed in clinics to calm bladder infections and relax the urinary area. It also has strong antimicrobial action similar to *Tribulus terrestris.*

Puncture Vine Leaf and Fruit (Tribulus terrestris) This plant is native to eastern Europe. Clinical research has shown that *Tribulus* generates a tonic effect on sexual organs and hormones, promoting an increase in sexual drive and maintaining healthy testosterone levels. This is due to the nutritional support that Tribulus provides to the body's production of hormones. See the men's section on this herb for information on lean muscle mass enhancement.

Wild Yam Wild yam contains plant steroidal sapogenins similar to the female hormone progesterone. It cannot be converted in the body into progesterone, DHEA (dehydroepiandrosterone), or other sex hormones. The herb may, however, have mild hormonal effects through other mechanisms. Many women successfully use wild yam to reduce the symptoms of PMS and alleviate discomforts associated with menopause. It is often taken to relieve menstrual or uterine cramps. Wild yam may also help prevent or treat dysmenorrhea and indigestion.

Folic Acid For years, naturopaths have suggested folic acid, a B vitamin, for women who are infertile. The CDC in Atlanta urges pregnant women to consume more folic acid because it prevents severe spinal birth defects. (Folic acid is found in edible jute, spinach, endive, asparagus, papaya, okra, and cabbage.)

Estrogen Dominance

The problem of excess estrogen levels, or estrogen dominance, in both men and women has become a huge health problem in the last few decades. Estrogen dominance, however, is not yet fully accepted by all medical professionals.

We are bombarded with an abundance of environmental pseudo-estrogens or xenoestrogens (literally, "foreign estrogens") in Western civilized societies, which creates an imbalance with our other hormones, primarily progesterone.

Estrogen replacement therapy (estrogen without supplemental progesterone), hysterectomy, birth control pills, exposure to xenoestrogens, and dietary abundance all contribute to estrogen dominance. Excess calories from an abundance of animal fats, sugars, refined starches, and processed foods lead to estrogen levels in Western women twice as high as those in women in Third World countries. This sets the stage for an exaggerated estrogen decline at menopause.

In addition to pre- and postmenopausal bone loss, other problems associated with estrogen dominance include

- Allergies
- Diminished sex drive
- Depression
- Fatigue
- Fibrocystic breasts
- Increased blood clotting
- Infertility (in men and women)
- Miscarriage
- PMS
- Uterine cancer

How to Have Great Sex

The following are lifestyle recommendations for men and women who want a healthy, active sex life:

- *Limit or omit alcohol.* Too much alcohol can affect sexual performance. Excess alcohol consumption decreases the body's ability to produce testosterone. In other words, the mind may be willing, but too much alcohol definitely diminishes a man's ability to have an erection.

  Also, long-term alcohol use has been associated with testicular atrophy, which can lead to increased estrogen and decreased testosterone. Studies also have linked alcohol use to benign prostatic hypertrophy (BPH), which can lead to prostate cancer.

- *Stop smoking.* Cigarettes can constrict blood vessels in the penis and cause impotence. Nicotine has the exact opposite effect of L-arginine. So if your love life is important to you, ignore those advertisements that depict smokers as sexy and desirable. And who wants to kiss a smoker? Also, avoid secondhand smoke.

- *Exercise regularly.* Exercise at least three days a week for one-half hour or more per day. (See chapter 7.) Exercise can have a tremendous positive impact on your sexual health. Men who exercise at least three to four times a week have sex more often. Women who exercise on a regular basis report they feel more sexy. Exercise stimulates blood flow throughout the body and has a rejuvenating, energizing effect.

  Note: Vigorous exercise, as well as hot tubs, saunas and tight underwear, can lead to increased temperature in the gonads and reduced sperm count.

- *Watch your weight.* Keep your weight under control and normal for your body structure. Excess weight may diminish blood flow to the sex organs, causing impotence and other problems.

- *Adjust your attitude.* Some people say, "It is all in your head!" It isn't all in your head, but the right attitude helps.

- Uterine fibroids
- Fat gain (especially around the belly, hips, and thighs)
- Water retention

Xenoestrogens are known to cause

- Infertility
- Premature puberty
- Fibrocystic breast disease
- Breast cancer
- PMS

Environmental pollutants play a key role in many of our current health problems, including breast cancer (now at epidemic levels), PMS, infertility, and fibrocystic breast disease. Xenoestrogens are found in everyday synthetic materials—materials previously thought to be inert. They include DDT (a pesticide), PCBs, and DDE (a DDT breakdown product).

The body's hormones are measured at levels of parts per trillion. To function in optimal health—and especially optimal sexual health—the sex hormones, including estrogen, progesterone, testosterone, and DHEA, all need to be at their proper levels and in balance with each other. If not, problems occur. However, pollutants that affect the human sex-hormone systems occur at 100 to 1,000 times greater concentrations than those of the body's normal hormones.

Thirty years ago, researchers showed that DDT and PCBs could induce mammary tumors in laboratory animals, a warning signal suggesting that they might do the same in women. But for more than a decade, the cancer establishment (the National Cancer Institute, the American Cancer Society, and researchers at the nation's leading cancer research centers) has largely ignored these findings.

Almost 20 years ago, researchers noted that human breast tumors contain higher levels of these toxic chemicals than surrounding cancer-free breast tissue. Still, little attention was paid to the subject.

In 1992, Dr. Frank Falck, then an assistant clinical professor in the Department of Surgery at the University of Connecticut School of Medicine, published an analysis of tissue samples from 40 women who had biopsies of suspicious breast lumps. Compared with lumps judged benign, those that were cancerous showed much higher levels of PCBs, DDT, and DDE.[26]

Common Pollutants around Us

The following information on some of the common environmental chemical pollutants affecting our sex lives and reproductive health is taken from *Our Stolen Future* by Theo Colborn:[27]

DDT A study published in the Proceedings of the Society of Experimental Biology and Medicine in 1950 by two Syracuse University zoologists, Lindeman and Burlington, described how doses of DDT prevented young roosters from developing normally. The researchers injected the pesticide into 40 young roosters for two to three months. The DDT did not kill the roosters or even make them sick. But it made them look like hens. The birds' testicles were only 18 percent of normal size. Their combs and wattles remained stunted and pale. The injections resulted in chemical castration.

Michael Fry, a wildlife toxicologist at the University of California at Davis, injected eggs from western and California gull colonies with DDT, DDE, and methoxychlor (another synthetic pesticide known to bind to estrogen receptors). He found feminization of the males' reproductive tracts. Typical female cells were found in the testicles, and in cases of higher doses, he noted the presence of an oviduct, the egg-laying canal normally found only in females. Despite all this internal disruption, the chicks looked normal.

DDT binds to estrogen receptor sites in the body—in males and females. It is now considered one of the classic xenoestrogens. DDT is metabolized to DDE in the human body within a few months. DDE then may last in the body for several decades.

DDT use was banned in the United States. However, worldwide production of DDT has never been higher. In fact, DDT is still manufactured in the United States and shipped to Third World countries.

Don't think that we in the United States have escaped DDT exposure: The DDT this country ships to Third World countries ends up sprayed on vegetables and fruits shipped to U.S. supermarkets. In 1991, the United States exported 96 tons of DDT.

Since DDT persists in soil for several centuries, those living in houses built upon or near former agricultural land are exposed to the chemical daily.

Plastics Manufacturers routinely add chemicals such as nonylphenols to plastic polystyrene and polyvinyl chloride (PVC). Nonylphenols are now known to cause estrogen-sensitive breast cancer cells to proliferate, multiply, and grow. Researchers have concluded that nonylphenols act like an estrogen. These are found in plastics we use every day, such as toys, bottles, nipples, storage containers, and so on.

One study showed that the food-processing and packaging industries used PVCs containing nonylphenols. Another reported contamination of water that had passed through PVC tubing. The breakdown of chemicals such as those found in industrial detergents, pesticides, and personal care products gives rise to nonylphenol. Global production of another estrogenic chemical, alkylphenol polyethoxylate, totaled 600 million pounds in 1990. Although the products purchased by consumers are not themselves estrogenic, studies have shown that bacteria found in wild animals, in the environment, and in sewage treatment plants degrade these alkylphenol polyethoxylates, creating nonylphenol and other xenoestrogens.

Detergent Breakdown Products John Sumpter, a biologist from Brunel University in Uxbridge, England, began to study sexually confused fish reported in English rivers by anglers. Many fish caught in the lagoons and pools just below the discharges from sewage treatment plants looked quite bizarre. Even experienced anglers could not tell if the fish were male or female, as they showed both sexes' characteristics at the same time. They were perfect examples of intersex (where individuals are "stranded" between both sexes).

Sumpter used a marker that helped identify female fish. Normally in females, vitellogenin, a special egg protein, is made in response to estrogen from the ovaries. On an estrogen signal from the ovaries, the liver produces vitellogenin and the protein is incorporated into the eggs. Since the response is dependent on estrogen, vitellogenin levels found in male fish would be a good indication of estrogen exposure.

Caged fish raised in captivity and then kept in the contaminated pools made 1,000 to 100,000 times more vitellogenin than control trout kept in clean water. Fifteen sites were sampled. The results demonstrated soaring vitellogenin levels and indicated a national problem. Alkylphenol levels from detergent breakdown products are high on the list of suspected causes. However, Sumpter suspects that the synergistic qualities of several xenoestrogens acting together are what really produce the problem.

Canned Foods Plastic coatings are often used by manufacturers to line metal cans to help reduce the metallic taste in canned foods. These linings are present in about 85 percent of the cans in the United States. Researchers analyzed 20 brands of canned foods purchased in the United States and Spain. They discovered bisphenol-A in about half of the food tested at levels up to 80 parts per billion. This is 27 times greater than the concentration of bisphenol-A that caused breast cancer cell proliferation in a Stanford University study. A vast majority of the cans available worldwide contain these plastic linings.

Commercially Raised Beef, Chicken, and Pork Commercially raised livestock are routinely given xenoestrogens to cause them to retain water. It is an effective, cheap, quick way to fatten them up, resulting in greater profits for the farmer. In the 1970s and 1980s, Puerto Rico saw an epidemic of very early puberty in girls (even of toddler age) and young boys, who developed breasts as a result of meat and dairy products containing high levels of estrogen. In the United States, the use of estrogen compounds is now slightly better regulated, but they are still very much used and abused.

Birth Control Pills Birth control pills contain a synthetic estrogen and a synthetic progesterone to force the body to cycle in a normal manner, even though conception may have occurred and different hormone levels are supposed to occur. Adding extra estrogen to a woman's body exacerbates fibrocystic breast disease.

Researchers also have shown the spermicide nonoxynol-9 breaks down in the body into nonylphenol—a known xeno-estrogen.

It is a known medical fact that estrogen stimulates breast cancer and other health problems. The breast cancer rate in the United States is now 1 out of 8 women. In the 1950s, the rate was 1 out of 20.

Even the pharmaceutical industry believes that excess estrogen is causing breast cancer and fibrocystic breast disease. A drug specifically made to block the estrogen receptor is sold as a fibrocystic breast disease cure.

Supplements to Fight Estrogen Dominance

While all the substances listed for men and women earlier in this chapter can be helpful for sexual function in general, the following are essential for combating the effects of estrogen dominance. Men and women can often greatly benefit by supplementing with natural progesterone, which needs to be in balance with another hormone, estrogen. Many individuals benefit from using wild yam. Other hormone-balancing herbs include *damiana* and *dong quai*.

Men, and oftentimes women as well, may need to increase their testosterone levels. This can be safely done with botanicals such as *Tribulus terrestris, Panax (Korean) ginseng,* and *sarsaparilla extract.*

Levels of the hormone DHEA are also often low in many individuals, especially those over the age of 50. Supplementation can be very helpful, but one does need to be careful with the dosage as side effects occur when one takes too much.

What Can We Do?

Several simple precautions can greatly reduce your exposure to xenoestrogens. For example:

• Use glass or ceramics whenever possible to store food.
• If you must use plastics, do not heat them in the microwave oven or leave them in the sun.
• Use a simple soap or detergent with fewer chemicals (no moisturizers, dyes, or perfumes).
• Use natural pest control (mousetraps, ladybugs, cayenne pepper) instead of pesticides.
• Avoid synthetic chemicals.
• Don't use herbicides.
• Buy hormone-free meats to eat.
• Buy "organic" produce—produce grown without pesticides, herbicides, or synthetic fertilizers or hormones.
• Avoid using spermicides and birth control pills.
• Drink distilled water.

Another important hormone that can be very helpful is *melatonin*. This hormone, produced by the pineal gland, helps regulate levels of many other hormones in the body. (See chapter 13 for many other benefits of melatonin.) This one is my favorite.

In summary, sex is a complex subject with physical, mental, emotional, and spiritual factors intertwined. What is good for the goose may not be good for the gander, so to speak. You need to be aware of all the many parameters that influence sex. Hopefully, this chapter can put you on the right road to answers you may be looking for.

—7

The Importance of Physical Activity

Paul Ward and Rod Burreson

The idea that humans need regular physical activity has been widely accepted by the general public, professional organizations, the medical community, and various levels of government. The problem that remains is how to motivate children and adults to seek higher levels of physical fitness so that the health of individuals and the nation can significantly improve.

During the last two decades, volumes of evidence about the importance of regular physical activity and its impact on health have been recorded by hundreds of exercise scientists worldwide. It is interesting to note that most of the vigorous research has been conducted in the United States.

A number of very credible reports, position papers, and digests have been released by professional groups, such as the American College of Sports Medicine (ACSM), the President's Council on Physical Fitness and Sports (PCPFS), and the American Heart Association (AHA), supporting the importance of physical activity for acquiring and maintaining good health. Moreover, governmental agencies, such as the Centers for Disease Control and Prevention (CDC), the National Institutes of Health (NIH), and the Surgeon General's Office, have issued reports that strongly agree with these professional groups.

The net result of all this research clearly demonstrates that regular physical activity lowers the risks for many diseases, fortifies most body systems, and improves mental health. The concept of "exercise as medicine" is a reality, and the benefits of regular exercise are backed by extensive scientific evidence. After many years of skepticism, authorities now recognize and accept the fact that physical activity can prevent, control, and ameliorate a number of health problems, such as heart disease, diabetes, cancer, high blood pressure, asthma, arthritis, osteoporosis, and low back pain, as well as enhance and improve rehabilitation.

What Is Physical Fitness?

Health is defined as the physical, mental, and social well-being of an individual and obviously includes the absence of disease. Physical fitness contributes to health and is focused on attaining enough vigor and energy to perform physical work and engage in physical activity and heavy exercise.

Most people define physical fitness incorrectly. They tend to include the attributes of motor fitness, general athletic ability, and specific athletic ability in their definition. However, most exercise scientists agree that physical fitness includes a set of physiological attributes—strength, local muscular endurance, cardiorespiratory endurance, and body composition (percentage of body fat) that allow individuals to perform physical activity.

Physical attributes such as flexibility, hand-eye coordination, foot-eye coordination, agility, speed, body balance, and muscular power are included in other movement concepts like motor fitness and general and specific athletic ability. These attributes do not have any bearing on health and disease prevention.

Nevertheless, all of these activities and abilities are dependent upon the attainment of a high level of the basic physical fitness components, i.e., strength, local muscle endurance, and cardiorespiratory endurance. Low levels of these components severely limit performance and predispose the participant to injuries—whether in games, recreational activities, or even the general movement patterns needed for everyday living.

Furthermore, a good level of physical fitness enhances the quality of life at all ages. It permits greater engagement and higher performance levels in sports and recreational pursuits, improves the performance of regular daily tasks, and enhances health and well-being. The only method of attaining physical fitness is engaging in various forms of moderate to vigorous physical activity.

Attributes of Physical Fitness

Descriptions of the physical fitness attributes are presented below.

Strength Strength is defined as the ability of a muscle or muscle group to execute one maximum contraction against a maximum resistance. A practical example is how *much* you can lift in a specific way, such as in a bench press, leg press, or squat. Strength is improved by engaging in weightlifting or resistance activities. In addition, free exercises that require a variety of movements of the body against the force of gravity can enhance strength but to a lesser degree than weightlifting. Practical examples of such exercises include push-ups, crunches, and squats.

Local Muscular Endurance (LME) Local muscular endurance is the ability of a muscle or muscle group to make repeated contractions. A practical example is how *many* particular movements you can perform with a specific weight using any desired exercise, such as a curl, pulldown, or bench press. LME is improved by using weight training or free exercises for the number of repetitions consistent with one's goal of muscular endurance. High strength levels of the muscles involved also positively influence LME. Any weightlifting exercise can be used, and innumerable free exercises can be used to develop LME.

Aerobic Fitness Aerobic fitness is also known as cardiorespiratory endurance (CRE). It is the ability to execute moderate-intensity general exercise over extended lengths of time. Cardiorespiratory endurance is enhanced by engaging in activities such as walking, running, swimming, circuit weight training, biking, stepping, rowing, or various exercise classes.

Aerobic fitness involves the ability of the heart and circulatory and respiratory systems to recover quickly after an exercise session.

Aerobic activity is any nonstop activity that requires you to increase your heart rate to between 120 and 160 beats per minute and maintain it for 30 minutes or longer, depending upon age, goals, and state of physical fitness.

Body Composition Body composition is defined as the proportions of bone, muscle, fat, and organ weight in the body. The average 18-to-26-year-old male has 12–15 percent body fat. The average woman in the same age range has 26–30 percent body fat. Male and female athletes have 6–20 percent body fat. Men and women who are older than 26 tend to become fatter as they age. This creeping obesity occurs mainly because of gross inactivity; however, a small portion may be due to decreases in the output of various hormones. Both weight training and cardiorespiratory endurance activities will help in the reduction and/or the maintenance of reasonable levels of body fat.

Total fitness is the development of all the basic components of physical fitness and concurrent maintenance of a low body fat level. Emphasizing one component of physical fitness at the detriment of the others diminishes optimal health and functioning. A bodybuilder who has difficulty walking up a flight of stairs and a marathon runner who is too weak to move furniture are extreme examples, but they illustrate the lack of wisdom of focusing on just one element of fitness. For optimal health and the ability to perform daily tasks with healthy levels of body fat, you must strive for a balance of the basic physical fitness attributes.

When all components of physical fitness are developed in a balanced manner, you will achieve optimal health and function and place yourself at lower risk for heart disease, cancer, diabetes, osteoporosis, and other chronic diseases.[28]

Hope for the Sedentary

Some people are caught in a time warp. They remember their physical education teachers using phrases such as "no pain, no gain" or "harder is smarter." Moreover, physical exercise was often used as a punishment. This has contributed to an aversion to exercise, which is superimposed on most people's innate dislike for exercise. Many people therefore minimize physical activity, which is detrimental to their health and physical appearance.

In 1993, the American College of Sports Medicine published its "Exercise Lite" recommendations with regard to meeting the goal of keeping the body fit to enhance overall health and decreasing the risk for heart disease, cancer, and other common diseases. The following key statements from the American College of Sports Medicine regarding regular moderate physical activity have implications for those who have an aversion to exercise. They will give you hope:

The current low participation rate may be due in part to the misperception of many people that to reap health benefits, they must engage in vigorous, continuous exercise. The scientific evidence clearly demonstrates that regular, moderate-intensity physical activity provides substantial health benefits.

Every adult should accumulate 30 minutes or more of moderate-intensity physical activity on most, preferably all, days of the week. One way to meet this standard is to walk two miles briskly.

Intermittent activity also confers substantial benefits. Therefore, the recommended 30 minutes of activity can be accumulated in short bouts of activity: walking up the stairs instead of taking the elevator, walking instead of driving short distances, doing calisthenics or pedaling a stationary cycle while watching television.

The health benefits gained from increased physical activity depend on the initial physical activity level. Sedentary individuals are expected to benefit most from increasing their activity to the recommended level.

Two other components of fitness, flexibility and muscular strength, should not be overlooked. Clinical experience and limited studies suggest that people who maintain or improve their strength and flexibility may be better able to perform daily activities, may be less likely to develop back pain and may be better able to avoid disability, especially as they advance into older age.

If Americans who lead sedentary lives would adopt a more active lifestyle, there would be enormous benefit to the public's health and to individual well-being. An active lifestyle does not require a regimented, vigorous exercise program. Instead, small changes that increase daily activity will enable individuals to reduce their risk of chronic diseases and may contribute to enhanced quality of life.[29]

THE BENEFITS OF EXERCISE

The current physical activity profile of adult Americans is not very encouraging. The 1996 Surgeon General's Report on Physical Activity and Health found that 60 percent—well over half—of Americans are not regularly involved in physical activity. Worse yet, 25 percent of Americans are not active at all. The Surgeon General's report goes on to state that in American youth, physical activity declines dramatically during adolescence. These trends are dangerous and need to be quickly reversed for the health of our citizens and our country. Healthcare costs could bankrupt our society, not to mention the misery of a sick and debilitated American population.

In adults, activity patterns and physical fitness levels mirror what they were taught during their school years. Schools at all levels have not succeeded in teaching physical fitness and instilling the need for lifetime physical fitness in our youth. We seem to have an inborn aversion to hard work and physical activity, which increases with age. This, combined with the failure of the school system to instill lifetime fitness attitudes, the emergence of the high-tech industry, passive entertainment such as television and movies, good economic times, and the burgeoning fast-food industry, has exacerbated the problem of inactivity, growing obesity, and poor health.

With the "American spirit" that built and developed this great nation, there is hope. That hope is the desire and resolve to improve our lives. Individuals can effectively strive and attain good health and well-being with a threefold strategy: (1) engaging in regular physical activity, (2) using nutritional supplements and eating healthy, and (3) reducing stress and allowing time to rest and recharge the body and mind.

Many Americans have taken such action, as demonstrated in the ever-growing membership to health clubs, now approaching 30 million. This represents approximately 11 percent of the total U.S. population. Millions more exercise at home. Just think of what would happen to our health status and the reduction in healthcare costs if we could increase the number of Americans who exercise regularly. With this, along with a spiritual and educational renewal, we would see a resurgence of American greatness and consequent leadership in the world.

In 1995, the U.S. Department of Health and Human Services presented the following physical activity-related health objectives for the nation for the year 2000 (see Table 7.1).

The following section presents the well-established and indisputable benefits of exercise. In 1996, the U.S. Surgeon General's office published its Report on Physical Activity and Health. Its main objective was to summarize existing research, which clearly demonstrates the benefits of physical activity in preventing disease and improving well-being and mental health. In addition, this report presented conclusions that can be helpful to people who are interested in improving and enhancing their health by physical activity.

The major conclusions of this report are presented below.

Overall Mortality

1. Higher levels of regular physical activity are associated with lower mortality rates for both older and younger adults.
2. Even those who are moderately active on a regular basis have lower mortality rates than those who are least active.

Table 7.1   Physical Activity–Related Health Objectives for the Nation for the Year 2000

#	Objectives
1.3	Increase to at least 30 percent, the proportion of people aged six and older who engage regularly, preferably daily, in light to moderate physical activity for at least 30 minutes daily.
1.4	Increase to at least 20 percent, the proportion of people over age 18 and to at least 75 percent the proportion of children and adolescents aged 6–17 who engage in vigorous physical activity that promotes the development and maintenance of cardiorespiratory fitness three or more days per week for 20 or more minutes per occasion.
1.5	Reduce to no more than 15 percent, the proportion of people over age six who engage in no leisure time physical activity.
1.6	Increase to at least 40 percent, the proportion of people over age six who regularly perform physical activities that enhance and maintain muscular strength, muscular endurance, and flexibility.
1.7	Increase to at least 50 percent, the proportion of overweight people age 12 and older who have adopted sound dietary practices combined with regular physical activity to attain an appropriate body weight.

Source: U.S. Department of Health and Human Services; Healthy People 2000: National Health Promotion and Disease Prevention Objectives—Midcourse Review and 1995 Revisions (Washington, D.C.: U.S. Government Printing Office, 1995).

Cardiovascular Disease

1. Regular physical activity or cardiorespiratory fitness decrease the risk of cardiovascular disease mortality in general and of coronary heart disease mortality in particular. Existing data are not conclusive regarding a relationship between physical activity and stroke.

2. The level of decreased risk of coronary heart disease attributable to regular physical activity is similar to that of other lifestyle factors, such as keeping free from cigarette smoking.
3. Regular physical activity prevents or delays the development of high blood pressure and exercise reduces blood pressure in people with hypertension.

Cancer

1. Regular physical activity is associated with a decreased risk of colon cancer.
2. There is no association between physical activity and rectal cancer. There is not enough data to draw conclusions regarding a relationship between physical activity and endometrial, ovarian or testicular cancers.
3. Despite numerous studies on the subject, existing data are inconsistent regarding an association between physical activity and breast or prostate cancers.

Noninsulin-Dependent Diabetes Mellitus

1. Regular physical activity lowers the risk of developing noninsulin-dependent diabetes mellitus.

Osteoarthritis

1. Regular physical activity is necessary for maintaining normal muscle strength, joint structure and joint function. In the range recommended for health, physical activity is not associated with joint damage or development of osteoarthritis and may be beneficial for many people with arthritis.
2. Competitive athletics may be associated with the development of osteoarthritis later in life, but sports-related injuries are the likely cause.

Osteoporosis

1. Weight-bearing physical activity is essential for normal skeletal development during childhood and adolescence and for achieving and maintaining peak bone mass in young adults.

2. It is unclear whether resistance-type or endurance-type physical activity can reduce the accelerated rate of bone loss in postmenopausal women in the absence of estrogen replacement therapy.

Falling

1. There is promising evidence that strength training and other forms of exercise in older adults preserve the ability to maintain independent living status and reduce the risk of falling.

Obesity

1. Low levels of activity, resulting in fewer kilocalories (calories) used than consumed, contribute to the high prevalence of obesity in the United States.
2. Physical activity may favorably affect the distribution of body fat.

Mental Health

1. Physical activity appears to relieve symptoms of depression and anxiety and improve mood.
2. Regular physical activity may reduce the risk of developing depression, although further research is required on this topic.

Health-Related Quality of Life

1. Physical activity appears to improve health-related quality of life by enhancing psychological well-being and by improving physical function in persons compromised by poor health.

Adverse Effects

1. Most musculoskeletal injuries related to physical activity are believed to be preventable by gradually working up to a desired level of activity and by avoiding excessive amounts of activity.
2. Serious cardiovascular events can occur with physical exertion but the net effect of regular physical activity is a lower risk of mortality from cardiovascular disease.[30]

Individual Americans resolving to increase their physical fitness levels and those of their family and friends can reverse this unhealthy trend. This objective can be easily attained because physical activity is a widely achievable means to a healthier life.

Governmental agencies can and should promote the need for daily exercise as a form of "preventive medicine." Individuals who heed the message will improve the body's defense functions and their quality of life.

AN IMPORTANT ADDITIONAL BENEFIT

Many people ask the question, "Why do I have to exercise?" In answering this, experts often overlook one of the most important aspects of exercise: The human body needs consistent exercise to improve the functioning of the lymphatic system. The lymphatic system is instrumental in eliminating toxins from the body and is a defense mechanism that fights infection, viruses, bacteria, fungi, and disease, but it does not have its own pump. Nevertheless, the lymph moves slowly and steadily along its vessels. Exercise increases the speed of lymph flow through the system by as much as 10–15 times the resting rate. This greatly enhances the clearance of toxins, wastes, excess fluids, and infection from all tissues of the body.

Unlike the cardiovascular system, which pumps blood with and through the heart muscle, the lymphatic system performs its function indirectly through the action of gravity, the rate and depth of breathing, the heart rate and force of contraction of the heart, and the contraction and relaxation of the muscles that occur with all types of physical activities. The lymph vessels have a large number of one-way valves that permit the lymph to flow in one direction.

The action of inhalation resulting from the descent of the diaphragm causes the intra-abdominal pressure to increase and the intrathoracic (chest) pressure to decrease. Research has shown that the lymph from the lower abdominal area is literally "pumped" into the veins of the upper chest during inhalation by this change in pressure in the chest and abdomen. An increased rate and depth of breathing produces a commensurate increase in the flow of lymph fluid toward the heart. This process operates at rest but is intensified during exercise.

As mentioned, the direction of lymph flow is assured by a system of one-way valves in the lymph vessels. An additional impetus is added to the forward motion of the lymph by the contraction of the segments of the vessel walls. This results in the movement of lymph from one valve segment to the next.

To stimulate the flow of lymphatic fluids, you must increase your breathing rate, increase your heart rate, and increase the mechanical pumping action by contracting and relaxing your muscles through exercise and frequent postural changes.

SENIOR FITNESS

Senior citizens are the fastest growing segment of the American population. According to the 1997 aging statistics of the U.S. National Center for Health Statistics, the average life expectancy for both males and females is increasing. The current average life expectancy is 76.5 years. By 2050, life expectancy is projected to exceed 82 years. The fastest growing segment of the senior population is the "very old" (85 and older). It is expected that this group will expand from 3.1 million in 1990 to approximately 17.7 million by the year 2050.[31]

Another way to look at the increase of the older population is to consider the relative number of Americans that are over 65 years of age. According to the U.S. Census Bureau, in 1900 only 4 percent of the American population was over 65. Now, people over 65 represent more than 12 percent of the American population. This is projected to increase to 20 percent by the year 2020.[32]

The absolute numbers of people over 65 years of age in the U.S. population are equally dramatic. The United States today has approximately 36 million people over 65. This number is expected to reach 70 million by the year 2030, which is almost double what it was in 1993.[33]

The most important concern for this growing segment of the American population is the quality of life. What advantage is it to live longer but in a debilitated state? The National Center for Health Statistics estimates that 15 percent of the average American's life is spent in an "unhealthy" state. This manifests itself as impairment by disabilities, injuries, and chronic diseases, all of which can be strongly impacted and minimized by employing regular exercise, good nutrition, cessation of smoking, moderate consumption of alcohol, nutritional supplementation, adequate rest, and effective stress reduction.

The World Health Organization has published three relevant summaries concerning the benefits of physical activity as it relates to physiological benefits, psychological benefits, and social benefits. Table 7.2 contains a summary of the physiological benefits of physical activity for older people. Table 7.3 shows a summary of the psychological benefits of physical activity for older people. Table 7.4 presents a summary of the social benefits of physical activity for older persons.

One of the great benefits of regular physical activity is that as a person improves in strength, local muscle endurance, and cardio-respiratory endurance, body fat is reduced and muscle and bone mass increase. In addition, when muscle is generated it gives one a youthful look and allows more calories to be burned at rest and in exercise. Research has shown that body fat doubles in people between the ages of 20 and 65. When fat accumulates, the body becomes distorted from its normal attractive form.

The basal metabolic rate (BMR) drops because of the loss of muscle mass and bone mass that occurs in sedentary older persons. This accelerates the increase in body fat, and a vicious cycle is created. Regular physical activity, especially strength-building calisthenics and weightlifting, help to maintain muscle and bone mass, which keeps the BMR at higher levels and helps control the accumulation of body fat.

Senior citizens are frequently confronted with a number of ailments, including

Table 7.2 A Summary of the Physiological Benefits of Physical Activity for Older Persons

Immediate Benefits

• Glucose Levels: Physical activity helps regulate blood sugar levels.

• Catecholamine Activity: Both adrenaline and noradrenaline levels are stimulated by physical activity. This increases use of fats and sugars for energy, among other things.

• Improved Sleep: Physical activity enhances sleep quality and quantity in individuals of all ages.

Long-Term Effects

• Aerobic/Cardiovascular Endurance: Substantial improvements in almost all aspects of cardiovascular functioning have been observed following appropriate physical training.

• Resistive Training/Muscle Strengthening: Individuals of all ages can benefit from muscle-strengthening exercises. Resistance training can have a significant impact on the maintenance of independence in old age.

• Flexibility: Exercises which stimulate movement throughout the range of motion assist in the preservation and restoration of flexibility.

• Balance/Coordination: Regular activity helps prevent and/or postpone the age associated declines in balance and coordination that are a major risk factor for falls.

• Velocity of Movement: Behavioral slowing is a characteristic of advancing age. Individuals who are regularly active can often postpone these age-related declines.

Source: World Health Organization; A Summary of the Physiological Benefits of Physical Activity for Older Persons; Healthy Living Guidelines 1997 (Geneva, Switzerland, 1997).

Table 7.3   A Summary of the Psychological Benefits of Physical Activity for Older Persons

Immediate Benefits

• Relaxation: Appropriate physical activity enhances relaxation.

• Reduces Stress and Anxiety: There is evidence that regular physical activity can reduce stress and anxiety.

• Enhanced Mood State: Numerous people report elevations in mood state following appropriate physical activity.

Long-Term Effects

• General Well-Being: Improvements in almost all aspects of psychological functioning have been observed following periods of extended physical activity.

• Improved Mental Health: Regular exercise can make an important contribution in the treatment of several mental illnesses, including depression and anxiety neuroses.

• Cognitive Improvements: Regular physical activity may help postpone age-related declines in central nervous system processing speed and improves reaction time.

• Motor Control and Performance: Regular activity helps prevent and/ or postpone the age-associated declines in both fine and gross motor performance.

• Skill Acquisition: New skills can be learned and existing skills refined by all individuals regardless of age.

Source: World Health Organization; A Summary of the Psychological Benefits of Physical Activity for Older Persons; Healthy Living Guidelines 1977 (Geneva, Switzerland, 1997).

Table 7.4 A Summary of the Social Benefits
of Physical Activity for Older Persons

Immediate Benefits

• Empowering Older Individuals: A sedentary lifestyle eventually threat-
ens to reduce independence and self-sufficiency. Participation in appropriate physical activity can help empower older individuals and
assist them in playing a more active role in society.

• Enhanced Social and Cultural Integration: Physical activity programs,
particularly when carried out in small groups and/or social environments, enhance social and intercultural interactions for many older
adults.

Long-Term Effects

• Enhanced Integration: Regularly active individuals are less likely to
withdraw from society and more likely to actively contribute to the
social milieu.

• Formation of New Friendships: Participation in physical activity, particularly in small groups and other social environments, stimulates
new friendships.

• Widened Social and Cultural Networks: Physical activity frequently
provides individuals with an opportunity to widen available social networks.

• Role Maintenance and New Role Acquisition: A physically active lifestyle helps foster the environment needed to maintain an active role
in society and to acquire positive new roles.

• Enhanced Intergenerational Activity: Physical activity can be a shared
activity, which provides opportunities for intergenerational contact
thereby diminishing stereotypic perceptions about aging and the
elderly.

Source: World Health Organization; A Summary of the Social Benefits of Physical
Activity for Older Persons; Healthy Living Guidelines 1997 (Geneva,
Switzerland, 1997).

1. Cardiovascular disease
2. Cancer
3. High blood pressure
4. Depression
5. Osteoporosis
6. Bone fractures
7. Diabetes
8. Arthritis
9. Orthopedic impairments
10. Hearing impairments
11. Cataracts
12. Visual impairments

Exercise has been shown to dramatically improve the first nine of these health problems.

The Seven Basic Health Habits

It has been shown that people who follow good health habits have much lower death rates than those who live reckless lives. The implementation of the following seven basic health habits can add health and years to your life:

1. Do not smoke.

2. Use alcohol moderately.

3. Eat breakfast daily.

4. Do not snack.

5. Get seven to eight hours of sleep per night.

6. Exercise regularly.

7. Maintain an ideal body weight.

A "two-fisted" (physical activity and practice of good health habits) approach to dealing with health and fitness for seniors is an effective battle plan. However, adding sensible eating, nutritional supplementation, and stress reduction and management creates a winning strategy for extending life and increasing the quality of life.

Most exercise scientists and medical authorities now believe that regular physical activity can produce tangible benefits for almost all older adults. Even the sedentary and physically frail can benefit from some type of physical activity that is consonant with their fitness level. In addition to the physical, psychological, and social benefits of regular physical activity, there is the potentially dramatic reduction of healthcare costs produced by preventive exercise interventions. It's about time that Americans look at exercise as preventive and curative medicine.

YOUTH FITNESS

Since the 1960s, we've seen a steady gradual decline in the emphasis on physical education in the American public school system. This, coupled with the introduction of videotape players, video games, computers, and other high-tech innovations as well as other distractions in modern American society have produced a generation of youth that is obese and unfit.

Many studies over the last two decades have identified the deficiencies in youth fitness, but the information has fallen on deaf ears. Moreover, this criticism can also be applied to most parents, who are ultimately responsible for the health and well-being of their offspring.

In 1983–84, the U.S. Office of Disease Prevention and Health Promotion conducted the National Children and Youth Fitness Study (NCYFS). The most important conclusion of this study was that our children were significantly fatter than in the 1960s.[34] Today, the situation is getting worse, as reported in the 1996 Surgeon General's Report on Physical Activity and Health.

A 1985 study by the President's Council on Physical Fitness and Sports supported and funded a survey called the "PCPFS 1985 National School Population Fitness Survey." It found:

1. " . . . there is a low level of performance in important components of physical fitness by millions of our youth."
2. "Upper arm and shoulder muscle girdle strength and endurance for both boys and girls was poor." Upper

arm and shoulder girdle strength and endurance for both males and females have been identified by the armed forces, police departments and fire departments as major physical fitness weaknesses for those who have applied for service with these entities.[35]

A summer 1987 newsletter published by the National Association of Governors' Councils on Physical Fitness and Sports reported the results of a study involving children in Maryland, Virginia, and the District of Columbia. These children were administered a Soviet youth physical fitness test. The conclusion of the testing project revealed that "Most American children who took the Soviet youth fitness test scored at the 'acceptable' or 'outstanding' level in events that required coordination, but were somewhat weak in the upper body strength test and were below expectations in the endurance categories as reflected in the distance runs."[36]

The current status of physical education in our schools is alarming. It appears that few students experience daily physical education activity. Younger children (elementary and middle school age youth) are more likely to engage in regular physical education classes than high school students. Even so, it has been reported that daily physical education is rare even for the lower grade levels.

The 1996 U.S. Surgeon General's Report on Physical Activity and Health made the following conclusions based on a study of adolescents and young adults:

1. Only about one-half of the U.S. young people (age 12–21 years) regularly participate in vigorous physical activity. One-fourth report no vigorous physical activity.
2. Approximately one-fourth of young people walk or bicycle (i.e., engage in light to moderate activity) nearly every day.
3. About 14 percent of young people report no recent vigorous or light to moderate physical activity. This

indicator of inactivity is higher among females than males and among black females than white females.

4. Males are more likely than females to participate in vigorous physical activity, strengthening activities and walking or biking.

5. Participation in all types of physical activity declines strikingly as age or grade in school increases.

6. Among high school students, enrollment in physical education remained unchanged during the first half of the 1990s. However, daily attendance in physical education declined from approximately 42 percent to 25 percent.

7. The percentage of high school students who were enrolled in physical education and who reported being physically active for at least 20 minutes in physical education classes declined from approximately 80 percent to 70 percent during the first half of this decade.

8. Only 19 percent of all high school students report being physically active for 20 minutes in physical education classes.[37]

It is very clear that in spite of all the reports containing significant evidence of a declining fitness state and growing obesity of American youth, the programs that have been in place in the past and those implemented today are inadequate and probably have an incorrect emphasis. There is insufficient accent on physical fitness activities and too much emphasis on recreation and sports. Statements of two highly placed federal government officials highlight this conclusion.

Donna E. Shalala, former secretary of health and human services, stated that "schools and universities need to reintroduce daily, quality physical activity as a key component of a comprehensive education."[38]

Surgeon General David Satcher characterizes poor youth physical fitness as a "major epidemic" in the United States. He stated, "I think we've made a serious error by not requiring physical education in grades K through 12. We are paying a tremendous price for this physical inactivity. People pay with pain and suffering and society pays with money and lost productivity."[39]

There is an important need to develop early in life a regular physical activity pattern other than play, as well as to instill in children the importance of continuing this pattern until death. The school and the home are the obvious places to develop a pattern of regular physical activity that promotes health, function, and fitness. However, as indicated in the 1996 Surgeon General's report, it is evident that these programs are failing.

There is hope! While education officials continue to be asleep regarding the deplorable state of youth fitness, the U.S. Senate is considering legislation that would address the problem. On May 27, 1999, Senator Ted Stevens from Alaska introduced the Physical Education for Progress Act. The purpose of this legislation is to provide grants and contracts to local educational agencies to enable these agencies to initiate, expand, and improve physical education programs for all kindergarten through 12th-grade students.

While this is a positive step forward, we need to demand that these programs require physical training and that physical fitness testing be implemented throughout the school year. Moreover, parents need to take matters into their own hands and require, provide, and supervise physical fitness training for their children beyond that provided (or not provided) at their local schools.

ACSM EXERCISE GUIDELINES

Many organizations (governmental and private) as well as commercial interests (companies and individuals) are involved in presenting varied forms of physical activity to the public. Because of the large number, guidelines for exercise prescription are needed.

The largest and most prestigious professional organization dealing with exercise science is the American College of Sports Medicine. As the philosophical and scientific leader for physical activity, the ACSM has developed guidelines for the prescription of exercise programs that enhance cardiorespiratory fitness, body composition, muscular strength, endurance, and flexibility in the healthy adult population.

The ACSM has 18,500 members in over 70 countries around the world. Its mission statement is the following: "The ACSM promotes and integrates scientific research, education and practical application of sports medicine and exercise science to maintain and enhance physical performance, fitness, health and quality of life."[40]

The ACSM was founded in 1954 and is committed to the diagnosis, treatment, and prevention of sports-related injuries and to the promotion of physical activity. It is an association of people and professions that have as a common goal the use of medicine, exercise science, and practical application of exercise to enhance the health of all Americans.

Below are the ACSM recommended guidelines for the quantity and quality of exercise for developing and maintaining cardiorespiratory and muscular fitness and flexibility in healthy adults. It is worthwhile to consider that a combination of frequency, intensity, and duration of regular exercise has been shown to be effective in producing a training effect (strength, flexibility, muscle endurance, and cardiovascular respiratory endurance). All of these factors interact to produce what is called "overload."

In general, the lower the total interaction of frequency, intensity, and duration (called the "exercise stimulus"), the smaller the training effect. Conversely, the greater the stimulus, the larger the effect.

It is recommended that well-rounded exercise programs be used, including aerobic exercise, resistance training involving all major muscle groups, and flexibility-enhancement exercises for all major muscle groups. The recommended number of days per week varies with the physical fitness state and goals of the exerciser and type of program.

An exercise program should be implemented for all people above two years of age. For older people entering an exercise program and anyone who has not engaged in regular exercise a slower, less intensive program should be considered. Younger people need to adapt their programs sensibly so that the frequency, intensity, and duration will not interfere with their growth process.

The application of these guidelines should be in the context of the exerciser's needs, goals, and current abilities. It is important to start slowly and to take into account the total interaction of frequency, intensity, and duration of exercise. All good exercise programs involve a general and specific warmup, which includes flexibility exercises, followed by the main exercise program, which is followed by a cooldown with relevant flexibility exercises.

The goal of any exercise program is to provide the correct amount of physical activity to achieve the maximal benefit with the lowest risk. Moreover, it is important to foster an attitude that leads to lasting lifestyle changes and promotes a lifetime of physical activity.

A WORD ABOUT SPORTS AND RECREATIONAL ACTIVITIES

Sports such as golf, baseball, and bowling and other recreational activities, although requiring specific athletic skills, do not promote the basic components of fitness. They do not stress the heart, lungs, and muscular systems with sufficient intensity, sustained for an adequate duration, to enhance strength, local muscular endurance, and cardiorespiratory endurance and to foster and maintain a low level of body fat.

However, depending upon the sport or recreational activity and the level of performance, some improvement of the basic fitness attributes may occur. To gain optimal levels of all the basic fitness attributes and to minimize injuries, you must engage in specific physical fitness programs besides participating in sports or recreational activities.

Improvement in the basic physical fitness attributes almost always improves one's performance levels in sports and recreational activities. An increase in strength enhances power development,

The ACSM Guidelines for Aerobic Exercise and Improving Body Composition

Aerobic exercise of sufficient intensity should be a part of an adult fitness program to enhance cardiovascular respiratory function and to control accumulation of body fat.

1. Frequency of training: 3–5 days per week.

2. Intensity of training: 60–90 percent of maximum heart rate or 50–85 percent of maximum oxygen uptake reserve. Lower intensities of 55–64 percent of maximum heart rate or 40–49 percent of maximum oxygen uptake reserve should be utilized for individuals who are quite unfit.

3. Duration of training: 20–60 minutes of continuous aerobic activity or intermittent bouts (2–6 ten-minute periods) accumulated throughout the day of aerobic activity. Lower intensity physical activity for a longer period of time is preferred to higher intensity for nonathletic and deconditioned individuals.

4. Mode of activity: Any activity that uses large muscle groups can be maintained continuously and is rhythmic and aerobic in nature, such as walking-hiking, running-jogging, bicycling, cross country skiing, dancing, rope skipping, rowing, stair-climbing, swimming, skating and various exercise classes and endurance games.

The ACSM Guidelines for Resistance Training and Improving Body Composition

Resistance training should be an integral part of an adult fitness program and of a sufficient intensity to enhance strength, muscular endurance and maintain fat-free mass. Resistance training should be progressive in nature, individualized, and provide a stimulus to all the major muscle groups.

1. Frequency of training: At least 2–3 days per week for each major muscle group.

2. Number of exercises: A minimum of 8–10 exercises involving all the major muscle groups.

3. Intensity of training: A minimum of one set of 8 to 12 repetitions to near fatigue.

4. Mode of activity: Resistance training (with weights) is recommended, but traditional calisthenics exercises "can still be effective in improving and maintaining strength."

The ACSM Guidelines for Flexibility Training

Flexibility exercises should be incorporated into the overall fitness program sufficient to develop and maintain range of motion (ROM).

1. Frequency of training: A minimum of 2–3 times per week.

2. Number of exercises: All the major muscle groups should be stretched.

3. Intensity of training: Stretching should not be forceful.

4. Mode of activity: All stretching methods are valuable and include: static stretching (stretch and hold), dynamic or ballistic stretching (nonstop motion) and resistive stretching (stretching with a partner).

Source: American College of Sports Medicine; The recommended quantity and quality of exercise for developing and maintaining cardiorespiratory and muscular fitness and flexibility in healthy adults. *Medicine & Science in Sports & Exercise*, Volume 30, Number 6, June 1998; 975–91.

while increases in local muscular endurance and cardiorespiratory endurance permit engagement in sports or recreational activities for a longer period of time. This adds to the enjoyment of participation.

Each sport or recreational activity has specific requirements for the amount of strength, local muscular endurance, and cardiorespiratory endurance. It is therefore wise to engage in a physical activity program that promotes improvement in these attributes and at least maintains them while one is participating in the sport or recreational activity. Moreover, each sport or recreational activity has its specific impact on enhancing the physical fitness attributes. While some benefit to the physical fitness attributes is gained by participating in sports and recreational activities, it is prudent to maintain a collateral physical fitness program to optimize performance and minimize injuries.

The bottom line is that whether we participate in sports or recreational activities or just want to improve our health and well-being, we must engage in a regular physical activity program. Such a program must have as its aim the improvement and maintenance of strength, local muscular endurance, and cardiorespiratory endurance and the achievement and maintenance of an optimal and healthy body composition (lower body fat). A balanced program is the prudent approach.

MY DAILY EXERCISE PROGRAM

Health is so necessary to all the duties, as well as pleasures of life, that the crime of squandering it is equal to the folly.
—SAMUEL JOHNSON

Engaging in my exercise program may allow you to improve your basic physical fitness attributes. Moreover, the program is effective and functional. Your performance in any sport or recreational activity may be improved by applying my exercise program three to four times per week. Furthermore, your health, well-being, and mental outlook may be enhanced.

Some of the positive aspects of my program are listed below:

- It requires no equipment yet is effective in developing the major attributes of physical fitness as well as helping to optimize body composition.
- It can be performed in a small space.
- The exercises are simple and can be easily performed.
- There is no need for special instruction other than reading the description of each exercise in my forthcoming book and then viewing the accompanying photographs.
- It meets the criteria recommended by the ACSM and 1996 Surgeon General's Report on Physical Activity and Health as researched by Paul Ward, PED.
- It can be completed in 45 minutes per day or less after the initial break-in period. When you have completed this program, you will have conditioned every major muscle group in the body to enhance strength, local muscle endurance, and extensibility, which will improve flexibility and range of motion of all the major joints in the body.

Beginning with a functional warmup, the program then moves into the Five Rites. Thereafter, the exercises work the major power center of the body: the legs, buttocks, and abdominal muscles. The program concludes with important and specific low-intensity stretching as a cool-down. If you do what you can as often as you can, soon you will see the results you desire. Other people will notice too!

The program blends potent ancient Tibetan rites, some very effective Eastern stretching exercises, and a few exceptionally effective contemporary Western exercises that strengthen the total body and increase functional mobility. After more than 30 years of piecing together these different exercises, I am proud to offer them to all who are willing to receive them in my next book, *Exercising with Rod Burreson.*

The following pages provide an overview of my exercise program, highlighting the health benefits one can expect from each phase.

- *Phase I* (warmup) prepares the body for more intense exercise. The basic purpose of this phase is to gradually and systematically prepare the total body for the exercise that follows. During this phase the heart rate, muscle temperature, blood flow to the muscles, and respiration and perspiration gradually increase. The total warmup phase includes 11 basic warmup exercises, which can be completed in 12–15 minutes.

- In *Phase II* the Five Rites are performed. These are derived from very powerful ancient Tibetan exercises. They are easy to perform yet potent enough to impact your life forever. Their general purpose is to normalize the speed of the seven "spinning energy centers," or vortexes. The normalization of the rotational speed of these vortexes is thought to regulate and enhance the output of the endocrine glands. The optimal number of repetitions for each of the Five Rites is 21, which can be performed in 15 minutes. This phase involves very deep breathing, which has additional health benefits.

- *Phase III* includes exercises that strengthen and condition the muscles of the legs, hips, and abdominal region. In addition, these exercises enhance the functional mobility of the attendant joints, which translates into better posture and improved performance in recreational sports. This phase includes four basic exercises that are performed for 15–20 repetitions. The performance time for this phase is 15 minutes.

- *Phase IV* involves specific stretching and cooldown exercises. This phase slowly returns the body to the resting state, while improving the flexibility and range of motion of the trunk, hips, legs, and ankles. Five

simple and effective exercises are performed for
15 repetitions, which take 8–10 minutes.

The plan is to start easy as you learn the routine. The order of
the exercises is very important. Perfect technique is not needed,
but it is the goal. You cannot expect to perform each exercise perfectly at the start, but this will come with practice and time.

The operating principal is this: *Do what you can and keep
working toward the goal and ideal performance for each exercise in
the program.*

While exercising, concentrate on what you are doing. The
mind controls the body. Those who have difficulty in controlling
the physical will benefit greatly from the discipline accrued by
performing my exercise program regularly. Most importantly, you
will grow to love it.

The program presents a sensible and balanced approach to
anti-aging and improved health and well-being. Engagement in a
physical exercise program is a necessary step to add years to your
life—and life to your years. So, start today—health is on the way!

— PART 2

The Importance of Diet

Nutrition involves the relationship between foods and the health of the body. Optimal nutrition is a diet that contains all essential nutrients that are supplied and utilized in a balanced amount to maintain good health.

Knowledge of these nutrients and their functions in the body is helpful for achieving good nutrition and a balanced diet. A balanced diet contains portions of each of the six main nutrient classifications of food—carbohydrates, proteins, fats, vitamins, minerals, and antioxidants—and water. Part 2 will cover each of these in detail.

Each nutrient has its own special function and relationship to the body, but no nutrient acts independently of the others. All the nutrients must be present in the right quantities in order for a person to maintain optimal health. Although everyone requires all of these nutrients, individuals do not necessarily require the same amounts. Quantities vary according to individual needs.

In spite of all the excuses we might have for not getting adequate nutrients, such as soil depletion, food processing, and cooking, it ultimately is our own responsibility to feed ourselves properly. Too often we sacrifice optimal nutrition for convenience, cost, or taste.

The Importance of Good Nutrition

Good nutrition is essential for

- normal organ development and functioning
- normal reproduction
- growth
- optimal energy and efficiency
- resistance to infection and disease
- repair of bodily damage or injuries

As a nation of convenience we want what is fast and easy. We have an abundance of fast-food restaurants, frozen foods, canned foods, boxed foods, and junk foods to choose from to satisfy our hunger and cravings. Unfortunately, the refining process, preservatives, and additives used prevent us from satisfying our nutritional needs.

Many people mistakenly believe that the typical American diet is well balanced and contains sufficient amounts of all the nutrients we need for optimal health. However, surveys in North America show that the diets of more than 60 percent of the people tested are deficient in one or more of the essential nutrients.[41]

Most surveys test for only 18 of the 45 known nutrients and use the standard Daily Values (DV), which are considered very low. Recognized as the minimal requirements for survival, they are inadequate to maintain optimal health. While these surveys look for common deficiencies such as iron; calcium; zinc; potassium; iodine; magnesium; selenium; manganese; vitamins A, C, E, B_1 (thiamine), B_2 (riboflavin), B_3 (niacin), and B_6; folate (folic acid); and iodine, they ignore equally important nutrients such as chromium and essential fatty acids.

Nutritional deficiencies result whenever tissues are deprived of adequate amounts of essential nutrients over a period of time. Deficiency symptoms are not necessarily obvious. Associated conditions develop slowly over time and can be very insidious and difficult to identify. One does not need to have scurvy to have a vitamin C deficiency. One does not need to have osteoporosis to have a calcium deficiency. Symptoms can be as subtle as appetite loss, bad breath, soft or brittle fingernails, fatigue, or insomnia.

Malnutrition does not occur only in areas of poverty or in underdeveloped countries. Although the United States is one of the most technically advanced and fast-paced nations, we do not seem to know how to feed ourselves properly so we can feel our best.

We are not exactly healthy as a population. We suffer from fatigue, frequent colds, allergies, excessive weight, diabetes, hypoglycemia, anemia, arthritis, mental problems, heart disease, cancer, and many other conditions that leave us unsatisfied with our health and feeling poorly. We too often do not even consider our own eating habits as the possible cause.

—8

Carbohydrates

Carbohydrates are the chief source of energy for all body functions and muscle uses. They are also needed for the digestion and assimilation of other foods. Carbohydrates provide immediately available calories for energy by producing heat when carbon in the system unites with oxygen in the bloodstream. Carbohydrates also help regulate protein and fat metabolism; fats require carbohydrates for their breakdown within the liver.

Carbohydrates are converted in the body to simple sugars such as glucose or fructose. Some of the blood sugar is used as fuel by tissues in the brain, nervous system, and muscles. A small portion of the glucose is converted to glycogen and stored by the liver and muscles. The excess is converted to fat and stored throughout the body. When fat reserves are needed for energy and converted to glucose to be used as body fuel, weight loss results.

The more complex the carbohydrate is (containing longer chains of sugar molecules), the longer it takes to break down and digest. Some very-long-chain sugars are not digested at all and are an excellent source of fiber. Examples are cellulose (found in celery), inulin (found in Jerusalem artichokes), and agar (found in some types of seaweed).

STARCHES

Starch molecules contain long chains of sugar molecules and are considered a complex carbohydrate, provided they are unrefined.

Refined starches include white flour, white rice, pasta, enriched flours (both white and dark), cornstarch, tapioca, and most breakfast cereals found on supermarket shelves, as well as all the products made with these ingredients. (These should be consumed only in limited quantities.)

Unrefined starches are not usually as detrimental to blood sugar levels as refined starches because they are more complex and are rich in vitamin and mineral cofactors needed by the body. They include starchy vegetables and fruits—yams, potatoes, corn, figs, bananas—and the many varieties of grains.

The main source of carbohydrates in the diet should be complex, such as fruits, vegetables, beans, nuts, seeds, and whole-grain breads, cereals, and other unrefined complex starches.

SIMPLE VERSUS COMPLEX

Simple carbohydrates are refined and are digested very quickly. They include all simple sugars including sucrose—brown sugar, powdered sugar, and white sugar, for example. Fructose occurs naturally in fruit. It can also be made from corn and other grains and is present in honey (a combination of fructose, glucose, maltose, and sucrose). Raw and turbinado sugars are slightly less refined than white sugar. Otherwise, they're identical.

Enzymes in the digestive tract quickly break down simple sugars, which can then be absorbed into the bloodstream. These sugars are referred to as high-glycemic-index sugars.

Complex carbohydrates take much longer to break down in comparison to simple carbohydrates. In general, the more unrefined the carbohydrate, the longer the digestion time required (with the exception of starches). These carbohydrates release a slow, constant stream of glucose into the bloodstream and therefore produce less impact upon blood sugar levels. These sugars are referred to as low-glycemic-index sugars.

SUGAR: AN AMERICAN ADDICTION

Most Americans consume a huge amount of sugar—approximately 40 teaspoons each day. Much of it, about 75 percent, is hidden in processed foods. In fact, sugar is the most commonly used food additive.

The top two sugar sources are soft drinks and cereals, which also happen to be the two best-selling foods in America. Other major sugar sources include candy, ice cream, baked goods, and other desserts.

The nine teaspoons of sugar contained in just one can of soda supply 180 calories, almost 10 percent of the daily calorie requirement for an average adult. Sugar accounts for an average of 640 calories consumed per day, or 24 percent of total calories,

Eating Carbohydrates

Most, if not all, of your carbohydrate intake should consist of unrefined complex carbohydrates. Sources include the following:

- All vegetables and greens
- All whole grains (including brown and wild rice)
- All whole cereals
- Nuts and seeds
- Legumes

Refined complex carbohydrates to avoid include the following:
- White flour
- Cornstarch
- White rice
- Potato starch
- Bread and crackers (white flour)
- Pasta

more than half of the carbohydrate content of the standard American diet.

Research has implicated excessive sugar consumption in the following health problems:

- Atherosclerosis (hardening/clogging of the arteries)
- Cancer
- Depression
- Diabetes
- Diverticulitis
- Gout
- High blood pressure
- Hormonal disorders
- Hypoglycemia
- Indigestion
- Kidney stones
- Liver disorders
- Mental and nervous disorders
- Migraine headaches
- Nutrient deficiencies
- Obesity
- Osteoporosis
- Periodontal disease
- Tooth decay
- Urinary infections

The True Junk Food

Processed sugar provides "empty calories," devoid of nutritional value. It has no fiber, no vitamins, no minerals, no essential fatty acids, no antioxidants, and no phytochemicals (chemicals found in plants with medicinal properties). To make matters worse, the body must tap into its precious supply of essential nutrients in order to process sugar. In effect, sugar's empty calories double the nutrient deficit. Laboratory animals fed sugar die significantly sooner than animals fed the same number of calories as complex carbohydrates such as whole grains and beans.

We need the simple sugar glucose to fuel cellular energy production. Cells generate energy by burning glucose in the presence of oxygen. Glucose is made from dietary carbohydrates, proteins, and fats. We burn glucose day and night, so we need a constant supply. A set of finely tuned mechanisms keeps blood glucose levels very stable.

Eating sugary foods, however, triggers excess insulin production. This sabotages the blood-sugar-regulating machinery, placing inordinate stress on the pancreas (which must make a lot of extra insulin to clear the extra sugar from the bloodstream), on the liver (which must transform sugar to glycogen in order to store it), and on the adrenal glands (which are stimulated to increase their output of adrenaline).

Sugar Turns to Fat

All sugars are rapidly digested, absorbed, and, unless you immediately burn them off through exercise, converted to fat. Acetates from sugar are the basic building blocks of both cholesterol and saturated fatty acids.

The more sugar (or white flour or other refined carbohydrates) you consume, the more acetate molecules you'll have in your system to support the production of saturated fat and cholesterol—and cellulite! Sugar literally becomes fat. The fat that is stored not only looks unattractive but contributes to hardening of the arteries, heart attacks, and many other health problems.

Because complex carbohydrates are burned much more slowly, they do not trigger fat production.

Recommended Dietary Intake

- 30 percent fat (mostly essential fatty acids)
- 40 percent protein
- 30 percent carbohydrates (mostly complex, unrefined)

—9

Protein

Protein is an important dietary component found readily in dairy products, meat (chicken, turkey, fish, and so on), soy, eggs, beans, peanuts, nuts, and seeds. Protein breaks down into amino acids, which are used for hundreds if not thousands of functions in the body, such as the formation of blood cells, antibodies, muscle tissue, and connective tissue.

DANGERS OF A HIGH-PROTEIN DIET

More common than inadequate protein consumption is the over-consumption of protein, especially among males. The popular meat-and-potatoes diet of today easily lends itself to being protein heavy.

Many people have become food phobics. They are afraid to eat carbohydrates—they think it will make them fat. They are afraid to eat fat—they think it will make them fat. What's left? Protein.

A number of popular diets encourage high protein intake, while limiting carbohydrates. This type of diet may cause weight loss but at what cost in the long run?

The average American diet, which is high in protein and low in fruits and vegetables, generates a large amount of acid, mainly as sulfates and phosphates. The kidneys respond to this dietary acid challenge by excreting it (via urination) and its by-product—ammonium. In order to buffer this acid, the body increases active resorption of calcium and other minerals. Where does it get these minerals? From our mineral storehouse—the bones. This means the body has to sacrifice valuable minerals needed for strong, healthy bones to buffer this excess acid. Indeed, bone density is directly related to acidity. Alkali buffers, such as those found in fruits and vegetables high in potassium, can help to reverse acid-induced urinary calcium loss.

Proteins in vegetable foods are accompanied by base precursors not found in animal foods, which provide predominantly acid precursors. Imbalance between dietary acid and base precursors leads to a chronic net dietary acid load that can have adverse consequences on bone. The Department of Epidemiology and Biostatistics, University of California, San Francisco, the Division of Endocrinology, and the General Clinical Research Center showed that "elderly women with a high dietary ratio of animal to vegetable protein intake have more rapid femoral neck bone loss and a greater risk of hip fracture than do those with a low ratio."[42]

According to Dr. Theodore Baroody, author of *Alkalize or Die*, acid wastes in the body can attack the joints, tissues, muscles, organs, and glands, causing minor to major dysfunction. If they attack the joints, you might develop arthritis. If they attack the muscles, you could end up with myofibrosis (aching muscles). If they attack the organs and glands, a myriad of illnesses could occur.[43]

One of the primary functions of the liver is to process acid toxins from the blood and to produce alkaline enzymes to defend against these acidic toxins. The load is much heavier on the liver when acid waste products are high due to excess protein.

I do recommend daily intake of one type of protein, and that is sulfur-rich whey protein, as well as low-fat cottage cheese and/or plain cultured yogurt. It is incredibly beneficial to cellular

High-Protein Diets

High-protein diets can be *dangerous*. They place a tremendous burden on the kidneys, liver, and bone structure and are detrimental to one's overall health. Many people have lost weight on these types of diets, but at a huge sacrifice to their overall health in the long run. The following health problems can result from a diet containing excess protein:

• Bone loss (osteoporosis)
• Kidney stones
• Increased risk for diabetes
• Acid/alkaline imbalances
• Liver dysfunction

There are much better, healthier ways to lose weight! (These are discussed later.)

metabolism when you also consume adequate amounts of essential fatty acids. The two products together, sulfur protein and EFAs, enrich the cells and stimulate natural metabolism. See Dr. Johanna Budwig's diet for cancer patients.[44]

—10

Fat

The Right Kind, the Right Amount

Not all fat is bad. The fact is that we need some fat in our diet, but we need the right kind. The following should help clear up the confusion.

ESSENTIAL FATTY ACIDS

Of the 45 essential nutrients that must be obtained from foods, two are fatty acids: omega-6 (linoleic acid), a polyunsaturated EFA, and omega-3 (alpha-linolenic acid), a superunsaturated EFA. Arachidonic acid is also considered essential, but it can be synthesized in the body if sufficient linoleic and linolenic acids are present. The reason they are called essential is the body cannot manufacture them and they must be ingested daily.

Essential fatty acids are unsaturated fatty acids necessary for normal growth and healthy arteries and nerves. Essential fatty acids are important for the transport and breakdown of cholesterol. They also keep skin and other tissues youthful and healthy. Essential fatty acids are the highest source of energy in nutrition.

Omega-3 is vital to brain development, normal blood pressure, healthy skin, and an effective immune system. It also lowers triglycerides and, if taken at high levels, lowers cholesterol. The antiaggregatory (blood thinning), antithrombotic (platelet normalization), and anti-inflammatory properties of omega-3 have all been clinically demonstrated.

Omega-3 oils are broken down into two active substances, EPA (eicosapentaenoic acid) and DHA. EPA has been specifically shown to play an important role in heart health. DHA is very important for proper brain growth and development.

The two major sources of omega-3 are fish and flaxseed oils, with flax being the richer of the two sources. Flaxseed oil requires less processing than fish oils, can be produced without pollutants, breaks down less readily, and is more cost effective to produce commercially.

Other good sources include soybeans and soybean oil; sunflower, sesame, and pumpkin seeds and oil; walnuts; and dark green vegetables, such as broccoli and spinach. To obtain essential fatty acids in the diet it is best to rely upon fresh, raw, unrefined foods or products such as fresh, unrefined, cold-pressed oils.

Omega-3 and omega-6 fatty acids are essential to health. These two EFAs form the membranes of every one of the billions of cells in our bodies. They are also needed for cellular energy production. Glands need EFAs to carry out the secretion of hormones and other regulating substances. Muscles require EFAs to repair damaged tissues and to speed healing. EFAs are critical to the immune response. Brain, eye, adrenal, and nerve cells require EFAs to function, and EFAs are necessary for growth and reproduction.

In addition, omega-3 and omega-6 are prostaglandin precursors (or raw materials). Prostaglandins are key body substances that regulate nearly every physical function. Prostaglandins support or control the following:

- Inflammatory process
- Healing and repair
- Immune system
- Neural circuits in the brain
- Cardiovascular system, including cholesterol levels and actions in the bloodstream

- Blood pressure
- Blood coagulation
- Digestive and reproductive systems
- Body thermostat and calorie burning
- Cell growth and proliferation

In the body, linoleic acid (omega-3) is converted first to gamma linolenic acid (GLA) and then to dihomo-gamma linolenic acid (DGLA), a chemical that does wonders for our health. DGLA is essential for the production of prostaglandin E1. This is an important hormone-like chemical that reduces inflammation, boosts immunity, lowers blood pressure, keeps platelets from sticking together, and improves blood vessel tone.

As we age, our bodies become less efficient at converting linoleic acid to GLA and therefore are less efficient at producing prostaglandins. Several diseases, including cancer, eczema, multiple sclerosis, and diabetes, also make the conversion less efficient.

This doesn't necessarily mean that supplementing with GLA will cure or prevent these diseases. In fact, some experts warn that GLA supplements have the potential to aggravate some symptoms because GLA and DGLA can actually promote inflammation.

Therefore, it is not only important to consume omega-3 and omega-6 fatty acids in the proper amount, it is also very important to consume them in the proper ratio. An excess intake of omega-6 in the diet is more common because this EFA is found in corn, safflower, and other commonly consumed vegetable oils.

In recent years, the incidence of asthma and allergies has increased. This rise correlates with the recent change in our dietary fat consumption—a reduced intake of saturated (animal) fats, an increase in the intake of polyunsaturated fatty acids from vegetable oils containing omega-6, and a decrease in the intake of oily fish, which contains omega-3.

Omega-6 is the precursor to arachidonic acid and prostaglandin E2, an *inflammatory* prostaglandin. Omega-3 and EPA *inhibit prostaglandin E2*, thereby helping to regulate our inflammatory response. It is easy to see how our anti-inflammatory response may be inhibited by a diet lacking in fish, flax, or other sources of omega-3.

EXCELLENT SOURCES OF OMEGA-3 AND GLA

The two best sources of omega-3 and GLA are flaxseed and borage oil.

Flaxseed

Flax is a small grain that contains the highest known vegetarian source of omega-3. One serving (20 grams) of flax contains 3,200 mg of omega-3 fatty acids plus 6 g of fiber, of which 1,600 micrograms (mcg) are cancer-fighting lignans. Flaxseed oil has nature's optimal balance of omega-6 and omega-3 for our diet.

The National Cancer Institute is looking closely at flax for possible chemopreventive effects. Flaxseeds are also one of nature's richest sources of lignans (also found in grains such as bran, buckwheat, and corn). Lignans deactivate potent estrogens that can initiate the growth of cancerous tumors, especially in the breast and reproductive system. In fact, studies have shown that women who consume a diet high in lignans have lower rates of colon and breast cancer.

The best way to supplement with flax is to grind up the whole seeds (in a coffee grinder) as you use it. The essential fatty acids quickly spoil after exposure to light and oxygen, so do not grind a large amount and use it over the next few weeks. The ground seeds will remain fresh only for a day or so if kept in a small container in the refrigerator. You can add flaxseed to salads, cottage cheese, yogurt, soups, cereals, and so on. Be sure to add ground flax to cooked foods *at the table,* not on the stove, as high heat will also destroy the integrity of the EFAs.

Using high-lignan flaxseed oil is also an option. In fact, it is much more convenient when taken in capsule form with other omega-3, 6, and 9 oils to give you the perfect balance of EFAs.

A Note on Breast Cancer

According to the National Alliance of Breast Cancer Organizations, breast cancer is the most common form of cancer in U.S. women: one of every nine women in the United States will develop breast cancer, and a woman dies of breast cancer every 12 minutes.

Currently, researchers are determining if fish oil in a woman's diet lowers her breast cancer risk. According to *Tufts University Health & Nutrition Letter*, in laboratory conditions, breast tumor production slowed in animals fed fish oils (omega-3). In another study, women with breast cancer taking fish oil supplements increased the Omega-3 fatty acids in their breast tissue after three months. It is too early in the study to determine whether fish oil actually reduces a woman's risk of breast cancer or whether fish oil will slow the progression of breast cancer, but researchers suspect that it might.[45]

Eating a diet of fresh fruits and vegetables, beans, nuts, and grains can also lower your chances of breast cancer and all other types of cancer as well.

Eating less meat is also recommend. Researchers have long wondered why American women are more prone to breast cancer than Japanese women. It is suspected to be because Japanese women eat less fat, more soy protein, and more fish.

Eliminating alcohol, caffeine, sugar, and high-fat desserts and not smoking can reduce the cancer risk. Taking supplements such as beta carotene; vitamins A, B complex, C, and E; chromium; selenium; coenzyme Q10; proanthocyanidins (PC-95); olive leaf extract (oleuropein), and EFAs (such as flaxseed oil or borage oil) may also help.

Herbs, such as cayenne, ginger, garlic, burdock root, milk thistle, red clover, and dandelion root, can cleanse the body (liver and bloodstream) of toxins that may be carcinogenic and increase cancer risk.

Borage Oil

Since the Middle Ages, people have used borage, an herb with bright blue flowers, to treat heart disease and rheumatism and to reduce inflammation. Borage oil is one of three major supplemental sources of GLA and is often used to treat a number of conditions, including rheumatoid arthritis, eczema, and PMS.

Besides borage oil, GLA comes from the seeds of the evening primrose plant and from black currants.

UNSATURATED VERSUS SATURATED FATS

Unsaturated fatty acids usually are liquid at room temperature, and many come from vegetable sources such as safflower, soy, and corn. Other sources of unsaturated fatty acids are wheat germ, seeds, and cod liver oil. Whole grains and green leafy vegetables are very low in fat, but the fat they do contain is unsaturated. Many animal products are high in monounsaturated fats but are also high in cholesterol and saturated fat.

Unsaturated fatty acids are important for respiration of vital organs and make it easier for oxygen to be transported by the bloodstream to all cells, tissues, and organs. Unsaturated fatty acids also regulate blood flow and help break up cholesterol deposits on arterial walls. They are essential for normal glandular activity, especially for that of the adrenals and thyroid. They nourish and maintain the health of the skin, mucous membranes, and nerves and have many, many more important functions.

Monounsaturated fats (short-chain fatty acids) in the diet seem to have no effect on total serum cholesterol levels and do not lower HDL, the "good cholesterol." Polyunsaturated fats (long-chain fatty acids) in the diet tend to lower serum cholesterol levels.

Saturated fatty acids are solid at room temperature and are usually found in animal products. Saturated vegetable fats are found in many solid and hydrogenated shortenings, such as coconut oil and cocoa butter. While these are sometimes adver-

Sources of Unsaturated Fats

Foods high in monounsaturated fats include (estimated percentages given are of total fat)

- Olives and olive oil (77 percent monounsaturated)
- Avocados (75 percent monounsaturated)
- Canola (rapeseed) oil (62 percent monounsaturated)
- Vegetable shortening (50 percent monounsaturated)
- Margarine (49 percent monounsaturated)
- Peanuts and peanut oil (49 percent monounsaturated)
- Sesame oil (42 percent monounsaturated)
- Most nuts (except coconut and walnuts)

Foods high in polyunsaturated fats include

- Safflower oil (77 percent polyunsaturated)
- Sunflower seeds and oil (66 percent polyunsaturated)
- Soybean oil (62 percent polyunsaturated)
- Walnuts (60 percent polyunsaturated)
- Corn oil (59 percent polyunsaturated)

tised to be cholesterol free, this may be misleading because these fats are unhealthy, altered, unnatural fats and should be avoided.

Saturated fats are metabolized more slowly by the body when compared to unsaturated fats. Saturated fats should be limited in the diet because they tend to raise serum cholesterol levels in the body. Elevated cholesterol levels in the blood have been associated with an increased risk for the development of coronary heart disease.

CHOLESTEROL—THE TRUTH

There is much confusion about cholesterol. Cholesterol has become something that people fear and want to avoid. Some people are afraid to consume any cholesterol whatsoever and are alarmed that their blood tests reveal they still have elevated levels.

Cholesterol is a fatty substance manufactured largely by the liver and intestines, but also by all cells in the body, for the production of the adrenal sex hormones, vitamin D, and bile salts. Cholesterol also has a vital role in nerve and brain function.

We also obtain cholesterol from foods—largely animal products, such as meat, seafood, dairy products, and eggs. Egg yolks, organ meats, cream, and butter are very high in cholesterol. Although low in total fat, shrimp, lobster, and sardines are fairly high in cholesterol. Foods of plant origin, such as fruits, vegetables, grains, cereals, nuts and seeds, contain no cholesterol.

Cholesterol is manufactured in the body from dietary saturated fatty acids and refined carbohydrates.

While deficiencies of cholesterol in the body are unlikely to occur, cholesterol commonly accumulates throughout the body if fats are eaten excessively. But if you are also eating the proper amounts of fiber and essential fatty acids and other nutrients you need to properly metabolize fats, you should be able to eat cholesterol-containing foods, in their natural state, in moderation, without any problem.

Dietary Sources of Cholesterol

The following are cholesterol amounts in common foods:

Egg (1 medium) 274 mg	Steak (8 oz) 208 mg
Lamb chop (6 oz) 168 mg	Veal cutlet (6 oz) 168 mg
Hamburger (6 oz) 162 mg	Pork chop (6 oz) 150 mg
Ham (6 oz) 150 mg	Ice cream (1 cup) 59 mg
Cheddar cheese (1 oz) 30 mg	Mozzarella (1 oz) 15 mg
Whole milk (1 cup) 33 mg	Butter (1 tsp) 12 mg
Mayonnaise (1 tbsp) 9 mg	Skim milk (1 cup) 4 mg

These foods are natural. I would eat butter over margarine any day—cholesterol or no cholesterol. The body has a much easier time dealing with natural fats than it does fake fats and altered fats (trans-fatty acids, which are covered in the next section).

Lecithin (found in egg yolks, liver, nuts, whole wheat, unrefined vegetable oils, soybeans, and corn), inositol, and the essential fatty acids (omega-3) are very important dietary factors that help break up and transport cholesterol in the body. Also important are fiber; vitamins A, C, and D; and proanthocyanidins (PC-95).

FATS TO AVOID

Hydrogenated and partially hydrogenated fats are fats that have been changed from their natural liquid form to become more solid. This processing alters the natural molecular structure of the fatty acids into an unnatural configuration. These fatty acids are unhealthy because they resemble saturated fats, but the body has a much more difficult time processing them. Trans-fatty acids also produce free radicals in the body. Because very small amounts of trans-fatty acids occur in nature, they are *foreign* to the body.

Hydrogenated fats are saturated-like fats made from plant oils and fats that have been heated to a very high temperature (as high as 458 degrees Fahrenheit) and pressure processed. Enzymes are killed at much lower temperatures; therefore, all active enzymes are eliminated.

Hydrogenated fats are created when an oil that is largely unsaturated, such as corn oil, has hydrogen added to it, causing fat to become more solid at room temperature. During hydrogenation, the unsaturated fat becomes more saturated. Hydrogenated oils are *artificially saturated.*

Most packaged foods list these fats on the label as partially hydrogenated or hydrogenated oil. The more solid and hydrogenated the fat, the more trans-fatty acids the product contains. Examples of hydrogenated fat products include margarine, margarine-based products, shortenings, and fats used for frying.

Unhealthy Fats

Hydrogenated oils are fats that have the same capacity to do harm as saturated fats.

Why Are Trans-Fatty Acids Bad?

Among other results, researchers have found that trans-fatty acids significantly raise LDL ("bad cholesterol") levels, while lowering HDL ("good cholesterol") levels. In the Framingham Heart Study (a 40-year study covering 5,209 individuals living in Massachusetts), high LDL levels combined with low HDL levels was indicative of coronary heart disease risk.[46]

Trans-fatty acids also can easily become trapped along arterial walls, creating an ideal environment for buildup of plaque and development of atherosclerosis.

Results from other human studies and recent large-scale epidemiologic surveys clearly show that dietary trans-fatty acids increase the risk of developing coronary heart diseases. Studies support the idea that lowering the intake of trans-fatty acids may lower the risk of coronary heart disease.

Butter versus Margarine

Butter contains easy-to-digest short-chain fatty acids but contains relatively few EFAs (only about 2 percent linoleic acid). It also contains about one gram of cholesterol per pound of butter and does not contain the factors needed for its metabolism. (Oil seeds and fresh seed oils contain these factors.)

Butter contains fatty acid chains that are more easily metabolized than the fatty acid chains found in hydrogenated oils, fats, shortening, and margarine. Butter can also be used for frying, baking, and other cooking methods because it consists mainly of saturated fats, which are relatively stable in the presence of light, heat, and oxygen.

Vegetable Oils versus Animal Fats

Modern-day diets high in hydrogenated vegetable oils instead of natural animal fats are implicated in causing a significant increase in heart disease and cancer.

Note: Many commercial dairies use antibiotics, which can be found in butter and other dairy products. These can cause allergies, tiredness, sugar craving, hypoglycemia, and several other health problems. Look for nongenetically modified, organic, drug-free, hormone-free butter in health food stores or larger grocery stores.

Margarine does not contain much short-chain, easily digestible fatty acid. The oil from which margarine is made contains a substantial amount of unsaturated fatty acids, but these are destroyed or changed into other substances in processing. Margarine contains less essential fatty acids than butter. The fatty acids it does contain are altered and interfere with the functions of essential fatty acids and often become concentrated in heart tissue. These fatty acids also are metabolized much slower than the ones in butter.

In addition, the following points should be considered:

- Margarine contains no cholesterol, but the body treats it the same as a saturated fat.
- Margarine contains no antibiotics or pesticides but contains many other nonnatural chemicals as a result of processing. The effect of these on health is yet unknown.
- Margarine and other hydrogenated products are not good for cooking because the unsaturated fatty acids they contain are further altered by heat, light, and oxygen.
- Margarine is advertised as the healthy choice, but the truth seems to be the opposite.

Because of the way margarine is manufactured, it can be actually more dangerous to one's health than butter. Butter is more healthy (in moderation, of course) in terms of digestibility, usefulness for frying, and naturalness. In addition, most people agree that butter tastes better.

To lengthen thy life, lessen thy meals.
—BENJAMIN FRANKLIN

FAT INTAKE: THE CONTROVERSY

Lack of fats and essential fatty acids in the diet can cause a change in cell structure, resulting in slowed growth and other disorders. Symptoms of inadequate fat intake include brittle and dull hair, nail problems, dandruff, allergies and dermatitis (especially eczema in infants), and cancer. The primary cause of cancers common to women is a low intake of essential fatty acids.

If too much fat is consumed, abnormal weight gain and obesity may result. Excessive fat intake will cause abnormally slow digestion and absorption, resulting in indigestion. If a lack of carbohydrates and water in the diet accompanies excess fat intake, fats cannot be completely metabolized and may become toxic to the body.

Most authorities now recommend fat consumption be 20–30 percent of the total calorie intake. For a 2,000-calorie-per-day diet, this is about 44–70 g of fat. *At least* one-third of this (about 15–23 g) should consist of essential unsaturated fatty acids. The American Heart Association currently recommends that monounsaturated fats should take precedence over polyunsaturated fats in a 1.5 ratio to 1. Saturated fats (and *especially hydrogenated fats*) should be avoided.

KNOW WHAT YOU ARE EATING

Avoid prepared foods that contain animal fat or tropical oils such as palm and coconut. These fats are often used because they are less expensive and produce aesthetically appealing products. To avoid saturated fats, manufacturers often instead use hydrogenated or partially hydrogenated oils. Prepare your own foods as much as possible, and *read labels carefully* before you buy or eat anything!

Many health problems are associated with excessive fat intake. Obesity represents a major threat to health and quality of life. Although obesity has strong genetic determinants, the increasing prevalence of obesity in populations around the world suggests that high-fat diets promote obesity. Carefully controlled laboratory studies, cross-sectional studies, clinical trials, and studies of individuals at high risk to develop obesity clearly demonstrate that a high-fat diet increases the likelihood of obesity and that the risk of obesity is low in individuals consuming low-fat diets.

The amount and type of dietary fat intake (especially high saturated fat intake) may be associated with increased risk for the following health problems:

- ARM (age-related macular disease)
- Breast cancer
- Colon/rectal cancer
- Prostate cancer
- Renal (kidney) cancer
- Endometrial cancer
- Pancreatic cancer
- Non-Hodgkin's lymphoma
- Type II diabetes

Keep in mind that whereas the high intake of saturated fat appears to increase the risk of cancer, the specific effects of EFAs (omega-3s, CLA [conjugated linoleic acid], and tocotrienols) in most cases can be very beneficial.

—11

Vitamins

Vitamins are organic compounds that are indispensable to body functions. Vitamins are used within the body's structures as building blocks and are necessary for various biochemical functions. Most vitamins must be ingested, although some may be synthesized within the body.

For optimal health, we must obtain an adequate quantity of each of the vitamins. The amount needed varies from person to person and is based on a number of criteria. The Foods and Nutrition Board of the National Research Council has established a recommended daily value for each of the vitamins, but many people disagree with its interpretation. For example, Nobel Prize winner Linus Pauling believed that the DV for a vitamin is not the amount that leads to the best health for most people. It is, instead, only the estimated amount that for most people would prevent death or serious illness from overt vitamin deficiency.

To obtain optimal nutrition, many people use supplements in addition to eating a proper diet. Because nutrients in the soil are not as plentiful as they once were, along with many other factors, one cannot be certain of the nutrient value of foods eaten today.

Vitamins taken in excess of what can be utilized in metabolic processes are not usually of any value and will either be excreted in the urine or stored in the body. Excessive consumption of some nutrients (particularly fat-soluble vitamins) may result in toxicity.

Vitamins are usually characterized as being water soluble or fat soluble. The water-soluble vitamins are B complex, C, and bioflavonoids, and they are usually measured in milligrams. If taken in excess, they are largely flushed out of the body. This means for the most part that they are pretty safe. Water-soluble nutrients are also more easily lost in cooking if water is used.

The fat-soluble vitamins are A, D, E, and K, and they are commonly measured in units. Fat-soluble vitamins are stored in the body in our fatty tissue; taking excess amounts on a long-term basis may cause problems with toxicity.

Following are brief explanations of the vitamins and their importance to our health.

VITAMIN A

Vitamin A is a fat-soluble nutrient found in nature in two ways: preformed (usually from animal products) or beta carotene (from plant sources such as carrots or sweet potatoes).

Vitamin A is essential for fat metabolism and for developing and maintaining healthy skin, hair, nails, eyes (especially night vision), teeth, bones, gums, mucous linings, membranes, and various organs (especially the lungs). Vitamin A helps the body resist infection and helps prevent premature aging and senility.

Natural sources include whole milk, eggs, liver, fruit, and leafy green and yellow vegetables.

Deficiency symptoms include night blindness; dry eyes; rough, dry, or prematurely aged skin; loss of sense of smell; loss of appetite; frequent fatigue; skin blemishes; diarrhea; dry hair; dandruff; and brittle fingernails. Vitamin A deficiency can also lead to loss of vitamin C.

Beta carotene (Provitamin A)

Beta carotenes must be converted by the body into vitamin A before they can be utilized by the body. That is why they are called a vitamin A precursor, or provitamin A. In addition to their provitamin A action, carotenes are an excellent protective antioxidant.

Natural sources include beets, broccoli, carrots, cantaloupe, mustard, papaya, parsnips, pumpkin, spinach, sweet potatoes, tomatoes, watercress, and yellow string beans.

Deficiency symptoms are the same as for vitamin A.

B COMPLEX VITAMINS

The B complex vitamins are all water soluble. They are often referred to as the "stress vitamins" as they are rapidly depleted during stress. In general, they are very important for healthy nerve function but also have various individual important actions throughout the body.

B complex vitamins usually work better when taken in conjunction with other B vitamins. An oversupply of any one B vitamin can result in significant depletion of the others.

Vitamin B₁ (Thiamine)

B_1 helps promote proper use of sugars and energy from food and is necessary for proper functioning of the heart and nervous system. Thiamine is a blood builder, maintains muscle tone, and prevents fluid retention and constipation.

Natural sources include whole grains and cereals, yeast, liver, pork, poultry, lean meat, eggs, and legumes.

Deficiency symptoms include difficulty in the digestion of carbohydrates, fatigue, loss of appetite, irritability, emotional instability, confusion, memory loss, abdominal pains, and constipation. A thiamine deficiency can also elevate pyruvic acid levels in the blood, which can result in a loss of mental alertness, difficulty in breathing, and heart damage.

Vitamin B₂ (Riboflavin)

B_2 aids in growth and reproduction; alleviates eye fatigue; aids in antibody and red blood cell formation; promotes healthy skin, hair, and nails; and aids in metabolism.

Natural sources include milk, liver, cheese, fish, eggs, whole grains, brewer's yeast, almonds, and sunflower seeds.

Deficiency symptoms include cracks or sores in the corners of the mouth; red, sore tongue; feeling of sand inside the eyelids; eye fatigue; dilation of pupils; light sensitivity; scaling around the nose, mouth, forehead, and ears; trembling; dizziness; inability to urinate; vaginal itching; oily skin; and baldness.

Vitamin B$_3$ (Niacin)

Vital for the use of carbohydrates, fats, and proteins, niacin is needed for the formation of hormones, aids circulation (dilates blood vessels), controls cholesterol levels, and tones the nervous system.

Niacin can lower LDL cholesterol and triglyceride levels and raise HDL cholesterol levels. Studies show niacin can slow and even reverse the progression of atherosclerosis when used with other cholesterol-lowering drugs, diet, and exercise. However, in the doses typically needed for these effects (usually greater than 1,000 mg), niacin is considered a medication. At doses of higher than 2,000 mg, niacin has potentially serious side effects, including liver damage, high blood sugar, and irregular heartbeat. As little as 50 mg can cause flushing, headaches, cramps, and nausea. Take increased doses only on your doctor's advice.

Natural sources include liver, lean meat, poultry (white meat), fish, eggs, peanuts, avocados, dates, figs, prunes, green vegetables, whole wheat products, brewer's yeast, wheat germ, and rice bran.

Deficiency symptoms include muscular weakness, general fatigue, loss of appetite, indigestion, bad breath, small ulcers, canker sores, insomnia, irritability, nausea, vomiting, headaches, tender gums, and pellagra (a disease characterized by dermatitis, dementia, and diarrhea).

Vitamin B$_5$ (Pantothenic Acid)

Needed for the formation of proteins and nucleic acids, B$_5$ helps maintain functions of the intestinal tract, prevents certain forms of anemia, and aids in wound healing, antibody formation, growth stimulation, and vitamin utilization. The brain contains high concentrations of pantothenic acid, so many mental symptoms can result from B_5 deficiency.

Natural sources include leafy green vegetables, beans, peas, nuts, liver, egg yolk, royal jelly, brewer's yeast, wheat germ, and wheat bran.

Deficiency symptoms include vomiting, restlessness, abdominal pains, burning feet, muscle cramps, skin disorders, low blood sugar, depression, insomnia, and fatigue.

Vitamin B_6 (Pyridoxine)

Vitamin B_6 facilitates the body's use of carbohydrates, proteins, and fats; is needed for the production of hydrochloric acid; and alleviates nausea. Hydrochloric acid is necessary for the breakdown and digestion of food in the stomach.

B_6 is crucial for a healthy immune system as it is necessary for the production of antibodies and red blood cells. Individuals with inflammatory conditions such as rheumatoid arthritis are frequently deficient in B_6. Inflammation worsens in individuals with a pyridoxine deficiency, and the peroxidation levels (free-radical damage to fats) are thought to increase by as much as 40 percent.

B_6 is needed for the body to use proteins, to build and maintain muscle tissue, and to metabolize fats. B_6, along with folic acid, protects us from heart disease by helping to break down a by-product of protein metabolism, homocysteine. B_6 also helps the liver detoxify poisonous chemicals and metabolic by-products and is recognized to aid in PMS and painful periods.

Natural sources include brewer's yeast, bananas, avocados, wheat germ, leafy green vegetables, whole grains and cereals, milk, eggs, blackstrap molasses, cabbage, soybeans, walnuts, peanuts, and pecans.

Deficiency symptoms include low blood sugar and low glucose tolerance, hair loss, water retention during pregnancy, cracks around the mouth and eyes, numbness and cramps in the arms and legs, visual disturbances, nervousness, irritability, and increased urination. Symptoms of B_6 deficiency are similar to deficiencies of niacin and riboflavin.

Folic Acid—Another B Vitamin

Folic acid helps prevent heart disease. Studies show that daily supplementation with 400 mcg of folic acid reduces homocysteine levels. Homocysteine is a by-product of protein metabolism that binds with low-density lipoprotein (LDL) cholesterol and causes damage to the arterial wall, leading to plaque buildup and atherosclerosis. This also increases one's risk for blood clot formation. High levels of homocysteine often result from dietary inadequacies of B_6, B_{12}, and folic acid.

Older individuals tend to have higher homocysteine levels, which have been linked to an increase in heart problems. The higher the level of folic acid, the lower the level of homocysteine. Therefore, increasing levels of folic acid can prevent a buildup of homocysteine in the blood. Individuals consuming a high-protein diet have an increased need for these important nutrients.

Folic acid also has many other important functions in the body. It helps build red blood cells and aids in the division of body cells, body growth, and reproduction. It is also needed for hydrochloric acid production and protein metabolism.

A known cancer fighter (especially cervical and colon cancers), folic acid is also an important antistress vitamin as it supports the immune and nervous systems. Additionally, it helps reduce inflammation and has been shown to relieve symptoms of psoriasis.

Folic acid is important for the prevention of neural tube defects. This makes it a very important nutrient for pregnant women and women who may become pregnant.

Natural sources include brewer's yeast, leafy deep green vegetables (such as spinach, broccoli, and asparagus), wheat germ, mushrooms, nuts, liver, lima beans, lettuce, bananas, and oranges.

Deficiency symptoms include poor growth, gray hair, gastro-intestinal disturbances, anemia, irritability, forgetfulness, and mental sluggishness. Prolonged deficiency can cause neurological changes and mental deterioration.

The requirements for this vitamin increase during pregnancy as the rapid growth of the fetus quickly depletes the mother's reserves. Deficiencies can cause deformities in the fetus, such as cleft palate, brain damage, and slow development or poor learning ability.

Vitamin B$_{12}$ (Cobalamin)

B$_{12}$ is needed for the formation of blood cells and promotes growth. It also increases energy and memory and is required for metabolism of fats, carbohydrates, and protein.

Natural sources include kelp, bananas, peanuts, Concord grapes, sunflower seeds, brewer's yeast, wheat germ, bee pollen, liver, beef, eggs, pork, milk, and cheese.

Deficiency symptoms are very slow to appear, taking as long as five years to manifest. They include changes in the nervous system, such as soreness and weakness in the legs and arms, diminished reflex response, loss of sensory perception, difficulty in walking, speech problems (stammering), and jerking of limbs. Also, nervousness, unpleasant body odor, menstrual disturbances, and neuritis are signs of deficiency.

B$_{12}$ deficiency can cause a type of brain damage similar to schizophrenia. Symptoms include a sore mouth, numbness or stiffness, shooting pains, and a pins-and-needles sensation.

If deficiencies are not detected early, permanent mental deterioration may result. See your doctor if you notice any of these symptoms.

VITAMIN C

Vitamin C is a water-soluble nutrient that accelerates healing and is needed for bone and teeth formation, collagen production,

prevention of the common cold, digestion, red blood cell formation, and shock and infection resistance. It is also a protective
agent against cancer.

The need for vitamin C is increased by smoking; alcohol consumption; stress; high fever; use of contraceptive pills, antibiotics,
cortisone, aspirin, painkillers, or sulfa drugs; a high-protein diet;
drinking of excess water; exposure to smog or petroleum fumes;
and use of copper utensils.

Natural sources include rose hips, citrus fruits, black currants,
berries, broccoli, cabbage, cauliflower, persimmons, guavas, sweet
potatoes, and green bell peppers.

Deficiency symptoms include impaired digestion; bleeding
gums; a tendency to bruise; swollen or painful joints; weakened
tooth enamel or dentin; nosebleeds; anemia; lowered resistance
to infections, including colds and flu; and slow healing of wounds
and fractures. A severe deficiency results in scurvy.

VITAMIN D

Vitamin D is a fat-soluble nutrient needed for strong teeth and
bones, heart action, nervous system maintenance, normal blood
clotting, and skin respiration. Specifically, vitamin D_3 is needed

Ester-C®

Ester-C® is a pH-neutral and specially buffered form of vitamin C
sold as a multimineral ascorbate complex.

Clinical studies show that Ester-C® is absorbed into the
bloodstream faster, in larger amounts, and penetrates white
blood cells more efficiently than other types of vitamin C. It is
three times more bioavailable than regular vitamin C and lasts up
to four times longer in the bloodstream at its maximum level. As
a nonacidic form of vitamin C, Ester-C® is gentle to the stomach.

Ester-C® is a registered trademark of Inter-Cal Corporation
(U.S. Patent No. 4,833,816).

for adequate absorption of calcium. It also helps in the proper utilization of vitamin A and phosphorus. Vitamin D can be acquired through sunlight. Ultraviolet rays act on the oils of the skin to produce the vitamin, which is then absorbed into the body.

Seniors and individuals who are not exposed to regular sunlight are at risk of vitamin D deficiency if dietary sources are lacking.

Natural sources include milk, fish liver oil, egg yolk, tuna, salmon, sardines, herring, sprouted seeds, mushrooms, and sunflower seeds.

Deficiency symptoms chiefly involve the bones. Calcium and phosphorus imbalances cause faulty mineralization of bone structures. In children, this deficiency can result in rickets. In adults, this condition is called "osteomalacia." Symptoms include softening of the skull and fragile bones, with bowing of the legs and spinal curvature; enlargement of the wrist, ankle, and knee joints; poorly developed muscles; and nervous irritability. Tetany (muscular numbness, tingling, and spasms) and dental problems are also vitamin D deficiency symptoms.

VITAMIN E (TOCOPHEROL)

Vitamin E is a fat-soluble nutrient that is an anticoagulant and antioxidant. It helps prevent oxidation of substances in the body such as cellular membranes and fatty acids. Vitamin E plays an essential role in the cellular respiration of all muscles, especially the heart and skeletal muscles.

Vitamin E alleviates fatigue, dilates blood vessels, and reduces blood cholesterol, as well as improves circulation, capillary formation and the functioning of red blood cells, muscle, and other tissues. It is also important for reproductive functions in men and women. Some individuals claim it improves libido.

Vitamin E shows great promise for protecting against cardiovascular disease. It is a potent antioxidant that attaches directly to LDL cholesterol in the blood and helps prevent damage from free radicals. Studies show vitamin E might prevent or slow progression of atherosclerosis in people with cardiovascular disease and diabetes. In addition, the vitamin may even slow the effects of Parkinson's disease and Alzheimer's disease.

At high doses (above 1,080 IU [international units]) vitamin E can cause side effects including bleeding (especially when taken with blood-thinning medications) and gastrointestinal discomfort.

Natural sources include vegetable oils, whole-grain cereals, wheat germ, lettuce, Brussels sprouts, leafy greens, soybeans, and eggs. It is estimated that 90 percent of the vitamin E content of grains is lost in the milling process.

Deficiency symptoms include rupture of red blood cells (the membranes become fragile and break), a tendency toward muscular wasting, abnormal fat deposits in the muscles, premature aging and dry skin, miscarriages in women, and infertility in men. Vitamin E deficiencies contribute to the development of heart disease and cancer.

VITAMIN K (MENADIONE)

Vitamin K is a fat-soluble nutrient that is required for normal blood clotting, activates energy-producing tissues, and is important for the liver.

Natural sources include kelp, alfalfa, yogurt, egg yolk, safflower and soybean oil, fish liver oil, and leafy green vegetables.

Deficiency symptoms include delayed ability or inability to form blood clots, which can cause hemorrhaging in any part of the body. Also common are bruising, nosebleeds, and miscarriages.

−12

Minerals

Minerals are another group of essential nutrients needed for our physical and mental health. In the body they form part of the tissue structures and are components of enzymes and hormones, which regulate processes such as the immune system, growth, and energy in the body. Each of these enzymes and hormones depends on minerals and trace minerals to function. Minerals help to regulate the flow of fluids and to maintain water and acid-base balance in the body. Minerals have the power to rejuvenate energy, to overcome fatigue, and to improve thinking and memory. They facilitate nerve impulse transmission and muscle contraction and help strengthen the nervous and skeletal systems. In addition, minerals are needed to grow new hair, to normalize the heartbeat, and much more.

The body functions best when all the needed nutrients, including minerals, are present in their proper proportions. If there is a shortage of just one mineral, the overall system will weaken and begin to lose efficiency. In fact, in the absence of minerals, vitamins have no function. Lacking vitamins, the body can still make use of minerals, but lacking minerals, vitamins are useless. With the mineral balance of the body off, functions of the body cannot operate optimally, and eventually disease will set in.

DEFICIENCIES

For a number of reasons, individuals often do not obtain through their diet the proper amounts of some minerals. Food plants are often grown in soil deficient in important minerals because synthetic and superphosphate fertilizers, pesticides, herbicides, growth regulators, and livestock feed additives destroy microbial soil life needed to make the soil nutrients available to the plant. In addition, many minerals are in the form of water-soluble salts, and unfortunately, rains and heavy irrigation over the years can wash away these salts, causing depleted soil conditions.

Variable amounts of minerals are also lost because of cooking and processing. Food preservation methods such as blanching, freezing, and smoking cause up to a 30 percent nutrient loss, and canning and sun-drying can cause up to a 50 percent loss of nutrients. Chemical additives may have a protective effect, a destructive effect, or no effect on the nutrient value in the foods.

Losses due to cooking vary with the method used, amount of water used, cooking time, and other variables. Boiling (cooking foods in water at a temperature of 212 degrees Fahrenheit) can cause significant nutrient losses. Minerals are lost when large amounts of water encourage leaching.

BIOAVAILABILITY

Many individuals have trouble assimilating and utilizing minerals, even from highly assimilable food sources. Although healthy people generally absorb more than 90 percent of the protein, carbohydrates, and fat in their diets, they do not generally absorb minerals as efficiently. In fact, in controlled studies, adults have been found to absorb an average of only about 5 percent of the manganese, 10 percent of the iron, 10–20 percent of the zinc, and 30–40 percent of the magnesium and calcium from their diets.

The foods and medications that individuals consume can cause large variations in the bioavailability of minerals in their diets. For example, healthy adults have been found to absorb anywhere from 1 percent to over 35 percent of their dietary iron intake, depending on the composition of their diets. The same range of absorption applies for zinc. Bioavailability of minerals can also be influenced by several other factors.

For example, a high-fiber diet can interfere with mineral uptake since it contains substances that combine with minerals to form insoluble compounds. In addition, fiber helps food move through the digestive tract faster, allowing less time for absorption of minerals.

Because diet alone may not provide all the needed minerals one needs, many nutritionists suggest combining a diet high in unprocessed and unrefined foods with adequate supplementation of the necessary minerals, which anticipates the problems of assimilation.

MAJOR AND TRACE MINERALS

Major minerals are those found in larger amounts in the body, such as calcium and magnesium. Trace minerals are found in very minute amounts, such as chromium and selenium. They are all necessary for normal functioning of the body.

Following are brief explanations of a few of the major and trace minerals, showing their importance to our health and the prevention of disease.

Calcium

Calcium is the most abundant mineral in the body with about 99 percent deposited in the bones and teeth. Soft tissues and blood contain the remaining percentage. The main function of calcium is to act in cooperation with phosphorus to build and maintain bones and teeth. It is also essential for healthy blood, helps regulate the heartbeat, and is needed for nerve and muscle stimulation and for blood-clotting processes. Strong stomach acid secretions are required to absorb calcium into the body. Usually, only about 20 percent of the calcium we consume is actually absorbed.

Mineral Composition in an Average Adult Male

Water*	45,000 g
Calcium	1,100 g
Phosphorus	600 g
Potassium	140 g
Sulfur	140 g
Sodium	100 g
Chlorine	95 g
Magnesium	19 g
Silicon	18 g
Iron	4.2 g
Zinc	2.3 g
Vitamin C*	1.2–2.0 g

* Amounts of water and vitamin C are included for reference.

Calcium is found in significant amounts in milk and dairy products but also is found in smaller amounts in fish, seaweed, blackstrap molasses, nuts and seeds, black beans, soybeans, tofu, and vegetable greens.

Deficiency symptoms include muscle cramps and numbness and tingling in the arms and legs, bone malformation (rickets in children, osteomalacia in adults), osteoporosis, joint pains, heart palpitations, slow pulse, tooth decay, and insomnia.

Chromium

Chromium is a trace mineral needed to escort glucose through cell walls. Insulin requires the cooperation of small amounts of chromium as a catalyst. Many documented cases of diabetes have resulted from a diet of chromium-poor processed foods. These cases could have been prevented by the use of chromium-rich foods, such as brewer's yeast, beef liver, chicken, whole grains, or supplements. Chromium can help reduce sugar cravings by helping the body to utilize sugar more effectively.

Deficiency symptoms involve the interference of insulin action. The effects of this can include depressed growth rates, aortic plaque formation, and diabetes.

Iron

Iron is a very "temperamental" mineral that requires adequate systemic amounts of vitamin C, calcium, copper, cobalt, vitamin E, vitamin F, and 19 different amino acids in order to be absorbed. It is concentrated in the blood and is essential for the formation of hemoglobin and myoglobin, which transport oxygen throughout the body. Iron is the ninth most abundant mineral found in the body, yet most biochemists consider it a trace mineral because of its very delicate balance in the body.

Certain groups can be at risk of having low iron levels. These include young children and early teens, menstruating women, and people with conditions that cause internal bleeding, such as ulcers or intestinal diseases. But for healthy men and postmenopausal women, iron supplementation may not be needed. In fact, some studies suggest that high iron levels may increase the risk of heart attack and atherosclerosis, although a link hasn't been proven. In addition, if you have the uncommon (but not rare) genetic disease hemochromatosis, iron supplements could cause a hazardous iron buildup in your body.

If you have above 400 mcg of iron per deciliter of blood, you may not need to supplement with iron. In fact, doing so may cause health problems. If you have below 400 mcg per deciliter, talk with your doctor about supplementation. If you require supplementation, you should know that colostrum contains lactoferrin (an iron-building protein), which can help you better utilize the iron in your foods by improving iron uptake into the cells.

Iron is found in liver, oysters, heart, lean meat, leafy green vegetables, whole grains, dried fruits, legumes, and molasses.

Deficiency symptoms may result from a reduced oxygen-carrying capacity of the blood, causing pale skin, abnormal fatigue, and difficulty breathing. This is termed "iron-deficiency anemia." Other symptoms include constipation and lusterless, brittle nails.

Magnesium

Magnesium is an essential mineral element found inside all cells, where it is involved in many metabolic processes. Magnesium supports many functions of the body such as calcium absorption, protein synthesis, enzyme reactions, adenosine triphosphate (ATP) release (energy release), neuromuscular contraction, and temperature regulation. It also helps in the utilization of vitamin C, vitamin E, and the B complex vitamins. Because magnesium is very alkaline, it helps regulate the acid-alkaline balance of the body. Magnesium, the seventh most abundant mineral in the body, is a natural relaxer.

Magnesium is found in fresh green vegetables, raw unmilled wheat germ, soybeans, milk, whole grains, seafood, figs, corn, apples, and almonds.

Deficiency symptoms include muscular twitches and tremors, confusion, irregular heart rhythm, depression, vasodilation (dilation of blood vessels), oversensitivity to noise, irritability, and clot formation in the heart and brain. Calcium deposits in the kidneys, blood vessels, and heart may also occur as a result of magnesium deficiency.

Manganese

Manganese is vital to the development of bones, ligaments, and nerves and is also important to proper digestion and sex hormone and milk production. Manganese also functions as a catalyst and enzyme activator. Recent studies show a manganese deficiency contributes to excess blood sugar.

Manganese is found in whole-grain cereals, egg yolks, nuts, seeds, and green vegetables. A great deal of manganese is lost in the processing and milling of foods.

Deficiency symptoms include seizures in epileptics, loss of muscular coordination, dizziness, blindness, ear noises, and deafness. A manganese deficiency can also interfere with the body's ability to remove excess sugar from the blood, causing diabetes, and can also lead to atherosclerosis.

Molybdenum

Molybdenum is a trace mineral important in the metabolism of fats and carbohydrates. It is needed for iron utilization and is therefore important to prevent anemia.

Molybdenum is found in dark green leafy vegetables, whole grains, and legumes.

Deficiency symptoms include male impotence and possibly tooth decay.

Phosphorus

Phosphorus is the second most abundant mineral in the body. It functions with vitamin D and calcium and is found in every cell in the body. It is essential for energy production, muscle contraction, digestion, and pH balance of the blood.

More common than phosphorus deficiency is an excessive intake of phosphorus. This is largely due to the excessive consumption of carbonated beverages. These contain phosphoric acid, which is a great contributor to mineral imbalances. This is covered in more detail in chapter 15.

Food sources of phosphorus include meat, fish, poultry, eggs, whole grains, and seeds.

Deficiency symptoms include bone disorders, stunted growth, arthritis, loss of appetite, and weight loss (and sometimes weight gain), irregular breathing, mental and physical fatigue, tooth decay, and gum disease.

Potassium

Potassium is the third (tied with sulfur) most abundant mineral in the body and constitutes approximately 5 percent of total mineral content. Potassium is an essential mineral found in the intracellular fluid and is very important to electrical, nerve, muscle, and heart functions. Potassium is water soluble and works closely with sodium and chloride to normalize heartbeat, help regulate the water balance in the body, and regulate nerve transmissions. These chemicals are called electrolytes because they carry an electrical charge. Sodium and potassium carry a positive charge and chloride carries a negative charge. Rapid water loss can deplete potassium from the body with serious consequences.

Good potassium sources include dried apricots, baked potatoes, dried prunes, cantaloupe, bananas, oranges, and spinach. Potassium is contained in all vegetables, whole grains, sunflower seeds, and mint leaves.

Deficiency symptoms include general weakness, poor reflexes, nervous disorders, insomnia, constipation, and slow and irregular heartbeat. Eventually, potassium deficiency can result in muscle damage due to impaired glucose metabolism.

Selenium

Selenium is a trace mineral that is known to be often interdependent with vitamin E. In some instances a low level of one of these nutrients can be partly compensated for by the presence of the other. Selenium is a component of an important enzyme that helps prevent damage to cell structure. Some studies have shown that selenium has a protective effect. Selenium is also an important antioxidant in the body and a powerful anticancer agent.

Food sources of selenium include brewer's yeast, organ and muscle meats, fish and shellfish, grains, cereals, and dairy products.

Deficiency symptoms include premature aging (selenium preserves elasticity in tissues such as the skin), infertility, and possibly high blood pressure.

Silicon

Silicon is a mineral present in the skeletal structures and connective tissues of the body, such as cartilage, tendons, and blood vessels. Silicon, phosphorus, and calcium combine to make strong bones and could be an important factor in the prevention of osteoporosis and atherosclerosis. Silicon is the eighth most abundant mineral in the body and the door opener for muscle and nerve cells to accept calcium.

The best sources of silicon are hard drinking water, plant fiber, and horsetail (an herb).

Deficiency symptoms include brittle bones and skin problems.

Sulfur

Sulfur is the third (tied with potassium) most abundant mineral in the body, following calcium and phosphorus. This fact seems to surprise a lot of people as we don't hear about the need for sulfur like we do about calcium or many of the other minerals we actually need much less of.

While sulfur is present in every cell of the body, the highest concentration is found in connective tissues, such as in cartilage, collagen, and elastin. Sulfur bonds are an important structural component of all connective tissue, which supports and connects our internal organs, forms the walls of blood vessels, and joins muscles to bones. One component of connective tissue is collagen, which holds water and gives connective tissue its flexibility.

The body uses sulfur as a structural component (in combination with vitamins, especially vitamin C, and amino acids) to continually create new healthy cells to replace old ones. If the body isn't receiving the proper nutrition, including sulfur, for this process, the body will instead produce weak dysfunctional cells. Scar tissue is an excellent visual example of the result of inadequate nutritional support as the body is trying to repair itself.

Sulfur is found in garlic, onions, egg, and (because some amino acids contain sulfur) some other protein sources, such as meat. The best source for supplemental organic sulfur is MSM (methylsulfonylmethane), which is available as a supplement in powder or tablet form.

Deficiency symptoms are associated with slow wound healing, scar tissue, arthritis and other joint disorders, and skin problems. In the last few years, MSM has become one of the hottest selling nutritional supplements as it is so beneficial in providing relief for individuals with joint disorders, such as arthritis and TMJ (temporomandibular joint) syndrome.

MSM supplementation can benefit the body because it has been demonstrated to

- Improve joint flexibility and reduce stiffness and swelling associated with arthritis-like conditions.
- Improve circulation and cell vitality.
- Reduce pain associated with systemic inflammatory disorders, such as arthritis.
- Reduce scar tissue, which further aggravates arthritis-like conditions, increasing pain and decreasing mobility.
- Break up calcium deposits: Arthritis may be induced by excess calcium as it can migrate to soft tissues and form deposits. The tissues become calcified and the cells cease to function normally. MSM is able to rupture the weak (water) bonds of calcium in the synovial fluid of the joints. This is likely to also be true for kidney stones.
- Reduce allergies: MSM fortifies the body's natural barriers against allergens. Oral MSM has alleviated the allergic response to pollen and to foods. MSM is as good as or better than the traditional antihistaminic preparations but doesn't have side effects.
- Improve asthma: MSM also strengthens the lungs against allergic responses. It may help regulate the fluid that covers the surface of the airways.
- Reduce snoring.
- Improve skin tone and reduce scars.
- Reduce nasal congestion (sinusitis).
- Improve digestive disorders, i.e., constipation, diverticulitis, ulcerative colitis, Crohn's disease, parasites, and so on.
- Improve oral tissues (gum disease).

Golfers, joggers, tennis buffs, baseball players, and athletes of all kinds greatly appreciate the pain relief they get from MSM. It helps keep joints moving smoothly.

Vanadium

Vanadium is a trace mineral present in most body tissues and is considered essential to human health. Bones, cartilage, and teeth require vanadium for proper development. Vanadium is important for metabolism of fats and for the inhibition of cholesterol formation.

Vanadium is commonly lost in food processing, but best sources include fats, oils, whole grains, seafood, and meats.

What Sulfur (and MSM) Is Not

Do not confuse MSM with sulfa-based drugs, sulfites, sulfates, or sulfuric acid.

Sulfa-based drugs (sulfonamides) are part of a group of high molecular weight compounds that have been known to cause allergic reactions. Sulfa drugs include erythromycin, sulfisoxazole, sulfacytine, sulfamethoxazole, and sulfasalazine. These are large complex molecules (drugs) used as antibiotics. It is highly unlikely that anyone would be allergic to MSM or sulfur, a substance naturally occurring in the body.

Sulfites are preservatives, antioxidants, and browning agents used in foods. Ingestion of these is associated with adverse reactions, such as asthma attacks, nausea, and diarrhea. Several sulfiting agents are now in use: sodium sulfite, sodium bisulfite, potassium bisulfite, sodium metasulfite, and potassium metasulfite.

Sulfates are sulfuric acid salts.

Sulfuric acid is a heavy corrosive oily acid used in producing fertilizers, chemicals, and petroleum products.

Individuals who are sensitive to these substances do not react in a negative way to MSM. MSM is perfectly safe!

Deficiency symptoms include reproductive problems and possibly elevated cholesterol levels.

Zinc

Zinc is essential for the proper development of the reproductive organs and the health of the prostrate gland. It is also necessary for proper B vitamin utilization, digestion, and healing. Zinc plays a critical role in the synthesis of RNA and DNA, crucial to cell division, repair, and growth. Zinc is also important in the detoxification of alcohol in the liver, digestion and production of protein, and maintenance of normal blood cholesterol levels. Zinc is also needed to produce prostaglandins, which regulate numerous body processes, including blood pressure and heart rate.

This mineral is also key to certain immune system functioning, and deficiencies may impair a variety of functions associated with the body's immune defenses. Low zinc levels have been found in lung cancer patients and kidney disease patients.

Zinc is required for normal testosterone and sperm production. It has been hypothesized that high levels of impotence in American males may be due to chronic zinc deficiency. This may explain why in ages past, oysters (which are loaded with zinc) were thought to be an aphrodisiac.

Since large amounts of zinc impair copper absorption, be sure to get 1 mg of copper for every 15–20 mg of zinc. Zinc is found in protein foods such as meat, unprocessed whole-grain products, brewer's yeast, wheat bran, wheat germ, and pumpkin seeds.

Deficiency symptoms include loss of taste and/or smell, prolonged healing of wounds, suppressed immunity, fatigue, delayed sexual maturity and retarded growth, impotency in young males, painful knee and hip joints in teenagers, stretch marks in the skin, white spots on the fingernails, brittle nails and hair, hair lacking pigment (gray hair), an enlarged prostate, and sterility.

Deficiencies are common among individuals with alcoholism, diabetes, ADD/ADHD, atherosclerosis, high cholesterol, night blindness, acne, prostatitis, dermatitis, eczema, and ulcers.

–13

Antioxidants

Researchers around the world tell us that free-radical damage throughout the body is a major cause of aging and age associated diseases. Free-radical damage is now widely known to shorten life. Health problems, including allergies, Alzheimer's disease, arthritis, atherosclerosis (hardening and clogging of the arteries), macular degeneration, cancer, cataracts, multiple sclerosis, infections, and Parkinson's disease are all associated with free-radical attack. In fact, researchers now agree that most common ailments, including virtually all chronic degenerative diseases, are either caused directly by or are closely associated with free-radical damage.

In 1954, the free-radical theory of aging was proposed by Denham Harmon, M.D., Ph.D. While at that time it was challenged with a great deal of opposition by the scientific community, today Harmon's free-radical theory has emerged as the best understood and most widely accepted explanation of the aging process. Having stood the test of time and countless research validations, it has become not just *a* theory but *the* aging theory.

A free radical is an incomplete, unstable molecule. It is incomplete because it is missing an electron, which exists in a pair in stable molecules. It is unstable because it will "steal" an electron from another molecule and thereby create another free radical and a chain reaction of events, which results in thousands of reactions.

Every time molecules lose or gain an electron, they are weakened, and ultimately the whole structure, whether it is an enzyme, a protein, a cell membrane, tissue, or an organ, is damaged. Some areas of the body are more susceptible to damage than others. In their search for electrons, free radicals do a great deal of structural damage to healthy cells. Injured cells can't function properly and may even die.

Free radicals are an unavoidable part of life as by-products of normal metabolism in the body. They are produced as cells use oxygen to convert food into energy. The only way to avoid these free radicals would be to stop burning oxygen. But then, your metabolism would shut down, too.

Prolonged exposure to free radicals fast-forwards the aging process. One of the clearest manifestations of cumulative free-radical damage is a phenomenon known as cross-linking.

When free radicals damage molecules, cells split off to repair the injury. The cells have to rejoin with others to reform and reshape themselves. This may cause cross-linkage—a bond between large amino acid molecules that are normally separate from each other. Additional free radicals are also formed when waste fragments of these molecules break off. Free radicals cause proteins (e.g., collagen tissue) and/or genetic material (e.g., DNA) to fuse. Healthy DNA is necessary to replicate and renew the body's cellular components. Altered DNA produces useless debris and sometimes cancerous cells.

A bit like handcuffing, cross-linking hampers the ability of its molecular "hostages" to perform their assigned tasks. In this way, cross-linking works to the detriment of the entire organism. Because of cross-linking, the elastic, flexible tissue of youth turns to the wrinkled skin, stiff joints, and hardened arteries of old age.

Cross-linking worsens with age, as the cellular wear and tear of several decades accumulates and the body becomes less adept at scavenging free radicals. The result is the general, bodywide impairment of function that's synonymous with degenerative disease and aging.

In skin cells, the cross-linking of molecules causes the wrinkles characteristic of aging. In arterial cells, cross-linking reduces flexibility, which in turn raises blood pressure and puts extra strain on the heart as it pumps harder to maintain a continuous flow of blood. In the brain, cross-linking impedes message transmission between nerve cells, interfering with quick thinking and a rapid flow of ideas. Memory and concentration problems are more likely.

Cross-linking's most damaging effects are upon DNA molecules. When these molecules are damaged, they compromise a cell's ability to correctly interpret its DNA-encoded genetic blueprint. This results in impaired DNA replication and protein assembly. The entire process of renewal in the body depends on cells being able to replicate themselves exactly.

Compounds that prevent free-radical degeneration (oxidation) are called *antioxidants*. Antioxidants are a class of nutrients that prevent the diseases associated with free-radical damage and help alleviate the symptoms and side effects of many of these conditions.

Low levels of antioxidants increase free-radical activity and increase our risk of health problems. Therefore, the use of antioxidant supplements to scavenge free radicals can potentially decrease the risks of cancer, cardiovascular disease, cataracts, macular degeneration, neuropathy, and other circulatory problems and degenerative conditions.

As long as the ratio of oxidants to antioxidants remains in balance, the negative effects of the free radicals can be controlled. When the balance becomes upset by excessive exposure to internal or external factors or a combination of both, the antioxidants produced by the body simply cannot cope with the increased amount of free radicals.

In addition to the free radicals we produce as a natural part of our metabolic process, factors that increase free-radical exposure and the need for antioxidants include

- Exercise
- Stress

- Exposure to toxins such as pollutants, smog, tobacco smoke, alcohol, drugs, and pesticides
- Illness, infection, inflammation, and many health problems, including diabetes, arthritis, asthma
- Elevated blood lipids (especially LDL)
- Elevated blood sugar
- Many stimulants and metabolic enhancers, such as caffeine and diet pills
- Radiation (including ultraviolet [UV] light)

THE TOP ANTIOXIDANT NUTRIENTS

Antioxidants are compounds that protect against cell damage inflicted by molecules called oxygen-free radicals, which are a major cause of disease and aging. In my opinion, anyone concerned about their health should include antioxidants into their daily regimen.

Beta Carotene/Vitamin A

Beta carotene, found in fruits and brightly colored vegetables, is just one of about 50 different carotenoids. Beta carotene shows great promise as an antioxidant. Several studies indicate that it decreases the risk of heart disease and cancer, especially oral and skin cancers.

Beta carotene is a "weak" antioxidant compared to vitamins E and C, but they all work better when used together. For example, while beta carotene is effective against some oxidants (such as singlet oxygen), other antioxidants may not be.

Beta carotene is one of the few carotenoids that can convert to vitamin A, a fat-soluble antioxidant. (Vitamin A is ineffective against singlet oxygen.) Vitamin A is one of the body's foremost antioxidant protectors and is the principal nutrient responsible for the health of our mucous membranes. Vitamin A supplementation

Sugar and Free-Radical Damage (Glycation)

High blood sugar levels cause protein damage as the nonenzymatic joining of sugar to protein forms highly destructive oxygen radicals. The process of forming sugar-damaged proteins is called *glycation,* which can be compared to the browning reaction of sliced apples.

Elevated sugar levels can be very damaging to the protein tissues in the body. Blood sugars react spontaneously with collagen, a major protein found in skin, blood vessels, and connective tissue, and other proteins to form cross-linked sugar-damaged proteins. These are called *advanced glycosylation end products* (AGEs). When these are formed, additional free radicals are released as well. The formation rate of AGEs (and free radicals) increases as the blood sugar level increases and the length of time the level is raised increases.

The spontaneous reaction of sugar with tissue proteins such as collagen and myelin is responsible for accelerated tissue aging in diabetics and is believed responsible for

- Kidney damage
- Atherosclerosis
- Cataracts and macular degeneration
- Polyneuropathy (abnormal condition marked by numbness throughout the body due to nerve death) and many other common diabetes complications

Glycation plays a role in normal aging in all of us—not just diabetics. Aging animals have increased concentrations of AGEs in their collagen, as do diabetics.

As we age, our average blood sugar level tends to rise and our tissues become less sensitive to the actions of insulin (insulin resistance). This creates higher levels of free radicals and a greater need for antioxidant supplementation. Maintaining even and optimal blood sugar levels (70 to 100 mg percent) as well as adequate antioxidant protection can guard our tissues against aging prematurely.

stimulates mucous production and keeps membranes well lubricated and strong. It also strengthens the integrity of the bowel wall to help prevent the absorption of large protein molecules that cause the body to react negatively.

Vitamin C

Vitamin C, as an antioxidant, is very effective against free radicals. Vitamin C also stimulates white blood cells and overall immune function. It is effective against superoxides, which are continuously formed in the body as a part of cellular energy production and immune response, but they also come from irradiation, car exhaust, cigarette smoke, and ozone.

It is also effective against hydroxyl radicals—the most aggressive and damaging species known. These are formed in the body as part of normal metabolism. They are particularly harmful to cellular membranes.

Vitamin C is found in citrus fruits and some green vegetables, but supplementation is usually required to obtain therapeutic effects.

Smokers and drinkers require extra vitamin C. Each cigarette is estimated to destroy 35–100 mg of vitamin C in the body. Alcohol is a diuretic, which causes C to be eliminated from the body at a faster rate.

Vitamin E

Vitamin E is a major fat-soluble membrane antioxidant found in cells that fights off damage from peroxyl radicals. Vitamin E also protects white blood cells and may slow down the decline of immunity, which accompanies aging.

Vitamin E is widely known to help protect us from heart disease as it reduces the harmful effects of LDL cholesterol, also known as "bad cholesterol." Literally hundreds of studies demonstrate the protective effects of Vitamin E against cataracts and certain cancers, such as skin and prostate cancer.

Selenium

Selenium works closely with vitamin E in many of its functions in the body. It helps preserve elasticity of tissues by protecting cellular membranes from oxidation.

Recent studies suggest that selenium may help reduce the risk of prostate, lung, and colon cancers.

Be sure not to take too much selenium. Anything over 1 mg per day can be toxic over time. Stay in the 200–400 mcg range for safety and efficacy.

Zinc

Zinc is an important antioxidant that acts as an anti-inflammatory nutrient. Zinc protects the lysosomal membranes from rupture. Lysosomes contain enzymes and free radicals that can cause a cell to self-destruct and cause inflammation if the membranes rupture. Zinc also helps reduce inflammation associated with chronic, noninfectious prostatitis (inflammation of the prostate gland).

The following botanicals—plants or plant extracts—are valued for phytochemical and antioxidant properties:

Proanthocyanidins

Studies show that proanthocyanidins (often referred to as procyanidins or PC-95) are more potent in their antioxidant abilities and provide antioxidant protection for both vitamins C and E in the body. Research indicates that on a cellular level, proanthocyanidins are incorporated within the cell membrane, protecting against both water- and fat-soluble free radicals.

Proanthocyanidins were discovered in France in 1947 by Professor Jacques Masquelier and are backed by 50 years of clinical research and worldwide use. A large body of scientific research clearly demonstrates the beneficial effect proanthocyanidins have on a variety of health problems, including heart disease, circulatory disorders, neuropathy, and premature aging.

Proanthocyanidins protect us from free-radical damage, which contributes to cellular changes and invites degenerative diseases. They help maintain optimal levels of other important antioxidants in the body, such as vitamins C and E and glutathione.

Proanthocyanidins also spare vitamin C and other antioxidants by making them work better and longer in the body. Research also shows that proanthocyanidins are even more effective than vitamin C in preventing LDL from oxidizing and causing plaque formation.

This antioxidant is so important that a separate chapter is devoted to it. (See chapter 14.) I believe PC-95 is the single most important nutrient one can put in his or her body on a daily basis. It can help children, adults, and seniors alike.

Olea Europa/Olive Leaf Extract (Oleuropein)

Olea europa is an herbal extract from the leaves of the Mediterranean olive tree containing the phenolic glycoside compound elenoic acid. This is a natural antioxidant providing important cell protection at the membrane level. The extract has a secondary immune system effect by increasing phagocytosis (gobbling up of foreign bacteria and viruses) in white blood cells.

This is an excellent and very important natural antimicrobial and antibiotic. Olea europa should be used instead of or in combination with drug antibiotics (if they are absolutely needed) as olea europa does not have the negative effects on the necessary bacteria in the body that antibiotics do.

Among the conditions it has been reported to help are chronic fatigue syndrome, colds and flu, AIDS, herpes, Epstein-Barr, bladder infections, skin infections, eczema, psoriasis, fungus and yeast infections, fibromyalgia, ulcers, hiatal hernia, malaria, hemorrhoids, arrhythmias, and rheumatoid arthritis.

Olea europa has also been shown to affect the body's glucose or blood sugar levels by working independently of insulin to increase metabolic uptake of glucose. However, this activity is believed to occur in concert with glucose-induced insulin releases.

Olea europa protects LDL cholesterol from free-radical attack, assists in maintaining a healthy heart and cardiovascular system, and promotes flexible arterial walls and a healthy blood flow.

Finally, olea europa is a vasodilator that lowers blood pressure and helps prevent angina attacks. One study showed that a component in the olive leaf extract lowered blood pressure by causing constricted arteries to become more flexible and relaxed.[47]

Silymarin

Silymarin (milk thistle extract) is a concentrated group of flavonoid plant compounds. Flavonoids in general are important antioxidants that devour free radicals. "Silymarin" describes a group of flavonoids that function as an antihepatoxic, meaning that it acts directly on the liver to protect it from poisons. It mounts defenses on two fronts. First, it binds to the membranes of liver cells and creates a tough shield so that toxins have a more difficult time penetrating the cell walls. If toxins do make it into the cells and cause damage, silymarin then stimulates the liver to speed up production of beneficial enzymes and proteins as part of a healing restoration.

Its antioxidant effects have been demonstrated to prevent or inhibit liver toxicity and various types of cancer, including skin, breast, cervical, and prostate.

Ginkgo

Ginkgo (*Ginkgo biloba*) is an ancient remedy for an array of problems, but most of the scientific support shows that it benefits the vascular system, improves circulation, improves mental functioning and the ability to concentrate, relieves symptoms of tinnitus (ringing in the ears), helps prevent cancer, and alleviates symptoms of Alzheimer's disease.

Ginkgo is known to pass through the blood-brain barrier and therefore offer its protective benefits in the brain as well as throughout the body. Among many other beneficial properties, ginkgo is a powerful antioxidant that protects us from depressed antioxidant levels and stress. It also plays a role in the body's neuroprotective functions.

With age, blood flow in the brain decreases, which means less food and oxygen for brain cells. Reduced brain circulation can mean dizziness, memory loss, tinnitus, macular degeneration (the most common cause of blindness in the elderly), and even deafness (cochlear deafness). Components in ginkgo help protect the sensitive brain cells from free-radical damage. Numerous studies show that ginkgo extract helps maintain adequate antioxidant nutrition for our brains to function—such as remembering where we put our keys or glasses, what we were supposed to pick up at the grocery store, or the directions to a place.

Studies where ginkgo was given to individuals with moderate dementia, such as Alzheimer's, resulted in an improvement of psychopathology and cognitive performance, which is reflected in an increased ability to cope with the demands of daily living.

Artichoke Extract

Artichoke extract is related to silymarin (milk thistle) and has similar use as a liver tonic. Its active compounds include flavonoids and chlorogenic acid, both powerful antioxidants. Researchers have demonstrated that artichoke extract does have a protective antioxidant effect for liver cells.

In addition to use as a liver tonic, artichoke leaves have a long history of use as a digestive aid, and science has also documented its cholesterol-lowering and cardioprotective effects. It also has potential applications in the treatment and prevention of HIV, cancer, and diabetes.

The antioxidant activity of artichoke extract relates in part to its constituent flavonoids and its ability to chelate (bond) with metal ions.

Red Wine

Red wine contains powerful polyphenols: anthocyanes and, in particular, one called malvoside. Researchers have shown a number of health-promoting effects, including helping the cardiovascular system. Moderate consumption of wine can reduce mortality from coronary heart disease by increasing HDL cholesterol and inhibiting platelet aggregation.

In countries where wine is the primary alcoholic drink, heart disease death rates are lowest. Interestingly, the opposite is true for beer. Red wine, *in the amount of one glass per day,* seems to elevate HDL, or "good cholesterol."

The many polyphenols and flavonoids in red wine have a variety of specific health benefits: They promote nitric oxide production, inhibit platelet aggregation, help regulate cholesterol levels, and arrest tumor growth, as well as inhibit cancer formation.

Polyphenols in wine are also antimicrobial. They are effective against cholera, the dreaded *E. coli,* and also *E. typhi.* The Greeks and others used to pour wine into wounds and over dressings to disinfect them. Unfortunately, today's wines contains sulfites (preservatives) that can be harmful to the body.

Bilberry

Bilberry, which is botanically related to blueberry, is a well-known folk remedy for vision, especially for night blindness. During World War II, Royal Air Force pilots were given bilberry jam as they claimed it significantly improved their visual acuity in the dark. Bilberries contain anthocyanosides, which are necessary for normal photosensitivities of the eyes and help them adapt to variations in light intensity.

Anthocyanosides are antioxidants that have a strengthening effect on the walls of the small vessels and capillaries. They have demonstrated ability to accelerate the production of rhodopsin (visual purple) in the retina. Visual purple is a pigment in the receptors in the eye needed to send nerve impulses to the brain.

People who work with bright light (such as working in front of a computer) and suffer from eye fatigue can benefit from bilberry anthocyanoside supplementation.

Green Tea

Green tea, like red wine, contains polyphenols, which have antioxidant and anticarcinogenic properties. The most important and most powerful polyphenol catechin is EGCG, which stands for epigallocatachin gallate. Green tea extract contains about 31 percent EGCG. This potent antioxidant is also an important element in the body's production of antibacterial factors, cholesterol stabilizers, and blood-clotting substances.

Exciting research has also demonstrated the beneficial protective relationship between green tea and cancer, hypertension, tooth decay, gingivitis, and cholesterol.

Much of the protective benefits in green tea stem from its antioxidant properties.

Alpha Lipoic Acid (Thiotic Acid)

Alpha lipoic acid has several unique properties. It is both fat and water soluble, meaning it can protect both the inside and outside of our cellular membranes. Alpha lipoic acid also has regenerative properties for other antioxidants, such as vitamins C and E and glutathione. Instead of being used up after donating an electron, alpha lipoic acid can recycle these antioxidants by offering them an electron.

Alpha lipoic acid demonstrates powerful therapeutic properties for diabetes and is used throughout Europe to treat and prevent polyneuropathy, cataracts, and macular degeneration.

Alpha lipoic acid is naturally found in foods such as potatoes, carrots, and yams.

Coenzyme Q10 (CoQ10)

CoQ10 is an important antioxidant nutrient necessary for cells' mitochondria to produce energy. CoQ10 is found in the body but is depleted through age, disease, or inadequate nutrition. As levels decline, immune deficiency opens the door for many disease states. Certain organs of the body require larger concentrations of CoQ10, such as the heart and liver. CoQ10 as a supplement has proven to reduce blood pressure, stimulate the immune system, and improve energy.

The benefits of CoQ10 to the heart and cardiovascular system have been extensively documented. As an antioxidant, CoQ10 protects LDL cholesterol from oxidation and reduces the negative effects of stress by protecting and stabilizing mitochondrial membranes.

Researchers at Mount Sinai Hospital and Medical Center, New York, claim that CoQ10 may be crucial for cardiovascular health. As an antioxidant, it plays a protective role and has membrane-stabilizing activity.

The importance of CoQ10 is now being established in clinical trials worldwide. Clinical trials have already investigated the relationship between CoQ10 and blood pressure, total LDL and HDL cholesterol, and blood platelets, which determine our clotting risk potential.

Melatonin

While melatonin is a hormone from the pineal gland in the brain and is usually more known for its ability to regulate sleep, evidence indicates a role for melatonin in aging and age-related diseases, probably related to its efficient free-radical scavenger (antioxidant) activity. While most antioxidants work only in certain parts of certain cells, melatonin can permeate any cell in any part of the body, protect cellular structures and genetic material, and stimulate the production of glutathione-based antioxidants.

The benefit of melatonin as an antioxidant is remarkable, suggesting that it may be of use in the treatment of many diseases, including various cancers, hypertension, pulmonary diseases, and a variety of neurodegenerative diseases such as Alzheimer's. Research shows melatonin levels decline with age.

ARE YOU A VICTIM OF A FREE-RADICAL ATTACK?

To find out what effect free radicals are having on you, answer these questions and then take the quiz that follows.

- Do you bruise easily?

Capillary fragility is the result of free-radical damage of the capillaries. Fragile capillaries are prone to leak blood with the slightest bump. You may not even remember how you obtained many bruises because the bump seemed insignificant at the time.

- Do you have a lot of wrinkles?

Wrinkles are the result of the breakdown of collagen tissues in the skin. UV radiation causes free-radical formation in the skin and rapid depletion of antioxidant supplies in these areas as well.

Most skin aging is traceable to damage caused by free radicals—the same unstable molecules that attack the skin's collagen—and elastin-based support structures, producing sagging and wrinkles. Antioxidants are the body's prime defense against free radicals. Research has proven that antioxidants have powerful protective and restorative effects on the skin.

- Do you have heart disease?

Oxidation of LDL ("bad cholesterol") creates free radicals and a chain reaction of events resulting in plaque buildup and clogged arteries.

- Do you have arthritis?

The pain and swelling of arthritis is also caused by free radicals, which in tissues generate more free radicals and the release of harmful inflammatory prostaglandins.

- Do you have cancer?

There are probably over 100 different types of cancer and probably hundreds of ways that free radicals can cause damage associated with cancer. Here are just a few examples.

Carcinogens and many other stimuli, such as radiation (including sunlight), form free radicals in the body and can activate oncogenes, which cause cancer.

Free radicals can also damage sensors on cell membranes that regulate cell growth and proliferation. If sensors are damaged, unregulated growth can occur. Unregulated growth and cancer go hand in hand.

Free radicals can damage the genetic material (DNA in the cell nucleus) causing mutation of the cell. Free radicals can also damage components of the immune system, such as white blood cells or enzymes, that would otherwise recognize and destroy mutated cells before they multiply and become cancerous.

• Do you have cataracts?

The sensitive protein tissues in the eye are highly susceptible to free-radical damage if there are inadequate antioxidants to stop the damage. Excess sunlight is a risk factor for cataracts. Free radicals created by sunlight and other factors can also damage the retina, causing retinopathy, or may damage the macula, causing macular degeneration.

• Do you have HIV?

Studies show that individuals with HIV (human immune deficiency virus) have lower levels of various antioxidants compared to individuals without HIV. This can further compromise one's state of health and susceptibility to illness.

• Do you have allergies or asthma?

Epidemiological studies show associations among oxidant exposure, respiratory infections, and asthma in children of smokers. Symptoms of ongoing asthma in adults appear to be increased by exposure to environmental oxidants and decreased by antioxidant supplementation. There is evidence that oxidants produced in the body by overactive inflammatory cells contribute to ongoing asthma and allergic hypersensitivities.

- Are you experiencing memory loss or Alzheimer's?

While it is not known entirely what the exact causes of Alzheimer's, memory loss, and senile dementia are, it is known that free-radical damage is responsible for neuron degeneration.

- Do you have a break, sprain, bruise, cut, or other injury?

Any time tissue damage occurs due to a cut or fall, the tissues in the surrounding area generate more free radicals through the release of harmful inflammatory prostaglandins.

- Are you aging "prematurely"?

Cellular damage by oxygen radicals is believed to be directly involved in aging, causing the pathological changes associated with aging. The higher the level of free radicals we have in our cells, the faster we age.

As we age, we become more susceptible to "age-related diseases," such as diabetes, arthritis, vascular diseases (including coronary artery disease), and hypertension. With antioxidants, these are all, to some extent, preventable.

While the simple life-necessitating acts of breathing and eating create free radicals in the body, many environmental factors and exposure to various substances increase our exposure to these reactive chemical structures, including

- Cigarette smoke
- Rancid fats—trans-fatty acids found in margarine and other "altered fats"
- Poor diet—especially a diet high in sugar
- Certain prescription drugs
- Metabolic stimulants, such as caffeine and cocaine
- Alcohol
- Car exhaust, smog, and other air pollutants
- Pesticides/herbicides
- Ultraviolet light
- X-rays and other forms of radiation

- Strenuous exercise
- Stress

What Is Your Antioxidant Profile?

Your antioxidant profile can tell a great deal about how well you are protecting your overall health by protecting the health of your cells. To learn where you stand, take the following quiz. Answer each of the following questions, then calculate your score by checking the answers at the end of this quiz.

1. *How many servings of yellow-orange fruits and leafy green or yellow-orange vegetables do you have daily?*
   a. 2–4 half-cup or equivalent size servings
   b. 5–9 half-cup or equivalent size servings
   c. less than 2 half-cup servings
2. *Are the vegetables that you eat mostly fried, baked, boiled, steamed, or raw?*
   a. fried
   b. baked
   c. boiled
   d. steamed
   e. raw
3. *Do you use "cold-pressed" vegetable oil?*
   a. yes
   b. no
4. *How often do you travel by airplane?*
   a. more than 6 times a month
   b. about 2–4 times a month
   c. less than once a month
5. *How much time do you spend outdoors?*
   a. more than 20 hours a week
   b. about 5–20 hours a week
   c. less than 5 hours a week

6. *Do you smoke cigarettes?*

   a. yes

   b. no

7. *Do you have more than one or two alcoholic beverages a day?*

   a. yes

   b. no

8. *How close do you live to a city or industrial manufacturing complex?*

   a. live in a city or near an industrial manufacturing complex

   b. live in the suburbs of city or several miles away from an industrial manufacturing complex

   c. live in a rural area, far from a city or an industrial manufacturing complex

9. *How often do you exercise?*

   a. 3–4 times a week for about 30 minutes per session

   b. more than 5 times a week for more than 30 minutes per session

   c. less than 2 times a week

10. *Are you taking an antioxidant formula to supplement your diet?*

    a. yes

    b. no

Your Score: Each response is given a numeric value. A value of 5 is the most positive, and lower values may indicate areas that need improvement. After answering the questions, add the scores to determine your antioxidant profile.

Question 1

   a. 2: You are not obtaining protective amounts of antioxidants from fruits and vegetables, leaving cells vulnerable to free-radical destruction; eat 3–5 more servings a day.

b. 5: You're getting valuable antioxidants from fruits and vegetables, especially if the vegetables are eaten raw.

c. 0: You're not getting any antioxidants from fruits and vegetables; to help protect cells from free-radical damage, eat 5–9 servings a day.

Question 2

a. 1: Frying is high in fat; heat destroys some antioxidants.

b. 3: Baking is healthy but usually requires the addition of fat and involves the loss of some antioxidants to heat.

c. 2: Antioxidants are lost through leaching and heat.

d. 4: Steaming is a healthy cooking option, but it destroys some antioxidants.

e. 5: Raw, fresh vegetables supply the most intact antioxidants.

Question 3

a. 5: More vitamin E remains in cold-pressed vegetable oil than in oil processed with heat.

b. 0: Certain vegetable oils are good sources of polyunsaturated fats, which are associated with helping to lower cholesterol levels. However, heat processing destroys vitamin E, increasing your need for this vitamin.

Question 4

a. 0: Research indicates that airline passengers may be exposed to relatively high levels of radiation; the more one flies, the greater the exposure. Studies show that radiation may be associated with increased free-radical activity, increasing the need for cell-protecting antioxidants.

b. 3: Moderate air travel exposes passengers to greater levels of radiation than if traveling by ground transportation. Even this amount of radiation exposure affects free-radical activity, increasing the need for antioxidants.

c. 5: Limited air travel lessens your exposure to elevated radiation levels associated with airline flights; therefore, your requirement for antioxidants is not affected by this activity.

Question 5

a. 1: Excessive exposure to sunlight and ambient radiation may increase free-radical activity, possibly increasing the need for protective antioxidants.

b. 2: Moderate exposure to sunlight and ambient radiation may have an effect on free-radical activity, possibly increasing the need for protective antioxidants.

c. 5: Limited outdoor activity decreases your exposure to the harmful effects of the sun.

Question 6

a. 0: Smoking may greatly increase the need for protective antioxidants. Vitamins E and C work synergistically to protect lung cells from free-radical activity caused by smoking.

b. 5: Yet another good reason not to smoke, as research shows that it may increase the need for antioxidants.

Question 7

a. 0: A high intake of alcohol may greatly increase the need for all the antioxidants, particularly selenium. Moreover, all nutrients may be affected by high alcohol intake.

b. 5: Moderate to no intake of alcohol does not affect your requirement for antioxidants.

Question 8

a. 2: Air pollution may increase your need for antioxidants.

b. 3: You may be exposed to some of the air pollution from a nearby city or industrial manufacturing plant.

c. 5: Even when living in a pollution-free environment, body metabolism requires antioxidants to battle free radicals.

Question 9

a. 4: Although exercise increases your need for antioxidants, experts recommend a moderate exercise program to maintain good health. Adding a vitamin and mineral supplement insures protective amounts of antioxidants, particularly during physical stress.

b. 3: Excessive exercise increases your need for many nutrients, including antioxidants.

c. 1: By not exercising regularly, you are likely to have more body fat, be overweight, and have an increased risk of associated diseases.

Question 10

a. 5: You are assured of getting the protective amounts of antioxidants.

b. 0: You may not be getting protective amounts of antioxidants every day.

Your Antioxidant Profile:

45 to 50: Excellent. You know how to live a healthy lifestyle and protect your cells with a diet rich in antioxidants—the nutrients that research shows may help to protect your body's cells from the ravaging effects of free radicals.

35 to 45: You are on the right track, but you may need to strengthen your cell-protecting antioxidant profile. Review the questions and determine which areas need greater attention.

Less than 35: You need help. By improving your antioxidant profile, you can help prevent the destructive damage of toxins on natural body processes.

—14

Can PC-95
(Proanthocyanidins)
Really Be That Good?

Many people ask me the question, "If I could afford to take only one supplement, what would you recommend?" The answer has to be PC-95.

To appreciate my unshakable conviction that proanthocyanidin (PC-95) is the single most important nutrient you can put in your body, you must understand the role it plays in maintaining one's health. Proanthocyanidin is a powerful antioxidant that neutralizes our greatest health enemies: free radicals and electrophiles (precarcinogens). Free radicals are scavengers in our bodies that weaken cells in a domino fashion. Unprotected, our bodies may endure devastating damage. Free radicals are a key contributor in as many as 60 different diseases and health problems, including the following:

- Allergies
- Alzheimer's disease
- Arthritis
- Asthma
- Cancer (all types)
- Cataracts

- Circulatory problems
- Cirrhosis of the liver
- Diabetes
- Emphysema
- Glaucoma
- Hangover
- Heart disease
- High blood pressure
- Inflammatory bowel disease and other inflammatory conditions
- Kidney failure
- Lupus
- Macular degeneration
- Multiple sclerosis
- Muscular dystrophy
- Neuropathy
- Pancreatitis
- Parkinson's, other neurodegenerative diseases, and all other degenerative conditions associated with aging
- Senile dementia
- Stroke
- Varicose veins

Production of free radicals is a normal part of the body's mechanism. We can't avoid them. Tens of thousands of free radicals are formed in the body every second. However, they are not all harmful; some actually help us. The body's immune system uses free radicals to kill potentially infectious microbes and viruses. This activity (called phagocytosis), however, at the same time creates even more free radicals (hydrogen peroxide and hydroxyl radicals) that may lead to severe tissue damage.

Free Radicals Accelerate Aging

Researchers around the world tell us that free-radical damage throughout the body is a major cause of aging and age-associated diseases. Free radicals "steal" electrons from other molecules. Every time molecules lose or gain an electron, they are weakened, and ultimately, the whole structure is damaged or destroyed.

Aging results from the loss of vital cells from free-radical reactions. Free radicals destroy the membranes of lysosomes, enzyme-containing organelles found inside most cells. If the membrane sac that stores these enzymes is ruptured, the enzymes will kill the cell. With each cell destroyed and without the ability to renew it, we become one cell older.

Free radicals can attack and damage cells from the inside or outside of the cell. The main targets for free-radical attack are the vulnerable lipid-composed membranes of cells and their inner structures: the mitochondria, the Golgi apparatus, the endoplasmatic reticulum, the nuclear membrane, and so on. Damage to genetic material (DNA and RNA) is associated with cell abnormalities and cancer.

Free radicals attack fatty compounds circulating in the bloodstream, causing damage and the release of more free radicals in a chain reaction. Damage to LDL and lipoprotein are associated with heart disease.

Free radicals destroy protein as seen in cataract formation, kidney damage, liver damage, and damage to hemoglobin cells and aging in general (collagen breakdown).

Free-radical reactions form age pigments—residues called lipofuscin. These residues accumulate with time and interfere with cell function and life processes.

When free radicals destroy cell membranes, they interfere with the cell's ability to absorb nutrients and expel waste products. Without this ability, the cell dies. Cell membrane damage can lead to numerous degenerative problems and accelerated aging.

What Is PC-95?

PC-95 is a trademark name of Roex, Inc. This proanthocyanidin complex is in compliance with U.S. Patent No. 4,698,360 and international patents. "PC" stands for proanthocyanidins, and "95" refs to the tablets, which contain no less than 95 percent pure proanthocyanidins. PC-95 is the most important supplement you can put in your body and is formulated with the highest quality proanthocyanidin extract available.

Proanthocyanidins were discovered in 1947 in France by Professor Masquelier. Their health benefits are supported by 50 years of clinical research and worldwide use. Professor Masquelier clearly demonstrated that proanthocyanidins support the body's antioxidant defense system by providing important cell protection at the membrane level, safeguarding the body against cellular destruction known as oxidation, which occurs as a natural result of the oxygenation process.

Proanthocyanidins are naturally occurring, health-supporting compounds found throughout nature and highly concentrated in plant barks, stems, leaves, and skins. Grape seed extract and pine bark powder are especially high in proanthocyanidins. Both the seeds and the skins of grapes contain proanthocyanidin, which is the molecule responsible for the protective and healing benefits. The most concentrated source of this bioflavonoid is the seeds of white and green grapes.

Proanthocyanidins are also found in berries and other fruits and plants. All proanthocyanidins are similar, no matter their source. The difference is in the varying concentrations in the various sources and their level of antioxidant activity. Grape seed extract proanthocyanidin seems to yield the greatest concentration, at least 10 percent higher than obtained from pine bark.

Research shows that grape seed extracts with high proanthocyanidin content are of outstanding therapeutic value and contain gallic acid esters. These are the most active antioxidants of all these substances. This is due to the unique structural arrangements of grape seed proanthocyanidins that reduce the total surface area of gallic acid ester exposure, protecting the surface from oxidizing agents. This makes them superior to other proanthocyanidin compounds in this regard.

Proanthocyanidins (which belong to the bioflavonoid family) are believed to be the most potent form of antioxidants available

The French Paradox

"The French Paradox" refers to findings indicating that although the people of southern France consume high amounts of cholesterol in their diet, they have a relatively low incidence of death from coronary heart disease. This phenomenon has been attributed to the high consumption of red wine polyphenols.

Flavonols (polyphenols included) are known to influence the permeability of both natural and synthetic membranes. These attributes are consistent with some of the biological properties of grape seed extracts used in pharmaceutical preparations to combat microvessel disease.

in nature. Proanthocyanidins are actually 50 times more effective than vitamin E and 20 times more effective than vitamin C as an antioxidant. At the same time, proanthocyanidins give power to these antioxidants, so they work better together.

Proanthocyanidins neutralize oxygen-free radicals in both water and fat environments, providing superior protection for intercellular structures, including the nucleus and mitochondria, from free-radical attack. Proanthocyanidins possess more reactive sites for neutralizing free radicals than any other natural antioxidant.

The recommended daily dose of PC-95 is 60–300 mg, depending on one's age and state of health. More is perfectly safe and may be necessary in some cases.

WHY WE NEED TO SUPPLEMENT WITH PC-95

Diet alone is inadequate to prevent free-radical damage!

We used to get antioxidants, such as proanthocyanidins, from the fruits and vegetables that we ate fresh, but now, due to processing and cooking, many of these important compounds are lost. A German research group proved that the quantity of the flavonols, such as proanthocyanidins, in fruits and vegetables is dependent upon the maturity of the produce.[48] The problem is that almost all of the produce we consume now is picked before it is ripe because of the time it takes to travel through the distribution channels across the United States and from beyond. Unfortunately, artificial ripening is induced with gas. Therefore, the levels of important antioxidant flavonols greatly suffer, and this is affecting our health.

Another important reason we need to supplement with antioxidants is that the vast majority of people in the United States do not even eat the recommended number of fruits and vegetables on a daily basis to start with.

HOW DOES PC-95 WORK?

Exceptional Free-Radical Scavenging Activity

Proanthocyanidins protect us from free-radical damage, which contributes to cellular changes and invites degenerative diseases. They help maintain optimal levels of other important antioxidants in the body, such as vitamins C and E and glutathione. Proanthocyanidins also enhance the effectiveness of nutrients such as vitamins A, C, and E in a synergistic fashion.

Proanthocyanidins are also a cofactor of vitamin C, working synergistically with vitamin C, protecting it from oxidation and promoting greater antioxidant activity. Additionally, because vitamin C is necessary for formation of collagen and connective tissue, such as skin, tendons, bones, and cartilage, the addition of PC-95 is effective in promoting the health of the tissues most strongly affected by strenuous physical activity.

Research indicates that proanthocyanidins work on a cellular level. They are incorporated within the cell membrane, protecting against both water- and fat-soluble free radicals. Proanthocyanidin can assist in maintaining optimal health without any side effects.

- It crosses the blood-brain barrier, scavenging free radicals within the brain.
- It protects against radiation, pesticides, chemical pollution, and heavy metals, all of which produce free radicals.

- It is assimilated into the body within seconds.
- It improves the collagen matrix of blood vessels, thereby reducing leakage and improving circulation. Capillaries are able to carry more oxygenated red corpuscles to tissues, expediting soft-tissue healing.

Proanthocyanidins protect vascular walls by bonding to and stimulating collagen and elastin, strengthening vascular membranes and assisting the body in protecting cellular structures. In Europe, proanthocyanidins have been the most widely used product for cardiovascular health. They are able to strengthen vascular walls, improving capillary flow and promoting elasticity and resiliency of vascular membranes such as the linings of the stomach, intestines, sinus, respiratory cavities, joints, and vertebral spaces. Furthermore, proanthocyanidins protect LDL cholesterol from free-radical attack, which further assists in maintaining a healthy heart and cardiovascular system.

Proanthocyanidins protect us against excess production of nitric oxide (NO). NO is an intercellular chemical messenger involved in transferring signals in our cells. It is an important bioactive signaling molecule that mediates a variety of normal physiological functions, which, if altered, could contribute to many pathological conditions, including diabetes, atherosclerosis, ischemia, and reperfusion. During inflammatory processes, the generation of free radicals contributes to the tissue injury associated with these processes.

An increase in free radicals can produce damage to lipids, proteins, and DNA and induce cell death.

Protect your health. Without it you face a serious handicap for success and happiness.
— HARRY F. BANKS

Atherosclerosis Prevention

Proanthocyanidins can be very effective in the treatment and prevention of coronary artery disease, congestive heart failure, and other related cardiovascular diseases.

Researchers in the United Kingdom have demonstrated that the antioxidant properties of proanthocyanidins protect lipids (such as LDL cholesterol) from oxidation. Their results indicate that grape seed extract is an effective agent in combating the onset of atherosclerosis, which is triggered or complicated by lipid oxidation. It is also clear that this extract acts as an antioxidant in the vascular system and prevents the evolution of arterial lesions.[49]

Japanese researchers report that feeding proanthocyanidin-rich extracts to rabbits on a high-cholesterol diet significantly reduced severe atherosclerosis in the aorta.[50]

Research shows that proanthocyanidins are even more effective than vitamin C in protecting LDL from oxidation.[51]

Protection against Damage from a Heart Attack

In Italy, researchers demonstrated that proanthocyanidin supplementation makes the heart less susceptible to tissue damage following a heart attack. In both young and aged rats supplemented with proanthocyanidins, the recovery of left ventricular developed pressure and the values of coronary perfusion pressure were maintained close to those of the preischemic (prior to oxygen loss) period. Proanthocyanidins significantly increased the total antioxidant plasma capacity (by 40 percent in young and by 30 percent in aged rats) and the plasma levels of vitamin C.[52]

Researchers in Germany have also observed the cardioprotective effects of the important orally active constituents of proanthocyanidin due to their radical-scavenging activities as well as the inhibitory activities of damaging enzymes such as elastase.[53]

Protection against Blood Clotting

In a Spanish study, researchers compared the effectiveness of proanthocyanidins, wine, and aspirin on platelet aggregation (clotting) and lipid metabolism. They found that proanthocyanidins specifically from grape seed affect lipid metabolism, while their active constituents in wine (catechin and epicatechin) do not.

Although the clotting effects of proanthocyanidins were comparable to those of aspirin, proanthocyanidins were superior to wine in lipid metabolism. In addition, there is no risk of side effects from proanthocyanidins, unlike aspirin and wine in excess.[54]

OTHER BENEFITS OF PROANTHOCYANIDINS

Besides providing heart-related benefits, procyandins can aid the body in a number of other ways.

Cataract Prevention

Many eye diseases are associated with free-radical damage, including macular degeneration, retina disorders, and cataracts. These conditions greatly benefit from PC-95 supplementation.

Proanthocyanidins support the stabilization of microcapillaries in retinal membranes, promoting eye health, optical acuity, and focusing abilities. Proanthocyanidins are also found to enhance the eye's ability to adjust from light to dark environments.

Animal studies show that proanthocyanidin supplementation decreases the incidence of cataract development and also delays the development of cataracts compared to control animals that did not receive supplementation.

The Cardiovascular Benefits of Proanthocyanidins

- Provide protection from tissue damage following a heart attack
- Reduce elevated cholesterol
- Prevent arterial lesions
- Protect arterial and capillary wall structure
- Prevent blood clotting
- Inhibit activities of damaging enzymes

Vascular Protection

Proanthocyanidins help treat and prevent vascular disorders such as vascular insufficiency (poor circulation), varicose veins, leg cramps, easy bruising from capillary brittleness (fragility), and hemorrhoids.

Proanthocyanidins inhibit protease enzymes that break down proteins. These enzymes are released in the body during inflammation. The inactivation of proteases may protect vascular walls in our vessels and capillaries.

A study of 24 patients with noncomplicated chronic venous insufficiency (poor circulation) were treated with an oral administration of 100 mg proanthocyanidins daily. Swelling, itching, heaviness, and pain were evaluated. Circulation in all of the patients improved 80 percent, with significant improvement in symptoms being observed within the first 10 days of treatment. The action of the proanthocyanidins explains the rapid reduction of swelling in the lower limbs, and there were no adverse effects. Particularly striking were the results observed for itching and pain. Complete disappearance of discomfort took place during treatment in 80 percent of those suffering from itching and 53 percent of those with pain. Researchers reported an overall improvement in 70 percent of the patients studied.[55]

Proanthocyanidins can benefit the vascular system in the following ways:

• Strengthen the cell wall of veins, arteries, and capillaries
• Promote optical acuity, focusing abilities, and eye health
• Delay onset of cataracts
• Encourage skin suppleness and elasticity
• Assist the body in the manufacture of new collagen and elastin
• Reduce bleeding of gums
• Reduce leg soreness, aching, weakness, or numbness, which is often due to peripheral vascular disease

- Reduce bruising
- Reduce capillary fragility—leakages or blockages

Reduction of Joint Inflammation

Proanthocyanidins can be extremely effective in reducing inflammation within the body. Inflammation plays a key role in disorders such as asthma, allergies, sinusitis, hives, and arthritis.

First, proanthocyanidins strengthen connective tissue by blocking the effect of histamines and inhibiting prostaglandin synthesis, which causes destructive elastase activity commonly associated with arthritis.

They also regulate the release of histamine in the body by blocking the activator and enzyme responsible for the release. Histamine is responsible for many of the uncomfortable symptoms associated with allergies and colds. Histamines are also responsible for the body's inflammatory responses and vasoconstriction. German researchers showed that proanthocyanidins may be beneficial against histamine-induced coronary artery constriction.[56]

NO has diverse physiological roles and also contributes to the body's immune defense against viruses, bacteria, and other parasites. However, excess production of NO is associated with various diseases, such as arthritis, diabetes, stroke, septic shock, autoimmune diseases, chronic inflammatory diseases, and atherosclerosis. Cells respond to activating or depressing stimuli by enhancing or inhibiting the expression of the enzymatic machinery that produces NO. Thus, tight regulation of NO production is important for human health. Phytochemicals have been traditionally utilized to treat a family of pathologies that have in common the disregulation of NO production.

Researchers at the University of California, Berkeley, investigated the scavenging activity of proanthocyanidins against reactive oxygen and nitrogen species and its effects on NO metabolism in white blood cells in mice. They reported that the combination of several different biological activities (i.e., its ability to scavenge and inhibit the negative effects of NO and other free radicals) provides the basis for understanding the biological activity of proanthocyanidins as therapeutic agents in various human disorders.[57]

Antiulcer Activity

The anti-ulcer properties of water-soluble proanthocyanidins were studied. Complexes of proanthocyanidins and cimetidine (an anti-ulcer drug) were prepared. The proanthocyanidins were found to increase the water-solubility of the cimetidine and may help prevent undesirable side effects on the stomach.[58]

The structure-activity relationship, bioavailability, and therapeutic efficacy of the antioxidants differ extensively. Proanthocyanidins, naturally occurring antioxidants widely available in fruits, vegetables, nuts, seeds, flowers, and bark, have been reported to possess a broad spectrum of biological, pharmacological, and therapeutic activities against free radicals and oxidative stress.

The concentration- or dose-dependent free-radical scavenging ability of a grape seed proanthocyanidin extract (GSPE), in both in vitro and in vivo models, was assessed and compared to the free-radical scavenging ability of vitamins C, E, and beta carotene. These experiments showed that grape seed proanthocyanidin is highly bioavailable and provides significantly greater protection against free radicals and free-radical-induced lipid peroxidation and DNA damage than vitamins C, E, and beta carotene. Grape seed proanthocyanidin also demonstrated cytotoxicity toward human breast, lung, and gastric adenocarcinoma cells, while enhancing the growth and viability of normal human gastric mucosal cells. Grape seed proanthocyanidin provided significantly better protection as compared to vitamins C and E, singly and in combination. It also demonstrated excellent protection against acetaminophen overdose–induced liver and kidney damage by regulating bcl-X(L) gene DNA damage and presumably by reducing oxidative stress. These results indicate that grape seed proanthocyanidin provides excellent protection against oxidative stress and free-radical-mediated tissue injury.[59]

Other Benefits

You can read about proanthocyanidins' powerful effects on cancer and diabetes in part 3. Here are a few other potential benefits of proanthocyanidins:

- *Protect against neurologic diseases,* including multiple sclerosis, stroke, and spinal cord injuries.
- *Protect against liver diseases,* including those caused by toxins; viruses such as hepatitis A, B, and C; alcohol; and drugs.
- *Protect other organs and remove heavy metals.*
- *Inhibit replication of viruses,* including HIV (the virus associated with AIDS).
- *Prevent radiation damage* (internal and external), such as from the sun or x-rays, and so on.
- *Prevent premature aging, wrinkles, and associated conditions.* Most researchers now agree that cellular-induced free-radical damage is a key factor of the aging process. Research shows that proanthocyanidins determine the strength and elasticity of connective tissue such as collagen and elastin. They inhibit the formation of certain enzymes that break down collagen and other connective tissues, including those found in the joints and skin. Proanthocyanidins can help reduce cross-linking. Excessive cross-linking causes the connective tissue to become hard and inelastic and is the main cause of wrinkles and aging.
- *Prevent and relieve dry skin.*
- *Prevent and relieve sexual dysfunction in some males,* especially if the problem is due to poor circulation.

- *Improve circulation,* experienced as cold hands, cold feet, cold nose, and so on.
- *Speed tissue healing and injury repair,* not only by helping to reduce inflammation, and the damage created by inflammation, but also by supporting collagen and elastin tissues.

For general health and maintenance of ideal antioxidant status in the body, proanthocyanidins should be used in combination with other antioxidants, including vitamin C, vitamin E, coenzyme Q10, and lipoic acid.

—15

Water

The True Story

Water is an essential nutrient required for life. Water makes up more than half the weight of the human body. Without it, humans would die in a few days. All cell and organ functions depend on water, which helps rid the body of contaminants within cells and tissues. It serves as a lubricant and forms the base for saliva and the fluids that surround the joints. Water regulates body temperature, cooling the body through perspiration. Water helps to alleviate constipation by moving food through the intestinal tract and thereby eliminating waste.

Water is the main ingredient of all the fluids that make up your body's systems. These fluids travel through your body, carrying nutrients and waste to and from all your cells and organs. Your heart, your eyes, your intestines, and even your big toe need water-based fluids to survive.

Water is the basis of blood, which you need in every part of your body. It is the main ingredient of lymphatic fluid and the basis of your digestive juices. It even makes up the biggest part of the urinary system, urine.

DEHYDRATION—
THE UNDIAGNOSED EPIDEMIC

Most people do not drink enough water. To function, our bodies require a certain amount of fluid intake daily. To be well hydrated, the average adult must consume at least eight 8 oz glasses of water per day. This is in addition to the water that we receive from solid foods (some foods are 85 to 95 percent water), which is approximately four cups. Juice and liquid (broth) soup cannot be substituted for water. Caffeinated (coffee, tea, and colas) and alcoholic beverages have a diuretic effect and therefore are not appropriate substitutes either.

Daily water requirements vary with activity and age. If we exercise or if other conditions are present, such as very warm weather, the amount needed increases. Basic fluid intake serves to replace the fluids required to perform normal bodily functions. If we take in less or lose more fluid than is needed, the end result is dehydration.

The Nationwide Food Consumption Surveys indicate that a portion of the population may be chronically mildly dehydrated. Several factors may increase the likelihood of chronic mild dehydration, including a poor thirst mechanism, dissatisfaction with the taste of water, consumption of the natural diuretics caffeine and alcohol, participation in exercise, and environmental conditions.[60]

Loss of as little as 2 percent of body weight through dehydration results in impaired physiological and performance responses. New research indicates that fluid consumption in general and water consumption in particular can have an effect on the risk of urinary stone disease; digestive disorders; cancers of the breast, colon, and urinary tract; childhood and adolescent obesity; mitral valve prolapse; salivary gland function; and overall health in the elderly.[61]

Low water consumption is also now associated with an increased risk of colorectal cancer. High levels of water intake have been shown to protect against distal tumors. Dehydration can cause constipation, which can also lead to hemorrhoids, pH disturbances, and many other health problems. Studies show that mild dehydration is common in severe acute childhood asthma.[62]

DO YOU KNOW WHAT YOU ARE DRINKING?

While drinking enough water is very important, the quality of the water we drink is just as important. We can choose from tap water, bottled water, filtered water, and distilled water.

Of the many health threats found in drinking water from the tap, the chief contaminants are these:

- Bacteria: Animal and human waste can contain disease-causing bacteria, such as coliform or salmonella.
- Chemicals, asbestos, and heavy metals: Included in this category are chemical and heavy metal contaminants such as lead, lindane, asbestos, dichloromethane, and others. Lead is known to leach into drinking water from home plumbing and municipal distribution systems. Even homes with copper plumbing can present a risk because, until recently, lead solder was used to connect the copper pipes.
- Chlorine: Chlorine kills disease-causing bacteria such as coliform and *Legionella* (the bacterium that causes legionnaires' disease), but it is ineffective against hard-shelled parasite cysts such as *Cryptosporidium*. Chlorination also produces undesirable tastes, colors, and odors. Unfortunately, chlorination of water can create toxic trihalomethanes and other volatile organic compounds.
- Trihalomethanes: Chloroform, bromoform, bromodichloromethane and chlorodibromomethane, called trihalomethanes, form when organic compounds in water combine with chlorine. They are most prevalent in chlorinated surface water supplies. Decomposition of leaves, wood, grass, and mineral waste can form humus-related compounds contributing to trihalomethane formation. Research clearly shows that trihalomethanes cause cancer.

Chlorine in Drinking Water Is Associated with Increased Cancer Risk

Chloroform and other chlorination disinfection by-products (DBPs) in drinking water are known to cause cancer, particularly bladder cancer. Chlorine may double the risk of bladder cancer, and people may absorb as much or more from hot showers (via skin absorption and vapor inhalation) than from drinking water.

Published reviews of the scientific literature come to worrisome conclusions. Given the widespread and prolonged exposure to DBPs and the epidemiologic evidence of associations with several cancer sites, future research may establish DBPs as the most important environmental carcinogens in terms of the number of attributable cancers per year. For example, in individuals in Iowa, cases of brain cancer were suspected to be due to exposure to trihalomethane (a DBP) in drinking water.[63] A high incidence of breast cancer in North Carolina has also been associated with trihalomethane in drinking water.[64]

Studies of water DBPs have suggested a possible increased risk of bladder and colon cancers, as well as adverse reproductive and developmental effects, such as increased spontaneous abortion rates and fetal anomalies. Approximately 2–17 percent of all bladder cancer cases in the United States may be due to DBPs.[65] Studies in other countries have reported a similar association between exposure to trihalomethane in drinking water and cancer.[66]

Other health problems associated with chlorine and its by-products include heart attacks, diabetes, kidney stones and inflammation, gout, and possibly muscular dystrophy and multiple sclerosis.

Because most drinking water is clear, one does not see what lurks in it. The following are a few other contaminants that tap water might contain:

- Cysts: Chlorine-resistant capsules containing single-cell parasites (protozoa), cysts cause disease with symptoms of severe abdominal cramping and diarrhea. Unlike bacteria, it takes only 30 to 132 individual cysts to produce infection. Cysts are found in drinking water supplies where surface water is the primary source. The most common are species of giardia (such as *Giardia lamblia* and *Cryptosporidium*).

- *Cryptosporidium parvum*: A parasite causing severe diarrhea and abdominal cramps, *Cryptosporidium parvum* is especially dangerous to the elderly, small children, and individuals with AIDS, cancer, or other immune system deficiencies. A 1993 outbreak of cryptosporidiosis in Milwaukee, Wisconsin, is the largest outbreak of waterborne disease in the United States. Over 400,000 persons were affected by the disease, more than 4,000 were hospitalized, and over 50 deaths (some counts are as high as 100) were attributed to the disease.

- Organic compounds, including nitrates: Organic compounds may end up in drinking water as a result of misapplication of agricultural chemicals, chemical spills, or industrial discharge during manufacturing. Excessive nitrate levels can result in a birth defect involving the heart known as "blue baby syndrome." If untreated, the condition could be fatal. Boiling water contaminated with nitrate increases the nitrate concentration and the potential risk.

- Volatile organic chemicals: These are chemicals that vaporize easily from water into air and include a number of both human-made and naturally occurring chemicals. Some of these, including pesticides, herbicides, and insecticides, seep into the groundwater after application. They are contained in a variety of solvents, insecticides, household cleaning compounds, industrial wastes, and underground storage tanks.

Water Contamination Grossly Underreported

Almost nine out of every ten violations of the federal Safe Drinking Water Act are never reported to the main government database set up to alert regulators and consumers to potential water-related health hazards, according to an audit conducted by the U.S. Environmental Protection Agency (EPA).[67] State and local water districts across the country apparently break safety rules tens of thousands of times more frequently than previously documented. Violations range from missed water quality tests to contamination problems. Consumers, thus, may face greater health risks from drinking water than suspected earlier.

The investigation was based upon a government review of the Safe Drinking Water Information System (SDWIS), a state and federal database that collects information on 170,000 public water systems nationwide. Government policymakers use the SDWIS database to help determine whether public water systems are complying with safe drinking water laws.

The new findings suggest that the database is far less complete than government regulators have claimed. Apparently, state regulators are quite lax in reporting violations. While it is true that the vast majority of the unreported violations involve failures to properly test water systems or missed deadlines for filing information, serious infractions also go unreported. These include significant numbers of cases in which water systems exceed legal limits for coliform bacteria, violate standards for contamination from fertilizer and pesticide residues, or fail to properly treat or filter water.

In the fall of 1999, 40,000 water systems nationwide violated testing and purity standards. Of those, 9,500 systems serving 25 million people had violations that the EPA deemed "serious threats to public health."[68]

Bottled Water—Just More Expensive

Bottled water is not as pure as many people think. Producers of bottled water are not even required to meet the same standards that are applied to tap water. Fluoride and bacteria content of bottled water varies widely.

Studies show that even though you are paying more for bottled water, it may not be any better than tap water. Researchers took tap water samples from four processing plants in Cleveland and compared them with five types of bottled water samples, measuring fluoride and bacteria levels in both. Only 5 percent of the bottled water purchased in Cleveland fell within the fluoride range recommended by the state, and nearly 90 percent of the bottled water samples contained less than a third of the fluoride recommended.[69]

While two-thirds of the bottled water samples did indeed have a lower bacterial count than the tap water samples, 25 percent had a whopping 10 times more bacteria. Bacteria in tap water samples varied only slightly.

Even though the EPA recently required that local water systems regularly report the quality of local tap water to the community, there are no similar proposals requiring producers of bottled water to report its quality on its label.

To make matters worse, many manufacturer's use low-grade plastics, which can leach toxins (such as methyl chloride and xenoestrogens) into the water and drinker. These can impair fertility and cause cancer of the reproductive tissues.

DISTILLED WATER—THE WAY TO GO

Most health authorities agree that distilled water is the best type of water to drink. Distillation is the only process that removes 99 percent of all impurities. Other purification systems attempt to remove the impurities from the water, while distillation removes the water and leaves the impurities behind. Here's how distillation works:

1. Tap water is heated to 212 degrees Fahrenheit, killing bacteria, cysts, and viruses.
2. Steam rises, leaving behind dissolved solids, salts, heavy metals, and other chemicals and substances.

3. Steam is condensed back into water in a stainless steel coil.

4. Low boiling light gases are discharged through a gaseous vent.

5. The distilled water is then filtered to remove any volatile organic compounds.

6. The distilled water is collected and stored. To maintain taste and quality integrity, it is ideal to use a poly-carbonate container when storing distilled water for periods of a week or greater.

Heat, as part of the distillation process, effectively kills bacteria and even the most resistant parasites. This is a definite advantage over tap water as *Cryptosporidium parvum* is resistant to chlorine and other cleaning and sanitizing agents. It can survive up to a year in cool, dark conditions. Distillation, however, effectively destroys these nasty creatures. While the immunocompromised are most susceptible to infections by this parasite, outbreaks across the country have been reported.

While you may feel safe boiling your water, the problem is that chemicals such as fluoride and heavy metals such as lead, copper, and cadmium become concentrated several times over and therefore even more harmful when you boil your water. Fluoride has been shown to interfere with thyroid hormone production and is added to tap water in most cities.

Distilled water filtration systems remove fluoride and chlorine. Charcoal or carbon systems don't. Reverse osmosis systems work by forcing water under high pressure through a semipermeable membrane to reduce the amount of inorganic material. These systems vary greatly in effectiveness for filtering out undesirables. In addition, this process wastes up to six gallons of water to produce one gallon of semiclean water. This is not exactly cost effective. Finally, these systems require frequent filter changes, and if these are not done correctly, the system tends to clog and the stagnant debris mixes with the water and becomes a breeding ground for more bacteria.

You can save yourself much money and the anxiety
of falling ill by paying attention to your body's constant
need for water.

—F. BATMANGHELIDJ, M.D.,
Your Body's Many Cries for Water

One of the controversies concerning distilled water is in regard to its mineral content—or lack of it. It's true that distilled water contains no minerals so you cannot rely upon it to supply these trace nutrients. However, most of the minerals found in water are inorganic and therefore not in a usable form for the body.

Inorganic minerals found in water can actually do more harm than good. Calcium deposits can become lodged in plaque, constricting blood flow through the arteries to the heart and other vital areas of the body. They can also lodge in the joint tissues, causing arthritis pain and disfiguration. Kidney stones and gallstones are also formed by buildup of these inorganic solids. Usable organic minerals should be obtained from a good mineral supplement and from pesticide-free fruits and vegetables.

Distilled water is the only electrically active water available. It is able to combine with toxic residues, inorganic minerals, and heavy metals so they can be removed from the body through the elimination systems.

Distillation takes the water out of the contaminants. All other forms of purification try to take the contaminants out of the water. Which makes more sense to you? Don't be confused by people who don't know the importance of distilled water or those trying to sell you something. Distilled water is safe, effective, and very beneficial to the body.

To help retard the processes of premature and decrepit
old age it is essential that you drink plenty of
distilled water daily.

—N.W. WALKER, PH.D.,
1875–1985 (109 years young)

SOFT DRINKS

One of the biggest concerns is the increased consumption of soft drinks (sodas) by both adults and children over the last few decades. Instead of water, juice, and other healthy beverages, many people are now drinking soda, creating numerous serious health problems.

Phosphoric Acid

While the sugar content in soda is a major factor contributing to obesity and dental problems, even more of a health concern is the phosphoric acid content. Many people will switch from regular soda to diet sodas thinking that the sugar content is the cause of their dental problems, but the more serious culprits are phosphoric acid, aspartame, and other dietary acids found in soda pop, especially colas.

Consumption of phosphoric acid increases phosphorus levels, which depletes the body of calcium. In simple terms the phosphoric acid commonly found in soda can rob the body of calcium, elevating the risk of osteoporosis.

In a study of premenopausal women, women in the case group had a higher consumption of soft drinks containing phosphoric acid. This group showed increased levels of the parathyroid hormone than those in the control group. A clear association with hypocalcemia (low calcium) and the consumption of one or more cola soft drinks per day was shown. The study concluded that the consumption of soft drinks containing phosphoric acid should be considered as an independent risk factor for creating low calcium levels in postmenopausal women.[70]

Over 100 published papers have reported the health-related damages resulting from excess consumption of soft drinks. Harmful effects related to soft drink consumption included cavities and other dental disorders, mineral metabolism disorders, acid-peptic disease, other acid-base imbalance disturbances, urinary stone disease, hypocalcemia and increased risk for osteoporosis, neoplasm (tumor growth), increased risk factors for cardiovascular disease, and effects on the central nervous system, reproduction, and allergies.

Calcium loss is not just a problem for adult women. Serum calcium concentrations in children were compared to controls to assess whether the intake of at least 1.5 liters per week of soft drinks containing phosphoric acid demonstrated a significant risk factor for the development of hypocalcemia (low calcium). The results indicated a significant association between intake of phosphoric acid–containing soft drinks and hypocalcemia. Carbonated beverage consumption is also associated with increased bone fractures in younger individuals—including teenage girls.[71]

Animal studies suggest that the impact may even be more detrimental to younger individuals. In just seven days, the animals receiving soft drinks, both adults and immature, developed significant hypercalciuria (the excretion of abnormally large amounts of calcium in the urine, seen in cases of hyperparathyroidism and hyperphosphaturia (high phosphorus). In immature animals, the plasma pH dropped from 7.45 to 7.33 (became more acidic) but did not change in adult animals. Calcium dropped significantly in immature animals.

Fluoride

Another problem associated with soft drinks is the fluoride they contain. Fluoride is an extremely hazardous substance that critically impairs many body functions. We have been told that it is good for us as it fights tooth decay, and therefore this known poison is deliberately added to our water supplies. We also add fluoride to toothpaste, mouthwash, medications, pesticides, herbicides, foods, and beverages.

Excessive fluoride intake can cause skin eruptions, collagen breakdown, headaches, gastric distress, immune system weakness, reproductive problems, genetic damage, kidney disease, hip fractures in the elderly, heart problems, cancer, and dental fluorosis. Dental fluorosis occurs as a result of excessive total fluoride intake during tooth development. Fluorosis is a chronic endemic form of hypoplasia of the dental enamel caused by drinking water with a high fluoride content during the time of tooth formation and characterized by defective calcification that gives a white chalky appearance to the enamel, which gradually undergoes brown discoloration. This is an increasing problem as many children may receive substantial fluoride intake from soft drinks.

Studies show that the fluoride levels of the soda products tested averaged 0.72 parts per million (ppm). Fluoride levels exceeded 0.60 ppm in 71 percent of the products. The U.S. Environmental Protection Agency safety standard for fluoride content in drinking water is 4 ppm; however, the agency states the potential for both bone disease and mottled teeth (children) from drinking it.[72] Since fluoride levels are not marked on the soft drink products and not easily available from the manufacturers, it is not possible for clinicians or consumers to directly estimate fluoride ingestion from carbonated beverages.

Aspartame

Finally, the last item of danger in sodas is aspartame. Aspartame has been linked to numerous health problems, including migraines, prostate cancer, memory loss, seizures, obesity, pain, infertility, and the list goes on and on. The official FDA list contains a total of 92 health complaints associated with this artificial sweetener from thousands and thousands of people. And we all know that most people (less than 1 percent) do not file a formal complaint with the government—and most other people don't know what is causing their problems. In my opinion, aspartame should never have been approved—for any type of purpose.

CAFFEINE

Most caffeine consumed in the United States comes from coffee, soda, and black tea. The kola nut is the caffeine source in colas, and the cocoa bean supplies the caffeine in chocolate. Caffeine

The Many Uses of Cola

Cola has many uses, but do you really want to put this product in your body?

- To clean a toilet: Pour a can of cola into the toilet bowl. Let it sit for one hour, then flush clean. The acid in the cola removes stains from vitreous china.
- To remove rust spots from chrome car bumpers: Rub the bumper with a crumpled piece of aluminum foil dipped in cola.
- To clean corrosion from car battery terminals: Pour a can of cola over the terminals to bubble away corrosion.
- To loosen a rusted bolt: Apply a cloth soaked in cola to the rusted bolt for several minutes.
- To bake a moist ham: Pour a can of cola into the baking pan containing the ham. Cover the ham in aluminum foil and bake. Thirty minutes before the ham is finished, remove the foil, allowing the drippings to mix with the cola for a brown gravy.
- To remove grease from clothes: Pour a can of cola into a load of greasy clothes, add detergent, and run a regular wash cycle. Cola will also help loosen grease stains and clean road haze from your windshield.

The active ingredient in cola is phosphoric acid. (Its pH is 2.8.) It will dissolve a nail in about four days.

To carry cola syrup (the concentrate), a commercial truck must use hazardous material placards reserved for highly corrosive materials. Some cola distributors have been using it to clean the engines of their trucks for about 20 years.

is also found in weight-loss products, pain relievers, and cold remedies.

The American appetite for coffee is ravenous. Upward of 500 million cups are consumed each day. The average person drinks 25 gallons a year. Here in California and in most major cities, it seems there are coffeehouses on every corner.

Caffeine is the most widely consumed drug in Western society. The intake of caffeine-containing beverages in many adults and children often reaches levels that can induce pharmacological effects. Ninety-nine percent of ingested caffeine is absorbed and distributed to all tissues and organs. The effects of caffeine intake differ greatly according to acute or chronic intake, level of intake, and the development of tolerance. Caffeine administered to nonusers or recent abstainers can induce high blood pressure, arrhythmias (abnormal heartbeat or heart function), altered myocardial function, increased plasma levels of stress hormones, plasma renin (blood-clotting) activity, increased serum cholesterol levels, increased production of urine, gastric acid secretion, and alterations in mood and sleep patterns. Tolerance to chronic caffeine intake develops in most individuals, with the cessation of its effects on the kidneys, the cardiovascular system, the gastrointestinal system, and, to some extent, the central nervous system.

Studies clearly show that caffeine increases blood pressure and has an even stronger effect in hypertensive individuals. Most researchers conclude that regular coffee consumption may be harmful to some hypertension-prone subjects. Is there a relationship in America between coffee consumption and the 8–10 million people on antihypertension medications?

As you age, your body (particularly your brain) becomes more sensitive to caffeine, so you are more susceptible to many of its adverse effects, including tremors, insomnia, anxiety, panic attacks, irritability, rapid heartbeat, muscle twitching, and abdominal pain. The amount of caffeine it takes to trigger these side effects varies from person to person, but many researchers suspect that as little as 300 mg (about three 6 oz cups of coffee) may be too much for some people.[73]

Women and Caffeine Don't Mix

Women seem to be more at risk for health problems associated with caffeine consumption. Research has shown that caffeine exacerbates premenstrual syndrome and causes fibrocystic breast disease, a painful, potentially precancerous condition. (The good news is that fibrocystic breast disease usually goes away on its own when caffeine and similar compounds are eliminated from a woman's diet.)

Caffeine intake is especially dangerous to women who are pregnant or desire to become pregnant. Caffeine intake has been associated with reduced fertility, increased risk for spontaneous abortion, premature births, low birthweight babies, birth defects, and also SIDS (sudden infant death syndrome). There is a small but statistically significant increase in the risks for spontaneous abortion and low birthweight babies in pregnant women consuming greater than 150 mg of caffeine per day. (That's only about one and one-half cups of coffee.)

Caffeine can cross the placenta to reach the fetus and, in animals, has been shown to cause malformed fetuses. According to one study, women who drank more than the equivalent of one cup of coffee per day were half as likely to become pregnant as women who drank less. For these reasons, women who are pregnant or who are trying to become pregnant should avoid all caffeine-containing products.[74]

High caffeine intake also has negative effects upon bone density, another good reason for women to watch their intake level.

The Heart Disease Debate

A review of eight studies of people who drank more than five cups of coffee per day indicated that they were 60 percent more likely to develop heart disease. Several other studies have shown that those who consume more than five cups of coffee per day have an increased risk of death from heart disease. There's also a correlation between a high coffee intake and high levels of total cholesterol and LDL cholesterol. When people with elevated cholesterol stop drinking coffee, their cholesterol levels drop by about 10 percent.[75]

Drinkers of boiled coffee have higher cholesterol levels than drinkers of filtered coffee. The filters may help remove cholesterol-raising culprits, several of which have been identified.

What's the Answer?

A low intake, 100 to 200 mg of caffeine (one to two cups of drip coffee a day, or two shots of espresso) has no proven link to disease. With higher intakes, 500 mg of caffeine (five or more cups of coffee a day), there is no question of increased risk of many serious diseases.[76]

Some people should avoid coffee and caffeine altogether. You should abstain if you have a heart rhythm disorder, high blood pressure, panic disorder, gallstones, or fibrocystic breast disease or if you are a pregnant woman or trying to become pregnant.[77]

If you drink more than two cups of coffee a day, you are probably addicted to caffeine. You should cut back until you can enjoy just an occasional cup. Abruptly quitting may cause severe headaches, fatigue, and depression, so you're better off gradually tapering your consumption. For adrenal support, take B-complex vitamins and additional B_5 (500 mg twice daily), vitamin C (1,000 mg four times daily), and PC-95 (100 mg twice daily).

If you are thinking of just switching to decaf, you may want to reconsider. When coffee is decaffeinated, some of the chemicals used to extract the caffeine are left behind, creating other health problems, especially in the liver. Trichloroethylene is a particularly nasty cancer-causing agent (the FDA allows up to 10 parts per million in instant coffee and 25 parts per million in ground, roasted decaffeinated coffee). But other commonly used chemicals—trichloroethane, ethyl acetate, and methylene chloride—are also potent carcinogens. Drink only water-extracted decaf.

ALCOHOL

While the negative health effects of alcohol are detailed in the section on alcoholism, they should be mentioned here as well. Alcohol, as a diuretic, increases the need for water as it increases water loss through the urinary system. Also flushed out are many water-soluble nutrients.

The federal Office of Technology Assessment estimates that alcoholism and alcohol abuse cost the United States up to $120 billion annually in lost productivity, law enforcement, property damage, healthcare, and alcoholism treatment programs. This sum doesn't reflect the immeasurable losses due to human pain and suffering. More than 100,000 deaths per year are directly attributable to alcohol. After cigarettes, alcohol is the second most avoidable cause of death in the United States.

The following are a few of the health problems associated with alcohol use and abuse:

- Anger/aggression
- Anxiety
- Birth defects
- Cancer
- Candida yeast infection
- Capillary fragility (bruising, spider veins, rosacea, varicose veins, etc.)
- Depression
- Diabetes
- Fatigue
- Headaches
- Hearing and sight problems
- Heart disease
- Immune system depression
- Liver damage
- Malnutrition
- Memory loss
- Neurological effects
- Osteoporosis
- Pancreatitis
- Sexual problems
- Sleep disorders
- Stomach ulceration
- Stress and irritability

ALCOHOL AND CAFFEINE DECREASE FERTILITY

In a study examining the effects of alcohol and caffeine on conception with 124 women at Johns Hopkins School of Medicine, Baltimore, Maryland, researchers found a greater than 50 percent reduction in the probability of conception during a menstrual cycle in which participants consumed alcohol. Caffeine may enhance alcohol's negative effect. Women who abstained from alcohol and consumed less than one cup of coffee or its equivalent per day conceived 26.9 pregnancies per 100 menstrual cycles compared with 10.5 per 100 menstrual cycles among those who consumed any alcohol and more than one cup of coffee per day. This study revealed an independent dose-related negative effect of alcohol consumption on the ability to conceive. The results suggest that women who are attempting to conceive should abstain from alcohol.[78]

CONCLUSION

An adequate amount of distilled water is the best choice to provide needed water to the body. The question is, where does one get it? Popular supermarkets and specialty stores carry distilled water. The best solution is to make your own with a good countertop water distiller. (Roex offers one that works very well, is reasonably priced, and requires no installation or plumbing.)

−16

Digestion
A Vital Key to Health

The importance of good digestive health cannot be overstated. The saying "Death begins in the colon" is very true. This has been stated by many of the greatest known natural healers, including Dr. Paul Bragg, Dr. Bernard Jensen, Dr. Paavo Airola and Dr. John Christopher.

Our modern lifestyle has taken its toll on our digestive/elimination organs. Refined, processed foods lacking fiber, excessive animal fats, lack of exercise, and high stress all contribute to our current gastrointestinal health crisis.

As unpleasant as it sounds, consider that a sluggish bowel can actually retain pounds of old toxic and poisonous fecal matter. In fact 30–40 and up to 65 pounds have actually been reported! Many times the real cause of health problems is the retention and reabsorption of built up toxic waste. The colon and digestive tract of nearly every adult is burdened with a lifetime of accumulation of toxic waste materials. The very best diet can be no better than the worst if the colon is clogged with accumulated wastes.

Digestion starts in the mouth. The process of chewing and mixing the food with saliva, which contains digestive enzymes, begins the digestion process. When it reaches the stomach, the food is broken down into the components that make up blood, tissues, hair, skin, bones, and so on by hydrochloric acid and the digestive enzymes secreted by the pancreas. If these two items are not present in adequate amounts, food that is only partially digested moves into the upper intestinal tract, where it begins to ferment with the bacteria naturally present there. This creates a breeding ground for yeast and toxins, which create problems there and also may be absorbed into the bloodstream.

COLORECTAL CANCER

Colorectal cancer is the third leading cause of cancer in males, fourth in females, in the United States. Colorectal cancer is a malignant tumor arising from the inner wall of the large intestine. The colon is the part of the digestive system where waste material is stored. The rectum is at the end of the colon adjacent to the anus. Together, they form a long, muscular tube called the "large intestine" (also known as the "large bowel").

Benign tumors of the large intestine are called polyps. Malignant tumors of the large intestine are called cancers. If benign polyps are not removed from the large intestine, they can become malignant (cancerous) over time. Most diagnosed cancers of the large intestine are believed to have developed from polyps. Removal of colon polyps can prevent colorectal cancer. Colon polyps and early cancer may have no symptoms; therefore, regular screening is important.

Risk factors for colorectal cancer include heredity, colon polyps, long-standing ulcerative colitis, and chronic constipation. (Please see the sections in part 3 on constipation as well as the chapter on detoxification and elimination.)

DIGESTIVE ENZYMES

Digestive enzymes assist the body in the breakdown and assimilation of proteins, carbohydrates, fats, starches, and dairy products that we ingest. They are found in all live foods. When we eat raw foods, these enzymes help us to digest the food in the body, thus relieving the burden on the pancreas. The pancreas is the source of many digestive enzymes produced in the body for the same process.

The importance of digestive enzymes is probably one of the least understood aspects of health by the general public. There are three categories of enzymes:

1. *Metabolic enzymes,* which stimulate various chemical reactions involving many various functions of the body
2. *Digestive enzymes,* which help digest the food we eat
3. *Food enzymes,* which are contained naturally in raw foods and jump-start food digestion

The more enzymes we ingest either by eating raw foods or by supplementing, the less the body has to borrow from its natural reservoir of metabolic and digestive enzymes to digest food. This is one reason for the tradition of eating a salad of raw greens and vegetables at the beginning of a meal. The naturally occurring enzymes in these raw foods help us digest our whole meal.

As we age, the quantity and quality of digestive enzymes we are able to produce decrease at a rapid rate. This problem is made worse by organizations around the world that process foods with methods that destroy these natural saviors of the digestive tract. Cooking or food processing easily destroys enzymes, as they are very sensitive to heat. As a result, our diets today do not supply adequate digestive enzymes, leading to many health problems now linked to this enzyme deficiency:

- Allergies
- Bloating and flatulence
- Constipation
- High blood pressure
- Indigestion
- Lack of energy
- Lowered immunity
- Memory Loss
- Obesity

Inadequate intake of enzymes stresses vital organs such as the pancreas, liver, and spleen and can even lead to a metabolic enzyme deficiency. For this reason, a broad-spectrum digestive enzyme supplement is imperative today if we are to enjoy optimal health.

The following digestive enzymes can be found in raw foods or a good supplement:

- Alpha-galactosidase: Helps digest long-chain carbohydrates that often cause gas
- Amylase: Digests sugars and starches
- Bromelain (an anti-inflammatory food enzyme from pineapple): Aids in the digestion of proteins and fats
- Cellulase: Digests cellulose, the fibrous component of most vegetable matter
- Cerecalase: Breaks up phytic acids in fiber and cereals
- Glucoamylase: Yields more glucose from starch
- Invertase: Breaks down sucrose
- Lactase: Digests the milk sugars
- Lipase: Digests fats and oils, converting them to heat and energy
- Papain: Helps digest proteins
- Peptidase: Helps digest proteins
- Protease: Helps break up proteins into amino acids

Note: A good digestive enzyme supplement should be chewable as digestion naturally starts in the mouth.

PROBIOTICS

"Probiotics" may be a new word to some. It may look familiar, however, as most people know what antibiotics are—drugs used to kill bacteria in the body. Probiotics are live microbial food supplements (good bacteria) that beneficially affect the host by improving its intestinal microbial balance.

"Probiotics" actually means "for life." It includes not only the commonly known lactic acid bacteria (found in yogurt) but all naturally occurring beneficial bacteria in our intestinal tract.

The number of bacteria present in the digestive system is so huge, it is expressed in powers of 10; 10^3 is 1,000 and 10^6 is 1,000,000. In the esophagus, the numbers are 10^3 to 10^6 per gram of contents. The small intestine contains about 10^3 to 10^6 bacteria per gram, and this increases in the large intestine or colon to 10^8 to 10^{11}. In the feces, 10–20 percent of the weight consists of bacteria, most of which are anaerobic; that is, they can grow without oxygen.

These organisms are also called "intestinal flora," "gut flora," or "microflora." To distinguish the good ones from the others, the term *probiotics* arose to prominence in the nutritional science world. Acidophilus, while a prominent player, is actually only one of over 400 different species of bacteria in our intestinal tracts—there are over 200 strains of acidophilus alone. *Lactobacillus acidophilus* is the most commonly known.

Throughout history, people have benefited from the use of probiotic cultures found in sour cream, cheese, kefir, yogurt, sauerkraut and kimchi (fermented cabbage), miso (fermented soy), and other foods. Live bacteria products can benefit the body because they

- Normalize (balance) the intestinal tract
- Suppress growth of pathogenic and putrefactive bacteria
- Increase resistance against infections
- Produce lactic acid, acetic acid, butyric acid, and natural antibiotics
- Manufacture biotin, B_1, B_2, B_5, B_6, and vitamin K
- Encourage growth of bifidus bacteria, another probiotic strain that benefits the gastric intestinal tract
- Produce hydrogen peroxide
- Support and strengthen overall immunity
- Increase the overall digestive abilities of the gastro-intestinal tract
- Produce their own antibacterial substances against invading organisms
- Help resist damage from pollutants and radiation

Probiotics Enhance Nutrient Absorption

Many nutrients are dependent upon probiotic cultures for adequate digestion and proper utilization. Absorption of optimal amounts may depend in large part on the overall health of the intestines and their resident "guests." Absorption of the minerals calcium, zinc, iron, manganese, copper, and phosphorus is enhanced with the use of probiotics.

Foods fermented with probiotics have proteins that are more easily absorbed. Amino acids, the protein building blocks, are also more available in fermented dairy foods, such as yogurt or cottage cheese, when compared to milk.

The huge numbers of bacteria in the colon actively affect the other constituents of the gut. These are mostly harmless bacteria, which tend to reduce the number of pathogenic organisms entering the gut. Without these beneficial bacteria, we are much more susceptible to intestinal infection, cancer, and other health problems, such as irritable bowel syndrome, ulcers, and Crohn's disease.

The use of antibiotics and other drugs inhibits the amount of vitamins supplied by the bacteria, increasing our need for these nutrients. Bacteria also digest small constituents of dietary fiber, enabling them to be absorbed. Intestinal bacteria also helps break down bile pigments and bile acids. Without a steady supply of probiotics in the gut, we cannot properly benefit from these intestinal flora.

Three of the most important probiotics to supplement with are *L. acidophilus*, *B. bifidum* and *S. thermophilus*. (All of these are included in Colon Essentials.)

FIBER

Fiber plays a major role in maintaining a healthy digestive tract. The term "fiber" refers to or encompasses several carbohydrates and lignans that resist breakdown by human digestive enzymes and that are fermented by the microflora of the colon.

Fibers Are Soluble or Insoluble

Soluble fiber is fermented to a high degree, showing a powerful trophic effect at the colon level. Soluble fiber

- Absorbs toxins for elimination
- Provides food for beneficial bacteria in the colon
- Controls blood sugar levels by slowing down blood sugar absorption
- Improves cholesterol levels in the blood by lowering the bad LDL and raising the good HDL
- Reduces heart disease risk
- Reduces colon cancer risk

Examples include oat bran, wheat bran, psyllium and apple and fruit pectin.

Insoluble fiber is barely fermentable and has a marked laxative and intestinal regulatory effect. Insoluble fiber

- Acts like a broom to sweep the intestines clean
- Assists with bowel regularity (constipation and diarrhea)
- Aids digestion
- Reduces colon cancer risk

Examples include lignan, cellulose, and chitosan. (Chitosan is a naturally occurring polysaccharide derived from the exoskeletons of shellfish, such as shrimp or crab.)

Types of Fiber

Fibers consist of lignans, cellulose and hemicellulose, pectins, and gums.

Lignan is a highly complex, insoluble molecule found in woody plant tissues, such as flax. It is virtually indigestible. It attracts bile to its surface, helping to reduce cholesterol levels.

Cellulose is the fibrous insoluble component of plant cell walls. Its high water-holding abilities explain its ability to increase fecal weight. Hemicellulose is more readily broken down by friendly microflora in the colon than cellulose. Psyllium is high in hemicellulose and has very high water-holding capacities.

Pectin is a gel-forming substance found in all fruits and many vegetables. Pectin changes from an insoluble material in an unripe or raw fruit to a more water-soluble substance in a ripe or cooked fruit (or vegetable).

Gums are water-soluble thickeners, which are generally indigestible. They provide water binding and bulk to the contents of the colon and make us feel full. They are often used this way in supplements to help one achieve weight loss. They also have been shown to lower cholesterol levels. Examples include guar gum and carrageenan.

How Much?

The recommended dietary fiber intake for adults is around 25–30 grams/day, or 10–13 grams/1,000 kilocalories. However, popular U.S. foods are not high in dietary fiber, and common serving sizes of grains, fruits, and vegetables contain only 1–3 grams of dietary fiber. In spite of the widespread dissemination of the recommendation for fiber consumption, however, the usual intake of dietary fiber in the United States remains far lower than the recommended level, averaging only 14–15 grams/day.

Lack of fiber is associated with cardiovascular disease, colon cancer, gallstones, ulcerative colitis, diverticulitis, hemorrhoids, and constipation.

Fiber and Cancer

Fiber plays a major role in cancer prevention. Studies have shown a link between high-fiber diets and a decreased risk of colon cancer. Since fiber increases the bulk of the stool, it may dilute cancer-causing substances in the colon. It also moves waste faster through the digestive tract, leaving less time for potentially harmful or even cancerous substances in the stool to have contact with the lining of the bowel.

In general, the typical adult U.S. diet provides only about half the appropriate fiber intake. To reduce the risk of certain cancers, diet must be optimized, primarily to reduce caloric and fat intake. Fat intake should be 20–30 percent of total caloric intake, and fiber should be increased to 25–30 grams daily.

Researchers at New York Medical College suggest a diet designed around adequate fiber intake from grains (especially cereals), vegetables, legumes, and fruits, thereby reducing both calorie and fat intake. Such dietary improvements will not only reduce cancer and other chronic disease risks but contribute to a healthy life to an advanced age.[79]

Scientific evidence supports the role of wheat-bran fiber in reducing the risk of colorectal cancer. Italian researchers investigating the relationship between various types of fiber and colorectal cancer risk used data from a case-control study between 1992 and 1996. The study included 1,953 colorectal cancer cases that demonstrated the independent effect of fiber on colorectal cancer, particularly bran-type fibers and fibers of vegetable or fruit origin.[80]

A large amount of data also indicates that certain vegetables and fruits may be cancer protective through mechanisms (phytochemicals) in addition to their fiber content.

One disturbing study we came across was conducted through the Department of Pediatrics, Ohio State University College of Medicine, at Columbus Children's Hospital. Approximately half of the children from families who were health conscious enough to request dietary evaluation fell below the recommended intake of dietary fiber per day. The children with chronic constipation were consuming less than one-fourth of the recommended fiber intake. This is not the disturbing part. When the families were instructed to administer a high-fiber diet to their children, they were unable to accomplish this unless they received intensive and ongoing dietary counseling. Even among health-conscious families, only half of the children received the recommended amounts of dietary fiber. The researchers recommended further public education in this regard.

Our children's eating habits are formed by what we, as parents, teach them—largely by example. If we are not able to teach them what a healthy diet is (which is high in fiber), what chance do they have to grow into healthy adults?

Fiber and Diabetes

Having adequate fiber in your diet is also very important for other health areas you may not consider related to the digestive tract, such as breast cancer and diabetes.

In a randomized, crossover study, 13 patients with type II diabetes mellitus were instructed to follow two diets, each for six weeks: a diet containing moderate amounts of fiber (total of 24 grams, 8 grams of soluble fiber and 16 grams of insoluble fiber), as recommended by the American Diabetes Association (ADA), and a high-fiber diet (total of 50 grams, 25 grams of soluble fiber and 25 grams of insoluble fiber), containing foods not fortified with fiber. Both diets, prepared in a research kitchen, had the same macronutrient and energy content.

After six weeks, the high-fiber diet, as compared with the sixth week of the ADA diet

- Lowered the 24-hour plasma glucose and insulin concentrations by 10 percent and 12 percent, respectively
- Reduced plasma total cholesterol by 6.7 percent
- Reduced triglycerides by 10.2 percent.
- Reduced very-low-density lipoprotein cholesterol by 12.5 percent

A high intake of dietary fiber, particularly of the soluble type, above the level recommended by the ADA, improves control of blood glucose, decreases hyperinsulinemia (excessively high blood insulin levels), and lowers plasma liquid (fat) concentrations in patients with type II diabetes.[81]

The Benefits of Increased Fiber Intake

Increasing fiber may also help prevent the following conditions:

- Breast cancer
- Colon cancer
- Constipation
- Diabetes
- Diverticulitis
- Heart disease
- Hemorrhoids
- High blood pressure
- High cholesterol
- Indigestion
- Irritable bowel syndrome
- Parkinson's disease
- Weight problems

Fiber Sources

All plant foods are good fiber sources. The best include

- Whole-grain cereals such as wheat, brown and wild rice, millet, corn, amaranth, oats, barley, and buckwheat
- Beans, peas, and lentils
- Root vegetables, such as potatoes, sweet potatoes, yams, carrots, parsnips, and beets
- Fruits and leafy vegetables, including dried fruits

Note: Animal products (meat and dairy products) contain no fiber.

Excellent fiber supplements include the following:

- *Chitosan* Chitosan and chitin are two polysaccharide fibers that are commonly found in weight-loss products. These fibers speed up the movement of food through the digestive system, and help prevent dietary fat and cholesterol from absorbing and from adding pounds to the body or fat to the bloodstream.

Chitin is obtained from shellfish and is similar in chemical structure to cellulose and starch. It's heated with a special solution to make chitosan.

Both are indigestible and help cleanse the colon, regulate bowel habits, and reduce blood pressure and tumors as shown by the results of an estimated 1,000 studies.[82]

- *Flax* Flax is high in both soluble and insoluble fiber. Flaxseed is by far the richest source of lignans. Lignans are thought to help prevent cancer and when used by colonic bacteria are transformed into powerful antioxidants.

- *Alfalfa* Alfalfa is an excellent fiber source used in Japan as a medicinal herb for hypertension, and in China it is traditionally used as a diuretic and an arthritis remedy. Studies indicate the saponins in alfalfa lower blood cholesterol levels and triglycerides and may help prevent heart disease and possibly some strokes. It seems to decrease intestinal absorption of dietary cholesterol. The herb also contains the anti-inflammatory bioflavonoid quercetin, which may account for its alleged benefits in cases of asthma and hay fever.

Alfalfa is often found in green-food powders, frequently containing blue-green algae and wheat or barley grass.

The following herbs (individually or in combination) are excellent for cleansing and rejuvenating the colon:

- *Aloe vera* Serves as a natural laxative and bowel toning agent.
- *Barberry root* A tonic herb beneficial to the liver in blood purification and bile formation.

- *Buckthorn bark* A gentle nonhabit-forming laxative and diuretic herb effective for constipation, liver congestion, and cleansing.
- *Burdock root* An ingredient in all blood cleansing and detoxification combinations. Also a strong liver purifier.
- *Cascara sagrada* A bitters tonic for the liver and gall- bladder and a nonhabit-forming tonic laxative. Increases the secretions of the stomach, liver, and pancreas and helps the body rid itself of gallstones.
- *Dandelion root* An excellent liver cleansing and toning herb that possesses soothing, healing properties for the digestive system and bowel inflammation.
- *Garlic* Supports development of beneficial intestinal flora, while killing pathogenic organisms such as *Candida* (fungus) and parasites.
- *Ginger* A warming circulatory and body cleansing herb.
- *Red clover* A powerful blood-purifying herb effective for many chronic and degenerative diseases.
- *Silymarin (milk thistle)* An ingredient in liver regeneration and rebuilding. Increases the flow of bile from the liver and gallbladder.

(Note: These herbs are provided in Roex's WOW formula.)

A healthy digestive system is of vital importance to good health; however, its importance is commonly overlooked. A few small changes can provide major benefits, no matter what your age or state of health.

−17

Detoxification
and Elimination

*Every tissue is fed by the blood, which is supplied by
the intestinal system. When the intestines are dirty, the
blood is dirty, and so are the organs and tissues. It is
the intestinal system that has to be cared for first before
any effective healing can take place.*
—BERNARD JENSEN, PH.D.

Internal cleanliness is a very important key to vitality, energy,
vibrant health, and impeding the aging process. Internal detoxification is an ongoing process that our bodies perform daily. In
much the same way that our hearts beat nonstop and our lungs
breathe consistently, our bodies continually encounter and dispose of a variety of toxins and poisons. The liver is one of the
most significant organs in the body for detoxification. It works
continuously, day and night, year in and year out, cleansing
between one and two quarts of blood per minute.

Besides the liver, the other components of the detoxification
system are the lungs, kidneys, skin, spleen, bowel, and immune
system. Of all these components, the liver is by far the most significant organ in the detoxification of the human body.

Toxins are compounds in the body that have a negative effect on cellular structure and function. They fall into four main categories:

- Heavy metals
- Liver toxins
- Microbial toxins from the intestines
- By-products from the breakdown of proteins

(Note: All four toxins are common in a high-protein, low-carbohydrate diet.)

Toxic materials can be cellular wastes—by-products of our own metabolic processes, or they may consist of environmental pollutants, pesticides, and poisons ingested into our systems through the air we breathe, the foods we eat, and the water we drink.

Under ideal circumstances, the body is equipped to neutralize and dispose of these toxins through the liver, spleen, and eliminative channels (bowel, kidneys, lungs, skin, and lymphatic system). But in modern-day society this is practically impossible. Most people today are overloaded with sugar, caffeine, saturated fats, alcohol, drugs, chemicals from the food supply, and polluted water. Their detoxification systems are so overworked that eventually they can function at only half speed or they nearly stop. Toxic overload is the foundation of all kinds of diseases, energy loss, and mental disorders, yet the medical establishment still bases its diagnosis primarily on symptoms rather than looking to the root of the problem.

THE CAUSES OF TOXICITY

Accumulated toxins in the body account for a myriad of health complaints ranging from something as simple as fatigue or weight gain to serious health disorders such as arthritis, cancer, and other degenerative conditions. Perhaps 99 percent of the time, the amount of toxicity in the body correlates directly with the seriousness of the condition.

Faulty digestion and elimination develop in an individual through years of improper lifestyle and dietary habits. When we are not eliminating properly, wastes may not be expelled for days, months, or years. Toxins back up in the colon, causing self-poisoning. This occurs when the bowel walls form a buildup of uneliminated fecal matter. Not only does this toxic material hamper the absorption of vital nutrients through the intestinal wall, but it also causes the blood capillaries lining the intestinal wall to absorb these toxins into the bloodstream, polluting all of our organs and cells.

This self-poisoning lowers our overall health and vitality, depleting us of energy. Symptoms of a toxic body include

- Arthritis
- Bad breath
- Body odor
- Constipation
- Depression
- Excessive mucus
- Fatigue
- Gas
- Poor digestion
- Poor memory
- Rashes/hives
- Skin breakouts
- Stomach bloat
- Weight gain

and almost every other noninfectious health problem.

These problems can all be alleviated through internal detoxification techniques. While we cannot cover the subject in detail here, check the suggested reading list for books by some very good authors, such as Michael Murray, James Balch, and Gary Null.

THE LIVER: YOUR PRIMARY ORGAN OF DETOXIFICATION

The liver is perhaps the least understood by the general public yet is one of the primary organs of the detoxification system. It is probably the most complex organ in the body—even more complex than the brain. While it has hundreds of very important functions, we are going to discuss only its detoxification responsibilities in this section.

Every drop of blood running through the body must be filtered through the liver. The liver is responsible for removing or rendering harmless toxic chemicals from the body and the environment. This organ works nonstop to accomplish this huge task.

The liver filters up to two quarts of blood per minute, every minute of the day, to rid the blood of toxins. This process is critical to health because the blood is loaded with endotoxins (such as bacteria in the body that die and by-products from our own metabolism and the immune system), dead blood cells, and various other toxins. When the liver is working properly, it clears about 90 percent of these toxins from the blood before recirculating it through the body.

Research shows that silymarin helps protect and support normal liver function through its powerful antioxidant properties.[83] For other supplements that help maintain the optimal functioning of the liver, see "Rod's Detoxification Cleansing Program" at the end of this chapter.

Synthesizing and secreting bile (which is made from cholesterol) is the second way the liver helps detoxify the body. Each day the liver manufactures about a quart of bile, an emulsifier that breaks down and eliminates excess fat and other fat-soluble toxins from the body. Bile carrying fat and toxins attaches to fiber in the intestinal tract. These are then excreted through the colon.

Using approximately 150 different enzymes, the liver neutralizes unwanted chemicals such as drug residues (including alcohol), pesticides, and other environmental chemicals we breathe, drink, and eat. Other chemicals, such as hormones and prosta-

Cancer Prevention

Researchers now recognize that *90 percent of all cancers are due to the effects of environmental carcinogens,* such as cigarette smoke, food chemicals, and polluted air and water, combined with nutritional deficiencies that impair the proper functioning of the body. Therefore, the proper functioning of the *liver detoxifying* system is absolutely essential for the prevention of cancer. When metabolic processes go awry, cancer can take over.

It is essential that the liver receives all the nutritional and antioxidant support it needs!

glandins (including inflammatory agents such as histamine), are also neutralized by this process.

As a by-product of this process, free radicals are formed. To neutralize these metabolic free radicals, the liver produces the antioxidant glutathione. Natural substances that can assist the liver in this process include silymarin extract and vitamin C (at least 3,000 mg daily). Also important are magnesium, zinc, potassium, and certain sulfur-based amino acids. Glutathione is also needed to eliminate fat-soluble toxins.

This is a highly effective system. Obviously, the more toxins one is exposed to, the harder the liver has to work. A deficiency in glutathione can be devastating when the body is overwhelmed with toxins. Free-radical damage can destroy a liver—as in cirrhosis. While research does not support oral glutathione supplementation, it does support supplementation of vitamin C (up to 3,000 mg daily) to greatly help the body synthesize glutathione.

NUTRITIONAL SUPPORT

No detoxification program is complete without proper elimination and nutrition. Recognize the necessity and importance of a high-fiber diet and of having one or two normal bowel movements per day. Avoid processed and junk foods that contain sugar,

THE BODY'S DETOXIFICATION SYSTEM

SKIN The body's largest organ releases its load of toxins through perspiration. By working up a sweat, you can help this process along. Cleansers include saunas, salt baths, exercise, and diaphoretic (increase sweating) herbs (such as yarrow, boneset, and elder flowers), and minerals (especially MSM).

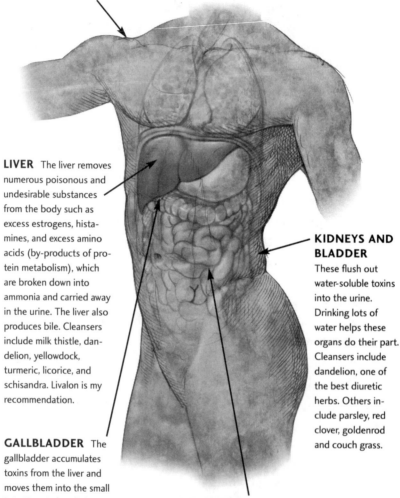

LIVER The liver removes numerous poisonous and undesirable substances from the body such as excess estrogens, histamines, and excess amino acids (by-products of protein metabolism), which are broken down into ammonia and carried away in the urine. The liver also produces bile. Cleansers include milk thistle, dandelion, yellowdock, turmeric, licorice, and schisandra. Livalon is my recommendation.

KIDNEYS AND BLADDER
These flush out water-soluble toxins into the urine. Drinking lots of water helps these organs do their part. Cleansers include dandelion, one of the best diuretic herbs. Others include parsley, red clover, goldenrod and couch grass.

GALLBLADDER The gallbladder accumulates toxins from the liver and moves them into the small intestines to be eliminated. It also stores and releases bile to help break down fats. Cleansers include turmeric, barberry, boldo, dandelion, yellowdock, milk thistle, fringe tree, and especially WOW.

INTESTINES The intestinal tract and the colon help in the breakdown of foods and the elimination of waste. Probiotics and fiber are necessary for this aspect of cleansing to be most effective. Fiber helps waste move quickly through the system. Helpful toxin binders include fruit pectin, bentonite clay, and laxative herbs, such as psyllium seed and flaxseed. Colon Essentials and EFAs are a must here.

Rod's Detoxification Cleansing Program

Supplements that can directly enhance the structure and function of the liver are

- *B vitamins,* especially niacin, folic acid, B_6, and B_{12}.
- *Vitamin C,* 3,000 mg or more daily, to enhance glutathione production and give antioxidant protection.
- *Minerals,* especially calcium, magnesium, zinc, sulfur (MSM), potassium, copper, and boron in a formulation like Roex's Ultimate Calcium Mineral Formula.
- *Silymarin* (milk thistle extract), such as in Livalon, which is 80 percent silymarin.
- *Artichoke extract*
- *Distilled Water,* at least eight 8 oz glasses every day. This is a must for anyone with liver, kidney, or gallbladder blockage because of its chelating ability with heavy metals and other toxins.
- *Probiotics* (as included in Colon Essentials), including DDS-1 *L. acidophilus, B. bifidum,* and *S. thermophilus.* (DDS-1 refers to the specific strain of *L. acidophilus* developed by Dr. Shahni of Nebraska Cultures.)
- *Digestive enzymes,* as in Digestive Balance (the complete formula).
- *Fiber,* both fat- and water-soluble, as in *CitriGenics II.*
- A good colon-cleansing and blood-purifying formula, such as in *WOW,* including
  - Aloe vera leaf powder
  - Barberry root
  - Buckthorn bark
  - Burdock root
  - Cascara sagrada
  - Cayenne
  - Dandelion root
  - Garlic
  - Ginger
  - Milk thistle seed
  - Red clover

salt, saturated fats, caffeine, nicotine, phosphoric acid, and alcohol. Avoid excess animal protein, which places a tremendous burden on the entire digestive system, especially the liver and the kidneys.

Our bodies need live foods—fresh, organic fruits, vegetables, and whole grains—that contain the necessary digestive enzymes to assure proper digestion and assimilation of nutrients as well as optimal glutathione synthesis.

Take care of your liver and your entire digestive tract and they will take care of you. Ignore and abuse these two systems and you will pay the penalty. It is just a question of when.

PART 3

The Nutritional Approach to Common Ailments and Conditions

The following provides information concerning common ailments and conditions. Not all of this information applies to every person suffering from the condition. Each causative factor, symptom, and therapeutic regimen must be considered separately according to the individual.

Minor disorders in their early stages can usually be treated at home effectively and safely. Serious conditions may require attention from a medical professional.

The science behind nutritional supplements is rapidly growing. While many of these remedies are old, they are still highly effective in promoting health. Nutritional supplements work with the body, often with little or no risk of side effects, unlike pharmaceutical drugs, which tax the body with toxins and by altering its normal operating functions. The overall cost of supplements also makes them an affordable alternative in maintaining our health.

ACNE

Acne is a common disorder of the skin characterized by recurring formation of pimples, whiteheads, and blackheads. Acne breakouts usually occur on the face, shoulders, and back, where sebaceous oil glands are the most numerous and active. It is caused by clogging and inflammation of the oil glands and ducts beneath the skin. In adolescents, acne affects about 75 percent of males and 50 percent of females, but it can occur in adults as well.

Contrary to what many physicians may say, acne is related to what we eat. (They will tell you that most cases of acne are related to hormonal imbalances.) Poor diet is the primary cause of hormonal imbalances—especially excessive saturated fat, hydrogenated fat, animal or dairy products, sugar, and refined carbohydrates. Nutritional deficiencies (particularly zinc, dietary sulfur [MSM], and vitamin B_6), poor elimination, buildup of toxins, and food allergies can also be contributing factors. Acne can be irritated by the use of cosmetics, poor hygiene, stress, and monthly menstruation.

What to Do

To prevent or treat acne, follow these tips:

- Wash your face twice daily. If you wear makeup, be sure to remove before it bedtime. Also remember to wash makeup applicator brushes and sponges often to avoid contamination.
- Apple cider vinegar mixed with baking soda may be gently used as an exfoliating and drying cleanser. Rub the mixture on the affected area gently in a circular motion, using a washcloth. Apply apple cider vinegar with a cotton pad as an astringent. Dilute it with distilled water if it is too harsh.
- Do not irritate and contaminate infections by touching or squeezing them with your hands and fingers.
- To stop a flareup when a pimple becomes visible, apply ice until it subsides.
- To take the red out of a blemish, combine 1 tbsp of lemon juice with 1 tbsp of salt. Apply this mixture to the red area and leave it on for 10 minutes and rinse.

- To get rid of a pimple overnight, dip a cotton swab in witch hazel or hydrogen peroxide and apply it to the pimple to dry it up. Then apply calamine lotion.
- Blemishes will also heal faster if you apply a drop of chamomile extract on them.
- Enemas or colon-cleansing herbs (ginger, aloe leaf powder, garlic, cascara sagrada, barberry root, dandelion, red clover, buckthorn, milk thistle, burdock root, alfalfa— such as provided in the WOW formula) may be used to speed the toxins out of the body and clear the skin.
- Supplemental vitamin A has been effective in the treatment of acne. Topical use of vitamin A from a capsule can also be effective.
- Zinc is an antibacterial agent and a necessary element in the oil-producing glands of the skin. A diet low in zinc will trigger acne flareups. Be sure your diet provides adequate amounts of zinc. Foods that are high in zinc, from highest to lowest concentrations, include oysters, herring, wheat germ, sesame seeds, torula yeast, blackstrap molasses, liver, soybeans, sunflower seeds, and egg yolk.
- Supplemental *zinc sulfate* (150 mg total daily, 50 mg after each meal) has also proven to be very beneficial for the skin and has cured numerous conditions of acne—even severe cases. Note: If bowel upset occurs, reduce the dosage and add 1–3 mg of copper. Selenium also may be required at 100 mcg daily.
- Eating a proper diet plays a large role in the health of your skin. Eat a balanced, healthy diet low in saturated fat, low in refined sugar and simple carbohydrates, low in salt, and high in complex carbohydrates.
- The final solution and one of the best is to supplement with the three most important nutrients that support the body against acne as well as help repair the skin. They are PC-95, Ester-C®, and MSM. The combination is very effective over time.

Beneficial Supplementation

The following supplements have been shown to be beneficial for people with acne:

- MSM: 2,500–3,500 mg daily
- Proanthocyanidins (PC-95): 150 mg daily
- Cleansing herbs: Ginger, aloe leaf powder, garlic, cascara sagrada, barberry root, dandelion, red clover, buckthorn, and milk thistle (such as found in WOW)
- Beta carotene and/or Vitamin A:
  Therapeutic: 50,000–100,000 IU daily for one month, then reduce dosage to maintenance level
  Maintenance: 10,000–25,000 IU daily
- Vitamin B complex: 50 mg two times daily
- Niacin: 100 mg three times daily
- Vitamin C (Ester-C®): 3–10 grams daily
- Vitamin E (internal and topical): 400 IU daily
- Flaxseed oil: 2–3 tbsp daily
- Zinc: 30 mg daily (zinc sulfate preferred)
- Probiotics: Such as *Lactobacillus acidophilus* (see page 228)
- Other herbs: Alfalfa, chamomile (extract-topical), chaparral, chlorophyll, coneflower, echinacea, and Oregon grape root

AGING

Aging, although a natural process that is inevitable as we grow older, is accelerated with poor dietary habits, lack of exercise, negative thinking, and abuse of the body.

Research shows that as we grow older, changes in metabolism and the conversion of food to energy cause an increase in the daily requirements of a number of important nutrients. According to some authorities, the RDAs in their present form may actually result in insufficiencies of certain nutrients, leading to increased risk for later-stage diseases. Many conditions are not necessarily "old-age diseases" but diseases resulting from suboptimal nutrition consumed over a period of time that increases the risk for these conditions later in life. Recognition is growing that specific nutrients, such as vitamins B_6, B_{12}, C, D, and E and the minerals calcium, sulfur, zinc, magnesium, potassium, iron, and chromium, may be required in significantly larger amounts as we grow older to optimize functioning in the body.

One of the most important steps we can take to help prevent premature aging is to make sure we have an adequate intake of antioxidants, especially proanthocyanidins (PC-95), which prevent free-radical damage. PC-95 and vitamin C are crucial antioxidants that prevent cross-linking, which is largely caused by free-radical damage and is commonly associated with aging of the skin. Cross-linking refers to the bonds that hold the outer surface skin cells together. As you grow older, these bonds become more cross-linked and stronger. The cells do not shed as easily as they did when you were younger. The outermost layer of skin cells therefore becomes "older" and thicker, causing a leathery look.

Every man desires to live long:
but no man would be old.

—JONATHAN SWIFT

Cross-linking at the molecular level causes the skin (and the body) to be less agile. Cross-linking can occur at all levels of cell functions, including the nucleic acids, DNA, and RNA, which are the master instructors of the cell. In this case, the cells cannot function properly and abnormal cells result.

Free radicals are believed to be the cause of destruction and death in nearly all living things. Compounded by environmental pollution, food additives, cured meats, tobacco smoke, alcohol, infection, stress, chemotherapy, asbestos, x-rays, pesticides, and other pollutants, free radicals can multiply at an alarming rate.

Free radicals can attack, damage, and ultimately destroy any material, not just the sensitive cells and tissues of the skin and inside the body. Free radicals degrade collagen and reprogram DNA and are implicated in more than 60 diseases.

Sunshine is a harmful influence to your skin. Years of exposure to the sun exaggerates and accelerates one's natural aging process. It is the primary cause of premature aging causing wrinkling, thinning of the skin, the appearance or darkening of brownish discolorations known as "age spots," and broken blood vessels. Sunshine accelerates the normal loss of moisture and elasticity of the skin. Twenty years of sunning can leave you looking 15 to 20 years older than you really are. UV rays are also a primary cause of skin cancer.

Because of its external exposure, the skin is subject to aging faster than our other organs. The epidermis is greatly affected by external factors, both good and bad. The dermis is affected only by internal factors, again, good and bad. The skin, especially the epidermis, is vulnerable to wear and tear and therefore, unlike the other organs in the body (provided we do not abuse them), is not maintenance free.

When the skin begins to age, the following occurs:

1. The skin becomes thinner.
2. Fewer skin cells are produced.
3. Skin cells grow more slowly.
4. The outermost layer (stratum corneum) becomes less effective for protection.
5. The skin retains less water.
6. Blood vessels become fewer.
7. Sweat and oil gland activity decreases, leading to dryness and itching.
8. Collagen and elastin fibers become more rigid and cross-linked, causing the skin to wrinkle and sag.

Loss and redistribution of fat tend to emphasize sagging and wrinkles. Wrinkles will usually appear first where the skin is the most thin, such as around the eyes and eyelids, the neck, and the jaw line. Eventually, jowls develop, the neck becomes creased, lines begin to radiate from the mouth, and "crow's feet" and "bags" develop around the eyes.

Dry skin contributes to skin problems such as scaling, cracking, eczema, irritation, and infection. Dryness of the skin also accentuates existing wrinkles, making them look deeper and more abundant.

What to Do

To prevent premature aging, follow this advice:

- Preventive nutrition is the best defense against mental and physical aging. The diet should include natural unprocessed foods that contain adequate amounts of all essential nutrients, as well as a plentiful supply of antioxidants, such as proanthocyanidins and vitamin C. Supplementation is crucial. Studies show proanthocyanidins provide a natural sunscreen against ultraviolet rays.[84]
- Free-radical damage can be greatly reduced by other antioxidants as well, including vitamins A and E, beta carotene, lipoic acid, bioflavonoids (i.e., activated quercetin), zinc, selenium, and the amino acids cysteine and glutathione.
- A diet very high in bromelain (pineapple) and papain (papaya) can help offset negative effects from the sun.
- Avoid alcoholic beverages or drink only in moderation.
- Do not smoke and avoid others that smoke.
- Exercise regularly. Walking, biking, swimming, or gardening are good choices.
- Get seven to eight hours of sleep each night.
- Eliminate or reduce stress.
- Get fresh air every day if possible.

- To prevent aging of the skin, use a sunscreen with a minimum SPF (sun protection factor) of 15, especially on the face, if you are going to be outdoors. Wear a hat to help keep the sun off your face. Also be sure to increase your intake of PC-95, vitamin C, and MSM whenever you are going to be spending time in the sun.
- Periodic baths of apple cider or olive oil can be very rejuvenating for the skin. They can also be used for massage.
- Keep the body cleansed of toxins by drinking lots of distilled water and using cleansing herbs.

Beneficial Supplementation

"Aging" is a relative term for toxic buildup in the cells of the body and/or nutritional deficiency. Both of these issues are addressed with the following supplements:

- Beta carotene (including marine carotenes): 10,000-30,000 IU daily
- Vitamin C: (Ester-C®) 2,000–6,000 mg daily
- B complex: 50 mg daily
- Vitamin E: 400 IU daily
- Chromium: 200 mcg daily
- Selenium: 200 mcg minimum daily
- Zinc: 30 mg daily
- MSM: 3,000 mg daily
- Antioxidants, such as PC-95: 180 mg daily
- Cleansing herbs: Ginger, aloe leaf powder, garlic, cascara sagrada, barberry root, dandelion, red clover, buckthorn, cayenne, and milk thistle extract (such as in WOW)
- Other herbs: Alfalfa, damiana, dong quai, garlic, ginseng, gotu kola, pau d'arco, spirulina, and chlorella

ALCOHOLISM

Alcoholism is a dependence on or an addiction to alcohol. Alcohol is a depressant that decreases the basic speed of all bodily functions. Heavy alcohol use can cause hepatitis, cirrhosis of the liver, gastritis (painful inflammation of the stomach lining), neuritis (inflammation of the nerves), damage to the brain, and vitamin and mineral deficiencies.

Alcohol is a carbohydrate, but it contains none of the vitamins or minerals that are needed for carbohydrate metabolism. Therefore, vitamins and minerals, especially B complex, vitamin C, zinc, magnesium, and potassium, are taken from other parts of the body and are readily depleted. In addition, vitamins A, B_1, B_2, B_6, B_{12}, and D, folic acid, sulfur, and calcium are lost.

Complications and symptoms of alcoholism include food allergies, blackouts, dizziness, slurred speech, incoordination, nervousness, irritability, tremors, heart disease, liver disease, increased cholesterol levels, high blood pressure, *Candida albicans* (commonly called "yeast") overgrowth, and blood-sugar disorders.

Alcoholism can be triggered by a poor diet consisting of refined foods and excess sugar. Other causes include vitamin and mineral deficiencies—especially B complex—excess coffee, hypoglycemia, stress, psychological addiction, and heredity.

Often the underlying cause is a candida infection creating strong sugar cravings. It is crucial that the yeast infection be treated along with the alcoholism.

What to Do

If you consume alcohol, follow these tips:

- Avoid overindulgence, and if symptoms of alcoholism occur or alcohol is consumed to a point where it interferes with the performance of daily activities, avoid alcohol completely. Consider counseling or outside assistance, such as Alcoholics Anonymous, for support.

- To help prevent a hangover, take a B complex supplement before going out, while you are drinking, and in the morning to help replace the B vitamins lost. Note: Vitamin B_1 deficiency (beriberi) is very common in the late stages of alcoholism.
- Vitamin C intravenously (20–30 grams daily) can help reduce withdrawal symptoms.
- For liver support and regeneration, supplement with the herbs silymarin (milk thistle extract), dandelion root, garlic, and barberry. Antioxidants such as PC-95 and lipoic acid are also very helpful. See also the section on the liver on page 337.
- Selenium also helps protect against alcohol-induced liver damage.
- To aid in recovery from alcoholism, one requires a stable blood sugar level. Eliminate refined carbohydrates, especially white sugar and white flour, maintain a diet high in protein, and note the suggested supplementation below.
- Because alcohol is a diuretic, drink distilled water while you are drinking and afterward to replenish lost fluids and supplement trace minerals to replenish lost electrolytes.

To treat candida yeast infection, see the section on yeast infection beginning on page 381.

To aid in detoxification, see chapter 17.

Cravings

To reduce cravings for alcohol, try the following:

- Vitamin B_3 (niacin) and the amino acid glutamine have been shown to help prevent the craving for alcohol. Glutamine also decreases the harmful poisoning effects of alcohol.

- MSM can also help reduce alcohol cravings.
- St.-John's-wort and angelica reduce alcohol cravings.
- Avoid coffee.
- Avoid nonnutrient junk foods and sugar, which tend to increase cravings for alcohol.
- Supplement with B complex.

Beneficial Supplementation

The following supplements have been shown to be beneficial for people with alcoholism:

- Beta carotene: 25,000–50,000 IU daily
- B Complex: 100–300 mg three times daily
- Vitamin B_3: 100 mg to 6 grams daily
- Vitamin C (Ester-C®): 3,000–10,000 mg daily
- Vitamin E: 1,000 IU daily
- Chromium: 200–400 mcg daily
- Magnesium: 1,000 mg daily
- Selenium: 200 mcg daily
- Zinc: 150 mg daily
- MSM: 4,000 mg or more daily
- Glutamine: 2,000 mg two to three times daily
- Silymarin (milk thistle extract): 300 mg daily
- PC-95: 200 mg daily
- Lipoic acid: 200–400 mg daily
- Probiotics (Colon Essentials): two to three times daily
- Herbs: Alfalfa, angelica, artichoke extract, cayenne, goldenseal, valerian, skullcap, chaparral, hops, and red clover

Let challenges make you a better person,
not a bitter person!

—ANONYMOUS

ALLERGIES

An allergy is a sensitivity to some particular substance known as an allergen. An allergen can be a food; an inhalant such as pollen, mold, dust, animal dander, or hair; an insect sting; chemicals; and a number of additional other substances. Most allergens are protein in nature.

An allergic reaction may take the form of hay fever (e.g., watery eyes, runny nose, sinus stuffiness), asthma, hives, eczema, high blood pressure, abnormal fatigue, abnormal hunger, stomach cramps, vomiting, anxiety, depression and other mental disorders, constipation, stomach ulcers, dizziness, headache, hyperactivity, insomnia, and hypoglycemia. Allergies are often difficult to detect. For example, an individual who suffers from recurring colds may actually be suffering from an unidentified food allergy.

Susceptibility to an allergen depends on heredity and the condition of one's immune system. Stress and hypoglycemia (adrenal exhaustion), poor diet (vitamin C and B complex deficiency), high copper levels, inadequate antioxidant levels, inadequate sleep, poor elimination, emotional trauma, and infection can weaken the immune system, making a person more susceptible to an allergic reaction.

What to Do

If you experience allergies, follow this advice:

- Be sure to take 300 mg of proanthocyanidins (PC-95) and 5,000 mg of vitamin C (Ester-C®) for the crucial antioxidant support you need. Vitamin C is essential to adrenal function and acts as an antihistamine as well. Proanthocyanidins also help remove histamine from the blood.

- MSM (4,000–6,000 mg daily) is also very important to support the health of mucus membrane tissues (such as inside the oral, nasal, and sinus cavities and also inside the lungs) to enhance cellular metabolism.

- Watercress is an old folk remedy for traditional allergy symptoms: sneezing, stuffy head, and watery eyes.
- B complex vitamins, especially B_6, are essential for adrenal function. B_5 is essential for cortisone production and acts as an antihistamine.
- Supplement with hydrochloric acid and digestive enzymes. A slowdown in production of these occurs in individuals over 40.
- Colostrum, which contains immune-regulatory factors and other vital immune support nutrients, may be beneficial because allergies are considered an immune dysfunction disorder.

  Note: If you have allergies in your family history and become pregnant, it is of critical importance that you breast-feed your infant to ensure optimal immune development.
- If possible, identify and remove or avoid allergens. Live in a clean environment: vacuum carpets and rugs daily, change vacuum bags frequently, dust daily with an oil-treated cloth so you do not spread dust around, enclose your pillow and box spring in plastic to reduce dust and dust mites, and avoid aerosol sprays and other irritating substances.
- Keep your bedroom free of objects that collect dust, such as carpet, books, and stuffed animals. If possible, get an air purifier or negative ion generator, especially for the bedroom.
- Get plenty of fresh air, especially when you sleep.
- Exercise daily to stimulate the immune system and promote blood flow.
- Avoid foods that have many chemical ingredients, such as commercial bread, catsup, and salad dressing. Hidden ingredients in canned and packaged foods can undo a nonallergenic diet. Many authorities recommend eating no processed foods.

Beneficial Supplementation

The following supplements have been shown to be beneficial for people with allergies:

- Vitamin A: 10,000–25,000 IU daily
- B complex: 50 mg three times daily
- Vitamin B_5: 100–200 mg daily
- Vitamin C (Ester C®): 5,000–7,000 mg daily
- Vitamin E: 400 IU daily
- Magnesium: 1,200–1,600 mg daily
- MSM: 2–6 grams daily
- Selenium: 200 mcg daily
- Zinc: 50 mg daily
- Proanthocyanidins (PC-95): 150–300 mg twice daily
- Colostrum: 1,000 mg three times daily
- Digestive enzymes: Before and after meals
- Herbs: Alfalfa, burdock, comfrey, echinacea, goldenseal, garlic, cayenne, and ginger

ARTHRITIS

Arthritis is a degenerative condition involving inflammation of the joints marked by pain and swelling. Over 100 different kinds of arthritis plague 15 percent of the U.S. population. Currently, managed-care health plans provide little in the way of support for patients with chronic conditions such as arthritis. Drugs intended to treat arthritis are both expensive and potentially risky and have side effects that may include ulcers and bleeding.

The cause of arthritis is not totally understood. Arthritis is thought to be related to the immune system (autoimmunity) and to poor diet, such as excess meat and soda drinks, excess refined carbohydrates (sugar and sweets) and other acid-forming foods, and inadequate raw vegetables. Poor elimination, glandular imbalances, psychological factors, lack of exercise, excess copper levels in the blood, and excess irritants (such as coffee, tea, salt, spices, and alcohol) may be additional causes or contributors.

Some authorities suggest that arthritis may be induced by the intake of too much calcium and the wrong forms of calcium—those the body cannot use. Insoluble calcium migrates to the soft tissues and deposits there. The tissues become calcified and the cells cease to function normally.

The two main types of arthritis are osteoarthritis and rheumatoid arthritis.

Osteoarthritis is the most frequently diagnosed type of arthritis. It involves continuous degeneration of the cartilage at the end of bone joints. These joints don't occur in just fingers and knees—the hips and the back also depend on healthy cartilage to move freely. For sufferers, pain can affect every aspect of life, from opening jars to performing well on the job.

Osteoarthritis usually affects the weight-bearing joints, such as the hips and knees, of elderly individuals. Onset of osteoarthritis is gradual with progressive pain, inflammation, deterioration, and joint enlargement. It may involve single or multiple joints but does not migrate from joint to joint.

Rheumatoid arthritis can affect the whole body instead of just one joint. Synovial membrane (connective tissue) thickens, and joints swell with redness and tenderness. Symmetrical joint involvement is common. Pain may migrate from joint to joint. Subcutaneous nodules are commonly found. Onset can be abrupt or insidious and may be related to physical or emotional stress, poor nutrition, or a bacterial infection.

What to Do

If you have arthritis, follow these tips:

- MSM supplementation supports formation of connective tissue (such as collagen and elastin, which make up cartilage), which is destroyed as part of the disease process. People with arthritis tend to lack the basic building blocks of cartilage.

Many, many people are now realizing that MSM can greatly reduce the joint and bone pain of arthritis. Two well-designed, preliminary studies suggest that MSM relieves arthritis pain at least as well as conventional over-the-counter NSAIDs (nonsteroidal anti-inflammatory drugs) such as ibuprofen (Advil, for example).[85]

In 1997, at the Oregon Health Sciences Center, researchers showed that MSM provided relief equal to that of Advil. Another study, conducted at the UCLA School of Medicine, found that of 16 patients with degenerative arthritis or joint disease, those taking MSM reported an 80 percent reduction in pain after six weeks of therapy. Only two of the patients on a placebo reported any kind of pain relief, and even then, relief was slight.[86]

MSM can relieve pain quickly—too quickly to result from collagen changes alone. Research conducted by MSM expert Dr. Stanley W. Jacob suggests that MSM actually blocks pain signals from traveling along a network of fibers from the site of damaged tissue to the brain. MSM also appears to reduce inflammation, enhance blood flow, and reduce painful muscle spasms.[87]

MSM is present in most foods, especially fresh fruits, vegetables, and dairy foods, but in varying quantities. Pollution, overfarming, irrigation, and deforestation influence soil MSM content. Cooking and food processing also destroy MSM.

- Vitamin C is very important because it is needed for the body to produce collagen and elastin as it works with MSM. Vitamin C also increases natural cortisone production, which is anti-inflammatory and helpful to the adrenals. While most people need at least 2,000 mg daily, individuals with arthritis may benefit from taking 3,000 to 20,000 mg daily.
- Magnesium supplementation will help keep calcium from despositing in the body. Calcium deposits often form in the joints, creating discomfort and disfiguration.
- Niacinamide can increase joint mobility by 85 percent if taken daily for three to four weeks. It is especially

beneficial for people with osteoarthritis, although those
with rheumatoid arthritis can also benefit. If nausea
occurs, reduce the dose.

- Proanthocyanidins (PC-95), as powerful natural antioxidants needed to help heal and reduce tissue damage
  caused by inflammation, are very effective for rheumatoid arthritis. PC-95 can also help reduce inflammation
  and enhance the effectiveness of other antioxidants in
  the body.

- Colostrum, which contains immune-regulatory factors
  as well as other vital immune support nutrients, may be
  beneficial because arthritis is considered an auto-immune
  disorder. Colostrum also contains anti-inflammatory
  agents, which can offer relief to individuals with arthritis.

- A diet free of red meat, white flour, white sugar, salt,
  citrus fruits, and/or the nightshade family (tomatoes,
  potatoes, green pepper, and eggplant) is helpful for relief
  of arthritis because it alkalizes the body.

- Get plenty of rest each day. Take naps if you need to.

- Do not skip exercise, even if you have a painful flareup.
  Exercise is very important to stimulate blood and lymphatic flow to the affected areas.

- Respect your pain. If a joint becomes painful for several
  hours after an activity, do not repeat the activity until
  the pains leaves.

- Use "contrast baths" for aching hands and feet. Place
  them in warm water for three minutes, then cold water
  for one minute.

Beneficial Supplementation

The following supplements have been shown to be beneficial for
people with arthritis:

- Vitamin A: 25,000–50,000 IU daily
- B complex (extra B_6 and B_{12}): 50 mg daily

- Niacin or niacinamide: 200–2,000 mg daily
- Vitamin C (Ester-C® or pharmaceutical grade C power): 3,000-20,000 mg
- Vitamin D: 1,600–3,000 IU daily
- Vitamin E: 400 IU daily
- Balanced mineral formula: 1,500 mg daily
- MSM: 3–10 grams daily
- Glucosamine: 1,200–2,000 mg daily
- Proanthocyanidins (PC-95): 300 mg daily or more if needed
- Colostrum: 1,000 mg four or more times daily
- Digestive enzymes: two to four tablets three times daily
- Essential fatty acids, especially EPA and DHA: 3,000 mg daily
- Cleansing herbs: Ginger, aloe leaf powder, garlic, cascara sagrada, barberry root, dandelion, red clover, buckthorn, cayenne, and milk thistle extract (such as found in WOW).

ASTHMA

Asthma is a chronic respiratory condition characterized by difficult breathing, coughing, and a feeling of suffocation. Attacks can last for several minutes or several days.

An asthma attack may be triggered by an allergen, irritants, emotions, low blood sugar, or disorders of the adrenal glands. Asthma may be associated with diet (excess carbohydrates and sweets, excess dairy products, and overeating), food additives (especially sulfites), and poor elimination.

What to Do

If you have asthma, follow these tips:

- Coffee, which contains caffeine, has been shown to relieve asthma symptoms. Caffeine, equivalent to two cups of coffee, can open constricted bronchial passages.

- In emergencies, the Chinese herb Ma Huang, which contains ephedrine, is very useful as a bronchodilator.
- Asthma weed is useful for most asthmatics. Use 25 drops of tincture in a small amount of water two to four times daily.
- MSM taken in high doses with water can greatly improve lung capacity.
- Magnesium is very important for asthmatics. Fairly high doses are needed.
- Visualization and meditation can be helpful to slow down breathing.
- During an asthma attack, it also may be beneficial to hold onto something above your head so that your arms are raised.
- Maintain a healthy body weight. Being even slightly overweight increases lung stress.
- Avoid common triggers for an attack. These include
  - Extremely cold air
  - Excessive humidity
  - Air pollution
  - Tobacco smoke
  - Overeating
  - Exercise
  - Infections caused by viruses
  - Laughing
  - Fumes: cologne, paint, paint thinner, bleach, or gasoline
  - Stress or emotions (anger, fear, excitement, etc.)
  - Allergens (pollen, mold, spores, animal dander, hair, feathers, grain dust, etc.)
  - Certain foods—chocolate, nuts, eggs, sweets, refined foods, excessive carbohydrates, excessive wheat and dairy products, additives, alcohol, tea—other nonfood irritants, and very hot and very cold foods.

- Sulfites (commonly found in restaurant salads and salad bars, frozen shrimp, potatoes, baked goods, sausage, wine, dairy products, and white sugar and white flour products)

Beneficial Supplementation

Asthma and allergies are closely related; therefore, similar supplement regimens are suggested. In addition, consider these suggestions:

- MSM: 10–20 grams (capsules or powder or a combination with eight 8 oz glasses of distilled water daily
- Magnesium: 1,200–1,600 mg daily

Rule your mind or it will rule you!

—HORACE

CANCER

While cancer is among the top two causes of death today, the most common types of cancer are generally preventable. Chemical and environmental factors may be responsible for 90 percent of all cancers. Exposure to these factors is largely our own responsibility. Additional cancer risk factors that are more difficult to control include genetics, age, hormone imbalances, and toxic buildup in the cells, especially the colon.

Environmental and chemical factors include the following: sexual practices, excessive use of alcohol, tobacco, many drugs and chemicals, and the presence of carcinogens and chemicals in food.

In the body, the major contributors to cancer can be categorized into four divisions:

1. Free-radical stress
2. Liver toxicity
3. Toxic buildup in the colon
4. Stressors, mental and physical (including chemicals)

This brief overview cannot possibly do this subject justice and therefore I strongly recommend four excellent books: *Cancer and Nutrition* by Dr. Charles Simone (Avery Publishing), *The Cancer Industry* by Ralph Moss (Paragon House Publishing), *A Cancer Therapy* by Max Gerson (Gerson Institute), and *Alkalize or Die* by Theodore Baroody (Holographic Health Press).

Cancer cells are abnormal cells that proliferate out of control in the body. They multiply to form tumors that invade neighboring tissues. They rob normal cells of essential nutrients, causing malnutrition and wasting. Cancer cells can also spread and progressively create havoc throughout the entire body. Symptoms depend on the type and location of the cancer.

Free radicals are largely responsible for the development of abnormalities and cellular damage. When free radicals damage the cell's genetic material, RNA and DNA, the cell mutates.

Fighting Cancer

The key to fighting cancer is to prevent it. Abnormal cells that are potentially cancerous are continually produced throughout the body. It is the responsibility of the white blood cells to rid the body of these abnormal cells before they can multiply and cause harm. But continued exposure to carcinogenic substances, such as tobacco, pesticide residues, and chemicals found in certain drugs, weakens the immune system. If the body is maintained in good health, not abused, and not overwhelmed with chemicals in foods or drugs, stress, obesity, or nutrient deficiencies, then the body can fight off cancerous cells, keeping them in check. Through diet and supplementation, we can provide the immune system all it needs to keep us healthy.

Cancer-fighting phytochemicals are found in various foods, such as broccoli, cauliflower, brussels sprouts, and grape seed. Such foods contain a host of disease-fighting, immune-promoting compounds that can render carcinogens harmless.

Broccoli is also a good source of vitamin C (a powerful antioxidant that also stimulates T lymphocytes [T cells] to produce interferon and reduces harm from nitrates), as are tomatoes and many berries and citrus fruits.

Flavonoids, found in all fruits and vegetables, especially citrus and berries, keep cancer-causing hormones from latching onto cells.

Garlic and onions contain sulfides that seem to protect against stomach cancer. They stimulate enzymes within cells that detoxify cancer-causing chemicals.

The health benefits of beta carotene are widely recognized. While carrots usually receive most of the glory for providing large amounts of this protective nutrient, beta carotene is also found in dark green leafy vegetables such as kale, spinach, and broccoli, and fruits such as cantaloupe and papaya.

Antioxidants are one of the keys to cancer prevention as they protect us from free-radical damage. Antioxidant nutrients donate one of their many electrons to stabilize a free-radical molecule and thereby neutralize its harmful effects. Without antioxidants, free radicals rob electrons from healthy cells, causing them to weaken and become susceptible to damage.

Over a hundred different studies suggest that eating fruits and vegetables rich in vitamin C, beta carotene, and proanthocyanidins or taking antioxidant supplements is linked to a reduced risk of virtually all cancers.[88]

Melatonin is another powerful antioxidant that should be part of any cancer prevention regimen or fight against cancer—especially for the prostate for men and breast and uterine cells for women.

Colostrum is a powerful immune enhancer. It is a rich source of transforming growth factors (TGFs)—which are polypeptides that promote cell proliferation, tissue repair, and wound healing—and has anticancer properties. Lactoferrin, also found in colostrom, is an iron-building protein and is believed to have the ability to bond to excess iron ions, therefore inhibiting the growth of microorganisms and tumors. Researchers have shown colostrum's effectiveness against cancer cells—specifically against lymphoma, bone, breast, and other cancer types.[89]

Proanthocyanidins protect us from damage from radical agents to DNA, cellular membranes, lipids, and proteins. Researchers at the Center for Cancer Causation and Prevention, AMC Cancer Research Center, Denver, Colorado, made the following powerful statement in the prominent medical journal *Carcinogenesis:* "Procyanidins present in grape seeds are known to exert anti-inflammatory, anti-arthritic and anti-allergic activities, prevent skin aging, scavenge oxygen free radicals and inhibit UV radiation-induced peroxidation activity." They continued, "Since most of these events are associated with the tumor promotion stage of carcinogenesis, these studies suggest that grape seed polyphenols and the procyanidins present therein could be anticarcinogenic and/or anti-tumor-promoting agents."[90]

Their research concluded, "These results show that grape seed polyphenols possess high anti-tumor-promoting activity due to the strong antioxidant effect of procyanidins present therein. In summary, grape seed polyphenols in general and procyanidin B5-3'-gallate in particular, should be studied in more detail to be developed as cancer chemopreventive and/or anticarcinogenic agents."[91]

Many other researchers have also demonstrated the powerful antioxidant and anticancer properties of proanthocyanidins. Most recently, Angelo John of the A.P. John Institute for Cancer Research got some remarkable results with his CAAT Therapy, PC-95, and oleuropein.

Sixteen Easy Steps to Cancer Prevention

Cancer is a disease that we all want to avoid. It causes pain and suffering to the afflicted and all those in support of them. Each day we are bombarded with toxic carcinogens in the foods we eat, the air we breathe, and the liquids we drink. I believe that our best defense is prevention, so I have included the following plan that I believe may help you get started.

1. *Maintain an ideal weight.* Even if you are only five pounds overweight, lose it. Decrease your daily caloric

intake (eliminate saturated fat) and exercise regularly. Stay active. Take the stairs instead of the elevator. Walk a few blocks instead of always taking the closest parking spot. Regular colon cleansing is also very beneficial.

2. *Eat a low-fat (good fats), low-cholesterol diet.* Increase the intake of vegetable protein sources, such as beans, which are naturally low in fat and contain no saturated fat. Fish and flaxseeds containing omega-3 fatty acids are also good. Eat nonfat dairy products instead of high-fat ones. Minimize your intake of meat, and avoid or eliminate processed meats, such as luncheon meats, which contain nitrates. Avoid or eliminate fried foods. Limit oils and fats. Learn to enjoy the taste of foods without fatty condiments.

   Animal fats increase unfriendly bacteria in the colon, which produce carcinogens. Animal fats do not break down rapidly, slowing the transit time (the time it takes to eliminate the waste products from the food consumed). The longer these carcinogens linger in the intestinal tract and colon, the more time they have to create trouble. Fiber increases transit time and helps carry fats out of the body.

3. *Eat lots of fiber, at least 30 grams a day.* The average daily consumption in the United States is probably less than 10 grams. Include fruits, vegetables and *whole* grains. For example, oatmeal is good, but whole oats or steel-cut oats are much better. Eat a variety of high-fiber foods, such as barley, millet, quinoa, amaranth, flaxseed, lentils, and beans.

   Colon cancer is the second most common form of cancer. Red meat, cholesterol, animal fat, and low fiber consumption, not enough water, along with a sedentary lifestyle, are the major contributors to a sluggish colon and colon cancer. Remember, animal products (meat and dairy) contain no fiber at all. The longer that old fecal matter remains in the colon, the more toxins are absorbed into the bloodstream and affect every cell and organ of the body.

4. *Eat lots of fruits and vegetables (especially cruciferous).* Broccoli, cabbage, cauliflower, brussels sprouts, tomatoes, and carrots have all been shown to contain numerous anticancer phytochemicals.

5. *Utilize nutritional and herbal supplements.* Supplement your diet with vitamins, minerals, antioxidants, and herbs in the proper dosages and combinations for your lifestyle.

6. *Avoid chemicals.* Eliminate MSG (monosodium glutamate), salt, nitrates, and food additives. Eat no barbecued, smoked, or pickled foods. Eat organically grown foods whenever possible.

7. *Avoid caffeine.* Coffee, tea, many soft drinks, chocolate, and many other substances contain caffeine, a harsh stimulant and diuretic.

8. *Avoid tobacco.* Do not smoke or chew tobacco or inhale other people's smoke.

9. *Avoid alcohol.* Consume only minimal amounts (three to five drinks per week—preferably red wine, which contains proanthocyanidins). Alcohol creates havoc on the liver, brain cells, and immune system.

10. *Avoid radiation and unprotected sunlight.* Have x-rays taken only when necessary. Use a sunscreen with an appropriate SPF when outdoors. (See the sections on aging and skin cancer for more information on these subjects.)

11. *Cleanse the colon and liver.* Use herbal formulas such as WOW and European silymarin (Livalon) to support regeneration of the liver (the major detoxification organ in the body).

12. *Maintain a healthy personal environment.* Keep the air, water, and workplace clean. Minimize electromagnetic

exposure (from power lines, cell phones, transfer stations, etc.).

13. *Avoid drugs.* Avoid hormones and any unnecessary drugs.

14. *Exercise.* Exercise is a great way to relax, stimulate immune function, stimulate the lymphatic system, and reduce stress. The lymphatic system does not have a "pump" as the heart does for the circulatory system, but exercise helps increase fluid movement and aids in toxin removal from the body.

15. *Meditate or pray.* Meditation and prayer have been shown to have a beneficial effect on the immune system and health and also to reduce stress.

16. *Be familiar with what is normal for you and your body.* Everyone is different. Learn the seven early warning signs of cancer:

   • Lump in breast
   • Change in wart or mole
   • Sore that will not heal
   • Change in bowel or bladder habits
   • Persistent cough or hoarseness
   • Indigestion or trouble swallowing
   • Unusual bleeding or discharge

   Other important signs are abnormal weight loss and unusually low energy.

An annual physical exam after age 40 is also very important. Find a physician whom you trust to monitor your ongoing health status through regular checkups. It is always better when a problem is detected early. Best, of course, is prevention through the 16 easy steps outlined above.

Beneficial Supplementation

The following supplements have been shown to be beneficial for cancer prevention:

- B complex (especially folic acid, B_2, B_5, B_6, and B_{12})
- Antioxidant nutrients such as
  - Vitamin A or beta carotene: 10,000 IU daily
  - Vitamin C (Ester-C® or pharmaceutical-grade powder): 5,000 mg or more daily
  - Vitamin D: 2,500 IU daily
  - Vitamin E: Up to 800 IU daily to strengthen cell membranes against invasion of viruses and toxins
  - Proanthocyanidins (PC-95): 300 mg daily
  - Zinc: 100 mg daily to boost anticancer activity of the T cells
- Selenium: 200 mcg daily to help build glutathione perioxidase, a powerful antioxidant in all cells
- Melatonin: 3–9 mg daily
- Colostrum: 4,000 mg daily
- Germanium: Up to 100 mg daily to boost interferon production in the body. Among many other sources, it is found in aloe vera and exists in extremely high concentrations in "healing waters" throughout the world.
- Chromium picolinate: 400 mcg daily
- Balanced trace mineral formula: 1,200 mg daily
- MSM: 10 grams or more daily
- Probiotics: Especially protective against colon cancer like *L. acidophilus*, *B. bifidum*, and *S. thermophilus.*
- Amino acids: Especially L-carnitine, which improves fat utilization
- Flaxseed: 2 tbl freshly ground seeds added to protein shakes, cereals, nonfat cottage cheese, nonfat yogurt, or baked goods; high in lignan fiber and omega-3 fatty acids
- Shark liver oil: 2,500 mg daily; product should contain a minimum of 20 percent alkylglycerols, which stimulate immunity through increased production of white blood

cells. This oil has also been shown to reduce injuries among individuals undergoing radiation therapy.

- Cleansing herbs: Ginger, aloe leaf powder, garlic, cascara sagrada, barberry root, dandelion, red clover, buckthorn, cayenne, and milk thistle extract (such as found in WOW).
- Other herbs: Alfalfa (high in fiber, saponins, and trace minerals), astragalus (potent antioxidant), burdock root (antitumor activity), chaparral (anti-inflammatory, promotes healing), echinacea (immune booster), garlic and onion (immune boosters), ginkgo (powerful anti-oxidant), ginseng (stimulates healing and immunity), goldenseal (stimulates immunity), and turmeric (anti-inflammatory, promotes healing)

And don't forget to drink a minimum of eight 8 oz. glasses of distilled water daily!

CIRCULATION PROBLEMS (VENOUS INSUFFICIENCY)

The circulatory system is responsible for transporting blood (carrying vital oxygen and nutrients) to every part of the body. A continuous supply is needed, and therefore the integrity of the circulatory system, made up of capillaries, arteries, and veins, is of crucial importance.

While venous insufficiency can be due to a number of causes, one important cause is pharmaceutical drug damage. Many drugs are very caustic to the vascular system, and extended use can lead to vascular insufficiencies.

Proanthocyanidins have clearly demonstrated their ability to enhance microcirculation throughout the body by inhibiting capillary permeability. Proanthocyanidins are also known to help normalize platelet aggregation in the blood.[92] See chapter 14 for more on this topic.

In the course of clinical testing with proanthocyanidins in the treatment of venous insufficiency, improvement was observable during the first weeks of treatment. This result, plus the absence of adverse effects and the benefit of a once-a-day administration, justifies the use of proanthocyanidins in the treatment of noncomplicated chronic venous insufficiency.

(Note: I suggest amounts of 300 mg or higher daily. I have witnessed faster improvement with even higher levels.)

Lipoic acid in doses of 600 mg (200 mg three times daily) has also shown to be very beneficial for various circulatory disorders.[93]

Problems Associated with Poor Circulation

The following are common circulatory problems.

Bruises Bruises are caused by breaks in small blood vessels in the soft tissue beneath the skin. These breaks leak blood, which causes a reddish mark on the surface of the skin. Bruises turn blue then yellow as the blood is gradually absorbed. Factors that make one susceptible to bruising are overweight, anemia, time of menstrual cycle, and lack of Vitamins C or D, bioflavonoids, or zinc. Too much aspirin can also cause bruising.

DMSO (dimethyl sulfoxide, a natural substance derived from wood pulp), applied externally, may prevent the discoloration of bruises. DMSO acts as a scavenger of free radicals that are produced when blood vessels are damaged.

Claudication Claudication is pain in the calf or legs that comes and goes. Claudication typically is felt while walking and subsides with rest. It is, therefore, commonly referred to as "intermittent claudication." In severe claudication, the pain is also felt at rest.

The usually intermittent nature of the pain of claudication is due to a temporary inadequate supply of oxygen to the leg muscles. The poor oxygen supply is a result of narrowing of the arteries that supply the leg with blood. This is felt especially when the oxygen requirement of the leg muscles rises with exercise or walking.

Intermittent claudication can be due to temporary artery narrowing due to spasm of the artery (vasospasm), permanent artery narrowing due to atherosclerosis, or the complete blockage of an artery of the leg. It is more common in men than in women. The condition affects 1–2 percent of the population under 60 years of age, 3–4 percent of persons age 60 to 70, and over 5 percent of persons over 70.

Polyneuropathy Polyneuropathy describes a problem with the functioning of the nerves outside of the spinal cord. The symptoms of a neuropathy may include numbness, weakness, burning pain (especially at night), and loss of reflexes. The pain may be severe and disabling. One of the most common causes of neuropathy is the decrease in microcirculation commonly seen in Type II diabetics as a result of free-radical stress.

Antioxidants such an proanthocyanidins and lipoic acid are very effective for relief of pain and restoration of circulation for healing.

Other causes include nutritional deficiencies, such as B_{12} and folate deficiency, medications, and chemical exposures.

Varicose Veins Varicose veins are veins that have become abnormally enlarged, twisted, and swollen. They may occur anywhere but are most commonly found in the legs. Varicose veins can be caused by weakened valves, weakened vein walls, or inflammation in the veins.

Factors that may contribute to development of varicose veins are obesity, heredity, tight clothing, sedentary lifestyle, crossing the legs, pregnancy, and nutritional deficiencies (especially a lack of antioxidants). Symptoms include leg pain, muscle cramps, fatigue of leg muscles, ankle swelling, and ulcers.

What to Do

For circulatory problems, try the following:

- Lipoic acid and proanthocyanidins (PC-95) are probably the most beneficial supplements to strengthen the capillary walls.
- B-Complex (Roex), 2 tablets daily, is recommended
- Other antioxidants (vitamins A, C and E, glutathione, zinc, selenium and bioflavonoids) can also help strengthen capillary walls.

- MSM and vitamin C can also help strengthen the veins as they are needed for healthy collagen tissue.
- Adequate amounts of the B complex vitamins and vitamin C are necessary for the maintenance of strong blood vessels.
- Vitamin E can dilate blood vessels and improve circulation.
- Topical application of white oak bark (i.e., oak bark poultice or salve) has proven to be helpful against varicose veins. It helps to strengthen the veins.
- Avoid refined carbohydrates (especially sugar).

Beneficial Supplementation

The following supplements have been shown to be beneficial for people with circulatory problems:

- Lipoic acid: 200 mg one to two times a day
- Proanthocyanidins (PC-95): 300-600 mg daily
- MSM: 2,000 mg or more three to four times a day
- Vitamin C (Ester-C®): 1,000 mg or more three to four times a day
- Vitamin A: 20,000 IU daily
- Vitamin D: 2,000 IU daily
- B complex (Roex): 2 tablets daily
- Vitamin E: 600 IU daily
- Flaxseed oil: 3–4 tbsp daily
- Herbs: Butcher's broom, capsicum, goldenseal, horsetail, kelp, oatstraw, parsley, white oak bark, and witch hazel

DIABETES

Diabetes is a metabolic disorder characterized by a decreased ability or complete inability of the body to utilize carbohydrates (glucose). Diabetics produce an insufficient amount of the hormone insulin, or they produce it but for some reason cannot use it. Insulin is essential for the conversion of glucose to energy. Therefore, in diabetics, glucose cannot be converted to energy and instead is accumulated in the blood, resulting in symptoms that range from mental confusion to coma.

Diabetes is a chronic degenerative disease, meaning all vital organs and tissues are affected by the condition in a negative manner. Diabetes can often lead to additional complications, such as atherosclerosis, loss of sight, kidney disease, gangrene, coma, and premature death.

Symptoms of diabetes include extreme thirst, frequent urination, sugar in the urine, increased appetite, loss of weight, fatigue, muscle cramps, impaired vision, itching, and slow-healing wounds.

The following factors are associated with the development of diabetes: high intake of simple carbohydrates (especially sugar), nutritional deficiencies, excess intake of saturated fat, pregnancy, surgery, physical or emotional stress, adrenal exhaustion, heredity, and obesity.

Types of Diabetes

Type I diabetes is insulin-dependent diabetes mellitus, also called juvenile-onset or congenital diabetes. Type I diabetes starts in children, tends to be unstable, and is hard to control.

Type II diabetes is noninsulin-dependent diabetes mellitus, also called adult-onset diabetes. The disease usually begins after the age of 40 but can occur at any age. Approximately 60–90 percent of diabetics are overweight. These individuals are not dependent upon insulin, although many may use it to control their symptoms.

Proanthocyanidins and Diabetes

Many studies have reported on the importance of antioxidant supplementation among diabetics. "In diabetes, a major cause of mortality is from cardiovascular causes, and low levels of antioxidants such as vitamin C have been associated with such complications."[94]

Free-radical production is increased in individuals with diabetes mellitus, and it has been suggested that elevated glucose levels may directly contribute to the generation of oxidative stress. Oxidative stress is a general term used to describe a state of damage caused by reactive oxygen species (ROS). This damage can affect a specific molecule or the entire organism. Reactive oxygen species, such as free radicals and peroxides, represent a class of molecules that are derived from the metabolism of oxygen and exist in all aerobic organisms.

Proanthocyanidins, as an exceptionally effective antioxidant group, are of great value to diabetics. Not only do they help prevent the many complications associated with the disease, most of which are a result of elevated levels of free radicals and low levels of antioxidants, but they also indirectly support insulin production and glucose regulation through protection of pancreatic islets of Langerhans beta cells.[95]

Excess production of nitric oxide (NO) is associated with various diseases, including diabetes. An excessive production of NO in response to cytokines has been shown to be the major cause of the destruction of pancreatic islet of Langerhans beta cells (where insulin is produced) associated with type I (insulin-dependent) diabetes mellitus.[96] Cytokines are nonantibody proteins, secreted by inflammatory leukocytes and some nonleukocytic cells, that act as intercellular mediators. They are produced by a number of tissue or cell types rather than by specialized glands and act locally in a paracrine or autocrine rather than endocrine manner.

The scavenging activity of proanthocyanidins is effective against the production of reactive oxygen and nitrogen species.[97] Vascular complications are major causes of morbidity and mortality in patients with diabetes mellitus. Nitric oxide has an important role in the regulation of vascular tone, and impaired nitric oxide activity could be implicated in the development of diabetic vasculopathy (deterioration of blood vessel walls).[98]

Proanthocyanidins have been used throughout Europe to safely treat and prevent complications associated with diabetes, including neuropathy, macular degeneration, retinopathy, cataracts, renal disease, and atherosclerosis.

What to Do

Treatment by natural means depends on the severity and the length of insulin dependency. While congenital or juvenile-onset diabetes can never be corrected completely through diet alone and requires insulin, proper diet does help.

Mild cases of adult-onset diabetes are easy to control. If insulin is used for prolonged periods, the pancreas may be suppressed to the degree that it has literally ceased to function. The body can become dependent upon exogenous insulin and may reduce its own insulin production.

The following are important considerations for a proper diet:

- A diet high in unrefined complex carbohydrates is the most beneficial for diabetics of all types. The diet should consist of no simple or refined carbohydrates (no sugar).
- Fats consumed should be vegetarian and unsaturated.
- No red meat should be consumed. Chicken and fish should be restricted to several times per week. Vegetarian protein sources are recommended, such as whole grains, nuts (almonds, cashews, peanuts, etc.), seeds (pumpkin, sesame, sunflower, etc.), soybeans, black beans, kidney beans, navy beans, and pinto beans.
- Some diabetics may need to avoid fruit and fruit juices, depending on their individual condition.
- Much of the diet should be composed of raw foods.
- Meals should be small and eaten five to six times a day.

- Liver cleansing and strengthening with milk thistle extract (silymarin) enhances glucose regulation.

- Antioxidants such as lipoic acid, oleuropein, and PC-95 are often used to prevent and treat neuropathy, macular degeneration, and other complications commonly associated with diabetes. Lipoic acid also supports liver health.

- Colostrum contains insulin-like growth factors that are very beneficial for diabetics. Many diabetics report great improvement while taking colostrum supplements.

- Olive leaf extract has a protective effect on capillary walls—very important for diabetics. It is also thought to have a beneficial impact on insulin.

- Exercise is very important to help manage body weight and to stimulate hormone production.

- Colon cleansing is very important to help keep toxins out of the body.

Important Foods for Diabetes

These foods have a natural insulin-like action in the body and should be considered for inclusion in the diet in high quantities.

- Brewer's yeast
- Brussels sprouts
- Buckwheat
- Cucumbers
- Fiber (flaxseeds, wheat bran, oat bran, guar gum)
- Garlic
- Green beans
- Jerusalem artichokes
- Oats
- Raw vegetables
- Soybeans/tofu
- Spirulina
- Wheat germ

Beneficial Supplementation

The following supplements have been shown to be beneficial for diabetes:

- B complex: 50 mg three times daily
- Vitamin C (Ester-C®): 4,000 mg or more daily
- Vitamin D: 2,000 IU daily
- Vitamin E: 400–1,000 IU daily
- Chromium picolinate: 400–600 mcg daily
- Magnesium: 500 mg daily
- Potassium: 200 mg daily
- Zinc: 50 mg daily
- Balanced mineral formula without iron: 1,200 mg daily
- Lipoic acid: 600 mg daily
- Proanthocyanidins (PC-95): 100–300 mg daily
- Olive leaf extract: 1,000–2,000 mg daily
- Milk thistle extract: 300 mg daily
- Digestive enzymes: Before and after meals
- Colostrum: 4,000 mg daily
- Cleansing herbs: Ginger, aloe leaf powder, garlic, cascara sagrada, barberry, dandelion, red clover, buckthorn, cayenne, and milk thistle extract (such as found in WOW)
- Other herbs: Alfalfa, burdock, goldenseal, uva ursi (bearberry, a trailing plant of the heath family [*Arctostaphylos uva ursi*]), watercress, and yellow dock

DIGESTIVE DISORDERS

Digestive disorders include gastritis, heartburn, and indigestion, which are symptoms of abnormal digestion. These are characterized by acute or chronic abdominal discomfort, pain, irritation, bloating, or gas and are often accompanied by general malaise, headache, nausea, and sometimes vomiting.

Contributing factors to digestive problems include improper diet (excess refined carbohydrates and sugar, insufficient chewing of foods, hurried meals, snacking, excess strong spices, salt, coffee, tea, alcohol, carbonated beverages, acid-forming foods, and food additives such as preservatives and colorings), food allergies, overeating, digestive enzyme insufficiency, constipation, cigarettes, *Candida albicans* overgrowth, bacterial overgrowth, aspirin and other drugs, stress, lack of exercise, heavy metals, obesity, and pregnancy.

First and foremost, diet changes are necessary:

- Eliminate consumption of refined carbohydrates, especially sugar. Refined carbohydrates are devoid of fiber—which is essential to the elimination process— and cause rapid secretion of gastric acid, resulting in heartburn and other gastrointestinal disorders. Green vegetables and distilled water are the best alkaline elements for maintaining proper pH balance.

- Eliminate excessively large meals. When the stomach is overloaded, the digestive enzymes cannot keep up with the workload, and food that is not completely digested is passed on to the lower small intestine. The result is indigestion, fermentation, and gas. Eating too often can create the same problem.

- Slow down and chew your food. Chewing food is part of the digestion process. Digestive enzymes in the mouth break food down into smaller particles for more adequate digestion in the stomach.

- Acute cases of various digestive problems may require fasting with water with a twist of lemon, diluted apple juice, carrot juice, carrot and cabbage juice, or slippery elm tea. Fasting of this nature can be safe for a period of one to seven days under the supervision of a competent naturopath. This may be followed by a diet regimen of eating simple foods such as brown rice for a few days and then slowly introducing additional foods after that.

Bad Breath

Bad breath (halitosis) can be caused by poor oral hygiene, nose or mouth infection, tonsillitis, tooth and gum decay, constipation, smoking, or the presence of foreign bacteria. Diabetes, nervous tension, chemicals (such as arsenic, lead, bismuth, and methane), or buildup of heavy metals may also be the cause of bad breath.

What to Do

If you experience bad breath, follow this advice:

- Brush your teeth and tongue and floss your teeth.
- Change your toothbrush often since bacteria can hide in toothbrushes and be reinoculated into the mouth.
- Store your toothbrush in a solution of hydrogen peroxide to kill microorganisms.
- Use a mouthwash containing zinc. Zinc is also anti-bacterial.
- Try chewing celery or carrots to help rid the teeth of bacteria and make the mouth cleaner.
- Avoid refined carbohydrates, which can cause tooth decay.
- Supplement with probiotics such as *L. acidophilus*. Bad breath is often associated with putrefactive bacteria living on undigested food in the stomach. This condition causes gas to be released through the breath.
- Supplement with chlorophyll, "nature's deodorant," which helps remove heavy metal poisons and sweetens the breath.
- Supplement with chewable natural digestive enzymes and HCl (hydrochloric acid), the acid component of gastric juice, three times daily immediately after every meal.
- Increase your intake of bran or other fiber: 1 tsp with water before meals.

Beneficial Supplementation

The following supplements have been shown to be beneficial in preventing bad breath:

- Probiotic formula: 20 billion CFUs (10 billion CFUs twice daily) (For best results look for formulations including B. bifidum, S. thermophilus and L. acidolphilus.)
- Chorophyll: 500 mg with each meal
- HCl (hydrochloric acid): 500 mg immediately after meals
- Chewable digestive enzymes: 2–3 with each meal (Look for plant-based formulations that contain amylase, cerecalase, phytase, lipase, glucomylase, peptidase FP, cellulase, invertase, lactase, protease, bromelain, papain, alpha-galactosidase, and acid-stable protease.)
- Herbs: Aloe vera, buckthorn bark, cascara sagrada, garlic, dandelion root, burdock root, red clover, and ginger (a combination provided in WOW)

Constipation

Constipation is characterized by difficulty in passing stools. Commonly, this is due to a diet low in bulk (fiber) and water and high in animal products (especially dairy) and a lack of exercise. Constipation can also result from the use of antacids and certain medications, such as codeine.

Severe chronic constipation is a common disorder among the elderly. This is commonly due to sedentary lifestyle and poor diet. Constipation is often caused by travel (due to changes in water, diet, and daily activities), pregnancy, hypothyroid function, aluminum toxicity, and stress.

In his book, Dr. Bernard Jenson reports that in 1990, a conservative $350 million was spent on laxatives. It is estimated that 200 million people or more in America are constipated.[99]

What to Do

If you suffer from constipation, try the following:

- Increase your intake of distilled water (at least eight 8 oz glasses daily).
- Try helpful foods, including garlic, flaxseed, and fruit—especially apples, papaya, pineapple, prunes, and figs.
- Increase the fiber in your diet—ground flaxseed, apple pectin, bran, psyllium seeds or husks, and so on.
- Increase the amount of exercise you get. At least go for a walk every day. Gradually increase your level of exercise if necessary.
- Take 800 mcg folic acid each day.
- Supplement with probiotics (such as *L. acidophilus*) or eat natural cultured yogurt that contains *L. acidophilus* daily. (Note: Avoid any yogurt that contains sugar, corn syrup, or other artificial sweeteners.)
- Harsh laxatives can rob the body of nutrients, as well as cause rebound constipation and laxative dependency. Laxative abuse can damage the internal wall of the colon and destroy intestinal muscle tone. Avoid harsh laxatives such as senna, castor oil, phenolphthalein, magnesium hydroxide, magnesium sulfite, and sodium sulfite.
- Utilize chewable active plant-based digestive enzymes.

Beneficial Supplementation

The following supplements may help prevent or relieve constipation:

- Folic acid: 800 mcg daily
- Probiotic formula: 20 billion CFUs (10 billion CFUs twice daily) (For best results look for formulations including *B. bifidum*, *S. thermophilus*, and *L. acidolphilus*.)

- Chewable digestive enzymes: with each meal (Look for plant-based formulations that contain amylase, cerecalase, phytase, lipase, glucomylase, peptidase FP, cellulase, invertase, lactase, protease, bromelain, papain, alpha-galactosidase, and acid-stable protease.)
- Herbs: Aloe vera, buckthorn bark, cascara sagrada, garlic, dandelion root, burdock root, red clover, cayenne, and ginger (a combination provided in WOW formula)

Diarrhea

Diarrhea, passing of loose, watery stools, can be caused by parasites, food poisoning, colitis, stress, viruses, chemicals, and allergies, including food allergies (such as to milk). It can also be caused by inflammation of the small pockets in the colon or bacterial imbalances.

Diarrhea can exist alone or as a symptom of other diseases. Diarrhea is commonly accompanied by increased thirst, abdominal cramps and bloating, intestinal rumbling, and loss of appetite.

Because of the rapid movement of food through the digestive tract, individuals with diarrhea do not properly utilize and absorb nutrients.

What to Do

When you have diarrhea, follow this advice:

- To avoid dehydration, drink lots of distilled water.
- Supplement with probiotics and eat lots of yogurt that contains friendly bacteria to help normalize bowel functions. Yogurt also has an antibiotic effect, especially against *E. coli,* the main cause of traveler's diarrhea. (Note: Avoid sweetened yogurt.)
- Carob, which is high in pectin, helps stop diarrhea.
- Fiber, such as bran and ground flaxseed, helps normalize bowel function.

- To replace lost nutrients, supplement with B complex vitamins, vitamin C, sodium, potassium, and magnesium, which are depleted with the water lost when you have diarrhea. Your diet should be rich in protein, carbohydrates, essential fatty acids, and other vitamins and minerals as well.

- If diarrhea lasts longer than two days, seek medical attention. Prolonged diarrhea can cause severe dehydration.

- Supplement with colostrum to support immune function and to ward off parasites and bacterial and viral causes of diarrhea.

Beneficial Supplementation

Consider taking the following supplements daily, until the problem is resolved:

- Calcium: 1,200 mg (avoid calcium carbonate)
- Magnesium: 600 mg
- Potassium: 99 mg
- Sodium (sea salt): ½ teaspoon
- B complex: 2 tablets (Look for a complete B formula, such as Roex B-Complex.)
- Vitamin C (Ester-C®): 1,000–8,000 mg
- Olive leaf extract: 2,000–4,000 mg
- Herbs: Alfalfa, comfrey, glucomannan, raspberry (tea), and slippery elm

Diverticulitis

Diverticulitis is a painful condition that occurs when small sacs form in the colon and become inflamed. Although diverticulitis is most common and most serious in the elderly, it can afflict anyone. Susceptibility is greater for people who take prednisone or other drugs that affect the immune system and increase the chances of an infection.

The primary cause of diverticulitis is a diet containing little fiber and lots of processed foods. The obvious way to prevent or treat diverticulitis is to improve your diet, although shifting too quickly to a high-roughage menu can irritate your colon even more. Once the problem has cleared up, you must slowly make dietary changes to prevent its return.

What to Do

If you suffer from diverticulitis, here are some tips:

- Ground flaxseeds, psyllium, and other fibers can keep your bowels moving normally.
- Supplement with probiotics.
- Chamomile, cramp bark, and peppermint can be helpful.
- Eating garlic or taking it as a supplement will directly attack the infection. (This is the main reason that garlic is the primary ingredient in Roex's Hurricane formula.)
- If you are nervous or stressed, also take herbs that increase relaxation, such as valerian, hops, and skullcap.
- Colostrum is also excellent to combat inflammation and help normalize bowel activity.
- For overcoming inflammation, proanthocyanidins, vitamin C, and olive leaf extract are recommended.

Beneficial Supplementation

The following supplements can be used to prevent or treat diverticulitis:

- Probiotic formula: 20 billion CFUs (For best results, look for formulations including *B. bifudum, S. thermophilus,* and *L. acidolphilus.*)

- Proanthocyanidin (PC-95): 300 mg daily
- Vitamin C (Ester C®): 4,000 mg or more daily
- Olive leaf extract: 4,000 mg daily
- Colostrum: 2,000 mg twice daily
- Herbs: Aloe vera, gentian, ginger, and peppermint

Warning: Do not confuse diverticulitis with appendicitis. An inflamed appendix can produce symptoms that are similar to those of diverticulitis, with pain in the lower right abdomen instead of the lower left. If you think you might have appendicitis, you must see a doctor. Once you are on the mend, however, you can follow the same treatments recommended for diverticulitis.

Heartburn

Heartburn is a symptom of abnormal digestion. Heartburn discomfort occurs when acidic digestive juices and partially digested food back up into the esophagus (the passageway between the mouth and stomach). This irritates sensitive tissues and causes "heartburn" discomfort.

Excess intake of fat, alcohol, and acidic foods, such as coffee, citrus, and tomatoes, can contribute to heartburn. Eating too fast or when emotionally upset or exhausted can also trigger heartburn.

What to Do

If you experience heartburn, try the following:

- Standing or sitting up straight will force acid and partially digested food back into the stomach.
- Drinking milk after eating can sometimes combat stomach acid and bring relief.
- Supplement with chewable digestive enzymes.
- Supplement with probiotics.
- Avoid antacids containing sodium bicarbonate. These may be helpful to neutralize excess acid but should not be overused. Used on a regular basis, they disturb the

body's acid/alkaline balance, creating a condition called "alkalosis." Sustained alkalosis with a substantial intake of calcium in the form of milk or calcium-containing antacids creates milk-alkali syndrome, which causes irreversible kidney damage. Antacids reduce hydrochloric acid, making it more difficult to break down foods. Antacids, by neutralizing all the acid in the stomach, also prevent efficient digestion and thus interfere with nutrient absorption.

• Avoid eating chocolate, onions, garlic, and cabbage and also avoid mixing these foods with alcohol.

• Avoid fatty foods (especially butter, cream sauces, gravies, salad dressings, etc.).

Beneficial Supplementation

The following supplements have been shown to be beneficial for people with heartburn problems:

• Chewable digestive enzymes: 2–3 with each meal (Look for plant-based formulations that contain amylase, cerecalase, phytase, lipase, glucomylase, peptidase FP, cellulase, invertase, lactase, protease, bromelain, papain, alpha-galactosidase, and acid-stable protease.)

• HCl (hydrochloric acid): 500 mg immediately after meals

• Probiotic formula: 20 billion CFUs (10 billion CFUs twice daily) (For best results look for formulations including *B. bifidum, S. thermophilus,* and *L. acidolphilus.*)

• Herbs: Aloe vera, gentian, ginger, and peppermint

Hiatal Hernia

A hiatal hernia occurs when a portion of the stomach protrudes above the diaphragm—the muscular wall separating the chest and abdominal cavity. This results in a loss of function of the valve at the bottom of the esophagus, allowing stomach acid to back up into the esophagus and produce heartburn, usually in the area underneath the breastbone. The pain most often occurs at night when the body is in a reclined position. Experts estimate that about 40–50 percent of the U.S. population suffers hiatal hernias.

What to Do

Use the suggestions given for heartburn.

Beneficial Supplementation

Follow the suggestions given for heartburn.

Indigestion

Indigestion (dyspepsia) is imperfect or incomplete digestion, manifesting itself in a sensation of fullness or discomfort in the abdomen accompanied by pains or cramps, heartburn, nausea, and gas. Headache, heart palpitations, and a disagreeable taste in the mouth can also accompany indigestion.

Usually, indigestion is the result of psychological stresses— anxiety, worry, or disappointment—disturbing the nervous mechanism that controls the contractions of stomach and intestinal muscles. Other causes are rapid eating (inadequate chewing), overeating, improper diet (overabundance of simple carbohydrates at the expense of other nutrients), unusual foods, fatty or spicy foods, or excess stimulants (such as coffee or tea) or alcohol. Continued use of antacids can exasperate indigestion over time.

What to Do

To avoid or treat indigestion, follow this advice:
- Eat a nutritionally well-balanced diet and avoid eating when emotionally upset or overtired.

- Take chewable digestive enzymes with each meal. Use a broad-spectrum supplement (including betaine HCl, bromelain, amylase, lipase, chymosin, trypsin, and lisotozyme) before and after meals.
- Supplement with probiotics.
- Hydrochloric acid tablets help to break down foods.
- Ginger is an excellent anti-inflammatory agent and helps calm the stomach.
- Peppermint also has a soothing effect on the digestive tract and stimulates digestive secretion. It may also be used as a tea.
- Fennel is a natural remedy for gas and stomach acid. This herb can be sprinkled on food to prevent stomach gas.
- Anise seeds are beneficial for a sour stomach. The seeds can be chewed or ground and sprinkled on food.
- Activated charcoal can relieve stomach gas because it absorbs it like a sponge. It also can absorb intestinal bacteria that can cause gas. Charcoal is also good for diarrhea and hiccups.
- Eat meals at regular intervals. This helps the stomach secrete digestive juices.
- Avoid large, heavy meals high in fat.
- Chew or supplement with ginger immediately after meals.

Beneficial Supplementation

The following supplements can be used to prevent or treat indigestion:

- Herbs: Ginger, anise, fennel, peppermint, spearmint, aloe vera leaf powder, garlic, cascara sagrada, barberry root, dandelion, red clover, buckthorn, and milk thistle (a combination provided in WOW)

Intestinal Gas

Intestinal gas (flatulence) is the most common digestive disturbance. Flatulence is abnormal amounts of gas passing upward or downward, with or without intestinal discomfort. It is commonly associated with constipation.

Eating too much food overwhelms the digestive enzymes. Undigested food becomes a breeding ground for putrefactive bacteria, which form gas.

Milk products can also cause flatulence in cases of lactase insufficiency. Fried foods, processed food, and concentrated sugar are other possible culprits.

In infants, flatulence is commonly termed "colic." It is accompanied by abdominal pain, distension, insomnia, fretfulness, and hysteria. The most common cause of infant colic in a totally breast-fed infant is the mother's diet. An inappropriate diet may include fried foods, junk food, and refined foods. Any food may cause the infant's distress, but the most common foods are cabbage, onion, garlic, wheat, yeast, brussels sprouts, and broccoli.

What to Do

Refer to the suggestions given for constipation, and read the following in addition:

- Probiotics and fermented foods such as yogurt and buttermilk aid in the digestion of high-fiber foods by increasing friendly bacteria in the colon.
- Carminative herbs stimulate digestion by increasing gastric juices, decreasing the amount of putrefactive bacteria, and stimulating intestinal motility. These include garlic, anise, fennel, and caraway.
- Charcoal tablets, which absorb gases in the digestive tract, are very beneficial. Take one to two per hour in acute cases.
- Fennel is a natural remedy for gas and stomach acid. This herb can be sprinkled on food to prevent stomach gas.

Beneficial Supplementation

The following supplements can be used to prevent or treat intestinal gas:

*   Herbs: Ginger, aloe leaf powder, garlic, cascara sagrada, barberry root, dandelion, red clover, buckthorn and milk thistle (a combination provided in WOW)

Irritable Bowel Syndrome

Irritable bowel syndrome (IBS), also called "spastic colon," is one of the most common gastrointestinal disorders. It has also been called "spastic colitis," "mucous colitis," and "nervous colon syndrome." It is characterized by abdominal pain, bloating, mucus in stools, and irregular bowel habits, including alternating diarrhea and constipation. It tends to be a chronic disorder. Some individuals experience alternating episodes of relapse and improvement.

An estimated 20 percent of the adult population may have IBS, which affects women about twice as often as men. The symptoms of IBS typically occur early in life, and half of the patients have onset of symptoms before they reach 30 years of age.

IBS is thought to be the result of abnormal contractions of the large intestine (colon). This largely involves impacted feces in the colon and bacterial imbalances resulting in inflammation, pain, and bloating. "Fecal impaction" refers to a firm, immobile mass of stool, most often in the rectum but also occurring in the sigmoid or descending colon. Impaction is common in elderly, inactive patients. Dietary, psychological, hormonal, or genetic factors may also play a role. In some patients, excessive contractions lead to spasms in the colon, causing abdominal pain, diarrhea, or constipation. Other patients with IBS are believed to have increased nervous sensitivity to normal events that occur in the intestine during digestion.

Altered bowel movements occur over periods of days to weeks. Occasionally, symptoms may be continuous.

During episodes of constipation, stools may be hard, small, pebble-like, and difficult to eliminate. This may be associated with a sense of incomplete evacuation. Passage of stool or gas may lead to alleviation of pain.

The diarrhea of IBS is usually of small volume but frequent. Episodes commonly occur during periods of stress.

Abdominal pain can range from mild to severe. It is usually felt in the lower abdomen, especially on the left side. The pain may be dull or sharp, crampy or continuous.

Other symptoms include abdominal distention, belching, and a sensation of bloating. On rare occasions, heartburn, nausea, and vomiting are reported. Depression, anxiety, and stress are commonly associated with IBS. Stress can reactivate a previous enteric inflammation and/or worsen the condition.

Inflammation of the intestine causes pain and altered motility. Inflammation of the mucosa of the gastrointestinal tract is accompanied by changes in intestinal nerve and smooth muscle function and in gut motility and sensation.

The causes of IBS are largely unknown. One prevailing theory is that partially undigested proteins irritate the upper intestinal tract, sometimes referred to as "leaky gut syndrome." Another possible cause is suspected to be irritation caused by bacterial or parasite infection. Lack of dietary fiber, probiotics, and digestive enzymes may also play a major contributing role.

What to Do

Some physicians have had success with a number of patients with irritable bowel using colostrum and lactoferrin. Studies suggest that anti-inflammatory therapy may be beneficial for individuals with IBS, opening the door of possibility for lactoferrin treatment. Colostrum can aid with digestion and overall immune support.[100]

- Proanthocyanidins (PC-95), olive leaf extract, ginger, and burdock root help to reduce inflammation.
- Probiotics should be started immediately.

- Increase dietary fiber (especially freshly ground flaxseeds or high-lignan flaxseed oil).
- Drink at least eight 8 oz glasses of distilled water daily.

Beneficial Supplementation

The following supplements should be considered for people with irritable bowel syndrome:

- Probiotic formula: 20 billion CFUs (10 billion CFUs twice daily). For best results, look for formulations including *B. bifidum, S. thermophilus,* and *L. acidophilus.*
- Chewable digestive enzymes: 2–3 with each meal. Look for plant-based formulations that contain amylase, cerecalase, phytase, lipase, glucomylase, peptidase FP, cellulase, invertase, lactase, protease, bromelain, papain, alpha-galactosidase, and acid-stable protease.
- Olive leaf extract: 2,000 mg twice daily
- Colostrum (from New Zealand): 2,000 mg twice daily
- Proanthocyanidins (PC-95): 200 mg minimum
- Stress-relieving herbs: Valerian, skullcap, and hops
- Demulcent herbs: Marshmallow, comfrey, slippery elm, and flaxseed (freshly ground)
- Soothing digestive herbs: Chamomile, peppermint, hops, and fennel
- Colon-cleansing herbs: Ginger, aloe vera leaf powder, garlic, cascara sagrada, barberry root, dandelion, red clover, buckthorn, milk thistle, and burdock root (a combination provided in WOW and Hurricane)

FATIGUE (LACK OF ENERGY)

Fatigue or lack of energy is probably one of the most common complaints heard in a doctor's office. Fatigue is a feeling of physical and mental weariness that can be caused by a variety of conditions, such as anemia, physical exertion, hypoglycemia, nutrient deficiencies, shallow breathing, medications, weight loss, obesity, boredom or emotional tension, stress, allergies, glandular imbalances, or almost any disease process. Fatigue is commonly accompanied by headache, backache, irritability, indigestion, and depression.

To obtain optimal energy levels or stamina, the entire body needs to be in good health. It may be necessary to take measures to improve digestion and circulation, to cleanse the colon, to nourish the glands and organs (especially the lungs and heart), and to strengthen the nerves.

A range of conditions may cause a person to feel a lack of energy. Research shows that most of these are due to nutrient insufficiencies. One needs to find the cause of the fatigue and then treat it. Supplementation can be very beneficial if deficiencies are present. For example, iron-poor blood cannot adequately carry oxygen throughout the body, which usually results in fatigue, and a diet poor in potassium causes muscular weakness, irritability, and a tired feeling.

Poor diet produces deficiencies of critical nutrients, particularly the B complex (especially the blood-forming nutrients: Folic acid, B_6, and B_{12}). These help to stimulate the body's synthesis of blood cells, which carry oxygen to the tissues in the body and give rise to the production of energy.

Lack of energy could also be a result of a mineral deficiency, particularly iron, zinc, and chromium. These are very important for the maintenance of proper energy levels. Trace minerals are very delicately balanced in the body. Too much of a mineral is as detrimental as too little.

High consumption of drugs and medications rob the body of energy. These poisons are too commonly used without regard to the effects they really have on the body. In addition, sugar, caffeine, and other stimulants and drugs can weaken the body in the long run. Essential fatty acid deficiency can also lead to both mental and physical fatigue.

Chronic Fatigue Syndrome

Chronic fatigue syndrome (CFS) is believed to be caused by the Epstein-Barr virus (EBV), the same virus that causes mononucleosis. EBV is a member of the herpes family and is related to the viruses that cause genital herpes and shingles. Many people can carry the virus and therefore pass it on because it is highly contagious but has no symptoms.

Chronic fatigue is characterized by extreme weakness and exhaustion, persistent apathy and depression, memory loss, headache, impaired concentration, recurrent achiness, low-grade fever, swollen glands, digestive problems, exaggerated allergic reactions, and aggravation of preexisting conditions. *Candida albicans* infection is often found in conjunction with EBV.

The condition is three times more common in women than in men. A person can be screened for EBV antibodies to determine if EBV is the cause of the many symptoms that can last for six months or longer. There is no drug cure for EBV. It may go into remission, but if the immune system is stressed, it will begin replicating again, causing symptoms to return.

The virus causes an overreaction of the immune system. The immune system becomes so overburdened that the result is immunity "burnout." The result is a feeling of complete exhaustion. Individuals with EBV require a comprehensive restorative program for the immune system. This involves not only eliminating immunosuppressive items (sugar, caffeine, alcohol, tobacco, and processed refined foods) but also introducing supportive supplements such as high doses of vitamin C, PC-95, CoQ10, probiotics, vitamins A and E, and olive leaf extract.

A 70-year-old woman with chronic fatigue couldn't walk to the front door of her house without becoming exhausted. After taking eight 30 mg tablets of PC-95 per day for one month, she was walking a mile a day. This is just one example of the power of this antioxidant.

Colostrum and Lactoferrin Inhibit Herpes Activity

Colostrum and lactoferrin can be very beneficial to activate, regulate, and balance the immune system. A number of studies show that colostrum and lactoferrin inhibit the replication of several strains of herpes viruses, including herpes simplex type 1 and 2.[101] Lactoferrin, found in colostrum, is also known to prevent virus absorption and/or penetration into host cells. Researchers state that lactoferrin possesses a potent antiviral activity and may be useful in preventing certain herpes viral infections in humans.[102]

Individuals with acute viral infections have reduced lactoferrin content. This suggests the white blood cells are not properly synthesizing lactoferrin.[103]

Hopefully, there will soon be human clinical trials to demonstrate the effect of colostrum and lactoferrin on EBV. Meanwhile, people with chronic fatigue syndrome continue to report the good results they have been experiencing by supplementing with colostrum daily.

What to Do

Energy levels and oxygen intake go hand in hand. Everyone, especially those suffering from low energy, should start and end his or her day with 10 to 20 minutes of deep breathing exercises.

Digestion, elimination, and dehydration must also be considered when plagued with fatigue. A sluggish elimination system results in a toxic load in the body, which saps energy and wreaks havoc on the immune system. Proper digestion is not only the breakdown and use of food but also the assimilation of nutrients: vitamins, minerals, antioxidants, and essential fatty acids. To ensure proper long-term functioning of these systems, we must maintain a healthy diet including a daily intake of fresh fruits, raw vegetables and at least 80 ounces of distilled water.

Get adequate rest and dedicate at least 40 minutes each day to participate in a stress relieving activity. Exercise—may it be running, walking, calisthenics, or yoga—is the best way to recharge your body and blow off some steam. Stress depletes your body of the fuel that powers it and affects your personal relationships, and estimates suggest it is the cause of more than 75 percent of patients' visits to their primary physician.

Beneficial Supplementation

The following supplements have been shown to be effective in preventing fatigue:

- Balanced multiminerals:*
  - Elemental calcium (preferably a combination of calcium citrate, chelate, aspartate, and lactate): 1,200 mg daily
  - Magnesium: 600 mg
  - Trace mineral combination (copper, molybdenum, potassium, selenium, zinc, boron, silica) without iron: 300 mg daily
- B complex:** three times daily with meals
- Vitamin C (Ester-C®): 3,000 mg
- Proanthocyanidins (PC-95): 200 mg (minimum) (Individuals suffering from CFS should increase their daily dosage of proanthocyanidins to a minimum of 300 mg)
- Oleuropein: 2,000 mg
- Chromium polynicotinate (especially for individuals with hypoglycemia): 200–400 mcg
- Lecithin: 1–2 grams
- CoQ10: 100 mg
- Colostrum (New Zealand Colostrum): 6,000–8,000 mg
- Essential fatty acids (omega-9 plus a 1:1 ratio of omega-3/omega-6):***

---

*Roex's Ultimate Calcium Mineral Formula contains all of the listed items.
** A quality B complex should include B_1, B_2, B_6, B_{12}, niacin, niacinamide, folic acid, biotin, pantothenic acid, magnesium, arginine, betaine hydrochloride, carnitine, choline, PABA, lecithin, bromelain, and alpha lipoic acid.
*** Roex EFAs contain omega-3, 6, and 9 in proper balance.

- Omega-3: 1,400–2,100 mg
- Omega-6: 1,400–2,100 mg
- Omega-9: 740–1,200 mg
- Herbs: cayenne, American gingseng/red deer antler combination, gotu kola, green oats

A wise man will be master of his mind.
A fool will be its slave.
—PUBLILIUS SYRUS

GUM DISEASE

Gum disease, also called periodontal disease or pyorrhea, is the inflammation and infectious condition of the structures that support the teeth. It is a progressive disorder caused by the bacteria found in plaque.

Plaque is an invisible bacterial film that forms on the teeth and consists of material found in saliva and other particles. It is constantly forming in the mouth. Everyone produces plaque, even those who care for their teeth. Plaque must be removed daily. If allowed to build up under the gum line, these bacteria thrive and multiply. Along the roots of the teeth, plaque will become calcified (often called tartar) and can be removed only by a dental professional. Eventually, this can cause tooth decay, tooth loss, and periodontal disease.

Smoking, a poorly fitted filling, dental bridgework, or an abnormality where the teeth meet all encourage bacterial growth.

Periodontal disease is the major cause of tooth loss among adults. It is estimated that by age 60, nearly 40 percent of the adult population needs false teeth as a result. The condition usually affects people over age 30 and becomes more prevalent with age, possibly due to the cumulative effects of bacteria. Without proper maintenance, even young people may experience some forms of periodontal disease.

After the common cold, gum disease is the most common infectious ailment in this country. According to the American

Academy of Periodontology, "Of the 125 million American adults who still have their teeth, 100 million are now infected and an estimated 32 million have an advanced case."[104]

Two common types of periodontal disease are gingivitis and periodontitis, each caused by a different type of bacteria found in plaque. Unfortunately, both diseases often go unnoticed by the affected individual since they are usually painless. The sooner one receives treatment the better, and of course, prevention is always the best treatment.

Gingivitis is a superficial inflammation of the gums. It usually begins with swollen, red gums that may bleed during brushing. Later, bad breath or a bad taste in the mouth may be present. Gingivitis usually does not result in tooth loss.

Periodontitis is caused by more harmful bacteria that affect not only the gums but the supporting bone, which can eventually result in bone loss. The bacteria colonize in gum crevices around the teeth and on the tooth root surfaces. The bacteria emit toxins that inflame the gum tissue, and the gums begin to pull away from the teeth. The inflammation can spread all the way into the underlying bone and cause serious damage by deterioration. As the infection advances, "pockets" can form between the teeth and the supporting tissues. Eventually the teeth will loosen and fall out.

Traditional methods of correction include surgery, reconstruction, and regeneration of damaged tissue and bone. Nonsurgical procedures may be attempted if disease conditions are treated early enough.

What to Do

The best treatment for tooth and gum problems is prevention. Daily removal of plaque and regular visits to your dentist will help keep your teeth and gums healthy.

- Brush and floss after every meal.
- Brush your teeth with baking soda or tooth powders containing baking soda.
- Rinse your toothbrush in hydrogen peroxide.

- Colostrum is a highly effective solution for gum disease. Before going to bed, open two capsules of colostrum and pour the contents onto the troubled area of the gums and leave it there. After about two weeks of doing this every day, you will be amazed at the results. It works wonders!
- Rub chlorella (a blue-green algae) onto the gum line.
- Vitamin C has been shown to help protect the gums against infection. In addition to supplements, some mouthwashes are available that contain vitamin C. Because zinc is antibacterial in the mouth, it also may be helpful to use a mouthwash containing zinc.
- PC-95 helps protect the sensitive tissues in the mouth from free-radical damage caused by the inflammation of gum disease. Chew two to three tablets during the day. Wait two to three minutes before swallowing.
- Avoid a high-phosphorus and refined-food diet, which is the major cause of tooth and gum disease. Eat a diet high in raw fruits, raw and lightly cooked vegetables, nuts, fermented dairy products, and whole refined grains. Avoid excess meat, soda, candy, refined cereals, and overcooked foods.
- A calcium deficiency can weaken the bones that support the teeth and can make the body more susceptible to infections. Calcium has been shown to be a key factor in the prevention and treatment of gum disease.
- A hydrogen peroxide and salt rinse can be used to kill bacteria and prevent gum disease.
- Drink lots of distilled water.

Beneficial Supplementation

The following supplements have been shown to be effective in maintaining healthy gums:

- Vitamin A: 25,000 IU daily

- B complex: 25–50 mg one to two times daily
- Vitamin C (Ester-C®): 1,000–2,000 mg three to four times daily
- Vitamin E (chewable): 400 IU daily, plus local application to gums
- Zinc: 15–25 mg one to two times daily
- Balanced mineral formula with an excellent source of calcium, such as microcrystalline hydroxyapatite (MCHC)
- Colostrum: Pour contents of two capsules directly onto the gums
- Probiotics: two to three times daily
- Proanthocyanidins (PC-95): 300 mg daily; also chew two to three tablets during the day
- Chlorella: Topically applied
- Herbs: Cayenne, coneflower, goldenseal, and myrrh

HEADACHE

Headache, or pain or ache in any portion of the head, is a symptom rather than a disease itself.

Headaches can be caused by stress, heavy-metal toxicity, insomnia, depression, constipation, indigestion, sinusitis, head injury, air pollution, hunger, hypoglycemia, poor circulation, and poor respiration. Additional causes include allergic reactions to MSG, chocolate, caffeine (and caffeine withdrawal), wheat, sulfites, dairy products, vinegar, poor dietary habits (sugar and refined carbohydrates, junk food), and alcohol. Toxins/fumes, liver disorders, menstrual disorders, anemia, high blood pressure, and eye strain can also result in head pain.

Tyramine-containing foods (red wine, sherry, champagne, beer, aged cheese, chicken liver, citrus, pickled herring, chocolate, avocados, bananas, plums) can initiate an attack because they seem to cause constriction of the blood vessels in the scalp, resulting in a reduced blood supply.

Sodium nitrate–containing foods (hot dogs, bacon, and other cured meats) can also cause headaches. Birth-control pills and estrogen supplements can cause headaches as can MSG, which is commonly added to Chinese food.

There are several types of headaches, including the following:

- *Sick headaches* are caused by undigested food in the stomach, stress, or menstrual disorders.
- *Bilious headaches* are caused by indigestion, overeating, and lack of exercise. They are experienced as dull pain in the forehead and throbbing temples.
- *Nervous headaches* are caused by tension, mental strain, and worry and are usually made worse by bright lights or noises of any kind.
- *Sinus headaches* are caused by allergies and hay fever, which inflame the mucous membranes of the nose, and are often brought on by changes in the weather, onset of menstruation, or a head cold.
- *Migraine headaches* are recurrent attacks of headaches often combined with visual and gastrointestinal disturbances. The pain is usually confined to one side of the head or one eye.

Headaches can also result from dehydration—not drinking adequate amounts of water. This is especially important to consider during the summer months or when traveling to warmer climates. Alcohol consumption and other factors can also play a role. The solution is simple: drink (or sip to avoid nausea) a lot of water. Eating fruits such as watermelon, which has a high water content as well as important trace minerals and electrolytes, can be very beneficial.

Repeated headaches may be a symptom of a serious disorder and therefore deserve medical attention.

What to Do

Treatment for headaches depends on the underlying cause:

- After a migraine has started, taking PC-95 can be very effective in easing symptoms. As soon as you feel a migraine coming on, take 10 PC-95 tablets (300 mg). Repeat in 30 to 60 minutes.

- Avoid sugar, which can make headaches worsen.

- Colon cleansing may be helpful for bilious headaches.

- For a nervous headache, it may be helpful to lie down where it is quiet and massage the neck muscles. Heat from a heating pad or a hot tub also helps.

- Soaking your hands in hot water (or taking a hot bath if you can) can relieve nervous or migraine headaches. Fill a sink with water as hot as you can stand it. Place both hands in the hot water up to your wrists for 30 minutes. The heat of the water expands blood vessels in your hands causing increased blood flow. This draws blood away from bloated arteries in the head, which cause the headache pain. The hot water also stimulates nerve endings in your hands, to send relaxation signals to your brain, and the hot water takes your focus away from your pain and directs it elsewhere.

- If a headache is caused by a drop in blood sugar or hunger, eat something, preferably complex carbohydrates or protein. Olive leaf extract can help manage sugar in the blood. For other helpful blood sugar regulating agents, see the sections on diabetes and hypoglycemia.

- Pressure on nerve endings can relieve persistent headaches. Apply pressure to pressure points. One is located at the second joint of the thumb. Use the thumb and index finger on the other hand to rub the joint vigorously. Use oil or hand lotion to lessen friction when massaging. Repeat the process on the other thumb. If a headache is severe, 10 minutes of vigorous massaging on each thumb may be required.

    Another pressure point is located in the palm area. Firmly massage the palm of one hand with the thumb of your other hand.

The third point is located near the eyebrows, centered above each eye. Using the knuckles of each of your thumbs press firmly for several minutes until headache pain subsides.

The last pressure point is located in the triangle of flesh between the thumb and index finger. With your other hand squeeze this area with your thumb and index pinching together. Concentrate on the most sensitive area.

- Drink a cupful of peppermint, catnip, red sage, or spearmint tea.
- Relax and get some fresh air.
- Magnesium supplements have been shown to reduce frequency and severity of migraine headaches. A magnesium deficiency increases one's sensitivity to noise, light, and other stimuli.
- Feverfew (an herb), when taken regularly, helps prevent migraine headaches.

Beneficial Supplementation

The following supplements have been shown to be beneficial in preventing headaches and reducing headache pain:

- B complex (extra niacin, B_{12}, and pangamic acid): 50 mg one to two times daily
- Vitamin C (Ester-C®) (with bioflavonoids): 4,000 mg daily
- Vitamin E: 400 IU daily
- Balanced mineral formula
- Olive leaf extract: 1,000 mg or more daily
- Proanthocyanidins (PC-95): 300 mg at onset—repeat in 30–60 minutes
- Herbs: Chamomile, feverfew, garlic, hops, peppermint plus catnip (tea for headaches of stomach origin), red sage, skullcap, spearmint (tea), white willow, and wood betony

In addition, drink lots of room-temperature distilled water. Ice-cold water is not recommended if you have a headache.

What a man thinks of himself determines,
or rather indicates his fate.

—HENRY D. THOREAU

HEART HEALTH

Coronary heart disease and stroke are the number one and number three causes of death in America, respectively. Those who survive often live with serious disabilities. According to the National Center for Health Statistics, cardiovascular disease (CVD) is classified into four major groups: ischemic (coronary) heart disease, hypertensive disease, rheumatic fever/rheumatic heart disease and cerebrovascular disease (stroke).

Many of the factors associated with development of CVD are lifestyle related and can be controlled, reversed, or eliminated entirely. The most common factors include smoking, little or no physical activity, excessive alcohol consumption, poor eating habits, obesity, and stress. Other risks include elevated levels of insulin, cholesterol, lipoprotein(a), and fibrin (hyperfibrinogenemia).

Folic acid helps prevent heart disease. Studies show that the higher the level of homocysteine in the blood, the higher the risk of heart problems.[105] Homocysteine is a by-product of protein metabolism, which binds with LDL cholesterol and causes damage to the arterial wall, leading to plaque buildup and atherosclerosis. This also increases the risk for blood clot formation. High levels of homocysteine often result from inadequacies of B_6, B_{12}, and folic acid.

What to Do

To maintain a healthy heart, try these suggestions:

- Studies show that increasing the intake of the B-vitamins B_6, B_{12}, and folic acid can prevent a buildup of homocysteine in the blood.[106] I would suggest taking 400 mcg folic acid daily to reduce homocysteine.

- Antioxidants prevent oxidation of LDLs. Researchers in Italy clearly showed that a diet enriched with proanthocyanidins enhances antioxidant activity and reduces myocardial postischemic damage (the damage that occurs following a heart attack due to free-radical damage) in rats. They found that a three-week supplementation of proanthocyanidins in rats (young and aged) makes the heart less susceptible to damage from a heart attack and that this is positively associated with an increase in plasma antioxidant activity.[107]

  German researchers have also recently demonstrated this very important heart protective aspect of proanthocyanidins and recommended that they be used therapeutically for cardiovascular diseases.[108]

  Researchers in Taiwan demonstrated that proanthocyanidins are effective against platelet aggregation. They stated that proanthocyanidins significantly inhibited platelet aggregation, and the potency of inhibition was comparable with that of aspirin, without the side effects.[109] Aspirin, of course, causes stomach upset in many individuals and cannot be used by them. Proanthocyanidins do not cause stomach bleeding or have any other negative side effects.

- There is evidence that flavonoid intake correlates inversely with coronary heart disease risk. Flavonoids are widely available in fruits, fruit juice, and other foods and act as antioxidants and iron chelators. Catechin demonstrated the ability to help minimize damage to the heart following a heart attack.[110]

- In women, elevated lipoprotein(a) levels are often reduced with estrogen hormone replacement therapy. Studies have also demonstrated similar benefits from phytoestrogens found in soy, flax, and herbs such as dong quai without the risk of side effects.[111]

- To reduce elevated cholesterol, see the section on hyper-cholesterolemia.
- For high blood pressure, see the section on hypertension.
- For weight problems, see the section on obesity.

Beneficial Supplementation

To keep your heart healthy, try the following supplements:

- Balanced Multiminerals:*
  - Elemental calcium (preferably a combination of calcium citrate, chelate, aspartate, and lactate): 1,200 mg
  - Magnesium: 600 mg
  - Trace mineral combination (copper, molybdenum, potassium, selenium, zinc, boron, silica) without iron: 300 mg
- Essential fatty acids (omega-9 plus a 1:1 ratio of omega-3/omega-6):**
  - Omega-3: 1,400–2,100 mg
  - Omega-6: 1,400–2,100 mg
  - Omega-9: 740–1,200 mg
- Proanthocyanidins (PC-95): 300 mg (minimum)
- CoQ10: 300 mg
- Vitamin C (Ester-C®): 3,000 mg (minimum)
- B complex:*** 1–3 capsules with meals
- Olive leaf extract: 2,000 mg

---

*Roex's Ultimate Calcium Mineral Formula contains all of the listed items.
**Roex's EFAs contain omega-3, 6, and 9 in proper balance.
***A quality B complex should include B_1, B_2, B_6, B_{12}, niacin, niacinamide, folic acid, biotin, pantothenic acid, magnesium, arginine, betaine hydrochloride, carnitine, choline, PABA, lecithin, bromelain, and alpha lipoic acid.

HEMORRHOIDS

Hemorrhoids are dilated veins around the anus and rectum. They may be either internal or external.

Poor eating habits (refined foods, lack of fiber) are largely responsible for hemorrhoids. This type of diet often leads to constipation, which causes the pressure inside the colon to increase. Hemorrhoids can also be due to strain on the abdominal muscles due to factors such as heavy or improper lifting, pregnancy, overweight, a sedentary lifestyle, and chronic constipation, which can result from the use of certain drugs and medication. Hemorrhoids may also be a sign of capillary fragility.

Symptoms of hemorrhoids include swollen veins that frequently become irritated and bleed. Hemorrhoids also cause itching and burning. The prevention of hemorrhoids is much easier than their cure.

What to Do

To prevent or treat hemorrhoids, follow these suggestions:

- Increase your intake of dietary fiber to about 20 grams or more per day. Eat high-fiber foods, a daily salad, and fresh fruits and vegetables. Chitosan is an important and beneficial fiber that encourages food to move through the digestive system, preventing dietary fat and cholesterol from absorption. It is indigestible and has been shown to help cleanse the colon, regulate bowel habits, and reduce blood pressure and tumors.
- Lipoic acid, proanthocyanidins (PC-95) and other antioxidants protect and strengthen the capillaries.
- Vitamin E can prevent and dissolve blood clots.
- Avoid commercial laxatives, which irritate the lining of the colon.
- Warm water soaks (sitz baths) can help relieve the discomfort of hemorrhoids and keep the area clean.

- Alternate hot and cold therapy.
- Hemorrhoids can be relieved by aloe vera gel, which also stimulates healing.
- Avoid lifting heavy objects.
- Moderate exercise has a generally beneficial effect on colonic function. However, strenuous exercise, such as weightlifting, can aggravate hemorrhoids.
- Eat bulky, high-fiber foods, such as whole grains, leafy vegetables, and fruits to help regulate bowel movements.
- Drink plenty of liquids every day.

Beneficial Supplementation

The following supplements have been shown to be beneficial in preventing and treating hemorrhoids:

- Vitamin A: 10,000 IU twice daily
- Vitamin D: 1,600 IU
- B complex: 50 mg three times daily
- Vitamin B_6: 100 mg three times daily
- Vitamin C (Ester-C®): 2,000 mg three times daily
- Vitamin E: 400 IU three times daily
- Proanthocyanidins (PC-95): 300 mg daily
- Lipoic acid: 100–200 mg two times daily
- MSM: 4,000 mg daily
- Balanced mineral formula with 1,200 mg calcium and 600 mg magnesium
- Fiber (such as bran or freshly ground flaxseeds): 1–2 tbsp with meals
- Chitosan: 3,000 mg daily
- Cleansing herbs: Ginger, aloe leaf powder, garlic, cascara sagrada, barberry root, dandelion, red clover, buckthorn, cayenne, and milk thistle extract (such as found in WOW formula—three capsules daily with your evening meal)

- Other herbs: Stone root (capsule and suppository) and goldenseal (suppository)

HYPERCHOLESTEREMIA (ELEVATED CHOLESTEROL)

High blood cholesterol levels increase the risk of heart attack and stroke. Here is why: Cholesterol is carried in the bloodstream, and some is deposited on the inner linings of the arteries. These fatty deposits build up, causing the artery walls to thicken and become less flexible. The artery narrows and restricts blood flow. Eventually the blood supply may be shut off completely. If the blockage is in an artery feeding the brain, a stroke may result. If the blockage is in an artery that feeds the heart, a heart attack may occur.

Two different types of blood cholesterol levels can be measured in the body: HDL (high-density lipoprotein) and LDL (low-density lipoprotein).

HDL refers to the type of cholesterol returning through the bloodstream back to the liver. It will then (hopefully) be converted into bile salts when fat is eaten and be excreted with fiber. HDL is sometimes called "good cholesterol" because ideally it is on its way out of the body.

LDL cholesterol travels through the bloodstream and delivers cholesterol to the tissues and glands that in turn use it to produce hormones. LDL is sometimes called "bad cholesterol" because it may very easily oxidize and become trapped in plaques and clogged arteries.

HDL cholesterol seems less likely to become so trapped. HDL helps clear LDL cholesterol from the bloodstream by transporting it to the liver where it gets broken down and excreted.

The HDL level may be as low as 30 or 40 mg or as high as 100 or 150 mg. This number is compared to the total serum cholesterol to form a ratio. For example, if the total serum cholesterol is 250 mg/percent and the HDL level is 100, the ratio would be 250 over 100, or 2.5 to 1. Generally, the lower the ratio, the better one's health.

Total serum cholesterol levels alone, without HDL and LDL levels, may be very deceiving. For example, a total level of 200 may look satisfactory to a physician. But if the HDL level is only 20 mg, the ratio would be 10 to 1, which indicates higher than twice the average risk of experiencing a heart attack.

We do not absorb 100 percent of the cholesterol contained in the foods we eat. Most people can absorb no more than 300–500 mg per day of cholesterol from foods. In fact, up to 80 percent of blood cholesterol comes from production in the liver, not from the cholesterol in food. Only 20–30 percent of the cholesterol in our blood comes preformed from cholesterol-containing foods we eat, no matter how much we eat.

Even if we ate absolutely no cholesterol, every day the liver would still make up to 1,500 mg of cholesterol from fats and sugars. The components for cholesterol production come from foods we actually should cut down on: saturated animal fats and simple sugars, including sucrose (white sugar), fructose, and corn syrup. The liver is an expert in converting sugars into cholesterol. On average, Americans eat 150 pounds of sugar per person a year, which gives the liver a tremendous amount of raw material to turn into cholesterol.

What to Do

To maintain healthy cholesterol levels, follow this advice:

- Avoid saturated animal fats and simple sugars, including sucrose (white sugar), fructose, and corn syrup. These are converted to cholesterol in the liver.
- Stress, caffeine, cigarettes, alcohol, and obesity are all factors that contribute to heart disease and should be avoided.
- Vitamin C helps increase HDL levels, lower LDL levels, and lower triglyceride levels. It also dramatically reduces high elevations of blood cholesterol by activating the conversion of cholesterol into bile salts.

- B complex, lost in the refining process of starches and essential in the metabolism of carbohydrates, is known to help keep cholesterol from collecting on artery walls.

- Vitamin E, also removed in the refining of grains and oils, helps dissolve clots, dilates blood vessels, and conserves energy so the heart can work less hard. Vitamin E is also an antioxidant.

- Niacin, known to reduce cholesterol levels as much as 25 percent, is even more effective when used with oat bran.

- Lecithin, which contains choline, is essential for the proper use of fat and cholesterol in the body. Lecithin in the diet significantly lowers cholesterol levels.

- Essential fatty acids, found in flaxseed oil, salmon, cod, and other cold-water-fish oils rich in omega-3, decrease platelet adhesion, thin blood naturally, reduce blood cholesterol, and increase HDL.

- Water-soluble fibers (such as guar gum, psyllium, and pectin) and nonwater-soluble fibers (such as chitosan and oat or soy bran) are effective in reducing blood cholesterol and triglyceride levels. They decrease LDL without decreasing HDL.[112] Fiber prevents cholesterol from recycling to the liver from the bowel, which signals a reduction of bile from the bowel back to the liver, which signals a reduction of cholesterol conversion to bile, causing a blood cholesterol increase.

- Alfalfa is an excellent and effective supplement that aids in cholesterol reduction. Alfalfa is rich in saponins, which provide a sort of sudsing action that prevents cholesterol and bile salts from being reabsorbed. Studies with alfalfa have demonstrated a 20 percent drop in total cholesterol. Ratios between HDL and LDL improved by 40 percent. Alfalfa also has been demonstrated to have a beneficial effect on high blood pressure.[113]

- Eating onion and garlic may help reduce heart disease as they both reduce the blood's tendency to clot. Raw onion and raw onion juice raise the levels of HDL. (Cooking reduces the beneficial chemical activity.) A clove or two of garlic can lower cholesterol and triglyceride levels in the blood.

- Eating apples (one to two daily) has been shown to lower total cholesterol levels by approximately 10 percent. In addition, while LDL decreases, HDL increases.[114]

- Probiotics such as *L. acidophilus*, cultured milk products, brewer's yeast, chromium, alfalfa, garlic, onion, and soy protein have all demonstrated the ability to lower cholesterol.[115]

- Proanthocyanidins (PC-95) have been demonstrated in clinical trials to help protect LDL cholesterol from oxidation.[116] LDL, remember, is at highest risk for oxidation in the body, making PC-95 an important cholesterol protector.

- Physical activity and exercise are also important factors necessary to reduce elevated cholesterol levels, particularly LDL levels.

- Red wine, in moderation, helps increase HDL and regulate healthy cholesterol and triglycerides in the body.[117]

- Chelation therapy, or EDTA (ethylenediaminetetraacetic acid), is a nonsurgical alternative aimed at increasing blood flow. It involves a simple binding of a metal ion within a carrier molecule, which allows the metal ions to be transported through the body. This causes a change or balancing of other ion metals.

EDTA, a man-made amino acid, collects calcium in the bloodstream (which otherwise binds cholesterol to artery walls) and toxic metals such as cadmium, mercury, and lead. The kidneys remove EDTA and any calcium or metals bound to it and flushes them out.

The body then readjusts and replaces the calcium in the blood by releasing calcium from other sources. This brings about gradual withdrawal of the calcium in the plaque of the arteries with a widening of the arterial lumen (interior diameter) and relaxation of the arterial walls, resulting in better circulation. The plaque in the arteries becomes softer, and the vessels become stronger, more supple, and better able to tolerate larger quantities of blood without raising the blood pressure. The cholesterol is either excreted or gobbled up by scavenger cells within the body.

Beneficial Supplementation

The following supplements have been shown to be beneficial for people with elevated cholesterol levels:

- B complex: 50 mg one to three times daily
- Niacin: 3,000 mg daily
- Vitamin C (Ester-C®): 3,000 mg or more daily
- Vitamin E: 400 IU two times daily
- High-lignan flaxseed oil: 2–3 tablespoons daily
- Lecithin (high in choline): 1–2 grams daily
- Chromium: 600 mcg daily
- Magnesium: 300–2,000 mg daily
- Potassium: 25 mg daily
- Vanadium and other trace minerals in a balanced mineral formula
- Selenium: 100 to 200 mcg daily
- Zinc: 50 mg daily
- Proanthocyanidins (PC-95): 300 mg daily
- Fiber, such as chitosan, freshly ground flaxseed, bran, and pectin (see CitriGenics II below)
- CitriGenics II (Roex's formula to normalize cholesterol): 6 tablets or more daily
- Alfalfa: 2,000 mg or more daily

- L-carnitine: 1,500–3,000 mg daily
- Colon-cleansing herbs: Ginger, aloe leaf powder, garlic, cascara sagrada, barberry root, dandelion, red clover, buckthorn, cayenne, and milk thistle extract (such as found in WOW formula)
- Other herbs: Angelica, black cohosh, hawthorn, hawthorn/walnut combination and mistletoe

In addition, these foods are beneficial in maintaining healthy cholesterol levels: alfalfa, apples, barley, beans (black, pinto, or navy), carrots, chili peppers, eggplant, flaxseeds, garlic, grapefruit, oat bran, olive oil, onions, salmon, seafood, seaweed, soybeans, spinach, yams, and yogurt.

HYPERTENSION (HIGH BLOOD PRESSURE)

Hypertension is an abnormal elevation of blood pressure. The average blood pressure for men is 120/80 and is slightly lower for women. Blood pressure that consistently exceeds 140/90 is considered high. The lower figure (diastolic pressure) was usually considered more important because it is the pressure the arteries are under even at rest, but new research shows that the higher, systolic number is also an important indicator of the health of the cardiovascular system.

Hypertension is a common disorder that often exists without symptoms and with an unknown exact cause, although in most cases diet is probably the primary factor. The risk of hypertension is increased by stress, excess weight, high sodium chloride intake, high cholesterol level, cigarette smoking, excessive use of stimulants (including excessive coffee consumption), use of oral contraceptives, and family history of high blood pressure.

Symptoms of hypertension may be nonexistent, or they may include headache, nervousness, insomnia, nosebleeds, blurred vision, edema, shortness of breath, dizziness, and ringing in the ears.

Presently, one-third of the American population suffers from hypertension. Some authorities report that one-half of these people do not even realize it. Because hypertension is one of the major contributors to cardiovascular disease, the number one cause of death in America, hypertension is now being examined more closely.

What to Do

Most people can lower their blood pressure by eating less meat and more vegetables. The following steps can also be helpful.

- A low-fat and high-fiber diet has been shown to help control hypertension in a significant way. Polyunsaturated omega-3 fatty acids (such as in fish and flax) are also very important in helping to regulate blood pressure.
- Diet deficiencies have also been identified as playing a role in hypertension. One survey conducted in 10 states over a two-year period showed that 66 percent of the study group was deficient in calcium, magnesium, iron, and vitamins A, C, and B$_6$, all of which are beneficial for people with hypertension.[118] These vitamins and minerals are cofactors that are needed by the enzyme systems of the body. They are of critical importance, in spite of the fact that they are not needed in large quantities.
- Individuals who are overweight and have hypertension can lower their blood pressure significantly by losing weight.
- Eliminate consumption of sodium chloride (salt). Sodium has long been thought to be a major contributor to hypertension, and while more work is still needed, chloride, more so than sodium, is now believed to be a primary variable.

Note: If you feel you must add salt to your food, sea salt is a much better option than regular table salt. It contains all other trace minerals to help keep the body's mineral levels in balance. However, be sure to use it in moderation.

- Eliminate stress whenever possible. When an individual is under stress, levels of vitamins B_1, B_2, B_6, B_{12}, and C and possibly magnesium are likely all very, very low in the body. A number of these play a big part in the regulation of blood pressure. In general, stress tends to lower the resistance of the immune system and increases the risk for free-radical proliferation throughout the body.

- *Garlic,* a time-proven, ancient remedy to reduce high blood pressure, may help to dissolve blood clots and reduce cholesterol, triglycerides, LDL cholesterol, platelet aggregation, and arterial plaque, which provides relief from chronic hypertension.

  Note: Roex's Hurricane formula supports the body in normalizing blood pressure due to its powerful garlic content.

- *Proanthocyanidins (PC-95)* are also beneficial in reducing hypertension. Research shows that free-radical pathology may contribute to impaired vasodilation in patients with hypertension. A number of studies have shown that proanthocyanidinss can lower blood pressure in a dose-dependent manner.[119]

- Colon cleansing is also very important.

Beneficial Supplementation

The following supplements have been shown to be beneficial for people with hypertension:

- B complex with extra niacin, B_6, B_{12}, and folic acid: 50 mg daily
- Vitamin C (Ester-C®): 3,000 mg or more daily
- Proanthocyanidins (PC-95): 300 mg daily
- Vitamin E: 200–600 IU daily
- Balanced mineral formula with calcium, magnesium, potassium, and silica

322 THE NUTRITIONAL APPROACH TO COMMON AILMENTS AND CONDITIONS

- Vitamin D: 1,000 IU daily
- High-lignan flaxseed oil: 2–3 tablespoons daily
- Olive leaf extract: 3,000 mg daily
- Lecithin: 1–2 grams daily
- Fiber, such as chitosan or freshly ground flaxseed: 3–4 grams or more daily
- Herbs: Cayenne (capsicum), garlic, glucomannan, dandelion, ginger, hawthorn berries, hibiscus flowers, hops, lady's-slipper, passionflower, skullcap, and valerian

Note: Two Roex products, Hurricane and WOW, contain powerful garlic, cayenne, and ginger, which are very supportive of healthy blood pressure.

HYPOGLYCEMIA (LOW BLOOD SUGAR)

Hypoglycemia, or low blood sugar, is an abnormally low level of glucose in the blood. There are three types of hypoglycemia. Two of them are rare organic forms involving the pancreas: tumors of the pancreas and enlargement of the island of Langerhans. The most common form is functional hypoglycemia, which is caused by an inadequate diet that is too high in refined carbohydrates. The result is impaired absorption and assimilation of ingested food. An overconsumption of carbohydrates causes the blood sugar level to rise rapidly, stimulating the pancreas to secrete an excess of insulin. This excess insulin removes too much sugar from the blood, resulting in an abnormally low blood sugar level.

An inadequate diet high in sugar or simple carbohydrates (excess consumption of soda, for example), stress, overwork, and skipping of meals can trigger the blood sugar level to drop, causing many of the following symptoms: cravings for sugars or sweets, lack of stamina, fatigue, constant hunger, tendency to gain weight, allergies, caffeine cravings, muscle cramps or spasms, mood swings or irritability, nervous habits, insomnia, anxiety, blurred vision or dry eyes, depression or crying spells, frequent headaches, inability to concentrate or poor memory, lightheadedness, dizzy or faint feelings, feelings of inadequacy or loss of confidence, cold sweats, indigestion, uncomfortable menstrual periods, low sex drive, and cold fingers or toes.

Symptoms are usually episodic, being related to the time and content of the previous meal, and are usually improved by eating. Hypoglycemia is commonly associated with food allergies.

What to Do

The therapeutic diet for hypoglycemia is high in protein, low in carbohydrates (unrefined complex) and moderate in fat.

- Carbohydrates should include only those that are slow absorbing, such as vegetables and whole-grain products. Avoid all sugar and refined carbohydrates as well as products that contain them.
- Eat small, frequent meals.
- Keeping the colon clean can help enhance nutrient assimilation and may reduce sugar cravings.

Beneficial Supplementation

The following supplements have been shown to be beneficial for people with hypoglycemia:

- B complex: 50 mg daily
- Niacin: 300–450 mg daily
- Vitamin C (Ester-C®): 1,000 mg two to five times daily
- Proanthocyanidins (PC-95): 200–300 mg daily
- Balanced multiminerals*
  - Elemental calcium (preferably a combination calcium citrate, chelate, aspartate, and lactate): 1,200 mg
  - Magnesium: 600 mg
  - Trace mineral combination (copper, molybdenum, potassium, selenium, zinc, boron, silica) without iron: 300 mg

---

*Roex's Ultimate Calcium Mineral Formula contains all of the listed items.

- Chromium: 200–600 mcg per day
- Probiotics
- Digestive enzymes: After each meal
- Herbs: Alfalfa, aloe vera juice, dandelion, hawthorn, juniper, kelp, licorice, safflower, and saffron

In addition, useful glucose-stabilizing foods include the following: whole grains (especially oats and oat flour), nuts, raw milk products (if no sign of allergy exists), avocado, brewer's yeast, and Jerusalem artichokes.

IMMUNE DEFICIENCY

A functioning immune system is essential for human survival. The immune system protects us from invaders such as yeasts, bacteria, and viruses, as well as fumes, chemicals, and substances such as alcohol, nicotine, and caffeine. Without a properly functioning immune system, good health simply cannot be maintained.

We are all provided a genetically active immune system and an acquired immune response. This means that part of our immunity is inherited and the rest is obtained through accumulated responses to foreign-body exposures.

The principal organs of the immune system are the thymus, bone marrow, spleen, and lymphoid tissue (for example, the tonsils). The immune system also consists of the lymphatic vessels, lymph nodes, specialized white blood cells—B cells, T cells (killer, helper, and suppressor), macrophage cells, and antibodies (also called immunoglobulins). Each has a different responsibility, but they all function together.

Without optimal immune protection we are susceptible to conditions including the common cold and flu, yeast overgrowth, parasite infection, fungus, various stages of immune deficiency syndrome, cancer, and even AIDS. We may take immunity for granted until we are threatened with losing it. Research now shows that the state of our immune system depends greatly upon our quality of behavior and environment.

General immune deficiency is experienced by all of us from time to time. This is largely due to stress, nutritional deficiencies, exposure to pathogens, and our general state of health.
Immune deficiency is characterized by

- Fatigue, loss of stamina and energy
- Swollen lymph nodes
- Frequent colds and infections
- Loss of appetite and weight loss
- Fever/night sweats
- Skin rashes and cold sores
- Diarrhea
- Candida yeast infection

The degree to which we are affected by immune deficiency depends on a number of factors, such as our general state of health and how we choose to maintain or improve it.

What to Do

Here are some suggestions maintaining a properly functioning immune system:

- Get plenty of rest. Studies have shown that the immune system functions best while we are asleep. Deep sleep is important for immune function; for example, B cell and macrophage activity increases. Some researchers even think of sleep as an aspect of immune function. The body needs to shut down in order for the immune system to effectively fight off what it has encountered. Most people know that we tend to sleep more when we are sick. It seems obvious that we must therefore need to. Lack of sleep, insomnia, and irregular sleeping habits (common with irregular work hours) have been shown to be detrimental to one's health and longevity.
  Melatonin is a hormone produced by the pineal gland at night during sleep. It appears to regulate biological

rhythms and may keep the body clock in sync. Bright light and alcohol consumption are known to inhibit melatonin production. Secretion of melatonin is known to decrease as a person ages, reportedly by as much as half. This may play a role in the aging process, and melatonin supplements are being investigated for potential anti-aging properties.

Melatonin is most effective as a relaxant when given in doses (such as 2–3 mg) that mimic the body's own production levels. Since the pineal secretes sufficient melatonin up to age 40 or so, daily supplements are probably unnecessary prior to then.

- Simple, nutritious, natural foods are important for optimal health. Increase your intake of soups, fresh fruits, vegetables, and juices. Drink lots of liquids (particularly pure water), which help flush toxins out of the body. Also, avoid processed foods, sugar, caffeine, alcohol, and tobacco.
- A positive attitude and desire for wellness is always of importance for optimal health.
- Maintain proper hygiene.
- Avoid stress.
- Colostrum contains immune support factors such as lactoferrin, immunoglobulins, antibodies, polypeptides, and transforming growth factors. Colostrum is a powerful immune stimulator and enhancer. It not only contains a multitude of agents that can fight off various pathogens directly, it also stimulates our own immune system components to work more effectively.
- B complex, vitamins C and E, and other nutritional support factors are critical for speedy recovery. Dr. Linus Pauling reported that the body requires large doses— 20,000 mg or more—of vitamin C per day in times of stress and illness.

- Vitamin C stimulates the production of interferon and increases the activity of certain white blood cells.
- Pantothenic acid (vitamin B_5) is important for making antibodies and for normal adrenal functioning.
- Vitamin A alone can greatly increase the size and effectiveness of the thymus, the key gland of the immune system.
- Zinc, containing antibacterial/antiviral properties, is important for the health of the immune system. Zinc is known to revive the thymus. Research shows that as little as 15 mg can restore immune function in even the elderly.[120] Zinc also provides antibacterial/antiviral properties in the mouth, so it may be beneficial to suck zinc lozenges or gargle with mouthwash that contains zinc.

  Note: Do not use high amounts of zinc for more than a week because it may upset your system and always take 1 mg of copper with each 15–20 mg of zinc.
- Consume an adequate amount of sulfur protein daily, which is needed to make antibodies.
- Vitamins C, A, and E, beta carotene, bioflavonoids such as proanthocyanidins (PC-95), zinc, selenium, and CoQ10 are extremely important antioxidants, which help prevent the formation of free radicals caused by pollutants in our air, food, and water.
- Olive leaf extract, also known as oleuropein, is a phenolic compound containing powerful disease-resistant properties. In 1969 the antimicrobial ingredient in oleuropein was identified by researchers at Upjohn pharmaceutical company. It was identified as the calcium salt of elenolic acid and was effective against the growth of every microbe the researchers tested it against—viruses, bacteria, fungus, yeast, and other protozoa.[121] Recently, it became popular as an immune-enhancing supplement. Its effectiveness is impressive.

- Echinacea is a natural, herbal antibiotic that counters the effects of most poisons in the body. It is the prime remedy to help the body rid itself of microbial infections. It is effective against both viral and bacterial attacks, not by killing these organisms but by supporting the body's natural defense system.

  Echinacea is a multifaceted beneficial herb. It has a number of positive properties in the body. It is not geared to just one activity as many drugs are. Due to the chemical composition of echinacea, it has a number of different modes of action, including antiseptic, antimicrobial, antisecretory, anti-inflammatory, and immunostimulant.

  Echinacea works extremely well in combination with other agents, such as vitamin C and garlic. Echinacea contains 17–18 percent vitamin C by dry weight in the form of bioflavonoids. If you add vitamin C to this formula, somehow the body assimilates the ascorbic acid more freely.

Note: Roex has a formula with several of these ingredients called "Hurricane" that supports the immune system and is especially helpful during the cold and flu season.

The Common Cold and the Flu

The common cold is a general inflammation of the mucous membranes of the respiratory passages caused by a variety of viruses. Because so many different types of viruses exist, it is difficult to develop a cure or cold vaccine. Colds are highly contagious.

Symptoms include nose and throat irritations, sneezing, runny or stuffy nose, watery eyes, headache, fever, chills, muscle aches, and temporary loss of smell and taste. On average, most people suffer from two or three colds per year. Most colds last about seven days.

Influenza, commonly called "the flu," is caused by viruses that infect the respiratory tract. Compared with most other viral respiratory infections, such as the common cold, influenza infection often causes a more severe illness.

Influenza viruses continually change over time, usually by mutation. This constant changing enables the virus to evade the immune system of its host, so people are susceptible to influenza virus infections throughout life.

Typical clinical features of influenza include fever (usually 100 to 103 degrees Fahrenheit in adults and often even higher in children) and respiratory symptoms, such as cough, sore throat, runny or stuffy nose, as well as headache, muscle aches, and often extreme fatigue. Although nausea, vomiting, and diarrhea can sometimes accompany influenza infection, especially in children, gastrointestinal symptoms are rarely prominent. The term "stomach flu" is a misnomer that is sometimes used to describe gastrointestinal illnesses caused by other microorganisms.

Most people who get the flu recover completely in one or two weeks, but some people develop serious and potentially life-threatening medical complications, such as pneumonia.

What to Do

Here are some suggestions for the prevention and treatment of colds and flu:

- Colostrum can be helpful for sore throat, cold, and flu. In a controlled study to determine the effectiveness of colostrum on a sore throat, often one of the first signs of an oncoming cold or flu, individuals showed significant reduction of some symptoms from the first day.[122] Other related studies (of the effectiveness of colostrum against tonsillitis-forming bacteria) have shown similar beneficial results.[123] Increase colostrum intake at the first sign of a cold or flu, preferably on an empty stomach.
- At the first sign of cold or flu symptoms, increase the intake of PC-95, olive leaf extract, garlic, and vitamin C.

Also increase the intake of foods that contain vitamin C, including citrus fruits, fruit juices, berries, cabbage, and green vegetables.

- It is important to replace lost vitamins and minerals due to the stress of a viral infection. The most prevalent losses are of vitamin C, B complex, and zinc. Zinc loss contributes to the loss of taste and smell commonly associated with colds and flu.

- Echinacea is very beneficial in the prevention and treatment of colds and flu, as well as upper respiratory infections, tonsillitis, and mouth and throat infections. The effectiveness of echinacea increases when used in conjunction with vitamin C and garlic.

- Beta carotene (vitamin A) protects the lungs.

- Hot herbal teas, especially those containing peppermint, are effective to help open nasal passageways.

- Increase liquid intake, especially hot liquids, which may help induce fever, which helps the body fight the virus.

- It also may help to inhale steam to warm the nasal passageways. Germs cannot thrive in an environment above 103 degrees Fahrenheit. For this reason, many authorities recommend not taking aspirin. Aspirin lowers the body's temperature, which is the natural immune response of the body. A heightened body temperature makes the white blood cells more mobile and more effective in killing germs. In addition, interferon, a protein produced by the body to fight off the virus, works less efficiently when a fever is brought down.

- If possible, stay home and in bed to reduce strain on yourself and avoid spreading the virus to others.

- If cold or flu symptoms persist longer than 14 days or if your temperature is above 103 degrees Fahrenheit, see your doctor.

- Hand-to-hand contact spreads more colds than does sneezing, coughing, or kissing. You can also catch a cold from a door handle, telephone receiver, or sink because a cold virus can remain alive upon such surfaces 72 hours after being touched by an infected individual. Hygiene is extremely important. Wash your hands often and avoid touching your face as much as possible.

Strengthen and Support Your Immune System Naturally

Every year, many individuals receive flu vaccines in order to ward off infection by the flu virus. It is important to keep in mind that with so many strains of the flu virus, it is impossible to create a vaccine that can protect against all of them. Vaccines are not without risk and side effects as they are created using killed or weakened viruses or bacteria. They can, in fact, be very dangerous and many people suffer serious consequences. Instead, why not strengthen your natural immunity against infection safely with colostrum, olive leaf extract, PC-95, Ester-C®, garlic, ginger, and echinacea?

Beneficial Supplementation

The following immune-enhancing supplements can be helpful:

- PC-95: 180 mg or more daily
- Vitamin C (Ester-C®): 3,000 mg daily

Do Antibiotics Help the Common Cold?

Antibiotics fight only bacterial infections. As colds are viral, antibiotics play no role in treating them. Using antibiotics when they are not necessary has led to the growth of several strains of common bacteria that are resistant to antibiotics (including one that commonly causes ear infections in children). For these and other reasons, it is important to limit the use of antibiotics to situations in which they are necessary. Sometimes a bacterial infection can follow the cold virus. This can be treated with antibiotics.

- Olive leaf extract: 3,000 mg daily
- Colostrum: 3,000 mg daily
- Melatonin (adults only): 3–9 mg in the evening
- Silymarin: 450 mg daily
- Probiotics (such as in Roex's Colon Essentials formula): Daily on an empty stomach
- Garlic, cayenne, ginger, and echinacea (as in Roex's Hurricane formula): 2–4 capsules daily

IMPOTENCE

One in four men over the age of 50 experience impotence. The causes may be varied, but the three main contributors are poor circulation, hormonal imbalances, and prostate problems. Women can also experience sexual difficulty, which becomes more prevalent with increasing age.

What to Do

To maintain healthy circulation, see the section starting on page 274.

- L-arginine can be beneficial. In one placebo-controlled study of 50 men with organic erectile dysfunction (ED), 9 of 29 (31 percent) reported a significant improvement in sexual function after receiving L-arginine for three weeks. Researchers concluded that high oral doses of L-arginine seem to cause significant subjective improvement in sexual function in men with organic ED.[124]
- Saw palmetto is an herb that has been shown in clinical studies to have beneficial effects in reducing symptoms of benign prostatic hyperplasia.
- Pygeum is the powdered bark from the *Pygeum africanum* tree found in northern Africa. As an herbal medicine, it has been used for prostate health in Europe for more than 20 years.

- A number of studies have confirmed the value of stinging nettle root for symptomatic relief of enlarged prostate by relieving symptoms such as frequent urination and weak urinary flow. The aboveground parts of the stinging nettle plant have no effect on the prostate but do possess a diuretic action that increases the production of urine. This makes them useful when its necessary to flush out the urinary system.

- Beta-sitosterols are plant compounds found in several herbs. Researchers believe they are key components in promoting and maintaining prostate health.[125] For more information on this subject, see the section on the prostate.

- *Tribulus terrestris* has been used by athletes in Eastern European countries to increase testosterone levels, as well as for its positive effect on the immune system and assistance in improving stamina and muscle strength without harmful side effects. Clinical research has shown that *Tribulus* generates a tonic effect on sexual organs and hormones by assisting the body in healthy sperm production, promoting an increase in sexual drive, and maintaining healthy testosterone levels. This is due to the nutritional support that *Tribulus* provides to the body's production of hormones.[126]

- Ginseng has been called the "king of all tonics" because it has been shown to help strengthen the body's normal functioning and to assist in overcoming the effects of stress and fatigue, promoting health and vitality. Among the significant components within ginseng are phyto-chemical triterpenoid saponins, known as ginsenosides. Many researchers believe these phytochemicals may be helpful in assisting the body to normalize hormone balance.

See chapter 6 for more information on natural ways to enhance your sex life!

Beneficial Supplementation for Men

To promote a healthy prostate, Roex's Advanced Men's Formula can be helpful. It contains

- Saw palmetto berry: 320 mg
- Saw palmetto extract: 100 mg
- Soy phytosterol: 150 mg
- Stinging nettle leaf root: 120 mg
- B_6, D_3, E, copper, zinc, glutamic acid, glycine, lysine, echinacea, *Pygeum africanum*, cranberry extract, pumpkin seed, beta sitosterol

To promote healthy reproductive system functioning, promote hormonal balance, and enhance libido and vitality, I recommend Immortale for Men. It contains

- *Tribulus terrestris:* 200 mg
- Panax ginseng root: 200 mg
- *Turnera aphrodisiaca* (damiana leaf): 200 mg
- *Avena sativa* (green oats): 200 mg
- Sarsaparilla root: 200 mg
- *Muira puama* (balsam and root): 200 mg
- Cayenne: 100 mg
- Wild yam: 100 mg

Beneficial Supplementation for Women

To assist the female body in promoting healthy reproductive system functioning, Immortale for Women can be helpful. It contains

- *Tribulus terrestris:* 300 mg
- Damiana leaf: 300 mg
- *Angelica archangelica* (dong quai) root: 300 mg
- Wild yam root: 300 mg
- Green oats (*Avena sativa*): 200 mg
- Cayenne (40,000 HU): 100 mg

For more information on menopause, see page 345.

INSOMNIA

Insomnia is a difficulty in falling asleep or staying asleep or an inability to fall back to sleep. It is actually very common and becomes more of a problem for many people with age. Part of the reason is that levels of one of the most important brain chemicals we need for sleep, melatonin, diminish with age. This hormone is produced in the pineal gland of the brain.

The majority of insomnia cases are caused by mental disturbances such as stress, depression, an obsessive-compulsive personality, anxiety, and physical pain or discomfort. Overeating and indigestion are also common causes of insomnia. Insomnia may originate from the diet or faulty digestion and be due to vitamin, mineral, enzyme, or amino acid deficiencies.

Deficiencies of B_6 and B_{12}, vitamin C, protein, calcium, magnesium, and potassium have been associated with insomnia. Vitamins B_6 and C are needed for the conversion of tryptophan into serotonin in the brain. Magnesium is a common deficiency that can trigger oversensitivity to noise, light, and other stimuli.

Stimulants (such as sugar, caffeine, salt, and ephedra) interfere with sleep as well as some depressants (including alcohol and antihistamines) and should be avoided.

What to Do

If a nutrient deficiency is responsible for the insomnia, one needs to correct the deficiency.

- The hormone melatonin is very important for sleep. At night, it is produced in the pineal gland of the brain. Levels decrease with age (reportedly by as much as half), and melatonin deficiencies are very common in the elderly.[127] Supplementing can greatly improve your ability to get a good night's sleep.
- If insomnia is due to jet lag, melatonin administration effectively synchronizes the sleep-wake cycle. It is also

beneficial for blind individuals and in subjects suffering from delayed sleep-phase syndrome—the inability to fall asleep quickly, not to be confused with insomnia.[128] Bright light and alcohol consumption also inhibit production of melatonin and can interfere with a good night's sleep.

- The amino acid tryptophan is necessary for sleep because it converts to serotonin (another important relaxation/sleep chemical) in the brain. Foods high in tryptophan include turkey, milk, cheese, and other dairy products. You may try eating these foods an hour before bedtime. One of the classic remedies for insomnia is to drink a glass of warm milk before bedtime.

- Supplementing with the botanical extract 5-HTP (5-hydroxy-tryptophan), which also converts to serotonin, can greatly enhance sleep.

- Inositol also converts to tryptophan once it gets inside the blood-brain barrier.

- Insomnia due to stress can be aided by exercise during the day.

- Warm showers and baths or a hot footbath with chamomile or other relaxing tea can help produce sleep.

- Do relaxation exercises or meditation before going to bed.

- Try to go to bed at approximately the same time every night and get up at the same time every morning. If you do not fall asleep in 20 minutes, get out of bed and do something relaxing.

- Avoid coffee or other stimulants.

- Avoid drinking alcohol before bedtime.

Beneficial Supplementation

The following supplements may be helpful if you experience insomnia:

- B complex: 50 mg two to three times daily with meals
- Vitamin B_5: 100 mg daily
- Vitamin B_6: 10–100 mg daily
- Vitamin B_1: 1,000 mcg two to three times daily
- Inositol: 1-10 grams before bedtime
- Niacin: 100 mg to 2 grams daily
- Vitamin C (Ester-C®): 1,000–5,000 mg daily
- Balanced mineral formula with calcium (2 grams) and magnesium (600 mg): Take at least half in the evening with melatonin
- Melatonin:
  Over age 40, take 1–3 mg in the evening
  Over age 50, take 3–6 mg in the evening
- 5-HTP: 100–200 mg at bedtime
- Herbs: Catnip, chamomile, hops, lady's-slipper, skullcap, valerian root, garlic, and ginger. Try the Roex Hurricane formula which contains many of these herbs.

LIVER TOXICITY

The liver is located in the upper abdomen and aids in digestion. In all, it has over 300 different functions. One of its primary functions is to remove waste products and worn-out cells from the blood. It breaks down toxins in the bloodstream and turns them into less harmful substances that are eventually flushed from the system.

The liver filters impurities out of one to two liters of blood every minute of our lives. This is a tremendous feat considering all the toxins we put into our bodies. If the liver becomes overwhelmed, such as from alcohol abuse or long-term use of certain medications, it may become damaged. Please see chapter 17 on detoxification and elimination for more information on the liver.

Hepatitis

Hepatitis is an inflammation of the liver due to infection or toxic substances. Infectious agents include viruses, bacteria and parasites. Infectious hepatitis can be contracted through blood, feces, contaminated food, water, and shellfish. Toxic agents include antibiotics, drugs, industrial solvents, anesthetics, carbon tetrachloride, and contaminated tap water.

Hepatitis begins with flu-like symptoms of fever, weakness, drowsiness, abdominal discomfort, and headache, possibly accompanied by jaundice. Soon, extreme fatigue and loss of appetite occur. The liver will be tender and enlarged. At this point, the liver is unable to eliminate poisons so they build up in the system; it cannot store and process certain nutrients that are vital for the body.

Hepatitis C is caused by the hepatitis C virus. Its infection and the complications it causes are the most common reasons for liver transplantation. One of the major problems is that 85 percent of individuals initially infected with this virus will become chronically infected. The hepatitis C virus can be transmitted through drug abuse, sexual contact, occupational exposure, occasionally by undetected methods, and, only rarely today, by blood transfusion.

Symptoms of hepatitis C include fatigue, muscle aches, poor appetite, low-grade fever, and infrequently, yellowing of the eyes. Patients who develop liver scarring (cirrhosis) from hepatitis C can have serious complications.

No remarkably effective "medical" treatments for chronic hepatitis C are in general use. Interferon and antivirals have less than a 30 percent response rate, and because of the residual viremia (virus that remains), a newly transplanted liver usually becomes infected again. However, colostrum, olive leaf extract, and silymarin can offer great benefit to the liver. Large doses can greatly reduce the viral load. Antioxidants such as PC-95 and lipoic acid also support liver function and enhance the effectiveness of the above-mentioned nutrients.

One case study followed three patients with hepatitis C using a triple-antioxidant combination of lipoic acid, silymarin (milk thistle extract), and selenium to protect the liver from free-radical damage, increase the levels of other antioxidants, and interfere with viral proliferation. The three patients recovered quickly and their laboratory values (conditions/markers being monitored in the evaluation) remarkably improved. Furthermore, liver transplantation was avoided and the patients were able to return to work, carry out their normal activities, and feel healthy. This treatment is a much less expensive alternative, as one year of the triple-antioxidant therapy costs less than $2,000, compared to more than $300,000 for liver transplant surgery.[129]

Cirrhosis

Cirrhosis is an abnormal liver condition characterized by irreversible scarring of the liver. Alcohol and viral hepatitis B and C are among the many causes of cirrhosis. Cirrhosis can cause yellowing of the skin (jaundice), itching, and fatigue. Diagnosis of cirrhosis can be suggested by physical examination and blood tests and can be confirmed by liver biopsy in some patients. Complications of cirrhosis include mental confusion, coma, fluid accumulation, internal bleeding, and kidney failure.

The effects of silymarin therapy were demonstrated in 36 patients with chronic alcoholic liver disease in a six-month double-blind clinical trial. The changes between the silymarin group compared to the placebo group were significant. These results indicate that silymarin exerts liver-protective activity and is able to improve liver function in alcoholic patients.[130] Other studies have shown similar benefits.[131]

Livalon from Roex includes a special silymarin extract from Europe that is 200 percent more bioavailable that any other silymarin product tested. It is one of the most effective liver detoxifiers available today.

What to Do

Here are some tips for maintaining healthy liver function:

- Silymarin therapy (alone or in conjunction with other antioxidants) has been used for some time to support and protect the liver against a variety of toxins. (Note: The extract bioavailability study mentioned above was conducted in Europe on Legalon, which is the same extract used in Roex's Livalon.)
- Consume absolutely no alcohol or saturated fats.
- A coffee (regular brewed, organic if possible) enema assists in removing toxins from the liver. Do this daily, if possible.
- I suggest performing a general liver detoxification at least once every two years for the average individual; however, those who consume fatty food diets, have more than an occasional alcoholic beverage, or routinely take drugs (pharmaceutical, over-the-counter, or recreational) should consider detoxifying at least once a year. To detoxify your liver, squeeze the juice of 12–15 lemons into a gallon of distilled water. Drink only this liquid for the entire day and consume no food (not recommended for hypoglycemic individuals).

Beneficial Supplementation

The following supplements can be beneficial for liver health:

- Vitamin A: 10,000–25,000 IU two to four times daily
- Folic acid: 5 mg three times daily
- B complex: 50 mg two to three times daily
- Vitamin B_{12}: 1,000 mcg daily
- Vitamin C (Ester-C®): 8,000–15,000 mg (1,000 mg hourly in acute cases)

- Vitamin E: 400 IU daily
- Flaxseed oil: 2–3 tablespoons daily
- Lecithin: 1–2 grams daily
- Silymarin (Livalon): 600 mg or more daily
- PC-95: 300 mg twice daily
- Lipoic acid: 200 mg three times daily
- Selenium: 200 mcg daily
- Artichoke extract: 900 mg daily
- Olive leaf extract: 2,000 mg four times daily
- Colostrum: 4,000–6,000 mg daily
- Chlorophyll: 1 tsp three to four times daily
- Spirulina: 1 tsp three to four times daily
- Beet and carrot juice: As desired
- Colon-cleansing herbs: Oregon grape root, ginger, aloe leaf powder, garlic, cascara sagrada, barberry root, dandelion root, red clover, buckthorn, cayenne, and milk thistle extract (such as found in WOW formula)

In addition, drink eight or more 8 oz glasses of distilled water daily.

MEMORY LOSS

Memory is the ability to remember and recall, through both conscious and unconscious means of association, previous sensations, impressions, ideas, concepts, and all information that has been consciously learned. The loss of memory (and mental faculties) is a growing concern in America as the incidence of different dementia diseases increases.

Poor memory can be a big part of aging (due to free-radical damage, for example) or can be a symptom of an underlying cause, such as nutrient deficiencies (B complex, antioxidants, and amino acids especially), alcoholism, hypoglycemia (low blood sugar), or Alzheimer's disease.

Alzheimer's disease is a form of brain disease that leads to confusion, memory loss, restlessness, difficulty in moving, speech difficulties, and more. The disease often starts in late midlife with slight defects in memory and behavior. The exact cause is unknown, but free-radical damage is believed to be a major contributor. High levels of aluminum have been found in brain tissue of affected individuals. Antioxidants and good nutrition may slow the progress of the disease. If begun early, they may serve as invaluable preventives.

What to Do

To help prevent memory loss, heed the following suggestions:

- PC-95 and *Ginkgo biloba* are two important antioxidant substances known to penetrate the blood-brain barrier and can protect the brain (as well as the vascular system, which feeds the brain) against free-radical damage. They also help enhance blood flow, which is very important for glucose delivery and metabolism. Melatonin is also an important antioxidant that serves to protect the brain cells.

  Ginkgo biloba leaf extract has been demonstrated to significantly decrease the symptoms of impaired brain blood flow, including poor short-term memory and decreased attention span. If one adds hot cayenne pepper when taking ginkgo and PC-95, it seems to make them even more effective.

- Choline, a member of the B complex family, also penetrates the blood-brain barrier and goes directly into the brain cells to produce a chemical that aids memory. It also facilitates the sending of nerve impulses, specifically those in the brain that are used in the formation of memory. Foods that contain choline include egg yolks, brain, heart, green leafy vegetables, yeast, liver, wheat germ, and lecithin.

- Niacin is a powerful vasodilator that helps increase blood flow to the brain.

- Vinpocetine, an extract of the periwinkle plant, is an excellent memory booster. It selectively dilates the arteries and capillaries in the head area, which improves circulation to the brain, thus alleviating cerebral insufficiency. Ongoing research around the world indicates that it may help improve memory, learning ability, insomnia, hearing, eyesight, and the effects of menopause. It also increases tolerance to damage caused by hypoxia (lack of oxygen, such as occurs with a stroke or heart attack).[132]

  Vinpocetine improves several different and fundamental aspects of cerebral metabolism. It increases the blood flow and therefore the use of glucose and oxygen in the brain. It also increases the rate at which brain cells produce ATP (which is cellular energy) and the production of neurotransmitters.[133]

  Vinpocetine works great when taken alone, and it also works well when combined with other memory-enhancing nutrients. Vinpocetine is normally taken orally with food, 5–10 mg, two or three times daily.

- Glutamine, which passes through the blood-brain barrier, is used as a fuel for the brain. This amino acid also helps keep excess amounts of ammonia from damaging the brain and helps to focus our thinking.

- Tyrosine, another amino acid, stimulates the production of norepinephrine, the "alertness" brain chemical, and has a role in sharpening learning, memory, and awareness and in elevating mood and increasing motivation.

- Taurine and methionine are amino acids that help nourish brain cells and help choline's effect of promoting thinking ability. It also helps stabilize brain cell membranes and helps minimize agitation, restlessness, and the inability to focus (an extreme form of which is epilepsy).

- Zinc is a coenzyme with vitamin B$_6$ that is needed to make all the major neurotransmitters, except acetylcholine.
- Magnesium supports the brain in producing energy as ATP. Once the body makes ATP, the ATP immediately combines with magnesium to stabilize and store it. The B vitamins require manganese or magnesium as their coenzymes to work properly.
- Manganese, an important trace mineral for normal central nervous system function, can help improve memory and can also help eliminate fatigue and reduce nervous irritability. Manganese helps stabilize acetylcholine so it is not prematurely used or discharged and has had success in epileptic therapy.
- Supplementation with tonic herbs such as ginseng, astragalus, or dong quai, either alone or in combination, is beneficial for individuals who are in a malnourished, weakened state. It is also helpful for preventing symptoms of aging, including poor memory. For superior results, tonic herbs should be taken at mealtime.
- American ginseng combined with red deer antler (in equal parts) is known as the most powerful energy-memory tonic for individuals of all ages.
- Siberian ginseng also has endurance-giving properties and is known as an adaptogen, which assists in the endurance of high levels of stress. (Using the brain all the time is a form of stress.)
- Gotu kola is a classic memory herb for brain fatigue.
- Ginger and cayenne stimulate circulation, which can also be helpful.

A feeble body enfeebles the mind.
—JEAN JACQUES ROUSSEAU

Beneficial Supplementation

The following supplements can be helpful in improving memory:

- B complex: 50 mg twice daily
- Choline: 1,500 mg twice daily
- Niacin: 100–500 mg daily
- Magnesium: 800 mg daily
- Manganese: 5–10 mg daily (adequate amounts should be available in a good balanced mineral supplement)
- Zinc: 50 mg daily
- PC-95: 300–400 mg daily (less is needed if using as a preventive)
- L-glutamine: 500 mg three times daily
- Amino acids: Methionine, taurine, and tyrosine
- Lecithin: 2 grams daily
- DMAE (dimethyl-amino-ethanol): 10–25 drops daily
- Herbs: Astragalus, calamus, cayenne, dong quai, *Ginkgo biloba* leaf extract, ginger, ginseng (American and Siberian), gotu kola, and red deer antler

MENOPAUSE

Menopause is defined as the time in a woman's life when menstrual periods have not occurred for 12 consecutive months and no other biological or physiological cause can be identified. It signals the end of her childbearing years. Perimenopause, the time approaching menopause, is when the menstrual periods start changing.

Natural menopause occurs when the ovaries naturally begin decreasing their production of the sex hormones estrogen and progesterone. *Induced* menopause occurs if the ovaries are surgically removed or damaged by radiation or drugs. Due to the abrupt cutoff of ovarian hormones, induced menopause causes the sudden onset of hot flashes and other menopause-related symptoms, such as a dry vagina and a decline in sex drive.

A simple hysterectomy (when the uterus but not the ovaries is removed) before natural menopause should not affect the production of sex hormones and so does not cause menopause (unless the nerves or blood supply to the ovaries is damaged during the hysterectomy).

The timing of natural menopause is variable. In the Western world, the average age is about 51. Natural menopause can begin, however, any time from age 30 to 60. Factors influencing the time of menopause include heredity (genetics) and cigarette smoking. Smokers (and former smokers) reach menopause an average of two years before women who have never smoked.

Other changes associated with perimenopause and menopause include night sweats, mood swings, vaginal dryness, fluctuations in sexual desire (libido), forgetfulness, difficulty in sleeping, and fatigue (probably from the loss of sleep).

Hormone-replacement therapy (estrogen with or without progestin) is the primary medical treatment for the symptoms and long-term risks associated with menopause. However, many women also are concerned about side effects and the increased risks for uterine and breast cancer with hormone-replacement therapy.

What to Do

Researchers at the Department of Obstetrics and Gynecology, Harbor UCLA Medical Center, Torrance, California, state that risk reduction for an array of health problems can be achieved through diet, exercise, and stress management. Specific vitamins, minerals, phytoestrogens, and essential fatty acid supplements are a vital component of the risk-reduction health program.[134]

Risk reduction for osteoporosis can be enhanced specifically through the use of ipriflavone and a comprehensive "bone-building" vitamin and mineral program.

Control of homocysteine levels for prevention of coronary artery disease, osteoporosis, and other health problems can be accomplished through B vitamin supplementation. The same interventions for risk reduction also may prove to be effective in the prevention and treatment of menopausal-related symptoms, particularly when the B vitamins, magnesium, isoflavones, and essential fatty acids are used. If lifestyle interventions and nutraceuticals do not adequately address symptoms, however, a woman has several alternative therapies from which to choose. Numerous excellent herbal and homeopathic therapies are available.[135]

- American ginseng (*Panax quinquefolius L.*) alleviates menopause symptoms because it provides natural beneficial estrogen-like compounds (phytoestrogens) and helps balance estrogen levels.
- A number of additional food plants contain beneficial phytoestrogens, such as soybeans and flaxseed. These, especially, may be partially responsible for the effects of herbal prescriptions for postmenopausal disorders in which estrogen deficiency is considered the primary cause. Some recent trials with oral isoflavone supplements report reductions in hot flashes, vaginal dryness, and breast pain.[136]
- The herbs damiana and dong quai contain phytoestrogens and promote hormone balance. Dong quai has been considered a "female ginseng," assisting the body in normalizing hormone balance and enhancing energy and vitality. Clinical studies have shown dong quai to be beneficial in promoting healthy menses and assisting the body during menopause. Dong quai has also been shown to promote blood flow, nutritionally supporting circulation in and to the pelvic area, and to provide nutritional support for blood flow to the heart, brain, and vascular system.[137]

- Wild yam also has phytoestrogen properties and is often used as a female hormone balancer for menstrual problems.[138]
- *Tribulus terrestris*, a plant native to Eastern Europe, has clinically shown a tonic effect on sexual organs and hormones by assisting the body in healthy hormone production.[139]
- St.-John's-wort preparations can be used successfully to relieve the psychological symptoms of menopause.[140]
- Italian researchers tested a plant product based on extracts of the leaves of *Salvia officinalis* (sage) and *Medicago sativa* (alfalfa) in 30 menopausal women with hot flashes and night sweating. The treatment eliminated these symptoms completely in 20 women, 4 women showed good improvement, and the other 6 showed a reduction in symptoms.[141]

The Roex formula Immortale for Women can be particularly beneficial for women in menopause as well as for younger women with PMS difficulties.

MENTAL HEALTH

The importance of a sound, well-functioning brain for health and happiness cannot be overstated. The brain is the master control biocomputer of the human organism. It generates every thought and mood. It controls our movements and regulates our breathing, heartbeat, body temperature, and hormone balance. Yet in spite of the importance of a smooth-running brain for health and vitality, the brain is usually the most poorly nourished organ in the human body.

The brain weighs about three pounds—less than 2 percent of our total body weight—yet it uses 20 percent of the body's total energy supply. The estimated 10 billion neurons (brain cells) have a voracious appetite for fuel (glucose), oxygen, vitamins, minerals, amino acids, and fatty acids, which must be satisfied every minute of every day of our lives. All these nutrients must be delivered to the brain constantly by our bloodstream. If the blood flow to the brain is interrupted even for 15–20 seconds, unconsciousness results. If deprived of blood or oxygen for more than 5–10 minutes, the brain dies.

Only slight changes in the molecular amounts of numerous chemicals can bring on changes in the brain affecting behavior, mood, and perception. Medical professionals have found that using megavitamin therapy for many mental disorders has doubled recovery rates.

Mental illness as a physical disease can result from low brain concentrations of vitamins B_1, B_5, B_6, and B_{12}, niacin, folic acid, vitamin C, various minerals (especially zinc), and amino acids. Psychological problems can also stem from undetected allergies (such as to milk, wheat, or corn) or from excess copper, aluminum, or other metals in the body.

About 30 percent of schizophrenics are deficient in vitamin B_6 and zinc. This condition is referred to as pyroluria and has had good results with B_6, zinc, and magnesium supplementation. Major symptoms of pyroluria include withdrawal and depression. Other indications include breath or body odor; intolerance to some proteins, alcohol, or drugs; morning nausea and constipation; crowded upper front teeth; white spots on fingernails; difficulty in remembering dreams; pale skin that does not tolerate sunlight; frequent abdominal pain; frequent head colds and infections; stretch marks; and irregular menstrual cycle or impotency.

What to Do

For good mental health, consider these suggestions:

- Avoid sugar. Research shows that 75 percent of patients suffering from anxiety and panic disorders had a dramatic increase in anxiety after eating as little as one candy bar daily. Sugar causes the body to release adrenaline, which is the major factor in panic attacks and also causes a draining of many of the nutrients required by the brain for optimal functioning.

- Avoid caffeine, which releases adrenaline in the body.
- Avoid all recreational drugs, including alcohol.
- Practice deep breathing from the diaphragm. Deep breathing initiates cell oxygenation and stimulates the lymphatic system to remove toxins.

Beneficial Supplementation

The following supplements have been shown to be beneficial in maintaining mental health:

- B complex:* two to three times daily
- Vitamin C (Ester-C®): 2,000–6,000 mg daily
- Manganese: 10 mg twice daily
- Zinc gluconate: 30 mg twice daily
- 5-HTP: 100 mg twice daily
- PC-95: 300 mg daily
- Melatonin: 3–9 mg daily as a natural mood enhancer
- Sulfur protein: 28–56 mg
- Balanced multiminerals:**
  - Elemental calcium (preferably a combination of calcium citrate, chelate, aspartate, and lactate): 1,200 mg
  - Magnesium: 600 mg
  - Trace mineral combination (copper, molybdenum, potassium, selenium, zinc, boron, silica) without iron: 300 mg
  - Essential fatty acids (omega-9 plus a 1:1 ratio of omega-3/omega-6):***
    - Omega-3: 1,400–2,100 mg

---

* A quality B complex should include B_1, B_2, B_{12}, niacin, niacinamide, folic acid, biotin, pantothenic acid, magnesium, arginine, betaine hydrochloride, carnitine, choline, PABA, lecithin, bromelain, and alpha lipoic acid.
** Roex's Ultimate Calcium Mineral Formula contains all of the listed items.
*** Roex EFAs contain omega-3, 6, and 9 in proper balance.

- Omega-6: 1,400–2,100 mg
- Omega-9: 740–1,200 mg
- Herbs: Cayenne, ginseng, gotu kola, and St.-John's-wort

Nervousness

Nervousness, a feeling of tension, unease, anxiousness, and excitability, can be caused by a large variety of circumstances and conditions. Overwork, lack of sleep, stress, poor diet, and lack of exercise and fresh air are only a few possible causes of nervousness.

What to Do

To relieve nervous tension,

- Massage the web structure of the hand between the finger and thumb. Apply hand cream for lubrication and start massaging the left hand first. After five minutes switch to the right hand. The webbing between the thumb and fingers contains many nerve endings that when massaged relax the entire body.
- Perform deep-breathing exercises.

Beneficial Supplementation

The following supplements have been shown to be beneficial for those experiencing nervousness:

- B complex:* two to three times daily
- Vitamin C (Ester-C®): 2,000–6,000 mg daily
- Manganese: 10 mg twice daily
- Zinc gluconate: 30 mg twice daily

---

* A quality B complex should include B_1, B_2, B_{12}, niacin, niacinamide, folic acid, biotin, pantothenic acid, magnesium, arginine, betaine hydrochloride, carnitine, choline, PABA, lecithin, bromelain, and alpha lipoic acid.

- 5-HTP: 100 mg twice daily
- PC-95: 300 mg daily
- Sulfur protein: 28–56 mg (varies proportionally with body weight, 160–250 lb)
- Balanced multiminerals:**
  - Elemental calcium (preferably a combination of calcium citrate, chelate, aspartate, and lactate): 1,200 mg
  - Magnesium: 600 mg
  - Trace mineral combination (copper, molybdenum, potassium, selenium, zinc, boron, silica) without iron: 300 mg
- Essential fatty acids (omega-9 plus a 1:1 ratio of omega-3/omega-6):***
  - Omega-3: 1,400–2,100 mg
  - Omega-6: 1,400–2,100 mg
  - Omega-9: 740–1,200 mg
- Herbs: Cayenne, ginseng, gotu kola, and St.-John's-wort

** Roex's Ultimate Calcium Mineral Formula contains all of the listed items.
*** Roex EFAs contain omega-3, 6, and 9 in proper balance.

Stress

Stress is any kind of physical or emotional strain on the body or mind. Stress is with us all the time. It is an unavoidable part of our lives. Stress is unique and personal to each of us. What may be stressful to one person may actually be relaxing to another.

Physical stress occurs when an external or natural change or force acts upon the body. Extreme heat or cold, overwork, injuries, malnutrition, illness, and exposure to drugs or poisons are examples of physical stress.

Emotional stress may be a result of fear, hate, love, anger, tension, grief, frustration, or anxiety. Too much emotional stress can cause the immune system to wear down, and physical illness, such as high blood pressure, ulcers, asthma, migraine headaches, strokes, cancer, and heart disease, can occur.

Emotional and physical stresses also may be combined in special body conditions such as pregnancy, adolescence, and aging. During these times, one's metabolism is increased or lowered, changing the body's physical functions, which, in turn, affects a person's mental and emotional outlook on life.

A certain amount of stress may be useful as a motivational factor, but too much of the wrong kind of stress can be detrimental. Recognizing early signs of stress and then doing something about it can make an important difference in the quality of life.

Physiologically, stress causes an increase in the production of adrenal hormones, which increases the metabolism of proteins, fats, and carbohydrates and produces instant energy for the body to use. As a result, an increased excretion of protein, potassium, phosphorus, and calcium occurs. Many of the disorders related to stress are not a direct result of stress but a result of nutrient deiciencies caused by the increased metabolic rate during stress. Vitamin C is utilized by the adrenal glands during stress, and any stress that is sufficiently severe or prolonged will cause a depletion of vitamin C in the tissues.

What to Do

The following tips and supplements can help reduce stress:

- Physical exercise is one of the most effective means of relieving emotional stress.
- Relax. Find activities that give you pleasure and are good for your physical and mental well-being, such as golf, walking, fishing, biking, listening to music, reading, playing with a pet or children, and so on.
- Think of something that produces an inner smile or glow. Picturing an adored person, an amusing situation, your pet, or some other "melt moment" induces calmness, reduces heart rate, relaxes muscle tension, and gives a sense of well-being.

- Do not keep problems bottled up inside you. If something is bothering you, let it out. Talking to someone can help relieve stress and make you feel better. Keeping a journal and writing letters can also help you get things off your chest and relieve stress.
- Crying can be a healthy way to bring relief if you're feeling anxious, and it might even prevent a headache or other physical consequence.
- Avoid drugs. Drugs are habit forming and create more stress than they take away.
- Chocolate may not be all bad! Chocolate contains high amounts of special chemicals called pyrazines, which stimulate the pleasure center in the brain. This chemical interrupts stress signals and helps to cheer you up. The sugar in chocolate also raises the level of brain serotonin, a natural chemical that soothes frazzled nerves.

  (Note: Sugar does have a great number of detriments and should almost always be avoided, especially by sugar-sensitive individuals, such as hypoglycemics. Chocolate treats also often contain saturated fats and/or hydrogenated oils, which should be consumed in limited quantities.)
- Replacement of lost nutrients, such as B complex (especially B_1, B_5, B_6, and B_{12}), vitamin C, magnesium, potassium, phosphorus, and zinc, is of critical importance to maintaining health. When you do not provide the body with adequate and complete nutrition, the body has difficulty recovering from the physical effects of stress.

  B complex vitamins help maintain the health of the nervous system. Even a slight deficiency can cause irritability and depression.

  Several dietary factors interfere with the ability of the body to utilize vitamin B_1 (thiamine). Tea (tannic acid), sugar, and alcohol consumption raise B_1 requirements in the body. Vitamin B_5 (pantothenic acid) improves the ability of even well-nourished people to withstand stress. Inositol converts into tryptophan and then into serotonin in the brain, which is crucial for sleep. Stress-related insomnia may be associated with a deficiency in this B vitamin.

- Physical and emotional stress can increase the need for vitamin C by 50 times. In addition, smoking (which often increases during stressful times) depletes the tissues of vitamin C.
- Magnesium is also drained from the body by stress. Studies indicate that a magnesium deficiency weakens the body's ability to cope with stress and makes one more sensitive to stimuli such as noise and bright lights.[142]
- GABA acts as an inhibitory neurotransmitter that prevents too many messages from being relayed across the brain.

Beneficial Supplementation

The following supplements have been shown to be beneficial for those experiencing nervousness:

- B complex:* two to three times daily
- Vitamin C (Ester-C®): 2,000–6,000 mg daily
- Manganese: 10 mg twice daily
- Zinc gluconate: 30 mg twice daily
- 5-HTP: 100 mg twice daily
- PC-95: 300 mg daily
- Sulfur protein: 28–56 mg (varies proportionally with body weight, 160–250 lb)

---

* A quality B complex should include B_1, B_2, B_{12}, niacin, niacinamide, folic acid, biotin, pantothenic acid, magnesium, arginine, betaine hydrochloride, carnitine, choline, PABA, lecithin, bromelain, and alpha lipoic acid.

- Balanced multiminerals:**
  - Elemental calcium (preferably a combination of calcium citrate, chelate, aspartate, and lactate): 1,200 mg
  - Magnesium: 600 mg
  - Trace mineral combination (copper, molybdenum, potassium, selenium, zinc, boron, silica) without iron: 300 mg
  - Essential fatty acids (omega-9 plus a 1:1 ratio of omega-3/omega-6):***
    - Omega-3: 1,400–2,100 mg
    - Omega-6: 1,400–2,100 mg
    - Omega-9: 740–1,200 mg
  - Herbs: Cayenne, ginseng, gotu kola, and St.-John's-wort

** Roex's Ultimate Calcium Mineral Formula contains all of the listed items.
*** Roex EFAs contain omega-3, 6, and 9 in proper balance.

In the middle of every difficulty lies an opportunity.
—ALBERT EINSTEIN

OBESITY

Obesity is a national health problem. It is estimated that 60 million Americans are above their ideal weight. Obesity increases numerous risks, such as for kidney disease, diabetes, high blood pressure, liver disorders, arthritis, and even premature death.

An individual becomes overweight when more calories are consumed than the body can burn off through activity. The excess calories are stored in the body as fat. The more calories taken in above what are burned off, the more fat accumulates. Each 3,500 excess calories equals one pound of body fat.

What to Do

The only way to lose weight permanently is to eat nutritionally balanced, low-calorie meals, exercise more, and drink lots of distilled water. Reduction of calorie intake alone, without exercise, is not likely to produce desired weight-loss results. When fewer calories are taken in than the body is accustomed to, the body's rate of metabolism slows down. Exercise increases the body's rate of metabolism, compensating for the difference. Crash diets are dangerous. Sudden weight loss can damage the heart, gastrointestinal tract, and metabolism. The following all can help regulate the body's weight:

- *Garcinia cambogia,* also known as hydroxycitric acid (HCA), is a fruit extract with a chemical composition similar to citric acid (found in citrus fruits). Clinical research has shown HCA is effective in promoting the body's ability to convert fats and carbohydrates into energy.[143] This reduces fats and fat metabolites produced by the body.

   Laboratory experiments and animal research suggest that HCA may be a useful weight-loss aid. HCA has been demonstrated in the laboratory to reduce the conversion of carbohydrates into stored fat by inhibiting certain enzyme processes. Animal research indicates that HCA suppresses appetite and induces weight loss. One case report found that eating one gram of fruit containing HCA before each meal resulted in the loss of one pound per day.[144]

- Thermogenic substances stimulate the alpha-II-adrenaline modulated pathways found on various tissues in the body. When these sites are stimulated, the metabolic activity of the tissues increases. High numbers of alpha-II receptors are present on the tissues of the body known to produce heat (which is why the term "thermogenic" is used). Thermogenics also act as an appetite suppressant. Thermogenic substances include ginger, yerba mate, green tea, ginseng, and caffeine. Cayenne and white willow are excellent catalysts.

- Chromium is necessary to regulate blood sugar and insulin levels, to assist in controlling food cravings, and in the efficient use of carbohydrates by the body.

- L-carnitine, inositol, choline, and other lipotropic factors assist and promote an increase in the body's ability to convert stores of fat into energy by increasing fat-burning capabilities.
- Fruits, vegetables, whole grains, and beans add bulk to the diet, make one feel full, and help carry excess fat out of the body. Excellent supplements include ground flaxseed, glucomannan, guar gum, and bran and should be taken with distilled water.
- Chitosan, a naturally occurring polysaccharide derived from the exoskeleton of shellfish, such as shrimp and crab, is chemically similar to the plant fiber cellulose. It provides bulk and assists in the elimination of toxic wastes. Chitosan has the unique ability to significantly bind to fats, acting as a "fat sponge" in the digestive tract. Chitosan is a positively charged fiber molecule that is magnetically attracted to negatively charged fat molecules. Clinical studies show chitosan can bind up to five times its weight in fat.
- Distilled water is a very necessary component in any weight-loss program. Drink eight 8 oz glasses every day!

Rod's Weight Loss Program

CitriGenics I is a unique blend of natural ingredients formulated to assist the body in converting fats and carbohydrates to energy. It can stimulate metabolic activity, promotes feelings of satiety, and controls food cravings. It contains

- CitriMax (Garcinia cambogia-HCA 50 percent, 750 mg): 1,500 mg
- L-carnitine: 300 mg
- Choline bitartrate: 100 mg
- Inositol: 100 mg
- Betaine HCl: 50 mg
- Chromium (ChromeMate): 200 mcg
- Green tea extract: 150 mg

- Panax ginseng: 100 mg
- Cayenne (40,000 HU): 100 mg
- Ginger: 100 mg
- Yerba mate: 100 mg
- Spirulina: 100 mg
- Kelp with trace minerals: 100 mg
- Vitamins A, C, E, B_2, B_3, B_6, B_{12}, biotin, folic acid, potassium, selenium, and iodine (sea vegetables)

Take 2–4 tablets with meals, twice daily.

GitriGenics II contains chitosan, which acts like a "fat sponge" for the digestive tract. It is enhanced with vitamin C and chromium polyniotinate to help control food cravings. Each tablet provides

- Chitosan (93 percent deacetylated): 250 mg
- Vitamin C (ascorbic acid): 100 mg
- Chromium (ChromeMate): 25 mcg

Take 4 tablets or more with evening meal.

WOW can be an excellent herbal combination for colon cleansing and blood purifying containing

- Aloe vera leaf powder
- Barberry root
- Buckthorn bark
- Burdock root
- Cascara sagrada
- Cayenne
- Dandelion root
- Garlic
- Ginger
- Milk thistle seed
- Red clover

Take 2 capsules daily after the evening meal; add 1 additional capsule daily until one has a significant bowel movement.

Individuals challenged with obesity should see positive results by eliminating processed foods from their diet and taking a more aggressive approach to the weight loss guidelines.

OSTEOPOROSIS

Osteoporosis is a loss of normal bone density, marked by the thinning of bone tissue and the growth of small holes in the bone. Osteoporosis may be very painful (especially in the lower back) and may cause frequent broken bones, loss of body height, and deformities (for example, the humpback look in the elderly). It occurs most frequently in women who have gone through menopause, individuals who are inactive or paralyzed, and individuals taking steroid hormones. Estrogen (a female sex hormone) is often used to prevent postmenopausal osteoporosis, but its use may cause uterine cancer.

A major cause of osteoporosis is an inadequate intake of calcium over a period of years. The minimum daily requirement for calcium for adults is 800 mg per day, while many people, especially the aged, get only 450 mg per day. It is estimated that over 30 percent of the American population suffers from calcium deficiency. In addition, calcium needs increase with age. Women who have passed menopause may need as much as 1,500 mg daily.

Calcium Facts

- 80 percent of American women are calcium deficient.
- Men and women over age 30 require up to 67 percent more calcium than do 16-year-olds.
- According to *The Calcium Bible* by Patricia Hausman, M.S., calcium not only is essential as a bone-building nutrient but also shows promise in helping control blood pressure.
- Research findings reveal that the time of day you take a calcium supplement is vital for maximizing its absorption and that the most effective time is nighttime.
- The form of the calcium taken and the conutrients it is taken with are important in achieving the most beneficial results from a calcium supplement. Vitamin D_3 is needed for optimal calcium absorption.

Other causes of osteoporosis are inability to absorb sufficient calcium through the intestines, calcium-phosphorus imbalance, lack of exercise, and lack of certain hormones. Individuals over the age of 50 should have a bone density test done every five years to check their mineral levels.

What to Do

To help prevent osteoporosis, follow these suggestions:

- A diet that is adequate in protein (but not excessive), calcium, magnesium, and vitamins C and D is the best treatment and prevention for osteoporosis.
- A calcium supplement is necessary to rebuild lost bone tissue and prevent further loss. Calcium hydroxyapatite, calcium gluconate, calcium citrate, calcium lactate, or chelated calcium are the best supplemental sources. Avoid calcium carbonate and oyster shell calcium.
- Consume foods that are high in calcium: milk and milk products, fish, eggs, cereal products, beans, many types of nuts and seeds, fruits (especially oranges and papaya), and vegetables (especially leafy green). (Note: Meat and dairy products do contain calcium but are not good sources to rely upon because they are high in protein and phosphorus, which can actually contribute to a calcium deficiency.)
- Some experts believe that a calcium deficiency is actually caused by a magnesium deficiency, which requires magnesium supplementation.[145]
- Proper stomach acidity is required for calcium to dissolve. If you are not sure you have adequate stomach acidity, try taking this old folk remedy with your calcium supplement: one tablespoon of apple cider vinegar mixed with one tablespoon of honey. Another suggestion is to take a hydrochloric acid supplement with calcium if you are not sure you have adequate stomach acidity.

The Amount of Calcium Found in Common Foods

1 cup lowfat yogurt	350–450 mg
1 cup skim milk	300–350 mg
1 ounce Colby cheese	293 mg
10 dried figs	270 mg
½ cup almonds	160 mg
1 cup broccoli	140 mg
1 tablespoon blackstrap molasses	140 mg
⅓ pound salmon	120 mg
1 cup rhubarb	120 mg
3½ ounces tofu	100 mg

- Avoid eating a diet high in animal protein, which induces a calcium deficiency.
- Avoid eating sweets and refined carbohydrates, which stimulate alkaline digestive juices, making calcium insoluble.
- Avoid prolonged stress, alcohol abuse, antibiotics, steroids, and cigarettes. (Tobacco leaches calcium from the bones.)
- Some experts say the answer to bone problems is silica. People who do not get enough calcium but have no bone problems, may be consuming large amounts of silica. In a newborn, the ratio of calcium to silica is very different from the ratio in an older person. This may be why babies' bones are so resilient. Silica is actually a youth factor. With the loss of silica, bones become older and more brittle. This decreases bone elasticity, which results in a greater propensity to fracture. Bone growth involves the process of adding calcium for hardness and increasing collagen, the tough connective tissue that binds

everything together and gives bones flexibility. Silica is essential for both these processes.[146]

Silica is important in the following ways:

- In the formation and repair of bone, cartilage, skin, and connective tissues of all kinds
- As a participant in several metabolic processes
- As an essential nutrient in the initial calcification of bones in newborns
- As a corrective dietary supplement in skeletal abnormalities resulting from silica deficiency
- In producing effects totally independent of the presence of vitamin D but synergistic with ascorbate

Beneficial Supplementation

The following supplements have been shown to be beneficial in preventing and treating osteoporosis:

- Vitamin B_{12}: 30–900 mcg daily
- Vitamin C (Ester-C®): 1,000–2,000 mg two to four times daily
- Vitamin D: 200 IU daily
- Vitamin E: 600 IU daily
- Calcium: 1,000–2,000 mg daily (in the proper forms)
- Magnesium: 500–1,000 mg daily
- MSM: 3–5 grams daily
- Copper: Amounts should be adequate in a balanced mineral formula
- Silica: Amounts should be adequate in a balanced mineral formula; at least 150 mg or more daily.
- Herbs: Comfrey and horsetail

Note: Roex's Ultimate Calcium Mineral Formula contains all the minerals in their proper balance, plus 150 mg silica for proper absorption. It includes the most bioavailable forms of calcium and does not include iron. Excess amounts of iron can easily oxidize and create free radicals in the body. You should not take iron unless blood tests have shown you are iron deficient.

PAIN

Pain is an unpleasant sensation caused by signals from some nerve endings. It is really a signal from the body that something is wrong. Pain is a basic symptom of inflammation and is an important clue to the cause of many disorders. In children, leg pains (especially at night) often are an indication of mineral deficiencies. (I have found that regular supplementation with a balanced multimineral formula [two to three tablets per night] eliminates the pain, allowing them to fall to sleep within 15 minutes!)

What to Do

To treat pain, try the following:

- Cold is the best remedy for the pain of injury. Ice numbs the affected area and decreases swelling by reducing the blood supply.
- MSM can be highly beneficial for pain associated with joint degeneration as seen with arthritis. Sulfur (taken with vitamin C) is an important component needed for connective tissue regeneration. The body is constantly in a state of self-repair, but if all necessary components are not present, healing cannot occur and scarring can take place. Results can usually be seen in two to four weeks of use. The higher the amount used, the faster results tend to be experienced.

  Researchers predict that MSM will soon be proven effective not only in the treatment of various types of arthritis (including rheumatoid and osteoarthritis) but other conditions as well—such as lupus and TMJ, which, like arthritis, involve connective-tissue degeneration, depletion of synovial fluid (which provides lubrication in the joints), tissue scarring, inflammation and pain.

- Calcium and magnesium help reduce muscle tension.
- Antioxidants such as PC-95 and lipoic acid help reduce tissue damage from inflammation. See chapter 14 for more information on PC-95.
- Zinc is also important to speed wound healing.

Beneficial Supplementation

The following supplements have been shown to be beneficial in treating pain:

- Vitamin C (Ester-C®): 2,000–10,000 mg daily
- MSM: 2 grams MSM per 1,000 mg vitamin C, four to five times daily
- Zinc: 25 mg daily
- Calcium: 1,200 mg daily
- Magnesium: 400 mg daily
- Trace minerals (properly balanced)
- PC-95: 300 mg or more daily
- Lipoic acid: 200 mg daily
- DLPA (DL-phenylalanine): 500–1,000 mg one to two times daily
- Herbs: Black cohosh, bugleweed, catnip, chaparral, wild yam, comfrey, corn silk, fenugreek, lady's slipper, mullein, white willow, and wintergreen

PROSTATE TROUBLE

The prostate is a small doughnut-shaped organ that encircles the urethra at its junction with the bladder. The urethra is the tube that carries urine from the bladder to the end of the penis. When the prostate is enlarged, it narrows the urethra, blocking the passing of urine. Urinary problems and painful and urgent urination are common prostate disorders.

Prostate trouble is one of the most common afflictions of men. Approximately 250,000 new cases were diagnosed in 1998 alone. At the current rate of growth, estimates suggest 1 in 3 American men will develop prostate cancer. It is a risk for all men that increases with age. African American men have the highest incidence of prostate cancer worldwide and a 50 percent greater risk of development than white Americans.[147]

Prostatitis is the inflammation of the prostate. The usual cause of prostatitis in men in their 20s and 30s is a bacterial infection from another area of the body that has invaded the prostate. Symptoms of acute prostatitis are local pain, fever, frequent urination, inability to empty the bladder fully (accompanied by a burning sensation), and blood or pus in the urine.

Prostatic enlargement (benign prostatic hypertrophy, or BPH) is the most common prostate problem. BPH is usually seen in older males and is often due to gradual enlargement over a period of several years. The prostate, which is normally the size of a walnut, can swell to the size of an orange. A majority of U.S. men over 45 are living with an enlarged prostate, many of whom do not even know it yet.

Symptoms of BPH include

- Painful urination (dysuria)
- Straining to urinate
- Dribbling after urination
- Hesitancy
- Decrease in force and caliber of urinary stream
- Sensation of incomplete bladder emptying
- Increased frequency of urination—especially at night

In addition, incontinence, involuntary urination, genital urinary infections, and blood in the urine could be symptoms of BPH. If you have any of them, ask your doctor to evaluate you for BPH and prostate cancer.

Prostate cancer is the second most common form of cancer for American men, following lung cancer. Although there are several common medical treatments (including radiation and surgery), men (like women with breast cancer) have options. The best cure, of course, is prevention. Refer to the section on cancer for suggestions.

What causes prostate enlargement? Hormonal changes. Dihydrotestosterone (DHT), a form of testosterone, is believed to be the major culprit of BPH. High levels of estrogen, progesterone, and prolactin also can enlarge the prostate.

A urologist from Mexico who was a Harvard graduate told me about another common, but little recognized, cause of prostate problems—parasites. Most people don't like to hear about the possibility of various worms or fungi setting up housekeeping inside us, but it is much more common than people realize. For this problem, I recommend Hurricane, WOW, and colostrum.

Proscar or Hytrin, an alpha blocker known to reduce blood pressure and tension in the prostate gland, is commonly prescribed, but far better treatments are available, including nutritional and herbal therapies. Studies have shown that saw palmetto lowers levels of DHT, estrogen, and progesterone, thereby reducing the chances of BPH. The active ingredients are fatty acids, esters, and sterols, including beta-sitosterol (also found in *Pygeum africanum*). Beta-sitosterols are believed to be the key components in promoting and maintaining prostate health.[148]

Both saw palmetto and pygeum offer similar benefits, but clinical research shows that pygeum is more effective. Taken together, they can alleviate BPH, reduce prostatitus, and even reverse impotence.

Because of my ongoing problem with the prostate, I think I have tried every formula on the market—with little success. I turned to European research and developed my Advanced Men's Formula. It has worked wonders for me. The result of my PSA (protein-specific antigen) blood test, which is an indicator for cancer of the prostrate at +5 or greater, was down to 1 last year, and my nighttime bathroom trips are now one or two, rather than six or eight as before!

Important Foods for the Prostate

Watermelon and tomatoes, which contain lycopene, improve prostate health. Ten servings of tomatoes a week, raw or in sauces, can reduce prostate cancer risk by over 40 percent.

Eat high-fiber, low-fat foods. Avoid hydrogenated oils and sugar. Cut back on red meat and eat more soy (tofu, tempeh, soy beans). Eating soy protein may be why Japanese men have a low incidence of prostate cancer. High serum levels of cholesterol have been associated with prostate disease.

Pumpkin seeds, which contain essential fatty acids, also nurture the prostate. Strawberry jam (despite the sugar) contains ellagic acids, which helps support the prostate.

Seafood, spinach, mushrooms, whole grains, and sunflower seeds are high in zinc, which can help relieve painful symptoms and swelling.

What to Do

The following steps support prostate health:

- Increase fluid intake to stimulate urine flow, preventing retention of urine. Drink 8 to 10 glasses of distilled water daily!
- Hot sitz baths and hot compresses can help relieve discomfort. Chamomile tea added to the water helps relieve pressure on the urethra and allows the bladder to empty fully.
- Avoid alcohol, caffeine, nicotine, and spicy foods, which have negative, irritating effects on the prostate.

Beneficial Supplementation

The following supplements have been shown to be beneficial for the prostate:

- Vitamin A: 25,000 IU one to two times daily
- B Complex: 50 mg three times daily
- Vitamin B$_6$: 50-100 mg two times daily
- Vitamin C (Ester-C®): 1,000-2,000 mg three times daily
- Vitamin D: up to 25,000 IU per week
- Vitamin E: 400 IU two to three times daily
- Calcium: 800-1,000 mg daily
- Magnesium: 400-500 mg daily
- Selenium: 100-200 mcg daily
- Zinc: 50 mg daily (supplement with 3-5 mg of copper per day to maintain proper zinc-copper ratio)
- Pumpkin seeds: Up to ¼ lb daily
- Flaxseed oil: 6-10 grams daily
- Herbs (as in Advanced Men's Formula): 2 tablets three times daily
  - Saw palmetto, 320 mg
  - Pygeum, 120 mg
  - Stinging nettle, 120 mg
  - Cranberry, echinacea, cayenne, false unicorn root, goldenseal, juniper berries, Siberian ginseng, and uva ursi

In addition, drink at least eight 8 oz glasses of distilled water daily.

SINUSITIS

Sinusitis is nasal congestion that restricts the amount of air allowed in for easy breathing. Sinusitis is often accompanied by headache, pain behind the eye, tenderness, fever, and loss of smell.

Nasal congestion and sinusitis may be due to an inadequate diet (for example, excess milk and dairy products, milk allergy, excess carbohydrates, raw vegetable deficiency), food or inhalant allergies, cold or flu virus, stress, or adrenal exhaustion.

Sinuses are air-containing spaces located within the skull. Their function is tied to the immune system. The membranes within them secrete mucus that cleans out the sinuses and nasal passages, protecting us from infection.

When the nasal passages are irritated (by smoke, pollution, allergies, and other irritants), the membranes secrete a lot more mucus to clean out the sinuses. Usually sinusitis develops when an individual has a cold or upper respiratory infection. This sets up an inflammatory condition of the nose and sinus cavities that obstructs the flow of secretions, causing infection and more secretions. If something is not done to break the cycle, it gets worse and worse.

What to Do

To avoid or relieve sinusitis, follow these suggestions:

- Eating hot soup speeds the flow of mucus out of the nose. Adding garlic, cayenne pepper, and raw onion may hasten relief. (I recommend Hurricane and olive leaf extract.)
- Place eucalyptus leaves in a pot of boiling water for five minutes. Turn the heat off and, with a towel draped over your head, lean over the pot and breathe in the herbal vapors. Be careful not to burn yourself.
- Take 2,000 mg of vitamin C every hour until you reach saturation. (Saturation can be indicated by the onset of diarrhea.) Vitamin C, taken in adequate high levels, acts as a natural antihistamine, anti-inflammatory agent and helps fight infection. Vitamin C and MSM also help heal damaged sinus membrane tissues.
- Adequate intake of vitamin A, which helps maintain the health of the mucous membranes of the nose and throat, can help in the treatment of sinusitis.
- Vitamin A, potassium, calcium, and zinc (which is necessary for vitamin A mobilization from the liver) aid the

work of the cilia in the nasal passageways that help expel mucus.

• Avoid nasal decongestants (sprays, drops, and inhalers). They work by shrinking swollen blood vessels in the nose. In time, vessels tend to "tire," making congestion worse.

Beneficial Supplementation

The following supplements may be beneficial for people experiencing sinusitis:

• Vitamin A: 25,000 IU up to six times a day in acute cases
• B complex: 25–50 mg two to three times daily
• Vitamin B$_6$: 100 mg twice daily
• Vitamin C (Ester-C®): 2,000 mg hourly in acute cases
• Vitamin E: 400 IU daily
• Zinc: 15 mg daily
• MSM: 4–10 grams daily
• Garlic: 500 mg three times daily
• Onion: Cooked and raw
• Onion syrup: 1 tsp per hour in acute cases
• Olive leaf extract: 2,000 mg daily
• Herbs: Comfrey, coneflower (*Echinacea angustifolium*), eucalyptus, fenugreek, and magnolia blossoms (tea)
• Hurricane (which contains garlic, echinacea, cayenne, ginger, and valerian): 2–3 capsules twice daily

SKIN CANCER

Cancer of the skin accounts for more than 40 percent of all cancers. Roughly 1.3 million Americans are diagnosed with non-melanoma skin cancer annually with an estimated 2,000 deaths during 2001. The risk of developing melanoma is about 1 in 120. Young children and teenagers are at the greatest risk.[149]

Malignant melanoma is the most deadly type of skin cancer. It is killing 30 percent more Americans today than it did less than 20 years ago. The reasons include

- The growing intensity of sunlight because of the depletion of the earth's ozone layer
- Trends in swimwear to expose more skin

Anyone can develop skin cancer, but having three of the following risk factors increases your chance of developing melanoma by three to four times. Having four or more of these factors carries a 25-fold greater risk. They are

- Being a blond or redhead
- Having blue or green eyes
- Having abundant freckles on the upper back
- Having fair skin that burns or freckles easily
- Having a tendency to develop a red, bumpy rash after exposure to the sun
- Having a relative who developed melanoma
- Having at least three blistering sunburns before age 20
- Working outdoors

Individuals with two or more risk factors should be alert to the first signs of melanoma because when caught early, the cancer is curable. It is almost always fatal after small black or blue tumors appear on the skin. An early melanoma lesion can resemble an ordinary mole with irregular edges, a red scaly patch, or a pale waxy nodule. Approximately 80 percent of skin cancers are found on the face, head, and neck. Other vulnerable areas include other highly exposed areas, such as the hands and forearms.

Skin cancer is not the only consequence of sun exposure. Premature aging (wrinkles, dry skin, age spots, and moles) may not be as dangerous as skin cancer, but much time, energy, and money are spent in futile attempts to undo the consequences.

Of all the factors that affect your skin—age, heredity, eating and drinking habits, smoking, stress, health, rest, and exercise—

your degree of sun exposure and how you protect your skin when you are outdoors is one of the most significant in maintaining the youthful look and feel of your skin.

Sunshine is the most harmful influence on your skin. Years of exposure to the sun exaggerates and accelerates one's natural aging process, causing wrinkling, thinning of the skin, the appearance of broken blood vessels, and brownish discolorations known as "age spots." Sunshine accelerates the normal loss of moisture and elasticity of the skin. Twenty years of sunning can leave you looking 15 to 20 years older than you really are.

What to Do

The American Cancer Society, the Skin Cancer Foundation, and the American Academy of Dermatology recommend these precautions:

- Avoid sun exposure between 10 A.M. and 3 P.M., when ultraviolet rays are most intense.
- Wear a hat, tightly woven protective clothing, and sunglasses (make sure they protect from UV rays) when exposed to the sun. Note: Sunglasses with lenses that do not provide protection from UV rays are very dangerous. Regular tinted lenses provide an illusion that it is darker than it is so your pupils dilate (like in a dark room), making your eyes extremely sensitive to damage.
- Before sun exposure, apply a sunscreen with a sun protection factor of 15 or more. Note: Remember to reapply your sunscreen if you are in extremely hot weather or are involved in activity causing you to perspire. If you are in or around water, the sun's rays are actually more intense because they are reflected; therefore, adequate protection is extremely important. You are not protected if you are underwater, either. You need to wear a waterproof sunscreen and reapply it often.

Cloudy weather conditions can give you a false sense of security when you are outdoors. As much as 80 percent of the ultraviolet rays of the sun can be transmitted through clouds and fog and can still cause a sunburn. Wind may also increase one's chances of overexposure to the sun because it may seem cooler, allowing you to remain comfortable in the sun for longer periods.

It is also very important to use sunscreen on your lips. Too much sun can cause cracking, peeling, and blistering of the lips. Individuals who are sensitive to fever blisters on their lips also need to take special protective care of the rest of their body.

In addition, antioxidants such as vitamins C and E, glutathione, polyphenols, and proanthocyanidins (PC-95) can be very important skin protectors used topically and taken internally. Increase your intake of high-antioxidant foods, especially those grown in tropical regions, such as mangos, pineapples, avocados, and papayas.

Proanthocyanidins (PC-95) have been clinically demonstrated to have antitumor effects for the skin.[150] They seem to have natural sunscreen capabilities. Before I play golf in the hot sun, I take between 6 and 10 PC-95 tablets and I rarely burn anymore.

THYROID PROBLEMS

The thyroid gland, located in the lower part of the neck, just below the Adam's apple, produces several important hormones. Thyroid hormones control the rate of metabolism of all the cells and therefore virtually all the organs of the body.

The thyroid uses iodine to make thyroid hormones. The two most important are thyroxine (T_4) and triiodothyronine (T_3). Thyroxine regulates the metabolism of energy and plays a key role in body weight.

Hypothyroidism

Thyroid disease affects more than six million Americans (3–5 percent of the population). Hypothyroidism (low thyroid hormone levels) is the most common thyroid illness. The condition is eight times more common in women than in men, and the risk of development increases with age.

Low thyroid hormone levels in the body can have profound effects. Hypothyroidism is generally characterized by fatigue, weight gain and difficulty losing weight, dry skin, dry and thinning hair, depression, headaches, low body temperature, unusual sensitivity to cold, decreased libido, slow reflexes, constipation, and mood swings. Women with this condition may experience PMS or irregular menstrual cycles. Men may experience impotence or low sperm count. Many so-called allergic diseases may in fact be due to thyroid disorders.

What to Do

The following recommendations are for people with hypothyroidism:

- Thyroid hormones are made from the mineral iodine and the amino acid tyrosine. Therefore, adequate levels of these in the body are crucial. Stimulating thyroid function can also be aided with zinc and vitamins A and E, which are needed to manufacture thyroid hormones. Vitamins C, B_2, B_3 (niacin), and B_6 are also necessary for normal thyroid hormone manufacture.
- Iodine is found in seafood, seaweed (such as kelp), mustard greens (which is also high in tyrosine), and iodized salt.
- Foods that contain tyrosine include carob, bean sprouts, soybeans, oats, peanuts, spinach, watercress, sesame seeds, butternut squash, chaya, chives, fava beans, pumpkin seeds, snow peas, and cabbage.
- For hypothyroidism, herbal pharmacologist Daniel Mowrey, Ph.D., author of The Scientific Validation of Herbal Medicine and Herbal Tonic Therapies, recommends combining gentian, cayenne, Irish moss, kelp, and saw palmetto.

- Exercise is particularly important in a treatment program for hypothyroidism. Exercise stimulates thyroid gland secretion and increases tissue sensitivity to thyroid hormones.

Beneficial supplementation

The following supplements have been shown to be beneficial for people with low thyroid hormone levels:

- Vitamin A: 25,000 IU one to two times daily
- Vitamin E: 300 IU daily
- Vitamin C (Ester-C®): 3,000–5,000 mg daily
- B complex: 50 mg twice daily
- Zinc: 25 mg daily
- Iodine or kelp: 4 mg daily
- Tyrosine: 50–100 mg daily
- EFAs: 5,000 mg daily

Hyperthyroidism

High thyroid hormone levels (hyperthyroidism) result in hyper-activity and nervousness. Graves' disease is the most common cause. Graves' disease is due to a generalized overactivity of the whole enlarged thyroid gland (goiter).

Symptoms of hyperthyroidism and Graves' disease include nervousness, irritability, fatigue, loss of weight, goiter, insomnia, tremor of the hands, intolerance of heat, rapid pulse, and easy perspiring.

Beneficial regulating herbs for both conditions include bugle-weed, lemon balm, self-heal, and verbena.

What To Do

The following recommendations are for people with hyperthy-roidism:

- Avoiding stimulants, such as caffeine, sugar, and nicotine, and replacing chlorinated water with pure distilled water is good advice for all of us and very important for those suffering from hyperthyroidism.
- To reduce inflammation, place ice packs or castor oil on the throat. Apply oil directly to the skin, then cover with a clean soft cloth and plastic wrap. Apply a heat pack and leave it in place for 30 to 60 minutes. For best results, do this for three consecutive days.

Consider incorporating some therapeutic treatments, such as acupuncture and massage. A good massage will relieve stress while acupuncture can correct hormonal imbalances and address underlying complications associated with hyperthyroidism.

Beneficial supplementation:

The following supplements have been shown to be beneficial for people with high thyroid hormone levels:

- Vitamin A: 25,000 IU one to two times daily
- Iodine or kelp: 2 mg daily
- Vitamin E: 1,000 IU daily
- Proanthocyanidins (PC-95): 180–200 mg daily
- B complex:* three times daily with meals
- Balanced multiminerals:**
  - Elemental calcium (preferably a combination of calcium citrate, chelate, aspartate, and lactate): 2,400 mg
  - Magnesium: 1,200 mg

---

* A quality B complex should include B_1, B_2, B_6, B_{12}, niacin, niacinamide, folic acid, biotin, pantothenic acid, magnesium, arginine, betaine hydrochloride, carnitine, choline, PABA, lecithin, bromelain, and alpha lipoic acid.
** Roex's Ultimate Calcium Mineral Formula contains all of the listed items.

- Trace mineral combination (copper, molybdenum, potassium, selenium, zinc, boron, silica) without iron: 600 mg
- Vitamin C (Ester-C®): 5,000 mg
- Essential fatty acids (omega-9 plus a 1:1 ratio of omega-3/omega-6):***
  - Omega-3: 1,400–2,450 mg
  - Omega-6: 1,400–2,450 mg
  - Omega-9: 740–1,500 mg

*** Roex's EFAs contain omega-3, 6, 9 in proper balance.

ULCERS

A peptic ulcer is a sore or hole in the lining of the stomach or duodenum (the first part of the small intestine). People of any age can develop an ulcer, and women are affected just as often as men. Over 25 million Americans will suffer from an ulcer at some point during their lifetimes. Most ulcers are caused by the bacterium *Helicobacter pylori* (*H. pylori*)—90 percent of all duodenal ulcers and more than 80 percent of all gastric ulcers. Before 1982, when *H. pylori* was discovered, spicy food, acid, stress, and lifestyle were considered the major causes of ulcers. The majority of patients were given long-term maintenance doses of acid-reducing medications, such as HCl (hydrochloric acid) blockers, without a chance for a permanent cure.

The most common ulcer symptom is gnawing or burning pain in the epigastrium. This pain typically occurs when the stomach is empty, between meals and in the early morning hours, but can also occur at other times. It may last from minutes to hours and may be relieved by eating or by taking antacids. Less common ulcer symptoms include nausea, vomiting, loss of appetite, and bleeding. Prolonged bleeding may cause anemia, leading to weakness and fatigue.

All about Iodine

Iodine is most recognized as an antiseptic for skin cuts, but it is far more important in thyroid hormone production. Of all the iodine in the body, 80 percent is found in the thyroid gland.

Iodine deficiency is most commonly seen with goiter, or an enlarged thyroid gland. Iodine deficiency was once prevalent in regions where soils were poor in iodine content. The incidence of this condition has now been reduced dramatically by the addition of iodine to salt. Iodized salt in the diet generally precludes the need for an iodine supplement.

Foods such as raw cabbage, turnips, cauliflower, soybeans, and peanuts contain substances called goitrogens, which inhibit thyroid activity. Prolonged consumption can lead to goiter, but cooking deactivates these compounds. People on a strict salt-free diet benefit most from an iodine supplement.

The normal recommended daily intake for iodine in adults is 150 mcg. Too much iodine can actually inhibit thyroid synthesis. Organic iodine, such as found in kelp, may be better retained in the body.

To determine if you are iodine deficient, dip a cotton swab into a 2 percent tincture of iodine (available at your local drugstore or supermarket) and dab the swab on your thigh or belly in an area about the size of a silver dollar. This will leave a yellowish stain that should disappear within about 24 hours if your iodine levels are normal. If the spot disappears in less than 24 hours, you are iodine deficient. If this happens, continue to apply the iodine spot every day until it remains visible a full 24 hours. You will then see reduced symptoms typical of hypothyroidism. (I have tried this on many people, and I know it works!)

Colostrum has been shown to be effective against *H. pylori*. Researchers at the Department of Clinical Pathology, Hospital for Sick Children, University of Toronto, Ontario, Canada, demonstrated the benefits of bovine colostrum for ulcers caused by *H. pylori*. They showed that bovine colostrum blocks the binding of *Helicobacter* species to select lipids, preventing adhesion of *H. pylori* to the lining of the stomach and intestinal tract, therefore inhibiting infection.[151]

Proanthocyanidins also have anti-ulcer activity, as does olive leaf extract.

What to Do

The most common causes for ulcers (peptic) are the proliferation of *H. pylori* (a bacterium found in the stomach), the overuse of NSAIDS (such as ibuprofen and aspirin), and an overproduction of stomach acids, in respective order. Stress and poor diet often trigger the discomfort but are rarely a direct cause.

- First and foremost, eliminate the triggers that cause the discomfort. Eat foods that are easily digestible, such as raw vegetables, and get rid of fatty, processed menu items. If you smoke, stop. Follow the guidelines for eliminating stress mentioned earlier. Incorporate natural products into your daily routine to address the discomfort associated with inflammation or to thin blood.

- Most importantly, you must know this: bacteria such as *H. pylori* cannot survive in an acid environment. Americans chew antacids like candy, which by design stop the production of stomach acid. In this nonacid environment, bacteria have the ability to proliferate, greatly increasing the risk of a bacteria-induced ulcer. Instead of opting for the short term relief offered by antacids, consider providing your body with digestive enzymes that safely and naturally break down every type of food group without negative long-term effects.

Beneficial Supplementation

The following supplements can be beneficial in preventing and treating ulcers:

- Probiotics (DDS-1 *L. Acidophilus, B. bifidum, S. thermophilus*): 5–15 billion CFUs
- Proanthocyanidin (PC-95): 120–180 mg
- Plant-based chewable digestive enzymes: 2–3 with each meal
- Oleuropein: 1,000–2,000 mg

You can double the dose of each item in the second week.

YEAST INFECTION (CANDIDA ALBICANS)

A yeast infection is a local or systemic colonization of the skin or mucous membranes of the yeast *Candida albicans*, also called "thrush."

Candida albicans is normally found in the mouth, digestive tract, vagina, and skin of healthy people. Under normal conditions, the body's defense barriers and immune system keep this fungus controlled and limited. However, if the body's defenses are weakened by an improper diet, or if the general or local ecology of the body or tissues is severely altered, such as occurs with antibiotic use, *Candida* begins to flourish. As the yeast takes hold, it produces local irritation and sends systemic toxins throughout the body, causing a number of symptoms: fatigue, depression, constipation or diarrhea, gas, bloating, abdominal pain, muscle or joint pain, headaches, allergies, rashes, nail fungus, and hypoglycemia.

Vaginal yeast infections are common and are accompanied by itching and discharge. *Candida albicans* infections often follow the use of antibiotic drugs and may occur with use of birth control pills, consumption of sugar and refined carbohydrates, nutritional deficiencies, improper hygiene, allergies, and pregnancy.

What to Do

To prevent and/or treat yeast infection, follow these suggestions:

- Eat no sugar or refined carbohydrates. Simple sugars weaken the immune system and feed yeast. Some individuals may wish to also avoid fruit and fruit juices, which contain natural sugars.
- Avoid foods and supplements containing yeast.
- Avoid antibiotics.
- Supplement with probiotics to restore normal intestinal flora.
- Eat fermented foods containing probiotics such as *L. acidophilus:* yogurt, kefir, cheese, and buttermilk.
- Avoid all other dairy products.
- Apply hydrogen peroxide solution (3 percent) topically.
- Supplement with vitamin C up to your individual bowel tolerance level. (This is considered the saturation level for the body, the level that causes loose stools. In some people, this may be 10,000 or 12,000 mg; in others it may be as high as 30,000–40,000 mg or more daily.)
- Supplement with colostrum to support the immune system and help normalize intestinal flora.
- Olive leaf extract is an excellent aid to fight yeast infection and support the immune system. Look for standardized extracts of 17–23 percent.
- Supplement with garlic. Raw cloves are the best.
- Aloe vera gel may be applied topically (to relieve itching), used as a douche, and also consumed internally (2 ounces four times daily).
- Echinacea is an effective antifungal agent and has a number of other immune-support properties as well.
- Roex's Hurricane formula is very beneficial for helping your immune system overcome this yeast.

Beneficial Supplementation

The following supplements have been shown to be beneficial in preventing and treating yeast infections:

- Vitamin A: 25,000 IU one to two times daily
- B complex (yeast free): 50 mg one to two times daily
- Vitamin C: Up to bowel tolerance
- Vitamin E: 400–800 IU daily
- Garlic (Hurricane): Fresh or 1,000 mg three to four times daily
- Colostrum: 2,000 mg two to four times daily
- Probiotics (Colon Essentials): 1-2 capsules four to six times daily; capsules may also be used as a suppository for vaginal infections
- Olive leaf extract: 2,000 mg twice daily

The Road Ahead

Many times in our lives we ask ourselves, "How did I get myself into this predicament?" Where we are today is primarily due to how we think. Where we will be tomorrow will largely be determined by the decisions we make now (today).

THE FORK TO THE LEFT

The road ahead is a forked road. If you take the fork to the left, you will continue to do pretty much what you have always done but you will expect different results. (By the way, that is my definition of *stupidity*.) That is, the road to the left is paved with

- Continuing to eat and drink what you know you should not.
- Being willing to try every new "cure-all" drug on the market, and simply going along with whatever the government, the majority of doctors, and the drug companies and their version of the truth tell you.
- Learning too late that the drug program you are presently on cannot and will not reinstate your health.
- Losing just a little more energy each week, each month.

- Being told to take just one more drug to overcome the side effects of the last drug a doctor said should solve your problem.
- Refusing to exercise or participate in regular physical activity.
- Arrogantly believing that people who take supplements, work out, and watch what they eat and drink are wasting their time and money.

THE RIGHT ROAD
(THE FORK TO THE RIGHT)

The road to the right has very different scenery along the way. You know instinctively or from past experience that there must be a better way than drugs, radiation, surgery, and long-term hospital stays. There are alternatives to the conventional approach to health problems that really do work and are safe, effective, and nontoxic to the body.

The road to the right emphasizes pure water; exercise; adequate intake of vitamins, minerals, essential fatty acids, and antioxidants; good sleep; and pleasing relationships in your personal life as well as your business life. On this road, you will learn how to think so you can learn how to live.

We all want to enjoy a long, viable, healthy life, but few people today go any further than wishing for it. As the farmer reaps what he sows, so shall you! We must *set goals* for our health, success, and future desires. We must give time and thought to whatever we desire, and then, if we truly believe we can reach these goals and never, ever, ever give up, we will succeed!

Read again about the mind-body connection in chapter 2, then see for yourself how changing your thinking can change your life. Realize that for thousands of years the Bible has taught us that "the leaves of the trees are for the healing of nations." Visualize yourself as vibrant, healthy, happy, and successful. Whatever your goal, if you think you can reach it, you will; if you think you can't, you won't. Either way, you are right.

TAKE THE HIGH ROAD TO HEALTH!

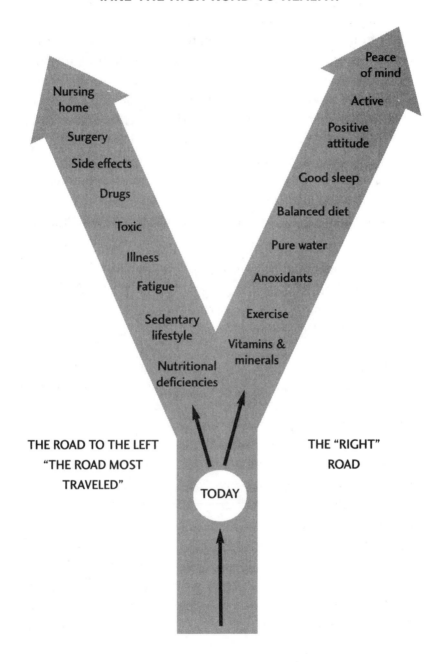

Personally, I chose to take the right road. It took me many years to finally make the right decision. It will probably take me a few more to diligently practice what I have now learned. I know I am far from perfection, but I am on the right road. You can learn from my mistakes by practicing and using the information presented in this book. You too can get on the *right road*. Work at it every day, every week, every month, and every year. Ask yourself, "Where do I want to be tomorrow?" Then *visualize* that place in your mind. See yourself as you want to be, and then put all your energy, thought, and resources into getting there. *Know* that the end result will be yours and *never, ever ever give up*! It is never too late—unless you *think* it is.

I am closing with my favorite interpretation of a Biblical scripture:

Ask and it shall be given unto you.
Seek and ye shall find.
Knock and it shall be opened unto you,
As all things are possible for he that believes!

Thank you for reading this book. May God bless you and keep you safe and healthy all the days of your life!

Appendix A

Suggested Nutritional Products

The following products are manufactured for and sold by Roex, Inc., a company I founded in 1994. They are suggested only as indicated in this book and subject to the disclaimer at the beginning of this book.

Procyanidin-95 (PC-95)

- In my opinion, the most potent free-radical scavenger antioxidant known in the world.
- Dr. Masquelier's original patented grape seed extract complex.
- Procyanidin has been shown to
  - Strengthen the cell walls of veins, arteries, and capillaries.
  - Promote optical acuity, focusing abilities, and eye health.
  - Encourage skin suppleness and elasticity.
  - Assist the body in the manufacture of new collagen and elastin.

Advanced Men's Formula

- Designed for men 35 and older for prostate health.
- Contains 17 different herbs, extracts, vitamins, and amino acids that synergistically support prostate health.
- Cranberry extract, saw palmetto, stinging nettle root, and essential amino acids help maintain healthy urinary function in the body.
- Also provides zinc, an integral component for a healthy prostate.

B Complex

- Contains B vitamins, which have been shown to build resistance to infection, disease, anxiety, and depression.
- Play a critical role in the body's conversion of carbohydrates into energy.
- Help maintain the health of the nerves, skin, eyes, hair, and mouth.
- Promote normal appetite and digestion.
- Improve fat metabolism and neurological function.

The Ultimate Calcium Mineral Formula

- A unique blend of minerals including calcium, magnesium, zinc, potassium, and trace minerals with vitamin D_3 to enhance absorption.
- Five different forms of calcium and three different forms of magnesium, formulated for better assimilation.
- Calcium and minerals have been shown to
  - Assist the body in promoting healthy bones, hair, skin, and nails.
  - Help regulate heartbeat, transmit nerve impulses, and contract muscles, as well as form and maintain strong bones and teeth.

- Generally be safe for children, adults, and seniors because they have no iron.

CitriGenics I

- Controls food cravings.
- All natural.
- Promotes feelings of satiety.
- Assists the body in converting fats and carbohydrates into energy.
- Contains 24 different vitamins, minerals, and herbal products.
- Stimulates metabolic activity and energy.

CitriGenics II

- All-natural marine fiber acts like a "fat sponge" for the digestive tract.
- Works within the body to absorb fat before it becomes part of your body.
- Enhanced with vitamin C and chromium polynicotinate.
- Helps to control food cravings.
- Assists in maintaining healthy levels of fats and lipids within the body.

Colon Essentials

- A scientific blend of three probiotics that compete with disease-causing microorganisms in the intestinal tract.
- Assists in the manufacture of B vitamins and vitamin K.
- Helps relieve constipation and general bowel irregularity.
- Increases the bioavailability of vitamins, minerals, enzymes, and fatty acids in the body.
- Excellent follow-up to antibiotics to replenish "friendly" flora in your digestive system.

Digestive Balance

- Contains all of the major digestive enzymes, including protease, alpha amylase, lipase, cellulose, lactase, papaya, melon, pepsin, bromelain, peppermint, chlorophyll, and more.
- Life as we know it could not exist without the action of enzymes—they act as catalysts for every activity in the body.
- Neutralizes acids in the mouth and stomach.
- Contains xylitol, which helps reduce cavities and fight plaque.

A&D with Mixed Tocopherols

- Naturally sourced from cold water fish oil.
- Necessary for healthy eyes, skin, bones, teeth, and mucous membranes in the mouth and intestines.
- Supports a healthy immune system and regulates the absorption and use of calcium and phosphorus, which is vital for normal growth, development, and maintenance of bones and teeth.
- Helps improve circulation, is protective of the heart, and aids in healing wounds and repairing tissue.
- Provides powerful antioxidant protection, enhances immunity, improves cardiovascular and skeletal health, and normalizes hormonal balance.

Oleuropein

- A powerful antioxidant made from Mediterranean olive leaf extract, the highest quality olive leaf extract in the world, containing 96 phytonutrients.
- Contains 17–23% pure oleuropein, the active ingredient that does all of the work.
- Beneficial support for viral infections, the common cold, skin irritations, heart trouble, and more.

- Assists the body in its natural defense against foreign pathogens.
- A powerful adjunct in any program of health, healing, and wellness.

Livalon

- The Roex name for the most bioavailable milk thistle extract in the world. An herb native to the Mediterranean region of Europe, it is the most ancient of all known medicines, having been used as a remedy for liver complaints for centuries.
- Made from a patented extract that is as much as 200 percent more bioavailable than other milk thistle products.
- Contains the active ingredient silymarin, which protects the liver by helping cells produce glutathione, which helps protect against free-radical damage.
- Exerts both a protective and restorative effect on the liver; stimulates the growth of new liver cells—by producing new protein—to replace old, damaged cells.
- May help the liver metabolize and clear alcohol from the body.

Mother's Gift Colostrum

- Comes from New Zealand pasture-fed cows certified to be free of antibiotics and hormones.
- Contains all four of the key immunoglobulins—IgM, IgG, IgA, and secretary IgA—which neutralize bacteria, viruses, and yeasts.
- Contains natural growth factors that are very important to promote wound healing and tissue repair, increase the breakdown of fat, and balance blood sugar levels.
- Has up to 100 times the mitogenic (cell-generation) potency of human colostrum.

- Reduces the damaging effects of free radicals (which are known to be cancer risk factors) because of its lactoferrin content.
- Has tremendous healing properties; capsules can be opened and applied directly to cuts, abrasions, or irritated skin and/or applied directly to gums in cases of sensitive teeth and mouth sores.

EFAs

- Contain an ideal 1:1 ratio of omega-3 to omega-6 oils, as well as omega-9 fatty acids. Omega-3 fatty acids (alpha-linolenic acid) are provided both by flaxseed oil and fish oil. Omega-3 oils are nature's richest source of EPA (eicosapentaenoic acid) and DGLA (dihomo-gamma-linolenic acid). Omega-6 fatty acids, also known as linoleic acids, are abundant in polyunsaturated saf-flower oil. Flaxseed oil, borage oil, and pumpkin seed oil are also sources of Omega-6 fatty acids. Omega-9 fatty acids are found in olive oil and pumpkin seed oil.
  - Flaxseed oil—The world's richest source of omega-3 fatty acids, which are beneficial for persons who have high cholesterol levels, strokes and heart attacks, angina (heart pain), high blood pressure, arthritis, ADD, multiple sclerosis, psoriasis, and eczema. They also promote smoother muscle action, foster clearer thinking, relieve allergies, and assist in weight loss. The flaxseed oil in Roex EFAs is extracted from unre-fined flaxseeds and is unique because it contains both essential fatty acids—alpha-linolenic acid and linoleic acid—in appreciable amounts.
  - Safflower oil—Supports the correct balance of prostaglandins. Prostaglandins are produced by every cell in the body and control functions such as repro-duction and fertility, inflammatory reactions, immunity, and cell communications.

- Borage oil—The richest source of GLA (gamma linoleic acid), which is almost nonexistent in today's standard American diet.
- Olive oil—A monounsaturated fat that has been shown to reduce harmful LDL cholesterol levels in the bloodstream.
- Pumpkin seed oil—Can be beneficial for individuals suffering from inflammation due to prostatitis and can provide a tonic effect on the male system.
- Support cognitive thinking.
- Provides beneficial support for eczema, dermatitis, psoriasis, lupus, heart disease, diabetes, arthritis, loss of memory, irritable bowel syndrome, allergies, and asthma.

MSM

- Provides the body with the sulfur necessary for the cellular transfer of fluids, toxins, and nutrients.
- An organic source of dietary sulfur (the missing mineral in our daily diet).
- Promotes healthy skin, hair, and nails.
- Assists the body in its natural detoxification processes.
- Enhanced with vitamin C to improve the absorption and action of MSM within the body.

WOW

- Designed to cleanse, purify, strengthen, and tone the entire gastrointestinal tract.
- Serves as a natural laxative and bowel toning agent.
- Includes barberry root, dandelion root, and red clover, which have been shown to be very supportive in cleansing the blood as well as detoxifying and supporting the function of the liver.

Melatonin

- Highest quality melatonin in the world, imported from Switzerland.
- Assists the body's natural circadian rhythm or sleep-wake cycle.
- Perfect for those whose schedules require resetting their internal time clocks.
- Enhanced with vitamin B_6 to facilitate the body's natural production of melatonin.
- Powerful antioxidant/free-radical scavenger.

Hurricane

- Contains *Echinacea purpurea*, garlic bulb, cayenne pepper, ginger, and valerian root and is formulated to benefit the body's immune system.
  - Garlic bulb—Supports the stimulation of macrophages, the white blood cells that engulf foreign organisms, such as viruses, bacteria, and yeast. Garlic can increase the activity of T-helper cells, the immune cells in the body, which are central to the activity of the entire immune system. Garlic can help inhibit the growth of parasites in the intestines, including amoebas that cause dysentery.
  - *Echinacea purpurea*—Has natural antiviral and anti-inflammatory properties that "kick-start" the immune system and stimulate the production of white blood cells. It contains polysaccharides, complex sugar molecules that stimulate the cells of the immune system, including the white blood cells. It is commonly referred to as a "natural antibiotic" and is used to fight infections caused by common colds and the flu. *Echinacea purpurea* may be helpful in reducing the inflammation caused by respiratory problems, bronchitis, strep throat, and enlarged prostate glands. It supports the produc-

tion of interferon, an important part of the immune system's response to viral infections that cause colds and the flu.

- Cayenne pepper—Stimulates blood flow, increases circulation, fights fatigue, stimulates blood flow to the brain, and strengthens the heart, arteries, capillaries, and nerves. It boosts the health of the entire cardio-vascular system. It stimulates the nerves of the stomach and promotes the secretion of digestive juices. It can be beneficial in the body's assimilation of nutrients and works as a catalyst speeding up metabolism, data transmissions of the brain, cellular respiration, and neural hormonal activity.
- Valerian root—Eases insomnia and calms the nerves. It helps people with insomnia get to sleep faster and sleep better without a groggy "morning after" effect. Chemicals in valerian root called valepotriates act as muscle relaxants, making the herb potentially useful against menstrual cramps and other spasms.
- Ginger—Contains compounds similar to the digestive enzymes found in the digestive tract, which may help digest a heavy, protein-rich meal. It can benefit those who suffer from heartburn, abdominal cramps, or a queasy stomach. Studies suggest that ginger can be useful in keeping cholesterol levels under control. It helps kill the influenza virus and helps the immune system wage war on infection.

Immortale for Women

- A special formulation of herbs and extracts that assists the body in normalizing hormone balance, enhancing vitality and inducing feelings of well-being.
- Helps stimulate sexual desire.
- Alleviates the physiological and psychological symptoms associated with menstrual cycles as well as menopause.

- May produce a generalized strengthening of the body and mind.
- Restorative properties foster healthy urinary function.
- Promotes lean muscle mass.

Immortale for Men

- Assists the body in overcoming the effects of stress and fatigue.
- A formulation of all-natural herbs and plant extracts designed to assist the body in fostering healthy reproductive system functioning, lean muscle mass, and increased sexual drive.
- Improves stamina and muscle strength.
- Contains green oats and Panax ginseng, which promote feelings of virility, vitality, and sexual desire.

Ester-C®

- Three times more bioavailable than regular vitamin C and lasts up to four times longer in the bloodstream at its maximum level.
- Nonacidic and gentle to the stomach.
- Promotes joint, skin, and cardiovascular health.
- Assists in the neutralization of free radicals.
- Intensifies the benefits of the super antioxidant PC-95.

PC-95 Daily Rejuvenating Cream

- Loaded with antioxidants and natural botanicals.
- Helps protect the skin and repair damage caused by the aging effects of sun exposure, environmental pollutants, and normal metabolism.
- Slows premature aging of the skin by stimulating and strengthening collagen synthesis.

- One of the few formulas available on the market today that features *Centella asiatica* as one of its primary ingredients. *Centella asiatica* assists in renewing a velvety softness of the skin by alleviating dryness, which is a major culprit in premature aging.
- Helps restore radiance to the complexion and promotes skin elasticity.
- Assists the body in reducing the appearance of weakened collagen, which results in wrinkles, crow's feet, age spots, and sagging skin.

Perfect Whey Meal Replacement

- A high quality protein powder, low in carbohydrates and sugar.
- Beneficial for a healthy weight maintenance program.
- Supports muscle repair and lean muscle production.
- Supports bone formation.
- Beneficial for the Immune system.

Appendix B

The Rise and Fall of the Killer Drug Rezulin

David Willman, *Times* Staff Writer

(Copyright 2000, *Los Angeles Times*. Reprinted with permission.)

People were dying as specialists waged war against their FDA superiors. Patient safety was at stake in the scramble to keep a "fast-track" pill on the U.S. market, research reveals.

WASHINGTON—The suffering persisted for more than two years. Initially, there were four known victims. Then 21. Then 33. Finally, 63 confirmed fatalities. All the while, federal authorities watched, waited and hoped the deaths would stop. It was not until a disparate collection of physicians inside the U.S. Food and Drug Administration waged a remarkable revolt that the agency was forced to reverse course. These specialists—dubbed the "Termites" by one medical officer—combined meticulous research and bluntly worded e-mail messages to upbraid their government superiors for contributing to the needless death of patients.

How the Termites prevailed in toppling Rezulin, a blockbuster diabetes drug that generated $2.1 billion in sales, illuminates one of the most important reversals in FDA history.

A reconstruction of Rezulin's rise and fall shows that senior government officials repeatedly played down the drug's propensity to cause liver failure and death. Before it was withdrawn on March 21, the FDA assured doctors and patients that Rezulin's potential benefits in lowering blood-sugar levels outweighed its grave risks.

Diary entries, internal correspondence and interviews with participants reveal the pivotal roles of separate factions inside the FDA: the Termites, spearheaded by the efforts of Dr. David J. Graham, and the agency's most senior officials, led by Dr. Murray M. "Mac" Lumpkin.

As deputy director of the FDA's drug-evaluation center, Lumpkin helped make Rezulin the nation's fastest-approved diabetes pill and, to the end, resisted its withdrawal.

Lumpkin said that he had no misgivings about keeping Rezulin on the market for so long. The drug finally was pulled, Lumpkin said, only when it became "outmoded" in comparison to newer pills for adult-onset diabetes.

After listening to Lumpkin defend the handling of Rezulin on May 19 at an FDA advisory committee meeting, one panelist, Dr. Jules Hirsch of Rockefeller University, shook his head.

"I don't share the point of view of a wonderfully happy outcome, of how well the system has worked," Hirsch said. "Because a lot of people died of this thing. And a lot more people than we know died."

Indeed, the FDA's sustained support of Rezulin had consequences: 63 confirmed deaths from liver failure and thousands of liver injuries. Because adverse events from prescription drugs are reported voluntarily, typically by doctors and hospitals, Rezulin's estimated toll is perhaps 10 times higher, experts say.

As the deaths kept escalating, the FDA responded by recommending multiple regimens of blood testing, called "monitoring," as a means of safeguarding patients from liver failure. From the fall of 1997 through mid-1999, the FDA and the manufacturer, Warner-Lambert Co. of New Jersey, agreed to four liver-monitoring recommendations.

Yet no scientific proof existed then, or now, that monitoring would protect Rezulin patients, according to the FDA's own research and interviews with physicians.

"It was a hope," said Dr. Srini R. Vasa, a liver specialist based in Kansas City, Mo., who treated three Rezulin patients with liver failure, two of whom died. "There were a lot of lives lost and a lot of lives changed. It did not make the drug safer."

The FDA has overseen withdrawals of nine prescription drugs since fall 1997, an unprecedented number within such a short span. However, of those nine, the agency granted "fast-track" approval to only one: the oval, tan pill marketed as a diabetes breakthrough.

Rezulin thus becomes a touchstone for federal policymakers and for the doctors, patients and family members so directly affected by the government's decisions.

This chronology of the struggle over Rezulin is based on previously undisclosed documents and scores of interviews conducted over the last three years with government and private physicians.

Doctor Learns of Liver Failure Deaths

Anxiety washed over him in a flash. It was Friday afternoon in early October 1997 and Dr. Robert I. Misbin had just gotten vexing news from two Warner-Lambert executives: Patients taking Rezulin were beginning to die of liver failure. When he hung up the phone at his government desk, Misbin felt a singular anguish. As an FDA diabetes specialist who advocated the approval of Rezulin, he had failed to confront the danger posed by the drug. After relaying word to his supervisor, Misbin was alone with a central question: How could this have happened?

Firm Seeks to Make Drug a "Blockbuster"

By May 15, 1995, Misbin's first day as an FDA medical officer, Warner-Lambert was moving to position Rezulin for heavy sales. The company launched a multi-tiered strategy for transforming Rezulin into a "billion-dollar blockbuster." Early slide-show pitches were made to Wall Street analysts, emphasizing the market of America's 15 million adult-onset diabetics and touting Rezulin's "new mechanism of action."

Warner-Lambert and its affiliates paid speaking or other fees to more than 300 doctors, from endocrinologists to family practitioners. The company flew diabetes specialists to the 1996 Olympic Games in Atlanta and provided accommodations at the Chateau Elan Winery and Resort.

Pills Stimulate the Pancreas to Secrete More Insulin

Patients with adult-onset, or Type 2, diabetes do not produce enough of their own insulin at the right moments or their bodies do not make efficient use of this hormone, which regulates the metabolism of blood sugar. Type 2 diabetes also can be treated effectively with changes in diet and exercise. Juvenile-onset, Type 1, diabetes patients cannot produce their own insulin and would die without daily injections or infusions.

Soon after Warner-Lambert submitted its new-drug application for Rezulin in July 1996, the FDA for the first time in its history granted a six-month fast-track review to a diabetes pill. The FDA then was taking a year or more to examine standard new-drug applications.

The assignment of vetting Rezulin's safety and effectiveness initially fell to Dr. John L. Gueriguian, a veteran FDA medical officer. Gueriguian "emphasized that [Rezulin] offered very little significant therapeutic advantage" over existing diabetes medications, according to a summary of an FDA staff meeting on Aug. 22, 1996.

By the fall of 1996, Gueriguian concluded that Rezulin was unfit for approval and warned of its potential to harm both the liver and the heart. But Gueriguian came under fire from Warner-Lambert executives, who contacted the FDA's Lumpkin to complain about Gueriguian's use of intemperate language.

Effective Nov. 4, 1996, Lumpkin ordered Gueriguian removed from the evaluation of Rezulin and any further dealings with Warner-Lambert, according to physicians familiar with the matter. Gueriguian's medical review also was purged from agency files.

These actions sent an early and enduring message within the FDA: Challenging Rezulin was not without risk to one's career.

More Study Brings Unsettling Conclusion

"We have real trouble," Misbin wrote in his personal diary in October 1997. He recalls being startled the afternoon of Friday, Oct. 10, when the two Warner-Lambert executives informed him of the first liver failures. Before recommending a regulatory response, Misbin studied Warner-Lambert's original research and the recent cases of liver damage. He reached an unsettling conclusion.

"We knew the essential truth—that Rezulin could cause liver failure," Misbin recalled. "There was a potential for a disaster." The FDA is obligated under federal law to ensure that new and existing prescription drugs are safe and effective for their intended use. The agency's quandary of what to do about Rezulin, medical experts say, was framed by this reality:

Compared to the constant risk of liver failure, patients would need to take Rezulin for years to gain potential benefits that could lessen the serious complications of diabetes, such as blindness or amputation. And Rezulin was one of 10 pills available to lower blood-sugar levels for adult-onset diabetics.

At the FDA, the official who manages the agency's response to unexpected deaths from a prescription drug is Lumpkin.

Pharmaceutical companies in the past have criticized the FDA for taking longer than European authorities to approve new drugs. Lumpkin and his boss, Dr. Janet Woodcock, are the two FDA officials directly responsible for meeting the agency's new objectives.

As deputy director of the FDA's Center for Drug Evaluation and Research, Lumpkin was the chief firefighter for Rezulin's wildfires. And by the fall of 1997—several months after its arrival on the U.S market in March—Rezulin had become a difficult-to-contain blaze.

Patient Monitoring Seen as a Remedy

Within three weeks of the first acknowledged liver failure cases on Oct. 10, 1997, the FDA and Warner-Lambert jointly devised a remedy: Rezulin patients should have their liver functions monitored by blood test every two to three months during the first year of use.

The FDA and the company hoped that blood testing would detect liver injury early enough to alert patients to stop taking Rezulin and avert the catastrophe of organ failure. The FDA predicted in a statement on Nov. 3, 1997, that "few, if any, of these patients will go on to develop permanent liver damage if the drug is stopped." At this point, the agency confirmed four liver failure deaths.

But less than a month after announcing this remedy, officials at the FDA learned of a disturbing development. Britain was planning to announce Rezulin's withdrawal from their market on Dec. 1, 1997. British officials, informed of six fatalities linked to Rezulin, had concluded that the drug's risks outweighed its benefits. The mind-set of British authorities was detailed in a Nov. 26, 1997, e-mail message from Lumpkin to Woodcock, his superior and director of the FDA's drug review center.

"They believe that the deaths and serious toxicities are primarily seen after greater than 3 months exposure," Lumpkin wrote in his e-mail. This

analysis made "the apparent incidence of serious toxicity much greater than originally thought."

Lumpkin told Woodcock that "unless there is some leak," the revelation from Britain would stay sealed five more days.

The FDA, viewed for decades as upholding the gold standard for drug safety, was about to be upstaged by its counterpart, the British Medicines Control Agency. But the FDA, together with Warner-Lambert, raced to offset the pending news out of London.

Warner-Lambert maintained that the frequency of liver failure was extremely rare and insisted that the drug should remain on the U.S. market. In a Nov. 27 e-mail to the FDA, a Warner-Lambert vice president wrote: "We are concerned about misleading physicians and patients as to the relative risk of Rezulin therapy."

The company's position was embraced at the FDA by Lumpkin. Instead of withdrawing Rezulin, the FDA and Warner-Lambert announced a second change in the drug's labeling. Rezulin patients were now advised to have their liver functions monitored monthly, instead of every two to three months, for the first half-year of use.

In a statement on Dec. 1, the same day that Rezulin's withdrawal was announced in Britain, the FDA said: "The increased monitoring of patients taking Rezulin is designed to detect those few patients in whom use of the drug can lead to serious liver damage." Five months later, tragedy struck in St. Louis with the liver failure and death of Audrey LaRue Jones, a vivacious 55-year-old high school teacher taking Rezulin. Jones had been monitored closely as a volunteer participant by the prestigious NIH. Her death on May 17, 1998, challenged the usefulness of monthly liver monitoring.

"It had terrible implications for the drug itself," the FDA's Misbin said. "Because if the NIH couldn't protect a patient, then who could?"

Since the nationwide clinical trial explored whether Rezulin could prevent diabetes, none of the 580 participants taking the drug had the disease.

Within three weeks of Jones' death, officials at the NIH banished Rezulin from the clinical trial, citing safety concerns. At the FDA, however, regulators did not broach even the possibility of withdrawing Rezulin, said several physicians familiar with the matter.

On July 28, Warner-Lambert announced that the company and the FDA had agreed to a third labeling change: Instead of monthly monitoring for half a year, patients were advised to submit to testing for the first eight months of use. By now, 21 patients had died of Rezulin-related liver failure.

The British, again citing safety concerns, later refused to allow reintroduction of Rezulin. One British official said that the benefits offered by Rezulin were "nothing that isn't already there with other drugs."

New Commissioner Seeks Reevaluation

Newly appointed FDA Commissioner Jane E. Henney ordered a reevaluation of Rezulin in January 1999, in response to a Los Angeles Times investigative series that disclosed at least 33 liver failure deaths attributable to Rezulin.

Graham, the agency's leading specialist in evaluating and preventing deaths caused by prescription drugs, was assigned the job. His responsibility is to examine medicines already on the market.

At a time when nearly half of all Americans regularly take one or more prescription drugs, Graham's work is of crucial importance. Delivering bad news about a hot-selling drug could stymie a career. Senior FDA officials could not be counted on to provide support. Full-throated opposition often would come from the product's manufacturer.

While Warner-Lambert tapped an array of specialists to defend Rezulin, Graham had the assistance of one colleague, pharmacist Lanh Green. They began studying the harm done to patients, the extent to which liver-monitoring recommendations had been followed and the ongoing risks of taking Rezulin.

Within two months, Graham amassed an indictment of Rezulin. He presented his research on March 26 to an FDA advisory committee—the same panel that had unanimously endorsed the drug's approval. Among Graham's findings:

- An estimated 430 or more Rezulin patients had suffered liver failure.

- Patients incurred 1,200 times more risk of liver failure by taking Rezulin.

- One of every 1,800 Rezulin patients could be expected to suffer liver failure, a far cry from the 1-in-100,000 risk espoused by a Warner-Lambert spokesman.

- Regular liver monitoring offered no safety guarantee, in part because Rezulin could so quickly and unpredictably damage the liver, sometimes within days. And more than 99 percent of patients taking Rezulin for four months or longer failed to follow the liver-monitoring recommendations.

Graham also described the deaths of Audrey Jones and another woman, Rosa Delia Valenzuela, who had died in a clinical trial despite undergoing monitoring. Valenzuela, 63, of Arcadia, Calif., was struck with liver failure about a month after taking Rezulin as a participant in a Warner-Lambert clinical trial.

Warner-Lambert's representatives told the advisory committee that Rezulin could not be held responsible for many of the liver failures. They cited factors such as preexisting medical conditions.

The committee was unpersuaded by Graham and voted, 11 to 1, to recommend keeping Rezulin on the market. Three of the panelists had received compensation from Warner-Lambert or an affiliate; they were granted conflict-of-interest waivers by the FDA.

Graham also was admonished by his immediate boss for the breadth of his report to the committee, he told acquaintances. The FDA declined to allow Graham to comment for this article.

As the advisory committee members dispersed from the March 26 meeting, tragedy again was unfolding. Another Rezulin patient, despite undergoing monthly monitoring in a Warner-Lambert clinical trial, lay near death.

Three days later, 37-year-old Adrian C. Seay died at nearby Washington Hospital Center. The District of Columbia medical examiner identified the cause of death as liver failure, "following treatment with" Rezulin.

On June 16, the FDA agreed to yet another labeling change, the fourth for Rezulin. Patients and doctors were advised that liver monitoring should be conducted monthly for the entire first year, instead of eight months. The FDA also said that new diabetes patients should no longer use Rezulin initially as a stand-alone treatment.

New Recommended Use for Drug OKd

But the FDA was hardly renouncing Rezulin. In addition to keeping the drug on the market, the agency approved Warner-Lambert's request for a new recommended use of Rezulin, in combination with two other popular blood-sugar-lowering pills.

The FDA's handling of Rezulin was ridiculed at a June conference sponsored by Georgetown University Medical Center. Dr. Alastair J.J. Wood, a Vanderbilt University professor and drug therapy editor of the *New England Journal of Medicine*, likened the FDA's label changes to managing the risk posed by a steep cliff. "The point was, you don't keep on putting up more and more signs if people continue to fall of a cliff, you try to do something more definitive, like try to prevent them from falling off. You put up a fence."

By late 1999, the tragedies persisted. The *Times* disclosed on Dec. 15 that the FDA had received reports of 21 additional liver failure deaths since Graham's presentation. Graham, acting with the knowledge of his supervisor, began preparing an updated analysis.

At the start of the new year, Graham told his fellow Termites that he was readying a knockout blow of Rezulin. He had amassed a case so strong that no one at the FDA could resist any longer.

Or so Graham hoped. On Jan. 6, 2000, Graham shared his latest findings regarding Rezulin's toll at an FDA staff meeting. In attendance was Dr. Robert J. Temple, one of the agency's most respected scientists. As director of one of the FDA's five drug review offices, Temple was a subordinate, on paper, to Lumpkin and Woodcock. But his reputation, built over 28 years inside the agency, was without peer. In a room of mostly mid-level medical officers, Temple's every word and gesture counted.

First, he raised the precedent of the "imminent hazard" withdrawal in 1977 of Phenforinin, the diabetes drug Misbin had dealt with at Ceiba-Geigy. This was a useful context. But where, his colleagues wanted to know, did Temple stand on Rezulin? All eyes were fixed on him.

Temple briskly slashed two fingers across his throat.

Specialists Asked to Look at Two Other Drugs

As the session ended, the Termites were emboldened. A consensus had formed for Rezulin's prompt withdrawal. But any such hope was doused on Jan. 13, when Lumpkin met with the same FDA specialists.

Lumpkin directed them to shift focus and assess the safety of two newer chemical cousins of Rezulin. The FDA had granted rapid approval to these diabetes drugs, Avandia and Actos, in mid-1999 after they were found to be far less toxic to the liver.

Several FDA physicians viewed Lumpkin's approach as diversionary. Rezulin, they said, should stand or fall on its own merits.

Lumpkin created further delay by scheduling two private meetings between FDA staff members and Warner-Lambert executives on Feb. 2 and March 1.

At the first meeting, Graham pointed out that the FDA had received reports of liver failure among patients who had taken Rezulin for eight to 18 months. This clashed with the company's earlier claim that the risk "substantially declines after six to eight months of therapy."

Some of the most pointed questions came from Temple and Misbin. They were skeptical of the company's claims that liver monitoring worked. "How many more unnecessary deaths will it take before you take action?"

Misbin asked the company.

As of early February, the FDA press office confirmed 85 cases of liver failure, including 58 deaths. This was nearly twice the number of liver failures acknowledged by the FDA a year earlier.

Nevertheless, the FDA brass continued to endorse Rezulin. On Feb. 24, Woodcock issued a statement reaffirming the agency's confidence in the drug, saying that "in many patients it has proven to be very effective." Her remarks showed that Rezulin continued to enjoy deep and well-connected support.

And doctors kept prescribing the drug. According to the pharmaceutical information company IMS Health, Rezulin during the preceding year generated $674 million in sales.

FDA Session with Firm Seen as Pivotal

The Termites, their ranks now swollen to about a dozen agency specialists, did not retreat. They made known to colleagues their conclusion that Rezulin should be withdrawn.

The March 1 meeting with Warner-Lambert loomed pivotal. The Termites were bracing for more resistance from the top. Senior FDA officials were determined to keep the session shrouded in confidentiality. Saying that they suspected a *Times* reporter was inside the agency's high-security headquarters in Rockville, Md., officials at midday shifted the 4 p.m. meeting a few miles north, to a conference room next to the sixth-floor offices of Woodcock and Lumpkin.

Behind closed doors, Lumpkin broached the option of bringing Rezulin for a third time to the FDA advisory committee, the panel that had overwhelmingly endorsed the drug in December 1998 and again Lumpkin's suggestion, several participants said, meant that the drug might stay on the market indefinitely.

Warner-Lambert proposed that Rezulin remain on the market for as long as two years while the company conducted new studies measuring the frequency of liver failure.

Medical officers with responsibility over diabetes drugs, Drs. Solomon Sobel and Saul Malozowski, also joined the Termites in pushing for Rezulin's withdrawal.

Lumpkin indicated to Warner-Lambert that no regulatory conclusion had been reached. But, Lumpkin made clear afterward, he was unconvinced that withdrawal of Rezulin was warranted. On March 2, one day after the meeting, Lumpkin wrote in an e-mail that his subordinates were relying on "soft hypotheses."

The Termites feared the FDA would stand pat and that avoidable deaths would continue.

By March 3, Graham had seen and heard enough.

He dropped a bomb: an e-mail addressed to Lumpkin and 13 other FDA officials. Graham's message could embarrass, if not render untenable, the position of Rezulin's defenders. He wrote that Warner-Lambert's claims of safety, long accepted by senior FDA officials, were "contradicted" by the scientific record.

"There are no existing data anywhere to suggest or support the hypothesis that monthly monitoring can or in fact does prevent drug-induced liver failure," he declared. "This idea, translated into policy through labeling, is entirely unproven and represents an imagined, artificial hope, not reality."

Graham concluded: "At each juncture in the management of Rezulin's liver failure risk, hindsight shows that we had little or no effect and that [Warner-Lambert's] assertions

that the liver failure problem was solved, were proved false. The data at hand should persuade us that Rezulin is unsafe compared to other available therapies and that its marketing be stopped."

Doctor Takes on Role of Whistle-Blower

Until early March, the Termites had confined their opposition to within the FDA. That was about to change.

Misbin, the longtime champion of Rezulin, had concluded that the drug must go. "I consistently underestimated the rapidity with which Rezulin could damage the liver," Misbin recalled in a recent interview. "I have underestimated the virulence of Rezulin."

Misbin seized the role of whistle-blower. He reached for an audience the FDA could not ignore—Congress. Misbin wrote to Rep. Henry A. Waxman [D-Los Angeles] and seven other lawmakers. He turned over internal e-mails regarding the agency's handling of Rezulin. He shared damning correspondence sent to him by a St. Louis physician who conducted early research for Warner-Lambert.

According to Dr. Janet B. McGill, the company "deliberately omitted reports of liver toxicity and misrepresented serious adverse events experienced by [Rezulin] patients in their clinical studies."

Misbin soon, however, found himself under an FDA internal-affairs investigation for allegedly disseminating confidential agency materials. The inquiry was initiated based on a complaint by Warner-Lambert that "someone had leaked nonpublic information" from agency files, according to Melinda K. Plaisser, an FDA associate commissioner.

On March 13, a senior FDA official warned Misbin: "You are required to cooperate with the investigation and failure to cooperate may result in disciplinary actions up to and including dismissal from federal service."

Misbin was undeterred. He refused to answer investigators' questions unless they were posed in writing.

Another agency medical officer, 72-year-old Dr. Leo Lutwak, also was targeted. Two internal affairs agents asked Lutwak if he had given the *Times* a Jan 24. e-mail written by Misbin. After the interrogation, Lutwak said, the agents warned that if his statements were proven to be untruthful he was at risk of imprisonment.

First the defrocking of Gueriguian. Then the admonishing of Graham. Now an investigation of Misbin and Lutwak. For many inside the FDA, the message was unmistakable: Oppose Rezulin at your peril.

FDA Briefing Yields No Pronouncement

The FDA at this point had linked 89 voluntarily reported liver failures, including 61 deaths, to the use of Rezulin.

On March 15, Woodcock and Lumpkin were summoned to the 14th-floor office of FDA Commissioner Henney for a confidential discussion of Rezulin.

Following the briefing, Henney again made no pronouncement about Rezulin. The drug's day-to-day fate remained in the hands of Woodcock and Lumpkin. They scheduled another staff meeting to discuss Rezulin.

For the Termites, this was perhaps their last chance. At 2:30 P.M. on March 21, Woodcock, Lumpkin, Misbin, Graham, Temple, Sobel and nearly a dozen other agency specialists gathered for a round-table discussion. Graham focused on how, in his view, patients incurred increased risk of liver

failure the longer they stayed on Rezulin. He estimated that 20 liver failures were occurring each month.

After two hours, Woodcock adjourned the meeting without declaring her or the agency's position. She then huddled in her office with a handful of subordinates, including Lumpkin and Temple. Lumpkin and Woodcock had captained the FDA's shift to accelerated approvals and less-adversarial relations with drug companies, a new paradigm epitomized by Rezulin.

By this point, the FDA had overseen the withdrawal of seven medications in 2 years. The fate of Rezulin posed unique sensitivity: It was the only therapy approved on a fast-track—and by the same FDA officials who were now sitting in final judgment of the drug.

Lumpkin and Woodcock had cited the absence of more withdrawals as evidence that the agency's faster approvals were not compromising safety. "The steady, if not declining, rate of withdrawals is particularly reassuring," they wrote in a May 1999 issue of the *Journal of the American Medical Association*.

All of which meant that, if Lumpkin and Woodcock sought the withdrawal of Rezulin, they risked further discrediting the FDA's faster, less-adversarial approach.

For Rezulin, the agency had confirmed 63 liver failure deaths by the deliberations of March 21.

Lumpkin made one last attempt to avert Rezulin's immediate withdrawal. He suggested scheduling another meeting with the advisory committee to reassess Rezulin. Temple objected, saying that more delay was unjustified.

The decision was now Woodcock's. It had been 29 months and 11 days since the FDA received the first reports of liver failure. She phoned executives at Warner-Lambert's headquarters in Morris Plains, N.J.

By 7:30 P.M., the FDA issued a statement disclosing that the company had agreed to immediately withdraw Rezulin. In the statement, Woodcock observed: "We are now confident that patients have safer alternatives."

Times researchers Janet Lundblad in Los Angeles and Sunny Kaplan in Washington contributed to this story, which originally appeared on June 4, 2000.

The complete series of *Times* investigative reports on the fast track approval of Rezulin is available on the *Times'* Web site: http://www.latimes.com/rezulin.

Notes

1. Grape seed extract is known by several names including procyanidin and proanthocyanidin and OPC (oligomeric proanthocyanidin).
2. Chopra D, Ageless Body, Timeless Mind, Harmony Books, New York, 1993;167–168.
3. Dawson-Hughes B, Dallal GE, Krall EA, Sadowski L, Sahyoun N, Tannenbaum S, A controlled trial of the effect of calcium supplementation on bone density in postmenopausal women. N Engl J Med 1990 Sep 27;323(13):878–83; and Sakhaee K, Bhuket T, Adams-Huet B, Rao DS, Meta-analysis of calcium bioavailability: A comparison of calcium citrate with calcium carbonate. Am J Ther 1999 Nov;6(6):313–21.
4. Weintraub S, Natural Treatment for ADD and Hyperactivity, Woodland Publishing Inc., Pleasant Grove, UT, 289.
5. Lambert NM, Hartsough CS, Prospective study of tobacco smoking and substance dependencies among samples of ADHD and non-ADHD participants. J Learn Disabil 1998 Nov–Dec;31(6):533–44.
6. Williams C, Wright B, Partridge I, Attention deficit hyperactivity disorder—A review. Br J Gen Pract 1999 Jul;49(444):563–71.
7. Burgess JR, Stevens L, Zhang W, Peck L, Long-chain polyunsaturated fatty acids in children with attention-deficit hyperactivity disorder. Am J Clin Nutr 2000 Jan;71(1 Suppl):327S–30S; and Mitchell EA, Aman MG, Turbott SH, Manku M, Clinical characteristics and serum essential fatty acid levels in hyperactive children. Clin Pediatr (Phila) 1987 Aug;26(8):406–11.

8. Coleman M, Steinberg G, Tippett J, Bhagavan HN, Coursin DB, Gross M, Lewis C, DeVeau L, A preliminary study of the effect of pyridoxine administration in a subgroup of hyperkinetic children: A double-blind crossover comparison with methylphenidate. Biol Psychiatry 1979 Oct;14(5):741–51.

9. Coleman M, Greenberg A, Bhagavan H, Steinberg G, Tippett J, Coursin D, The role of whole blood serotonin levels in monitoring vitamin B_6 and drug therapy in hyperactive children. Monogr Neural Sci 1976;3:133–6.

10. Requejo AM, Ortega RM, Navia B, Gaspar MJ, Quintas E, Lopez-Sobaler A, Folate and vitamin B_{12} status in a group of preschool children. Int J Vitam Nutr Res 1997;67(3):171–5.

11. Bottiglieri T, Courtwright KH, Summers, JW, Folate, vitamin B_{12}, and neuropsychiatric disorders. Nutr Rev 1996 Dec;54(12):382-90.

12. Starobrat-Hermelin B, The effect of deficiency of selected bioelements on hyperactivity in children with certain specified mental disorders. Ann Acad Med Stetin 1998;44:297–314.

13. Starobrat-Hermelin B, Kozielec T, The effects of magnesium physiological supplementation on hyperactivity in children with attention deficit hyperactivity disorder (ADHD). Positive response to magnesium oral loading test. Magnes Res. 1997 Jun;10(2):149–56.

14. Carter CM et al., Effects of a few foods diet in attention deficit disorder. Arch Dis Child 1993 Nov;69(5):564–8.

15. Boris M, Mandel F, Foods and additives are common causes of the attention deficit hyperactive disorder in children. Annals of Allergy 1994 May; 2:162–8.

16. Schoenthaler S, Moody J, Pankon L, Applied nutrition and behavior. Journal of Applied Nutrition, 1991 Nov;43.

17. Bendvold E, Gottlieb C, Bygdeman M, Eneroth P, Depressed semen quality in Swedish men from barren couples: A study over three decades. Arch Androl 1991 May–Jun;26(3):189–94.

18. Osser S, Liedholm P, Ranstam J, Depressed semen quality: A study over two decades. Arch Androl 1984;12(1):113-6.

19. Berg MJ, The importance of folic acid. J Gend Specif Med 1999 May-Jun;2(3):24-8; Favier A, Current aspects about the role of zinc in nutrition. Rev Prat 1993 Jan 15;43(2):146–51; and Uhland AM, Kwiecinski GG, DeLuca HF, Normalization of serum calcium restores fertility in vitamin D–deficient male rats. J Nutr 1992 Jun;122(6):1338–44.

20. Salvati G, et al., Effects of Panax Ginseng, CA Meyer saponins on male fertility. Panminerva Med 1996: 38:249–254.

21. Murray MT, The Healing Power of Herbs. 2nd ed. Rocklin, CA: Prima Publishing, 1995, pp. 370–1.

22. Moody JA, Vernet D, Laidlaw S, Rajfer J, Gonzalez-Cadavid NF, Effects of long-term oral administration of L-arginine on the rat erectile response. J Urol 1997 Sep;158(3 Pt 1):942–7.
23. Zorgniotti AW, Lizza EF, Effect of large doses of the nitric oxide precursor, L-arginine, on erectile dysfunction. Int J Impot Res 1994 Mar;6(1):33–5.
24. Scibona M, Meschini P, Capparelli S, Pecori C, Rossi P, Menchini Fabris GF, L-arginine and male infertility. Minerva Urol Nefrol 1994 Dec;46(4):251–3.
25. Chen J, Wollman Y, Chernichovsky T, Iaina A, Sofer M, Matzkin H, Effect of oral administration of high-dose nitric oxide donor L-arginine in men with organic erectile dysfunction: Results of a double-blind, randomized, placebo-controlled study. BJU Int 1999 Feb;83(3):269–73.
26. Falck F Jr, Ricci A Jr, Wolff MS, Godbold J, Deckers P, Pesticides and polychlorinated biphenyl residues in human breast lipids and their relation to breast cancer. Arch Environ Health 1992 Mar–Apr;47(2):143–6.
27. Colborn T, Dumanoski D, Peterson M, Our Stolen Future: Are We Threatening Our Fertility, Intelligence, and Survival? Dutton/Penguin, 1997.
28. Ward P, Ward R, The Encyclopedia of Weight Training (Laguna Hills, CA, QPT Publications, 1997); pp.24–27.
29. Pat RR, Pratt M, Blair SN, et al., Physical activity and public health: A recommendation from the Centers for Disease Control and Prevention and the American College of Sports Medicine. Journal of the American Medical Association 1995: 273; 402–407.
30. U.S. Department of Health and Human Services; A Report of the Surgeon General: Physical Activity and Health (Pittsburgh, PA: Superintendent of Documents, 1996).
31. U.S. Department of Health and Human Services, Centers for Disease Control and Prevention, National Center for Health Statistics—Division of Data Services; 1997 Aging Statistics Report (Hyattsville, MD).
32. U.S. Department of Commerce, U.S. Census Bureau; Geographic Profile, 1993 (Washington, D.C.). Quoted in Physical Activity and Fitness Research, Series 3, No. 4, December 1998; President's Council on Physical Fitness and Sports (Washington, D.C. 1998).
33. Ibid.
34. Ross JG, Gilbert, GG, The national children and youth fitness study. Journal of Health, Physical Education, Recreation and Dance (January 1985).
35. President's Council on Physical Fitness and Sports; 1985 National School Population Fitness Survey, S/N 017-001-00463 (Washington, D.C.: U.S. Government Printing Office, 1985).

36. National Association of Governor's Councils on Physical Fitness and Sports; Newsletter (Suer 198).
37. U.S. Department of Health and Human Services; A Report of the Surgeon General.
38. Ibid.
39. National Association of Sport and Physical Education—American Alliance for Health, Physical Education, Recreation and Dance; Surgeon general nominee promotes physical education. NASPE News (Winter 1998):6.
40. American College of Sports Medicine; Mission Statement: http://www.acsm.org/.
41. Hamilton E, Nutritional Concepts and Controversies, 3rd Edition, West Publishing Company, St. Paul, MN, 1982; 49–50; and Health promotion: Improved nutrition. Public Health Rep. 1983 Sep–Oct;Suppl:132-55.
42. Sellmeyer DE, Stone KL, Sebastian A, Cummings SR; A high ratio of dietary animal to vegetable protein increases the rate of bone loss and the risk of fracture in postmenopausal women. Study of Osteoporotic Fractures Research Group. Am J Clin Nutr 2001 Jan;73(1):118–22.
43. Baroody T, Alkalize or Die, Holographic Health Press, 1991, 23–8.
44. Budwig J, Flax Oil as a True Aid against Arthritis, Heart Infarction, Cancer and Other Diseases, Apple Publishing Co., Vancouver BC Canada; and Budwig J, The Oil-Protein Diet Cookbook, Apple Publishing Co., Vancouver BC Canada.
45. Mukutmoni-Norris M, Hubbard NE, Erickson KL, Modulation of murine mammary tumor vasculature by dietary n-3 fatty acids in fish oil. Cancer Lett 2000 Mar 13;150(1):101–9.
46. Korsgaard Thomsen K, Larsen S, Schroll M, Cardiovascular risk factors and age: A cross-sectional survey of Danish men and women from the Glostrup population studies, 1991. Am J Geriatr Cardiol 1995 Jan;4(1):31–41.
47. Petkov V, Plants with hypotensive, antiatheromatous & coronarodilatating action. Am. Journal of Chinese Medicine, 1979; VII(3):197–236.
48. Teuber H, Herrmann K, Flavonol glycosides of apples (Malus silvestris Mill.). 10. Phenolics of fruits (author's transl). Z Lebensm Unters Forsch 1978 Feb 24;166(2):80-4. German.
49. Nuttall SL, Kendall MJ, Bombardelli E, Morazzoni PJ, An evaluation of the antioxidant activity of a standardized grape seed extract, Leucoselect. Clin Pharm Ther 1998 Oct;23(5):323–5.
50. Yamakoshi J, Kataoka S, Koga T, Ariga T, Proanthocyanidin-rich extract from grape seeds attenuates the development of aortic atherosclerosis in cholesterol-fed rabbits. Atherosclerosis 1999 Jan; 142(1):139–49.

51. Bagchi D, Bagchi M, Stohs SJ, Das DK, Ray SD, Kuszynski CA, Joshi SS, Pruess HG, Free radicals and grape seed proanthocyanidin extract: Importance in human health and disease prevention. Toxicology 2000 Aug 7;148(2-3):187–97.

52. Facino RM, Carini M, Aldini G, Berti F, Rossoni G, Bombardelli E, Morazzoni P, Diet enriched with procyanidins enhances antioxidant activity and reduces myocardial post-ischaemic damage in rats. Life Sci 1999;64(8):627–42.

53. Chatterjee SS, Koch E, Jaggy H, Krzeminski T, In vitro and in vivo studies on the cardioprotective action of oligomeric procyanidins in a Crataegus extract of leaves and blooms. Arzneimittelforschung 1997 Jul;47(7):821–5. German.

54. Ardevol A, Blade C, Salvado MJ, Arola L, Changes in lipolysis and hormone-sensitive lipase expression caused by procyanidins in 3T3-L1 adipocytes. Int J Obes Relat Metab Disord 2000 Mar; 24 (3):319–24.

55. Costantini A, De Bernardi T, Gotti A, Clinical and capillaroscopic evaluation of chronic uncomplicated venous insufficiency with procyanidins extracted from vitis vinifera. Minerva Cardioangiol 1999 Jan-Feb;47(1-2):39–46.

56. Melzer R, Fricke U, Holzl J, Vasoactive properties of procyanidins from Hypericum perforatum L. in isolated porcine coronary arteries. Arzneimittelforschung 1991 May;41(5):481–3.

57. Rimbach G, Virgili F, Park YC, Packer L, Effect of procyanidins from Pinus maritima on glutathione levels in endothelial cells challenged by 3-morpholinosydnonimine or activated macrophages. Redox Rep 1999;4(4):171–7.

58. Vennat B, Gross D, Pourrat H, Pourrat A, Bastide P, Bastide J, Antiulcer activity of procyanidins preparation of water-soluble procyanidin-cimetidine complexes. Pharm Acta Helv 1989;64(11): 316–20.

59. Bagchi D, Bagchi M, Stohs SJ, Das DK, Ray SD, Kuszynski CA, Joshi SS, Pruess HG, Free radicals and grape seed proanthocyanidin extract: Importance in human health and disease prevention. Toxicology 2000 Aug 7;148(2-3):187–97; and Department of Pharmaceutical and Administrative Sciences, Creighton University School of Pharmacy & Allied Health Professions, 2500 California Plaza, Omaha, NE 68178, USA. debsis@bluejay.creighton.edu.

60. Batmanghelidj, F, Your Body Cries for Water, Global Health Solutions, Falls Church, VA, 1997.

61. Ibid.

62. Ibid.

63. Cantor KP, Lynch CF, Hildesheim ME, Dosemeci M, Lubin J, Alavanja M, Craun G, Drinking water source and chlorination byproducts in Iowa. III. Risk of brain cancer. Am J Epidemiol 1999 Sep 15;150(6):552–60.

64. Marcus PM, Savitz DA, Millikan RC, Morgenstern H, Female breast cancer and trihalomethane levels in drinking water in North Carolina. Epidemiology 1998 Mar;9(2):156-60.

65. Waller K, Swan SH, DeLorenze G, Hopkins B, Trihalomethanes in drinking water and spontaneous abortion. Epidemiology 1998 Mar;9(2):134-40.

66. Villanueva C, Kogevinas M, Grimalt J, Chlorination of drinking water in Spain and bladder cancer. Gac Sanit 2001;15(1):48-53; King WD, Marrett LD, Woolcott CG, Case-control study of colon and rectal cancers and chlorination by-products in treated water. Cancer Epidemiol Biomarkers Prev 2000 Aug;9(8):813-8; and Kuo HW, Chiang TF, Lo II, Lai JS, Chan CC, Wang JD, Estimates of cancer risk from chloroform exposure during showering in Taiwan. Sci Total Environ 1998 Jul 11;218(1):1-7.

67. U.S. Environmental Protection Agency. http://www.epa.gov/.

68. Ibid.

69. U.S. Environmental Protection Agency, National Secondary Drinking Water Regulations. http://www.epa.gov/safewater/mcl.html.

70. Fernando GR, Martha RM, Evangelina R, Consumption of soft drinks with phosphoric acid as a risk factor for the development of hypocalcemia in postmenopausal women. J Clin Epidemiol 1999 Oct;52(10):1007-10.

71. Mazariegos-Ramos E, Guerrero-Romero F, Rodriguez-Moran M, Lazcano-Burciaga G, Paniagua R, Amato D, Consumption of soft drinks with phosphoric acid as a risk factor for the development of hypocalcemia in children: A case-control study. J Pediatr 1995 Jun;126(6):940-2.

72. U.S. Environmental Protection Agency. http://www.epa.gov/OGWDW/mcl.html.

73. Stavric B, Methylxanthines: Toxicity to humans. 2. Caffeine. Food Chem Toxicol 1988 Jul;26(7):645-62; and Darragh A, Kenny M, Lambe RF, O'Kelly DA, Adverse effects of caffeine. Ir J Med Sci. 1981 Feb;150(2):47-53.

74. Bolumar F, Olsen J, Rebagliato M, Bisanti L, Caffeine intake and delayed conception: A European multicenter study on infertility and subfecundity. Am J Epidemiol 1997 Feb 15;145(4):324-34.

75. Davis BR, Curb JD, Borhani NO, Prineas RJ, Molteni A, Coffee consumption and serum cholesterol in the hypertension detection and follow-up program. Am J Epidemiol 1988 Jul;128(1):124-36; Kokjohn K, Graham M, McGregor M, The effect of coffee consumption on serum cholesterol levels. J Manipulative Physiol Ther 1993 Jun;16(5):327-35; and Superko HR, Bortz W Jr, Williams PT, Albers JJ, Wood PD, Caffeinated and decaffeinated coffee effects on plasma lipoprotein cholesterol, apolipoproteins, and lipase activity:

A controlled, randomized trial. Am J Clin Nutr 1991 Sep; 54(3): 599–605.

76. Darragh A, Kenny M, Lambe RF, O'Kelly DA, Adverse effects of caffeine. Ir J Med Sci 1981 Feb;150(2):47–53.

77. Leitzmann MF, Willett WC, Rimm EB, Stampfer MJ, Spiegelman D, Colditz GA, Giovannucci E, A prospective study of coffee consumption and the risk of symptomatic gallstone disease in men. JAMA 1999 Jun 9;281(22):2106–12.

78. Hakim RB, Gray RH, Zacur H, Alcohol and caffeine consumption and decreased fertility. Fertil Steril 1998 Oct;70(4):632–7.

79. Uksan V, Korsic M, Posavi-Antonovic A, Metabolic diseases and the high-fiber diet. Lijec Vjesn 1997 Mar-Apr;119(3–4):125–7; and Spiller GA, Freeman HJ, Recent advances in dietary fiber and colorectal diseases. Am J Clin Nutr 1981 Jun;34(6):1145–52.

80. Negri E, Franceschi S, Parpinel M, La Vecchia C, Fiber intake and risk of colorectal cancer. Cancer Epidemiol Biomarkers Prev 1998 Aug;7(8):667–71.

81. McIntosh M, Miller C, A diet containing food rich in soluble and insoluble fiber improves glycemic control and reduces hyperlipidemia among patients with type 2 diabetes mellitus. Nutr Rev 2001 Feb;59(2):52–5.

82. Kimura Y, Onoyama M, Sera T, Okuda H, Antitumour activity and side effects of combined treatment with chitosan and cisplatin in sarcoma 180-bearing mice. J Pharm Pharmacol 2000 Jul;52(7): 883–90; Tokumitsu H, Hiratsuka J, Sakurai Y, Kobayashi T, Ichikawa H, Fukumori Y, Gadolinium neutron-capture therapy using novel gadopentetic acid-chitosan complex nanoparticles: In vivo growth suppression of experimental melanoma solid tumor. Cancer Lett 2000 Mar 31;150(2):177–82; Tokumitsu H, Ichikawa H, Fukumori Y, Chitosan-gadopentetic acid complex nanoparticles for gadolinium neutron-capture therapy of cancer: preparation by novel emulsion-droplet coalescence technique and characterization. Pharm Res 1999 Dec;16(12):1830–5; and Jameela SR, Latha PG, Subramoniam A, Jayakrishnan A, Antitumour activity of mitoxantrone-loaded chitosan microspheres against Ehrlich ascites carcinoma. J Pharm Pharmacol 1996 Jul;48(7):685–8.

83. Fehr T, Schoedon G, Odermatt B, Holtschke T, Schneemann M, Bachmann MF, Mak TW, Horak I, Zinkernagel RM, Crucial role of interferon consensus sequence binding protein, but neither of interferon regulatory factor 1 nor of nitric oxide synthesis for protection against murine listeriosis. J Exp Med 1997 Mar 3;185(5):921–31.

84. Bagchi D, Bagchi M, Stohs SJ, Das DK, Ray SD, Kuszynski CA, Joshi SS, Pruess HG, Free radicals and grape seed proanthocyanidin

extract: Importance in human health and disease prevention. Toxicology 2000 Aug 7;148(2-3):187–97; and Department of Pharmaceutical and Administrative Sciences, Creighton University School of Pharmacy & Allied Health Professions, 2500 California Plaza, Omaha, NE 68178, USA. debsis@bluejay.creighton.edu.

85. Jacob, S, Lawrence, R, Zucker, M, The Miracle of MSM, Putnam Publishers, New York, 1999.

86. Ibid., 57.

87. Ibid.

88. De Stefani E, Brennan P, Boffetta P, Ronco AL, Mendilaharsu M, Deneo-Pellegrini H, Vegetables, fruits, related dietary antioxidants, and risk of squamous cell carcinoma of the esophagus: A case-control study in Uruguay. Nutr Cancer 2000;38(1):23–9; de la Taille A, Katz A, Vacherot F, Saint F, Salomon L, Cicco A, Abbou CC, Chopin DK, Cancer of the prostate: Influence of nutritional factors. Vitamins, antioxidants and trace elements. Presse Med 2001 Mar 24;30(11):557–60; and Nishino H, Tokuda H, Murakoshi M, Satomi Y, Masuda M, Onozuka M, Yamaguchi S, Takayasu J, Tsuruta J, Okuda M, Khachik F, Narisawa T, Takasuka N, Yano M, Cancer prevention by natural carotenoids. Biofactors 2000;13(1-4): 89–94.

89. Tokuyama H, Tokuyama Y, Bovine colostre transforming growth factor-beta-like peptide that induces growth inhibition and changes in morphology of human osteogenic sarcoma cells (MG63). Cell Biol Int Rep 1989 Mar;13(3):251–8; Hooton JW, Pabst HF, Spady DW, Paetkau V, Human codosinim contains an activity that inhibits the production of IL-2. Clin Exp Immunol 1991 Dec:86(3):520–4. Viander B, Ala-Uotila S5, Jalkanen NI, Pakkanen R, Viable AC-2. A new adult bovine serum- and colostrum-based supplement for the culture of mammalian cells. Biotechniques 1996 Apr;20(41):702–7.

90. Zhao J, Wang J, Chen Y, Agarwal R, Anti-tumor-promoting activity of a polyphenolic fraction isolated from grape seeds in the mouse skin two-stage initiation-promotion protocol and identification of procyanidin B5-3'-gallate as the most effective antioxidant constituent. Carcinogenesis 1999 Sep;20(9):1737–45.

91. Ibid.

92. Fine AM, Oligomeric proanthocyanidin complexes: history, structure, and phytopharmaceutical applications. International Clinical Research Center, Scottsdale, AZ.

93. Haak E, Usadel KH, Kusterer K, Amini P, Frommeyer R, Tritschler HJ, Haak T, Effects of alpha-lipoic acid on microcirculation in patients with peripheral diabetic neuropathy. Exp Clin Endocrinol Diabetes 2000;108(3):168–74; and Ruhnau KJ, Meissner HP, Finn

JR, Reljanovic M, Lobisch M, Schutte K, Nehrdich D, Tritschler HJ, Mehnert H, Ziegler D, Effects of 3-week oral treatment with the antioxidant thioctic acid (alpha-lipoic acid) in symptomatic diabetic polyneuropathy. Diabet Med 1999 Dec;16(12):1040-3.

94. Ngkeekwong FC, Ng LL, Two distinct uptake mechanisms for ascorbate and dehydroascorbate in human lymphoblasts and their interaction with glucose. Biochem J 1997 May 15;324 (pt 1): 225-30.

95. Rocic B, Vucic M, Knezevic-Cuca J, Radica A, Pavlic-Renar I, Profozic V, Metelko Z, Total plasma antioxidants in first-degree relatives of patients with insulin-dependent diabetes. Exp Clin Endocrinol Diabetes 1997;105(4):213-7.

96. Nakata M, Uto N, Maruyama I, Yada T, Nitric oxide induces apoptosis via Ca2+-dependent processes in the pancreatic beta-cell line MIN6. Cell Struct Funct 1999 Dec;24(6):451-5.

97. Virgili F, Kobuchi H, Packer L, Procyanidins extracted from Pinus maritima (Pycnogenol): Scavengers of free radical species and modulators of nitrogen monoxide metabolism in activated murine RAW 264.7 macrophages. Free Radic Biol Med 1998 May;24(7-8): 1120-9.

98. Chan NN, Vallance P, Colhoun HM, Nitric oxide and vascular responses in Type I diabetes. Diabetologia 2000 Feb;43(2): 137-47.

99. Jenson B, Dr. Jenson's Guide to Better Bowel Care, Avery Publishing Group, Garden City Park, NY, p55.

100. Collins SM, Stress and the gastrointestinal tract. IV. Modulation of intestinal inflammation by stress: Basic mechanisms and clinical relevance. Am J Physiol Gastrointest Liver Physiol 2001 Mar;280 (3):G315-8.

101. Marchetti M, Pisani S, Antonini G, Valenti P, Seganti L, Orsi N, Metal complexes of bovine lactoferrin inhibit in vitro replication of herpes simplex virus type 1 and 2. Biometals 1998 Apr;11(2): 89-94; Siciliano R, et al., Bovine lactoferrin peptidic fragments involved in inhibition of herpes simplex virus type 1 infection. Biochem Biophys Res Commun 1999 Oct 14;264(1):19-23; and Hasegawa K, Motsuchi W, Tanaka S, Inhibition with lactoferrin of in vitro infection with human herpes virus. Jpn J Med Sci Biol 1994 Apr;47(2):73-85.

102. Hasegawa K, Motsuchi W, Tanaka S, Inhibition with lactoferrin of in vitro infection with human herpes virus. Jpn J Med Sci Biol 1994 Apr;47(2):73-85.

103. Baynes RD, Bezwoda WR, Mansoor N, Neutrophil lactoferrin content in viral infections. Am J Clin Pathol 1988 Feb;89(2):225-8.

104. Position paper: Epidemiology of periodontal diseases. J Periodontol 1996 Sep;67(9):935-45.

105. Turgan N, Boydak B, Habif S, Apakkan S, Ozmen D, Mutaf I, Bayindir O, Plasma homocysteine levels in acute coronary syndromes. Jpn Heart J 1999 Nov;40(6):729–36.

106. Bunout D, Garrido A, Suazo M, Kauffman R, Venegas P, de la Maza P, Petermann M, Hirsch S, Effects of supplementation with folic acid and antioxidant vitamins on homocysteine levels and LDL oxidation in coronary patients. Faculty of Medicine, University of Chile, Santiago, Chile.

107. Facino RM, Carini M, Aldini G, Berti F, Rossoni G, Bombardelli E, Morazzoni P, Diet enriched with procyanidins enhances antioxidant activity and reduces myocardial post-ischaemic damage in rats. Life Sci 1999;64(8):627–42.

108. Chatterjee SS, Koch E, Jaggy H, Krzeminski T, In vitro and in vivo studies on the cardioprotective action of oligomeric procyanidins in a Crataegus extract of leaves and blooms. Arzneimittelforschung 1997 Jul;47(7):821–5.

109. Chang WC, Hsu FL, Inhibition of platelet aggregation and arachidonate metabolism in platelets by procyanidins. Prostaglandins Leukot Essent Fatty Acids 1989 Dec;38(3):181–8.

110. van Jaarsveld H, Kuyl JM, Schulenburg DH, Wiid NM, Effect of flavonoids on the outcome of myocardial mitochondrial ischemia/reperfusion injury. Res Commun Mol Pathol Pharmacol 1996 Jan;91(1):65–75.

111. Chiechi LM, Dietary phytoestrogens in the prevention of long-term postmenopausal diseases. Int J Gynaecol Obste 1999 Oct; 67(1):39–40; and Liu J, Burdette JE, Xu H, Gu C, Van Breemen RB, Bhat KP, Booth N, Constantinou AI, Pezzuto JM, Fong HH, Farnsworth NR, Bolton JL, Department of Medicinal Chemistry and Pharmacognosy, UIC/NIH Center for Botanical Dietary Supplements Research, College of Pharmacy, M/C 781, University of Illinois at Chicago, 833 South Wood Street, Chicago, Illinois 60612, USA.

112. Knopp RH, Superko HR, Davidson M, Insull W, Dujovne CA, Kwiterovich PO, Zavoral JH, Graham K, O'Connor RR, Edelman DA, Long-term blood cholesterol-lowering effects of a dietary fiber supplement. Am J Prev Med 1999 Jul;17(1):18–23; and Truswell AS. Meta-analysis of the cholesterol-lowering effects of dietary fiber. Am J Clin Nutr 1999 Nov;70(5):942–3.

113. Molgaard J, Von Schenck H, Olsson AG, Alfalfa seeds lower low density lipoprotein cholesterol and apolipoprotein B concentrations in patients with type II hyperlipoproteinemia. Atherosclerosis 1987 May;65(1–2):173–9.

114. Sicart R, Sable-Amplis R, Agid R, Diminution of blood and hepatic cholesterol induced by an apple-supplemented diet in the hamster. Trials in man. C R Seances Soc Biol Fil 1979;173(5):937–43.

115. Brashears MM, Gilliland SE, Buck LM, Bile salt deconjugation and cholesterol removal from media by Lactobacillus casei. J Dairy Sci 1998 Aug;81(8):2103–10; and Buck LM, Gilliland SE, Comparisons of freshly isolated strains of Lactobacillus acidophilus of human intestinal origin for ability to assimilate cholesterol during growth. J Dairy Sci 1994 Oct;77(10):2925–33.

116. Yamakoshi J, Kataoka S, Koga T, Ariga T, Proanthocyanidin-rich extract from grape seeds attenuates the development of aortic atherosclerosis in cholesterol-fed rabbits. Atherosclerosis 1999 Jan;142(1):139–49.

117. Soleas GJ, Diamandis EP, Goldberg DM, Wine as a biological fluid: History, production, and role in disease prevention. J Clin Lab Anal 1997;11(5):287–313.

118. Johnson K, Kligman EW, Preventive nutrition: Disease-specific dietary interventions for older adults. Geriatrics 1992 Nov;47(11): 39–40, 45–9.

119. Sherman DL, Keaney JF Jr, Biegelsen ES, Duffy SJ, Coffman JD, Vita JA, Pharmacological concentrations of ascorbic acid are required for the beneficial effect on endothelial vasomotor function in hypertension. Hypertension 2000 Apr;35(4):936–41; and Chang WC, Hsu FL, Inhibition of platelet aggregation and arachidonate metabolism in platelets by procyanidins. Prostaglandins Leukot Essent Fatty Acids 1989 Dec;38(3):181–8; and Sanz MJ, Terencio MC, Paya M, Isolation and hypotensive activity of a polymeric procyanidin fraction from Pistacia lentiscus L. Pharmazie 1992 Jun;47(6):466–7; and Terencio MC, Sanz MJ, Paya M, Antihypertensive action of a procyanidin glycoside from Rhamnus lycioides.J Ethnopharmacol 1991 Jan;31(1):109–14.

120. Macknin ML, Piedmonte M, Calendine C, Janosky J, Wald E, Zinc gluconate lozenges for treating the common cold in children: A randomized controlled trial. JAMA 1998 Jun 24;279(24):1962–7; and Mossad SB, Macknin ML, Medendorp SV, Mason P, Zinc gluconate lozenges for treating the common cold. A randomized, double-blind, placebo-controlled study. Ann Intern Med 1996 Jul 15;125(2):81–8.

121. Walker M, Olive Leaf Extract, Kensington Publishing Co, New York, 1997, pg 55–57.

122. Aabakken, Lam, Short term effect of bovine colostrum in patients with throat angina. A placebo controlled study. Statistical Report No. 309, Vuramed, Norway. Norges Apatekares tidsskritt, 98 nr 22. April 1990.

123. Urban T, The oponizing ability in antibodies from some health care products containing bovine colostrum. State Laboratory, State Pharmaceutical Company, Stockholm. Swedish Pharmaceutical Association, Yearly Congress, 1990.

124. Chen J, Wollman Y, Chernichovsky T, Iaina A, Sofer M, Matzkin H, Effect of oral administration of high-dose nitric oxide donor L-arginine in men with organic erectile dysfunction: Results of a double-blind, randomized, placebo-controlled study. BJU Int 1999 Feb;83(3):269–73.

125. Klippel KF, Hiltl DM, Schipp B, A multicentric, placebo-controlled, double-blind clinical trial of beta-sitosterol (phytosterol) for the treatment of benign prostatic hyperplasia. Br J Urol 1997 Sep;80 (3):427–32; and Goepel M, Hecker U, Krege S, Rubben H, Michel MC, Saw palmetto extracts potently and non competitively inhibit human alpha1-adrenoceptors in vitro. Prostate 1999 Feb 15;38(3): 208–15.

126. Dimitrov M, Georgiev P, Vitanov S, Use of tribestan on rams with sexual disorders. Vet Med Nauki 1987;24(5):102–10.

127. Zisapel N, The use of melatonin for the treatment of insomnia. Biol Signals Recept 1999 Jan–Apr;8(1–2):84–9.

128. Nagtegaal JE, Laurant MW, Kerkhof GA, Smits MG, van der Meer YG, Coenen AM, Effects of melatonin on the quality of life in patients with delayed sleep phase syndrome. J Psychosom Res 2000 Jan;48(1):45–50; and Zisapel N, The use of melatonin for the treatment of insomnia. Biol Signals Recept 1999 Jan–Apr; 8(1–2):84–9.

129. Berkson BM, A conservative triple antioxidant approach to the treatment of hepatitis C. Combination of alpha lipoic acid (thioctic acid), silymarin, and selenium: Three case histories. Med Klin 1999 Oct 15;94 Suppl 3:84–9.

130. Feher J, Deak G, Muzes G, Lang I, Niederland V, Nekam K, Karteszi M, Liver-protective action of silymarin therapy in chronic alcoholic liver diseases. Orv Hetil 1989 Dec 17;130(51):2723–7.

131. Salmi HA, Sarna S, Effect of silymarin on chemical, functional, and morphological alterations of the liver. A double-blind controlled study. Scand J Gastroenterol 1982 Jun;17(4):517–21.

132. Kiss B, Karpati E, Mechanism of action of vinpocetine. Acta Pharm Hung 1996 Sep;66(5):213–24; and Kiss, B., Szporny, L. et al., On the possible role of central monominergic systems in the central nervous systems actions of vinpocetine. Drug Dev. Res 1988 14, 263–279.

133. Miyata N, Yamaura H, Tanaka M, Muramatsu M, Tsuchida K, et al., Effects of VA–045, a novel apovincaminic acid derivative, on isolated blood vessels: Cerebroarterial selectivity. Life Sci 1993; 52(18):PL181–6; and Gaal L, Molnar P, Effect of vinpocetine on noradrenergic neurons in rat locus coeruleus. Eur J Pharmacol 1990 Oct 23;187(3):537–9.

134. Kass-Annese B, Alternative therapies for menopause. Clin Obstet Gynecol 2000 Mar;43(1):162–83.

135. Kass-Annese B, Alternative therapies for menopause. Clin Obstet Gynecol 2000 Mar;43(1):162–83.
136. Shiizaki K, Goto K, Ishige A, Komatsu Y, Bioassay of phytoestrogen in herbal medicine used for postmenopausal disorder using transformed MCF-7 cells. Phytother Res 1999 Sep;13(6):498–503; and Zava DT, Dollbaum CM, Blen M, Estrogen and progestin bioactivity of foods, herbs, and spices. Proc Soc Exp Biol Med 1998 Mar;217(3):369–78.
137. Zava DT, Dollbaum CM, Blen M, Estrogen and progestin bioactivity of foods, herbs, and spices. Proc Soc Exp Biol Med 1998 Mar; 217(3):369–78; and Liu J, Burdette JE, Xu H, Gu C, van Breemen RB, Bhat KP, Booth N, Constantinou AI, Pezzuto JM, Fong HH, Farnsworth NR, Bolton JL, Evaluation of estrogenic activity of plant extracts for the potential treatment of menopausal symptoms. J Agric Food Chem 2001 May;49(5):2472–9.
138. Zava DT, Dollbaum CM, Blen M, Estrogen and progestin bioactivity of foods, herbs, and spices. Proc Soc Exp Biol Med 1998 Mar;217(3):369–78; and Page L, ND, Ph.D., How to Be Your Own Herbal Pharmacist, Healthy Healing Publications 1997, p218.
139. Wright, J; Muscle and Fitness, 1996 September:140–142, 224.
140. Grube B, Walper A, Wheatley D, St. John's Wort extract: Efficacy for menopausal symptoms of psychological origin. Adv Ther 1999 Jul–Aug;16(4):177–86.
141. De Leo V, Lanzetta D, Cazzavacca R, Morgante G, Treatment of neurovegetative menopausal symptoms with a phytotherapeutic agent. Minerva Ginecol 1998 May;50(5):207–11.
142. Langley WF, Mann D, Central nervous system magnesium deficiency. Arch Intern Med 1991 Mar;151(3):593–6.
143. Lowenstein JM, Effect of (-)-hydroxycitrate on fatty acid synthesis by rat liver in vivo. J Biol Chem 1971;246(3):629-32; and Triscari J, Sullivan AC, Comparative effects of (-)-hydroxycitrate and (=)-allo-hydroxycitrate on acetyl CoA carboxylase and fatty acid and cholesterol synthesis in vivo. Lipids 1977;12(4):357-63.
144. Cheema-Dhadli S, Harlperin ML, Leznoff CC, Inhibition of enzymes which interact with citrate by (-)hydroxycitrate and 1,2,3,-tricarboxybenzene. Eur J Biochem 1973;38:98–102; Sullivan AC, Hamilton JG, Miller ON, et al., Inhibition of lipogenesis in rat liver by (-)-hydroxycitrate. Arch Biochem Biophys 1972;150:183–90; Greenwood MRC, Cleary MP, Gruen R, et al., Effect of (-)-hydroxycitrate on development of obesity in the Zucker obese rat. Am Phys J 1981;240:E72–78; and Sergio W, A natural food, the Malabar Tamarind, may be effective in the treatment of obesity. Med Hypotheses 1988 Sep;27(1):39–40.
145. Rude RK, Kirchen ME, Gruber HE, Meyer MH, Luck JS, Crawford DL, Magnesium deficiency-induced osteoporosis in the rat:

Uncoupling of bone formation and bone resorption. Magnes Res 1999 Dec;12(4):257–67; and Johnson S, The multifaceted and widespread pathology of magnesium deficiency. Med Hypotheses 2001 Feb;56(2):163–70.

146. Kaufman K, Silica: The Forgotten Nutrient. Alive Books, Burnaby, BC, 1990, pp. 17–22.

147. Rubin P, M.D.; Affiliations: Learn More about Prostate Cancer, University of Rochester, Posted Date: August 2, 1998; Last Revision Date: July 5, 2001.

148. Marks LS, Hess DL, Dorey FJ, Luz Macairan M, Cruz Santos PB, Tyler VE, Tissue effects of saw palmetto and finasteride: Use of biopsy cores for in situ quantification of prostatic androgens. Urology 2001 May;57(5):999–1005.

149. American Cancer Society, Cancer Resource Center, http://www3.cancer.org/cancerinfo/; and Lucci A, Citro HW, Wilson L, Assessment of knowledge of melanoma risk factors, prevention, and detection principles in Texas teenagers. J Surg Res 2001 May 15;97(2):179–83.

150. Gali HU, Perchellet EM, Gao XM, Karchesy JJ, Perchellet JP, Comparison of the inhibitory effects of monomeric, dimeric, and trimeric procyanidins on the biochemical markers of skin tumor promotion in mouse epidermis in vivo. Planta Med 1994 Jun;60(3):235–9.

151. Bitzan MM, Gold BD, Philpott DJ, et al., Inhibition of Helicobacter pylori and Helicobacter mustelae binding to lipid receptors by bovine colostrum. J Infect Dis 1998 Apr;177(4):955–61.

Suggested Reading List

A Cancer Therapy: Results of 50 Cases. 6th Ed. Max Gerson (Gerson Institute, Bonita, CA, 619-585-7600)

Alkalize or Die, Dr. Theodore Baroody (Holographic Health Press, Wayneville, NC, 1-800-566-1522)

The American Training Pattern, Dr. Paul Ward, Dr. Tom Rosandich, and Bob Lawson (Olympia Sport Publications)

Ancient Secret of the Fountain of Youth, Peter Kelder (Harbor Press)

Cancer and Nutrition, Charles Simone, M.D. (Avery Publishing)

The Cancer Industry, Ralph Moss (Paragon House Publishing)

Encyclopedia of Weight Training, Dr. Paul Ward and Dr. Robert Ward (QPT Publications)

Fats and Oils, Udo Erasmus (Alive Publishing, Vancouver, Canada)

Freedom from Disease, Hari Sharma, M.D. (Beda Publishing, Toronto, Ontario)

MAKKO—HO (Five Minutes of Physical Fitness), Haruka Nagai (Japan Publications)

Nutritional Guidance Program, Dr. Paul Ward (Health & Tennis Corporation of America)

Olive Leaf Extract, Dr. Morton Walker (Kensington Publishing Co, New York)

The Power of the Supermind, Vernon Howard (Prentice Hall)

The Science of Mind, Earnest Holmes (Putnam, New York)

Self Hypnosis (The Complete Manual for Health and Self-Change), Brian M. Alman, Ph.D., and Peter Lambrou, Ph.D.

Super Life, Super Health, The Editors of FC@A Publishing

The Wisdom of the Body, Sherwin B. Nuland (Alfred A. Knoff, Inc.)

The Wizard Within, A. M. Krasner, Ph.D. (American Board of Hypnotherapy Press)

Index

to, 84, 128, 146–147, 235, 241, 278, 297;
and physical activity, 100
olea europa/olive leaf extract (oleuropein),
178–179, 392–393
olive leaf extract, 68
omega-3 (alpha-linoleic acid), 147; conversion
of to GLA, 137; dietary sources, 138–140;
health benefits of, 135–136; sources of,
138–140
omega-6 (linoleic acid), 135
Opopka, Lake, 74
oral problems. *See* mouth/mouth problems
organic compounds, 211
organic minerals, 215
orthopedic impairments, 107. *See also* bones
osteoarthritis, 99, 261
osteoblast process, 12
osteoporosis (bone loss), 99–100, 107, 128,
133, 223, 360–364
Our Stolen Future (Colborn), 86
outdoor activity, 190
overweight. *See* obesity
oxidants, 185
oxidation, 173, 184, 200
oxidative stress, 279
oxygen, 172
oxygen radicals, 186

P
packaged foods, 143
Packer, Lester, 69
pain, 364–365; addiction to drugs due to, 52–
53; arthritis, 260–264; in calf (claudication), 275–276; headache/head pain,
305–309; joint inflammation reduction,
203–204; mind-body connection for overcoming, 33–34; reduction, 168; relief, 169
Panax ginseng, 75–76, 89
pancreas/pancreatic disorders, 129; cancer, 147;
pancreatitis, 194, 223. *See also* blood sugar
problems; diabetes; insulin
papain, 228
Parkinson's disease, 69, 235
partially hydrogenated fats, 143
Pauling, Linus, 9, 41, 149
PC-95 Daily Rejuvenating Cream, 398–399
PCBs, 85–86
pectin, 232
peptidase, 228
Perfect Whey Meal Replacement, 399
periodontal disease, 128, 302
personal environment, 271–272
perspiration, 245
pesticides, 73, 186
phagocytosis, 194
phosphates, 132
phospholipids, 65
phosphoric acid, 216–217, 219
phosphorus, 165
physical activity: American College of Sports
Medicine (ACSM) guidelines, 111–113;
attributes of physical fitness, 93–94; benefits of, 96–102, 103; definition of physical
fitness, 92–93, 92–94; reports on importance of, 91–92; sedentary people, 94–96;
senior fitness, 102–108; sports/recreational
activities, 113–116; youth fitness, 108–111

Physical Education for Progress Act, 111
physicians, 9, 10
Physicians' Desk Reference (PDR), 52, 60
phytochemical triterpenoid saponins, 76, 267
pineal gland, 90
placebo effect, 33–34, 262
plant foods, 235
plaque (arterial), 144
plaque (dental), 302
plastics, 87
platelet aggregation, 274. *See also* blood clotting
pleasure, 75
pollutants, 73, 74, 85–89, 186, 190
polyneuropathy, 175, 276
polyphenols, 181, 182
polyps, 226
polysaccharides, 235–236
polyunsaturated EFAs, 135
polyvinyl chloride (PVC), 87
poor circulation, 274–277
pork, 88–89
postmenopausal women, 38
potassium, 165–166
power drinks, 44
praying, 272
precarcinogens, 193
pregnancy, 221
premature aging, 175, 186, 205, 251
premenstrual syndrome (PMS), 82, 83, 85,
220
President's Council of Physical Fitness and
Sports, 108–109
prevention/treatment: acne, 248–249; alcoholism, 255–257; allergies, 258–260;
arthritis, 261–263; asthma, 264–266; atherosclerosis, 199–200; bad breath, 284; blood
clotting, 200–201; cancer, 232–234;
269–272; cataracts, 201; cholesterol levels,
314–318; circulatory problems, 276–277;
colds/flu, 329–331; constipation, 286;
damage from heart attacks, 200; diabetes,
280–281; diarrhea, 287–288; digestive
problems, 283; diverticulitis, 289; fatigue,
300–301; gum disease, 303–304; headaches, 306–308; heartburn, 290–291; heart
health, 309–311; hemorrhoids, 312–313;
high blood pressure, 320–321; hyperthyroidism, 376–377; hypoglycemia, 323;
hypothyroidism, 375–376; immune deficiency, 325–328; impotence, 332–333;
indigestion, 292–293; insomnia, 335–336;
intestinal gas (flatulence), 294; irritable
bowel syndrome (IBS), 296–297; liver function, 340; memory loss, 342–344; menopause, 346–348; mental health problems,
349–350; nervousness, 351; obesity, 356–
358; osteoporosis, 361–363; oxidation, 200;
pain, 364–365; premature aging, 251, 253–
254; prostate problems, 368–369; sinusitis,
370–371; skin cancer, 373–374; stomach
ulcers, 380–381; stress, physical/emotional,
352; U.S. Office of Disease Prevention and
Health Promotion, 108; yeast infections,
382. *See also* beneficial supplementation;
nutritional approaches to treatment; supplements
preventive medicine, 101

About the Authors

"If it is to be, it is up to me."
—Rod's Mantra

Some forty-eight years ago ROD BURRESON began his journey into health, primarily to learn how to rehabilitate his body from a very serious knee injury. This journey took him down a long, arduous road leading to an understanding of the body, the mind, and rehabilitation.

Rod has always had an active lifestyle and enjoys pushing his body to the limit. Often, however, this practice has put him in a perilous state. In fact, in his lifetime, Rod has broken many bones in his body, some repeatedly, including his facial bones, back, knees, hands, fingers, toes, and shoulder. As a key member of the U. S. Navy wrestling team and an avid student of the martial arts, Rod formed his basis of understanding for the importance of exercise and its benefits using his mind to direct his rehabilitation. It was also during his tour of duty that he first learned of his own vitamin deficiencies. This began his quest to learn as much as possible about the structure and function of the human body, and to this day, he continues to study medical and biomechanical research. Rod has discovered that the more he learns, the more he has yet to learn.

Rod has overcome so many personal, health, and emotional problems. It was, however, the loss of his son in an airplane crash that provided him the inspiration to dedicate his life to educating himself and as many people that would listen on the importance of enhancing the function of the human body. He wanted people to know it is *never, ever too late* to get on the road to health! Rod decided that it was time to form a company that would make products available to the general public that really work, that are affordable, and that function synergistically to support the structure and function of the body.

Armed with the super-antioxidant PC-95 he imported from Europe, Rod formed Roex, Inc., a company dedicated to finding solutions for many of the problems associated with aging and disease. He subsequently developed the *Roex Health Update* an hourlong, unscreened call-in health-talk radio show broadcast out of New York City.

The show can be heard in major metropolitan markets throughout the nation and has provided Rod the opportunity to touch many people's lives and give them the motivation to improve their health and vitality.

PAUL EARL WARD, PED is a highly regarded expert in the field of physical conditioning. He began his career in professional football, playing for both the Chicago Bears and the Detroit Lions. He has coached collegiate sports U.S. Olympic track and field teams, and he has been a consultant for the Dallas Cowboys and Los Angeles Rams.

He received his master's degree in physical education from the University of Washington and later earned his doctorate in physical education from Indiana University. He has devoted most of his life to researching and improving on methods, equipment, and nutrition for physical training and athletic performance. Dr. Ward's level of knowledge is so regarded that the majority of all the exercise equipment used today has been researched, conceptualized, tested, or improved with his guidance.

In addition to his contribution to *Never, Ever, Ever Give Up— Health Is on the Way*, Dr. Ward's writing accomplishments include more than 50 articles published in scientific journals and fitness magazines, authoring his book *Nutritional Guidance Program;* and co-authoring *The American Training Pattern* and *The Encyclopedia of Weight Training.*